Professional

Web Parts and Custor
with ASP.NET 2.

Professional

Web Parts and Custom Controls with ASP.NET 2.0

Peter Vogel

Wiley Publishing, Inc.

Professional Web Parts and Custom Controls with ASP.NET 2.0

Published by
Wiley Publishing, Inc.
10475 Crosspoint Boulevard
Indianapolis, IN 46256
www.wiley.com

Published simultaneously in Canada

ISBN-13: 978-0-7645-7860-1
ISBN-10: 0-7645-7860-X

Manufactured in the United States of America

10 9 8 7 6 5 4 3 2 1

1B/SR/RQ/QV/IN

Library of Congress Cataloging-in-Publication Data

Vogel, Peter, 1953–
Professional Web parts and custom controls with ASP.NET 2.0 / Peter Vogel.
p. cm.
Includes bibliographical references and index.
ISBN-13: 978-0-7645-7860-1 (paper/website : alk. paper)
ISBN-10: 0-7645-7860-X (paper/website : alk. paper)
1. Active server pages. 2. Web sites—Authoring programs. 3. Web site development. 4. Microsoft.net. 5. User interfaces (Computer systems) 6. Computer software—Development. I. Title.
TK5105.8885.A26V64 2005
005.2 76—dc22
2005021557

For general information on our other products and services please contact our Customer Care Department within the United States at (800) 762-2974, outside the United States at (317) 572-3993 or fax (317) 572-4002.

Wiley also publishes its books in a variety of electronic formats. Some content that appears in print may not be available in electronic books.

About the Author

Peter Vogel (MBA, MCSD) is a principal in PH&V Information Services. PH&V provides consulting services in client/server and Web development. Its clients include Volvo, Christie Digital, the Canadian Imperial Bank of Commerce, the Government of Ontario, and Microsoft. Peter's white papers appeared in the Visual Studio .NET and Office 2003 release package. Peter is the editor of the *Smart Access* newsletter from Pinnacle Publishing, and wrote *The Visual Basic Object and Component Handbook*, which has been called "The definitive guide to 'thinking with objects.'" Peter was the founding editor of the *XML Developer* newsletter. In addition to teaching for Learning Tree International, Peter wrote their ASP.NET 1.1, ASP.NET 2.0, and Technical Writing courses. His articles have appeared in every major magazine devoted to VB-based development and can be found in the Microsoft Developer Network libraries.

Peter lives in Goderich, Ontario, Canada, and presents at conferences all over the world, frequently as the keynote speaker.

Credits

Senior Acquisitions Editor
Jim Minatel

Development Editor
Sara Shlaer

Technical Editors
Derek Comingore
Richard Purchas

Copy Editor
Nancy Rapoport

Editorial Manager
Mary Beth Wakefield

Production Manager
Tim Tate

Vice President and Executive Group Publisher
Richard Swadley

Vice President and Executive Publisher
Joseph B. Wikert

Graphics and Production Specialists
Denny Hager
Joyce Haughey
Barbara Moore
Alicia South

Quality Control Technicians
John Greenough
Leeann Harney

Media Development Specialists
Angela Denny
Kate Jenkins
Steve Kudirka
Kit Malone
Travis Silvers

Media Development Coordinator
Laura Atkinson

Proofreading and Indexing
TECHBOOKS Production Services

This book is for my beautiful sons, in order of appearance:
Christopher, Jamie, and Jason.

Contents

Acknowledgments

A book is the product of many minds, only a few of whom have their names on the cover. The acknowledgments are where the author admits the truth: The book wouldn't be here (let alone be any good) without the work of Sara Shlaer, an editor of both skill and patience (who is *not* in Australia), and Richard Purchas of Factotum Information Services, Sydney, a technical editor with more good ideas than should have been possible (and who *is* in Australia). The book that you're reading is better because I got to work with Sara and Richard. Thanks, guys — you are the best things that could have happened to this book.

The reason this book exists comes down to two people: Neil Salkind of StudioB and Jim Minatel of Wiley Publishing. Neil got me this job — I didn't think I needed an agent until I worked with Neil. The linchpin of this project was Jim Minatel, who kept seeing the opportunities for this book as we worked through its various incarnations.

Introduction

Custom controls and Web Parts can make you more productive by enabling you to create re-usable components for your WebForms. You can package up a piece of your user interface and re-use it within your Web site or across many Web sites. But that's only one way that these controls make you more productive. If you've ever had an ASP.NET control that you wished worked slightly differently, you can now create the control that you want. When you build your own custom controls and Web Parts, you can have the control do as much (or as little) as you want.

If you've worked with ASP.NET you're familiar with ASP.NET server controls. You may even have tried building user controls or your own custom controls and have seen what ASP.NET controls look like from the inside. However, Web Parts are new with ASP.NET 2.0, and provide functionality that is very different from what you've seen with ASP.NET controls. Web Parts enable you to give your users the ability to customize your application to meet their needs. By using Web Parts, you can involve your users in creating their own user interfaces — yet another way of making you more productive.

This book's focus is on how to use Visual Studio 2005 most effectively to create your controls (although the information you need to create custom controls, user controls, and Web Parts using any text editor is also included). Visual Studio 2005 provides you with the best support for creating ASP.NET applications and creating your own controls.

The approach in this book is simple: "If you want this, code this; if you code this, you'll get this." Throughout the book, the emphasis is on the code that you need to create controls that you can use when building Web applications. There's no code in here, for instance, on how to calculate the square root of every number less than 2,000. The code in this book is based on business-related applications.

This also means that this book does not provide much background on how ASP.NET works, unless it makes a difference to you when you're writing code. If you're familiar with how ASP.NET works "under the hood," that knowledge will deepen your understanding of the material in this book. On the other hand, if you've been able to create applications without knowing that material — well, you won't need to know it to understand the examples in this book, either.

Where there is more than one way to accomplish a goal, I describe the costs and benefits of each method and identify the typical scenarios in which you would use each technique so that you can make an informed decision about what you want to do.

There's probably material in this book that you won't need, at least not initially. But when you do need that information, it's in here with lots of examples (in Visual Basic 2005 and C#) to show you how to do it. For instance, when you first build a custom control you may not intend to distribute that control outside of your company. As a result, you won't need to read the section on licensing. If, later on, you need that material, it's here (in Chapter 7, to be exact).

Whom This Book Is For

This book is written for the professional Web developer. I assume that you know how to create a WebForm and now want to take advantage of the features to create your own controls. I do not, however, assume that you are an experienced object developer. If you do have some experience with creating objects, you'll find a few pages of review material in here covering basic object-oriented (OO) concepts and how to implement them in Visual Basic 2005 and C#. I also assume that you're new to creating objects in Visual Studio 2005, so I've included some information at the start of Chapter 3 on how to set up your development environment to make you as productive as possible.

A note on the syntax: You'll probably realize that much of the sample code in this book could be a great deal terser — what is done in the sample code in three or four lines could often be done in one. The code in this book is written to be both readable and obvious: You shouldn't have to puzzle anything out when reading the sample code. The naming convention I use throughout (for example, putting a three-character prefix on all variable names) is also designed to be obvious. Newer naming conventions no longer use this style (what used to be called "Hungarian Notation"), but it still has advantages in a learning environment. You can tell that <strTextName> is a string without having to hunt for the variable's declaration.

In addition, I use the same style for both the C# and the Visual Basic 2005 code samples to make it easier to compare the two versions. In most cases I use the full object names (for example, System.Web.UI .WebParts.WebControl instead of just WebControl) to ensure that the code should run as advertised. While these practices makes sense for a book designed to help you understand how all of this technology works, you'll probably want to take advantage of the many shortcuts that both Visual Basic 2005 and C# offer you to write terser code.

How This Book Is Structured

This book is divided into four parts. Part I (Chapters 1 and 2) introduces the basic concepts of custom controls, user controls, and Web Parts. Part II (Chapters 3 through 7) covers everything that you need to know to implement all three types of controls. Part III (Chapters 8 through 11) explains how to build on the basics of the three controls to add business-specific functionality and build specialized controls, and addresses other advanced topics. Part IV contains Chapter 12, a custom control case study.

The following is a summary of the topics covered in each chapter:

- **Chapter 1, "Creating Your Own Controls":** This chapter describes the role of user controls, custom controls, and Web Parts. You also see what the differences are between the three types of controls and when to use each. This chapter discusses how to know when you have a problem that can be solved with one of the three types of controls and how to pick the right kind.
- **Chapter 2, "Creating Customizable Pages":** New to ASP.NET 2.0 is the ability to create customizable pages, which is where Web Parts are used. In this chapter you see, through a case study, how customizable pages can be used in an application and how this changes the process of building Web pages. This chapter includes the components of the Web Part framework that you will use with your Web Part.

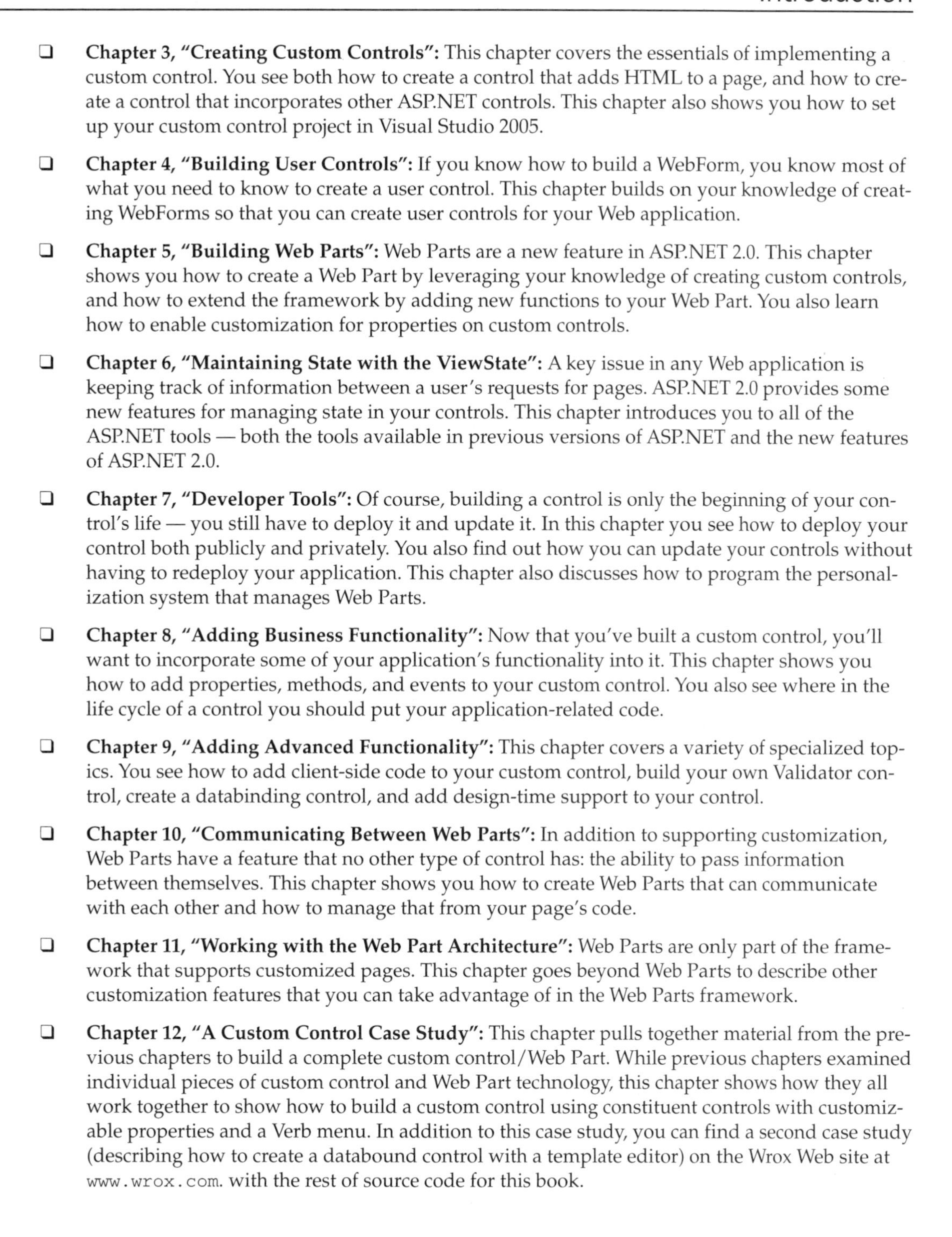

- **Chapter 3, "Creating Custom Controls":** This chapter covers the essentials of implementing a custom control. You see both how to create a control that adds HTML to a page, and how to create a control that incorporates other ASP.NET controls. This chapter also shows you how to set up your custom control project in Visual Studio 2005.
- **Chapter 4, "Building User Controls":** If you know how to build a WebForm, you know most of what you need to know to create a user control. This chapter builds on your knowledge of creating WebForms so that you can create user controls for your Web application.
- **Chapter 5, "Building Web Parts":** Web Parts are a new feature in ASP.NET 2.0. This chapter shows you how to create a Web Part by leveraging your knowledge of creating custom controls, and how to extend the framework by adding new functions to your Web Part. You also learn how to enable customization for properties on custom controls.
- **Chapter 6, "Maintaining State with the ViewState":** A key issue in any Web application is keeping track of information between a user's requests for pages. ASP.NET 2.0 provides some new features for managing state in your controls. This chapter introduces you to all of the ASP.NET tools — both the tools available in previous versions of ASP.NET and the new features of ASP.NET 2.0.
- **Chapter 7, "Developer Tools":** Of course, building a control is only the beginning of your control's life — you still have to deploy it and update it. In this chapter you see how to deploy your control both publicly and privately. You also find out how you can update your controls without having to redeploy your application. This chapter also discusses how to program the personalization system that manages Web Parts.
- **Chapter 8, "Adding Business Functionality":** Now that you've built a custom control, you'll want to incorporate some of your application's functionality into it. This chapter shows you how to add properties, methods, and events to your custom control. You also see where in the life cycle of a control you should put your application-related code.
- **Chapter 9, "Adding Advanced Functionality":** This chapter covers a variety of specialized topics. You see how to add client-side code to your custom control, build your own Validator control, create a databinding control, and add design-time support to your control.
- **Chapter 10, "Communicating Between Web Parts":** In addition to supporting customization, Web Parts have a feature that no other type of control has: the ability to pass information between themselves. This chapter shows you how to create Web Parts that can communicate with each other and how to manage that from your page's code.
- **Chapter 11, "Working with the Web Part Architecture":** Web Parts are only part of the framework that supports customized pages. This chapter goes beyond Web Parts to describe other customization features that you can take advantage of in the Web Parts framework.
- **Chapter 12, "A Custom Control Case Study":** This chapter pulls together material from the previous chapters to build a complete custom control/Web Part. While previous chapters examined individual pieces of custom control and Web Part technology, this chapter shows how they all work together to show how to build a custom control using constituent controls with customizable properties and a Verb menu. In addition to this case study, you can find a second case study (describing how to create a databound control with a template editor) on the Wrox Web site at `www.wrox.com`. with the rest of source code for this book.

What You Need to Use This Book

To try out the examples in the book, you need the following:

- The .NET 2.0 Framework
- Internet Information Services (IIS) on Windows 2000 or later

While Visual Studio 2005 has been used throughout this book, you can build custom controls with any text editor, as described in the book.

Conventions

To help you get the most from the text and keep track of what's happening, I've used a number of conventions throughout the book:

> **Boxes like this one hold important, not-to-be-forgotten information that is directly relevant to the surrounding text.**

Tips, hints, tricks, and asides to the current discussion are offset and placed in italics like this.

Source Code

As you work through the examples in this book, you may choose either to type all the code manually or use the source code files that accompany the book. All the source code used in this book is available for download at `www.wrox.com`. Once at the site, simply locate the book's title (either by using the Search box or by using one of the title lists) and click the Download Code link on the book's detail page to obtain all the source code for the book.

After you download the code, just decompress it with your favorite compression tool. Alternatively, you can go to the main Wrox code download page at `www.wrox.com/dynamic/books/download.aspx` to see the code available for this book and all other Wrox books.

Errata

We make every effort to ensure that there are no errors in the text or in the code. However, no one is perfect, and mistakes do occur. If you find an error in one of our books, like a spelling mistake or faulty piece of code, we would be very grateful for your feedback. By sending in errata you may save another reader hours of frustration; at the same time, you will be helping us provide even higher quality information.

To find the errata page for this book, go to `www.wrox.com` and locate the title using the Search box or one of the title lists. Then, on the book details page, click the Book Errata link. On this page, you can view all errata that has been submitted for this book and posted by Wrox editors. A complete book list including links to each book's errata is also available at `www.wrox.com/misc-pages/booklist.shtml`.

If you don't spot "your" error on the Book Errata page, go to `www.wrox.com/contact/techsupport.shtml` and complete the form there to send us the error you have found. We'll check the information and, if appropriate, post a message to the book's errata page and fix the problem in subsequent editions of the book.

p2p.wrox.com

For author and peer discussion, join the P2P forums at `p2p.wrox.com`. The forums are a Web-based system for you to post messages relating to Wrox books and related technologies and interact with other readers and technology users. The forums offer a subscription feature to e-mail you topics of interest of your choosing when new posts are made to the forums. Wrox authors, editors, other industry experts, and your fellow readers are present on these forums.

At `http://p2p.wrox.com` you will find a number of different forums that will help you not only as you read this book, but also as you develop your own applications. To join the forums, just follow these steps:

1. Go to `p2p.wrox.com` and click the Register link.
2. Read the terms of use and click Agree.
3. Complete the required information to join as well as any optional information you wish to provide and click Submit.
4. You will receive an e-mail with information describing how to verify your account and complete the joining process.

You can read messages in the forums without joining P2P but in order to post your own messages, you must join.

Once you join, you can post new messages and respond to messages other users post. You can read messages at any time on the Web. If you would like to have new messages from a particular forum e-mailed to you, click the Subscribe to this Forum icon by the forum name in the forum listing.

For more information about how to use the Wrox P2P, be sure to read the P2P FAQs for answers to questions about how the forum software works as well as many common questions specific to P2P and Wrox books. To read the FAQs, click the FAQ link on any P2P page.

Part I
Introducing Controls

1

Creating Your Own Controls

ASP.NET comes with its own set of server-side controls — so why create your own? And why would you need three different kinds of controls: custom controls, Web Parts, and user controls?

By creating your own controls, you can build powerful, reusable visual components for your Web application's user interface, including components that allow your users to customize and personalize your application. This chapter introduces you to the two primary types of controls (custom controls and Web Parts) along with user controls. You'll also see how creating your own controls can simultaneously improve the quality of your Web applications, make you more productive, and improve your user interfaces.

The Three Kinds of Controls

Why three different kinds of controls? Part of the reason is historical: Custom controls and user controls were introduced in the first version of ASP.NET, while Web Parts are new to ASP.NET 2.0 and add functionality that wasn't available in user controls and custom controls. So, from one perspective, Web Parts are different from user controls and custom controls because they are "newer" — not a very important difference. As you'll see, Web Parts are really just an extension of custom controls, but that new functionality provides developers with the opportunity to deliver something new: the ability for users to customize Web pages. But even that description doesn't really help distinguish among the three types of controls: while Web Parts are a special class of control, you can use both user controls and custom controls as Web parts (although they won't have all the customization facilities of a full-fledged Web Part).

Web Parts, custom controls, and user controls all allow you to create reusable components that can be used, in turn, to create Web pages in ASP.NET. Web Parts, custom controls and user controls in ASP.NET 2.0 look very much alike when you are using them to build Web pages. All can be used in Design view, for instance — you can drag them onto a page, resize them, and set their properties in the Property window. The major difference is that you drag custom controls and Web Parts from the toolbox in Visual Studio .NET but you drag user controls from Solution Explorer. However, because both user controls and custom controls can be used as Web Parts, you can drag customization components from both the Toolbox and Solution Explorer (full-fledged Web Parts appear in the Toolbox). Whether you are building Web Parts, custom controls, or user controls, you can add your own properties, methods, and events to them.

User Controls

While the focus of this book is on custom controls and Web Parts, user controls shouldn't be ignored. For developers, the major difference between user controls and custom controls is in ease of development — a powerful incentive to use user controls. User controls provide an easy way to create reusable controls: If you know how to create a Web page in ASP.NET, then you know how to create a user control. As an example, you can add controls to your user control the same way that you add controls to a Web page: by dragging and dropping the controls onto a design surface. Figure 1-1 shows a user control in Design view in Visual Studio .NET.

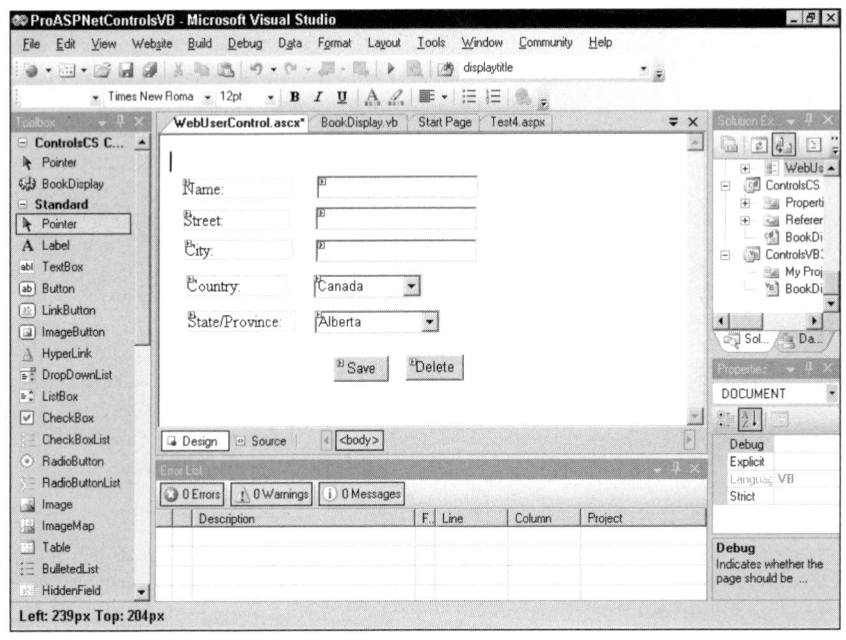

Figure 1-1

Of course, nothing comes for free: In order to gain this ease of development, user controls have several limitations. The first major limitation in the functionality of user controls is that they cannot inherit from other ASP.NET controls, while a custom control can inherit from other controls. The capability to inherit from other controls enables you, for instance, to create a custom control that inherits from the ASP.NET ListBox control and extends that control.

However, this limitation often just means thinking about the problem differently: If you want to create a user control that functions like a ListBox, you could just drop a list box on your user control and then add any new methods, properties, or events that you want (with a custom control, you would have to do all of your development without the benefit of a drag-and-drop designer). As you'll see in this book, all the features that you can take advantage of in a custom control are available to you in a user control — it's just that the user control's drag-and-drop designer means that you don't need them.

The second major limitation of user controls is in their reusability: user controls can't be shared among projects or Web sites. A user control can be used only on Web pages in the project that the user control is part of. There is no way around this limitation.

Custom Controls

Custom controls are a more code-intensive way to create reusable components for Web applications. For instance, to add new controls to your custom controls, you must write code that will create the controls and add them to the Controls collection of your custom control — there is no drag-and-drop facility as in a user control. In return for taking longer to create, custom controls offer you more power.

Custom controls are more flexible than user controls. You can create a custom control that inherits from another server-side control and then extend that control. You could, for instance, create a custom control based on another custom control — even one as complex as the TreeView control — and then add new methods or properties to create your own, even more powerful control.

Custom controls are more reusable than user controls. You can share a custom control among projects. Typically, you'll create your custom control in a Web Custom Control library that is compiled separately from your Web application. As a result, you can add that library to any project in order to use your custom control in that project.

Web Parts

It's not really correct to compare Web Parts with user controls and custom controls. User controls and custom controls can be used as Web Parts, although they will lack all of the features of a full-fledged Web Part. But, if you want to take full advantage of the Web Part feature set, then you must build your control as a Web Part right from the beginning. As you'll see, Web Parts are an extension of custom controls — think of full-fledged Web Parts as custom controls with superpowers.

Web Parts actually first appeared not in ASP.NET but in Windows SharePoint Services (in 2003, when SharePoint was re-architected to run on top of ASP.NET). SharePoint is Microsoft's Web-based tool for creating document-based solutions that can be customized by the user. As part of visiting a SharePoint site, users can build pages in SharePoint by adding Web Parts to a SharePoint page or modifying the Web Parts already on the page. With ASP.NET 2.0, a version of Web Parts was added to ASP.NET.

For most developers, the statement that "users can build pages in SharePoint" seems counterintuitive. The usual division of labor is to have developers build Web pages and users . . . well, users just use the pages. SharePoint, however, was designed to empower users, to let users build the pages they needed without having to call on the IT staff. In ASP.NET, Web Parts can be used to fulfill the same function: to let users build the pages they need from the inventory of Web Parts available to a page. Because of this ability, Web Part developers have a new and more interesting job to do. Web Part developers don't just build applications; they build components that enable users to build applications.

This description of how a Web Part is used on a SharePoint site omits an important step. After a Web Part is created it is added to one of several Web Part galleries available to the SharePoint site. Once a Web Part is available to a site, developers then add the Web Part to a page. Users can add Web Parts to a SharePoint page only if the Web Part is in one of the galleries for the site. Galleries aren't part of the ASP.NET 2.0 implementation of Web Parts.

> **While Web Parts have become part of the toolkit for all ASP.NET developers, currently Web Parts developed in ASP.NET 2.0 can't be used in SharePoint (and Web Parts built for SharePoint can't be used outside of SharePoint). However, Microsoft has committed to providing an upgrade to SharePoint that will allow ASP.NET 2.0 Web Parts to be used in SharePoint in the near future.**

The Benefits of Reusable Controls

By creating your own controls, you can build a toolkit of controls to draw on when building a Web application. Think of these controls as reusable *visual* components. A control can range from something as simple as displaying a title to being a complete business application in itself.

Much of the talk about the benefits of creating objects and components seems to revolve around abstract features (encapsulation, polymorphism, and so on). For a developer working in the real world, creating components really provides three practical benefits in terms of reusability:

- **Productivity:** By creating reusable components, you don't have to re-invent the wheel when implementing similar functionality in different applications (or parts of the same application).
- **Standardization:** By using the same components to perform operations that are common to different pages, you are guaranteed that the functionality is implemented in a common way.
- **Simplification:** By dividing functionality between specialized components and other parts of the application (such as workflow management, business logic, data access), the complexity in any one part is reduced.

Web Parts, custom controls, and user controls provide all three of these benefits. Web Parts add features that custom controls and user controls do not. These features include:

- **Integration:** Web Parts on the same page can find one another and exchange information.
- **Property settings that can be changed by the user:** At run time, users can change property settings for a Web Part to further customize the application for themselves or others.
- **Page design:** Web Parts can be added or removed from the page, relocated to other parts of the page, or just minimized to "de-clutter" the page.

The benefits of reusability with object-oriented development are so well known that they form part of the conventional wisdom of modern application developers. But Web Parts also provide another benefit: customization. The benefits of customization are not as commonly known, however, so the next section describes why customization matters to you.

Beyond Reusability with Web Parts

Through customization, Web Parts give you the opportunity to gain a new and more challenging class of benefits: you can create Web Parts that end users can add to their pages in order to create their own solutions. Think of Web Parts as reusable visual *tools* (rather than just visual components): Web Parts are tools that users employ to meet their goals. When you create a user control or a custom control you design it to help you and other developers solve problems in creating applications. With Web Parts you create controls designed to let end users solve problems, often in situations that you may not have even thought of.

This opportunity is challenging because it's difficult to predict all the ways that users will find to employ a genuinely useful Web Part. If building a reusable visual tool isn't enough of a challenge, you can also offer users the capability to customize your Web Part to meet their needs. In addition to adding your Web Part to a page, users can also modify the way that your Web Part behaves.

Developing with Web Parts isn't about what you can do for your users. Web Parts are about what you can allow your users to do for themselves — how you can empower your users. You can give users the ability to add Web Parts to pages, remove Web Parts from pages, move Web Parts from one location to another on the page, customize the Web Parts on a page, and join Web Parts together so that they can pass information between themselves. Users can perform all of these activities through your site's user interface — other than a browser, no additional tools are required. So, in addition to building applications, you can provide the tools that allow users to build their own solutions.

Allowing Customization with Web Parts

Initially it may seem that incorporating Web Part *tools* into your application isn't all that different from incorporating Web Part *components* into your page. When you decide to use a control as a Web Part, it may appear that all you've done is delay when the control will be incorporated into a page or when the control's properties will be set. For instance, instead of adding your control to a page at design time, you've delayed adding the control to the point when the page is being used at run time. You may be thinking that all that's required is some additional planning to ensure that your page will work correctly no matter when controls are added. You may even be thinking that all you'll really need to do is add some more error handling to your code in order to deal with conditions that may not have been considered at development time. If you do, then you're missing the point of Web Parts.

Here's the point: Incorporating Web Parts into your application development makes it possible to create a new kind of Web application. SharePoint, where Web Parts first appeared, was designed to empower users to build solutions that met their needs. With Web Parts now part of the ASP.NET developer's toolkit, you (and every other ASP.NET developer) also have the ability to empower your users. Instead of just designing an application to perform some task, you can consider the entire range of activities that your users need to perform and build tools that support those activities in any combination. Instead of delivering a rigid system that implements your design, you can build a discrete set of tools that allows users to meet their own needs. As your users' needs change and grow over time, they can call on your tools to deal with those changes.

Piggy Banks and Lego Kits

What's the difference between building a standard application and building a customizable solution? Let's say that you have some spare change rattling around in a drawer (or, worse, in several drawers). The obvious solution is to go out and buy a piggy bank. The piggy bank is a great tool for collecting and holding coins — but that's all it can do. Most piggy banks don't even do a very good job of holding paper money, let alone all the other things that you might want to save.

So instead of buying a piggy bank, you could buy a Lego kit. With a Lego kit you can build your own piggy bank — perhaps even figure out how to build a bank that works well with all the different things that you want to save. You can also build a tower, a plane, a car, and anything else that you can think of.

In addition, different Lego kits have different building blocks. The greater the variety of Lego building blocks available to you, the greater the variety of things that you can build and the easier it is to build specific items (a car is considerably easier to build if your kit includes wheels and axles, for instance). Within any application domain, domain-specific tools are more useful than general-purpose tools.

With Web Parts, your job is to provide your user with a set of building blocks that your users can build solutions with. And, besides, who doesn't enjoy playing with Legos?

Undoubtedly, the user community for your application will contain a variety of users, many with specialized needs. It's entirely possible that every user has a unique set of needs. As a result, different users may assemble the Web Parts that you've built in different ways. Instead of building a single application that must meet the diverse needs of all of your users, you build the Web Parts that your users need, and let your users each build a set of unique applications that meet their needs. Instead of building a single application, you enable the creation of an infinite number of applications, each tailored to its user. This is the ultimate goal of user customization: Each user builds a custom application for himself. With customization, each user sees her own custom version of the underlying application, as shown in Figure 1-2.

This is X-customization: eXtreme customization. But you don't have to go that far in order for Web Parts to be useful to you. If you do allow users to customize your application, it's likely that you'll support only limited customization of restricted portions of your application. And, in all likelihood, rather than each user building a unique application, a single customization will be implemented by many users in the user community.

But you can still consider X-customization as the ultimate goal of Web development — empowering your users with the tools they need to meet their goals.

Customization doesn't have to be limited to your application's users. You probably already recognize that you have different kinds of users in your user community. As a result, you may be planning different parts of your site to serve different user types. As part of this design process, you can create a series of roles for your application, where each role represents a different segment of your user community. The next step is to create a set of controls that can be assembled in different ways to create the pages that make up your application. You can then go one step further and, after adding your controls to the Web page, use the controls as Web Parts and customize them for various types of users. The final step is to assign users to roles so that when a user logs on, she receives the pages designed for her role.

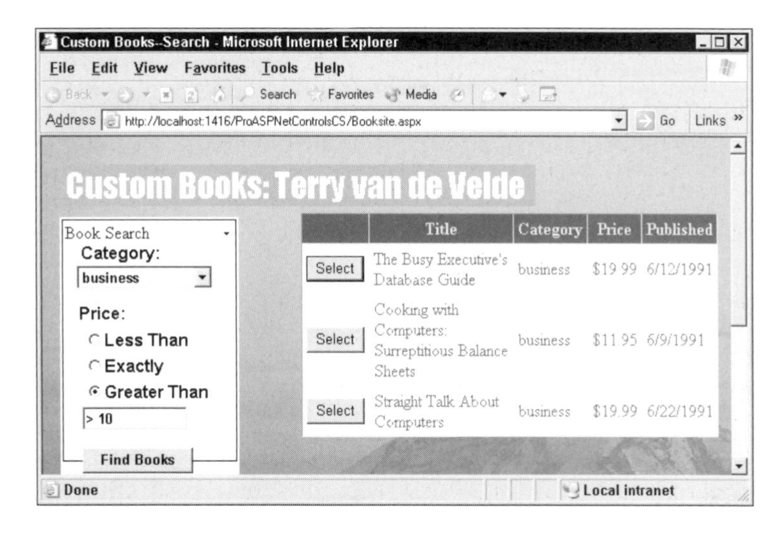

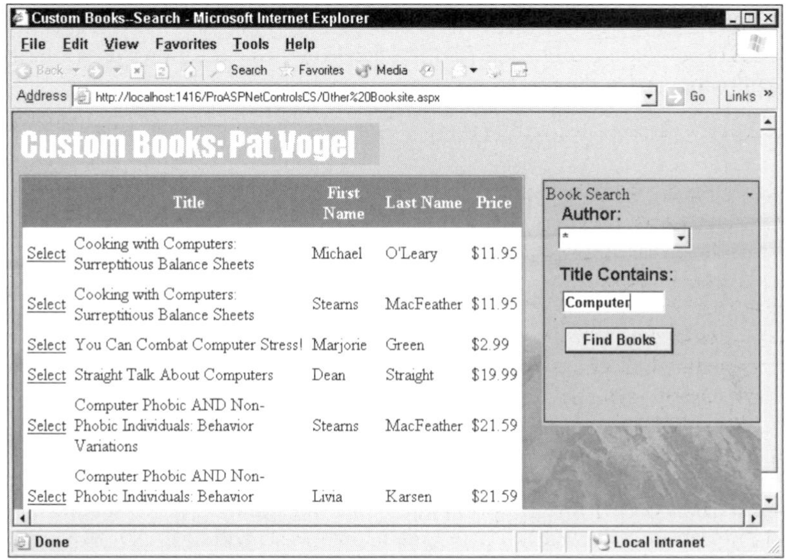

Figure 1-2

Implementing Reusability with Controls

One of the key ways to improve your productivity as a developer is through the re-use of components. If you've been building any kind of application, you've been using (or thinking about using) reusable objects. If you've been developing with ASP.NET, then you've been using (or thinking about using) custom controls and user controls as a means of creating reusable components.

When most developers think of "objects" they think of middleware components — items used to encapsulate business logic and data access that are called from the application code to perform some task. One example of these kinds of objects is the ADO.NET objects that are used in .NET to retrieve and update data (or the DAO and ADO objects in the COM world). There are two fundamental differences between that definition of objects and the ASP.NET-specific tools (custom controls, user controls, and Web Parts).

The first difference is that ASP.NET custom controls, user controls, and Web Parts can be used only with ASP.NET. The ADO.NET objects, for instance, can be accessed from any kind of code. It doesn't matter if your code is in a Windows Form, an ASP.NET page, or a middle-tier object, you can use the ADO.NET objects. However, limiting user controls, custom controls, and Web Parts to ASP.NET has its compensations: the ASP.NET tools, because they are tailored to ASP.NET, leverage the capabilities of the ASP.NET environment.

The second difference between the ASP.NET tools and what most developers think of as "objects" is where the ASP.NET tools are used. Most of the objects that developers create are designed to implement business logic and to reside in an application's middle tier — between the presentation layer (the user interface) and the data layer (the database). As part of creating a sales order system, for instance, a developer might create Customer, SalesOrder, and Invoice objects to handle all the activities involved with managing the application data. These objects would be called from code in the application's user interface and, in turn, update the application data in the database.

The ASP.NET tools, however, work only in the presentation layer, where they become an integral part of the user interface. In terms of the three benefits of using objects (productivity, standardization, simplification), the ASP.NET tools allow you to create a consistent user experience across many Web pages (and, with custom controls/Web Parts, across many Web sites). In addition, middle-tier objects can execute only on the Web server and are accessible only from application code that executes on your Web server. Web Parts, on the other hand, support writing code that will execute on both the server and in the browser, on the client. With the ASP.NET tools you can include client-side code that will be added to the HTML page that goes to the user and, as a result, executes in the Web browser.

Controls in Action

As an example of using controls to implement reusability in a user interface, consider a Web-based application that allows users to browse a catalog of books and order books. A user can log on to the application, search for a book by a list of criteria, read the details on a book, and place an order. Before they can access the site, users must register by entering information about themselves. In addition, when buying a book a customer must enter (or review and confirm) her billing, shipping, and contact information.

In this book application, users can list books in many different ways (for instance, wish lists, gift registries, recommended books, reminder lists). The application supports a variety of different customer types (such as individual consumers, companies, or libraries) and a variety of ways for customers to order books (individual orders, bulk orders, recurring orders, and so on). Customers can buy books using several different purchase mechanisms such as credit card, check, or purchase orders. Refer to Figure 1-2 to see typical pages from the bookstore Web site, listing books that match criteria entered by the user.

Obviously, many components in this application can be written once and then reused. For instance, a set of business rules that calculate a customer's creditworthiness or calculate the discounts available on an order shouldn't be duplicated in all the places where an order can be made — there's just too much danger that different versions of this code will get different answers. However, this code is implementing business rules and should be put in an object that is accessed by the parts of the application that need that processing.

There are a number of places in this application's user interface where a standardized, reusable control would be useful. Each page, for instance, should have the company logo and basic page information at the top. ASP.NET's master pages sound like a solution to this problem — but the page information isn't exactly the same for every customer (the customer name is included in the page's title bar, for instance). A Web Part would allow you to build a standard title bar for the top of the page that a user could modify to include their name as they want to be addressed and that would be automatically reloaded when that user returns to the site. For this Web Part, very little code may be required — just a set of properties that allow the Web Part's text and graphics to be updated may be sufficient. Figure 1-3 shows the title bars from two different pages implemented through the same Web Part.

Figure 1-3

While the application allows many different ways to list books, the way each book is displayed should be the same. By standardizing the way that book information is displayed, users can quickly figure out where to find particular information (such as price, genre, and so on). To meet this need, a custom control that can display a single book's information would be very useful. Because most of the book information is kept in a database, this Web Part could include the code to gather the information from the database either directly or by interacting with a middle-tier object. All that the application would have to do is pass a book's unique identifier to the custom control and the control would take care of displaying the book's data.

In fact, there's probably a need for two controls: a detailed book control that would display all the information on a book, and a summary book control that would display only basic information. Because the detailed information control would use a wide variety of controls and formatting to display all the information, it might be easiest to create it as a user control. Because the summary information control requires fewer controls, it might be easily created as a custom control. Figure 1-4 shows examples of these two Web Parts, with the detailed display above the summary display.

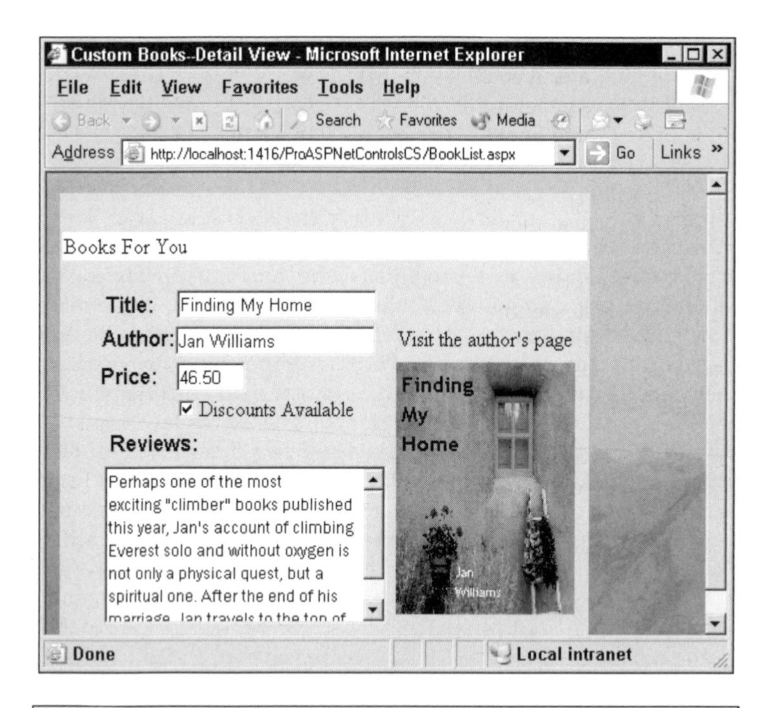
Custom Books--Detail View - Microsoft Internet Explorer
File Edit View Favorites Tools Help
Back Search Favorites Media
Address http://localhost:1416/ProASPNetControlsCS/BookList.aspx Go Links
Books For You
Title: Finding My Home
Author: Jan Williams
Visit the author's page
Price: 46.50
Discounts Available
Reviews:
Perhaps one of the most exciting "climber" books published this year, Jan's account of climbing Everest solo and without oxygen is not only a physical quest, but a spiritual one. After the end of his
Finding My Home
Done
Local intranet

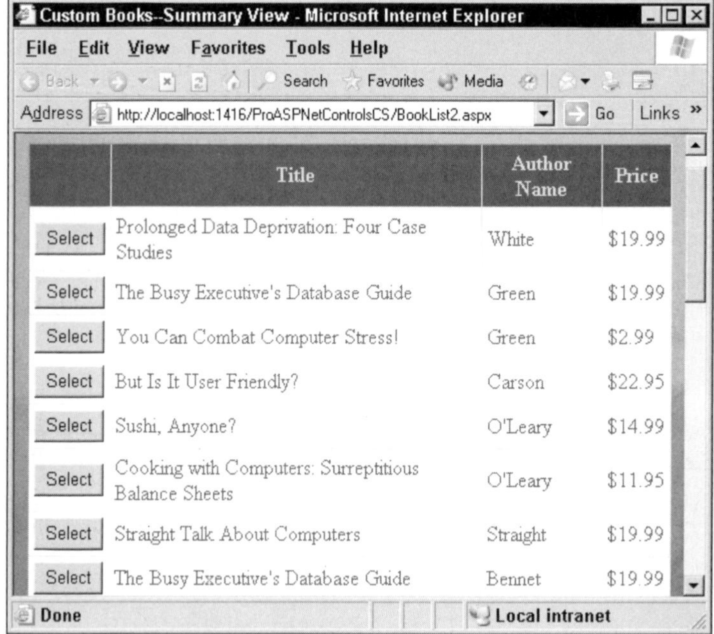
Custom Books--Summary View - Microsoft Internet Explorer
File Edit View Favorites Tools Help
Back Search Favorites Media
Address http://localhost:1416/ProASPNetControlsCS/BookList2.aspx Go Links
Title | Author Name | Price
Select | Prolonged Data Deprivation: Four Case Studies | White | $19.99
Select | The Busy Executive's Database Guide | Green | $19.99
Select | You Can Combat Computer Stress! | Green | $2.99
Select | But Is It User Friendly? | Carson | $22.95
Select | Sushi, Anyone? | O'Leary | $14.99
Select | Cooking with Computers: Surreptitious Balance Sheets | O'Leary | $11.95
Select | Straight Talk About Computers | Straight | $19.99
Select | The Busy Executive's Database Guide | Bennet | $19.99
Done
Local intranet

Figure 1-4

It would be convenient to have a single control that could be used to build all lists. This control could be implemented in one of two ways: it could either accept a set of criteria for building a list of books, or accept a list of book identifiers generated by some other part of the application. Either way, this control would use the previously created book summary control to display the individual books on the list in a standard way.

Throughout the application, customer information is gathered and displayed. Rather than make the user work with several different formats for customer information, why not create a customer information control? This control would work in two modes: data entry and data display. In the data display mode, the control would retrieve customer information from the database and display it. In the data entry mode, the control would accept customer information and do whatever validation is appropriate to the user interface (ensuring the customer phone number is correctly formatted, for instance). Once the data has passed validation, the control would take care of updating the database.

Here is a case where using a Web Part would be the best choice. If, for example, the Web page contains multiple controls, how do these controls commit their changes to the database? For instance, the Web page that lets customers order books might contain the control for entering customer information and a control for entering sales order header information. If these controls interact with the database (or middle-tier objects) individually, processing updates from the page could be very inefficient. The code on the Web page could coordinate updates from the controls, but then you lose some of the benefits of reusability that controls are supposed to provide. By taking advantage of the capability of Web Parts to find other Web Parts on the page and communicate with them, the code in the Web Parts could coordinate their updates. All the display-oriented Web Parts could look for an "update" Web Part on the page and send their updates to that Web Part for processing.

In either display or update mode, the customer control would have a set of properties that would expose the customer information to the application that's using the Web Part. Figure 1-5 shows the customer information Web Part in two different pages.

It's not hard to see that in addition to the benefits of standardization, there exist significant opportunities to improve the productivity of the person building or extending this application. When it's time to build a page that displays all the books for a specific customer, the developer who's building the page can start by adding the customer information control and the book listing control (which, in turn, uses the book summary control). From that point on, the developer just needs to add any specialized code required by the particular page.

Exploring the Different Kinds of Controls

Now that you've been introduced to the possibilities of Web Parts, custom controls, and user controls, you may be wondering how to decide which control to use in which situations. In this section, I offer guidelines on when you should use a user control or a custom control (remember that Web Parts are just a kind of custom control). Nothing is free, of course, so you also see what costs you incur by picking each type of control.

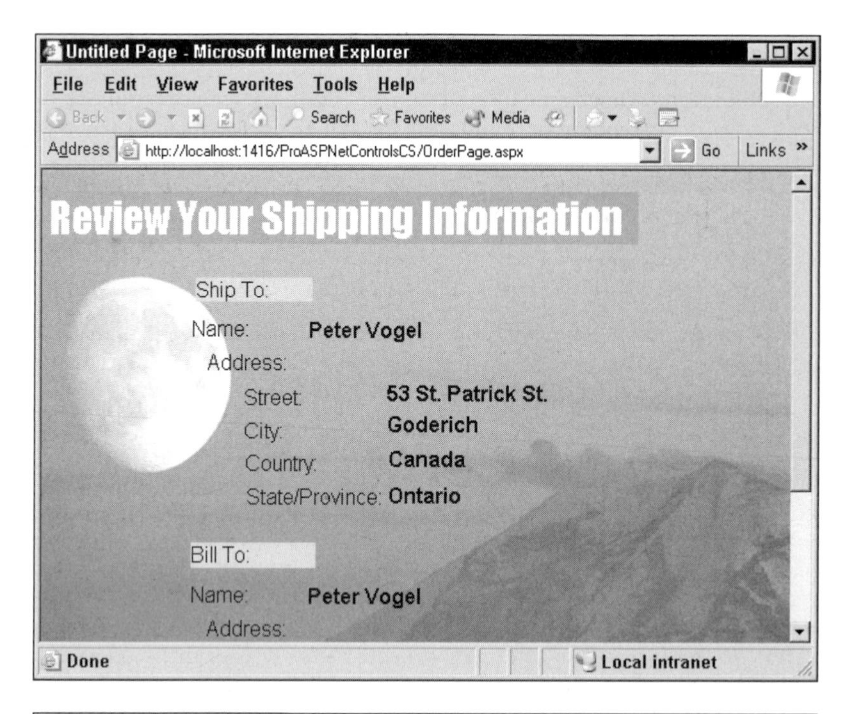
Untitled Page - Microsoft Internet Explorer
File Edit View Favorites Tools Help
Back Search Favorites Media
Address http://localhost:1416/ProASPNetControlsCS/OrderPage.aspx Go Links
Review Your Shipping Information
Ship To:
Name: Peter Vogel
Address:
Street: 53 St. Patrick St.
City: Goderich
Country: Canada
State/Province: Ontario
Bill To:
Name: Peter Vogel
Address:
Done
Local intranet

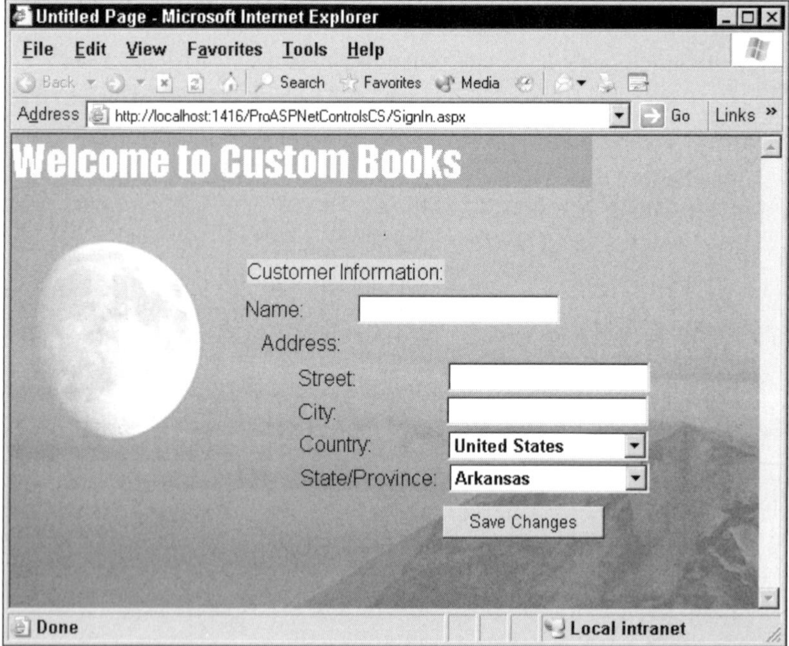
Untitled Page - Microsoft Internet Explorer
File Edit View Favorites Tools Help
Back Search Favorites Media
Address http://localhost:1416/ProASPNetControlsCS/SignIn.aspx Go Links
Welcome to Custom Books
Customer Information:
Name:
Address:
Street:
City:
Country: United States
State/Province: Arkansas
Save Changes
Done
Local intranet

Figure 1-5

When to Use a User Control

User controls should be your first choice for creating Web Parts where the control will be used on a single Web site only and isn't extending some other control. There are many benefits to using user controls:

- The drag-and-drop design interface supported by user controls is the simplest and fastest way to create your controls' user interface.
- You can put any amount of server-side code behind a Web user control, so you can have your Web Part perform any server-side processing that you want.
- You can give your Web Part custom properties, methods, and events, increasing the flexibility of the Web Part.
- You can include client-side code and HTML in your Web Part along with ASP.NET WebForm controls and server-side code just by switching to HTML view. This also lets you take advantage of Visual Studio .NET's support for writing client-side code (including IntelliSense).
- In addition to being more powerful than pure HTML, ASP.NET WebForm controls generate their HTML at run time and can configure the HTML they generate to match the device that is requesting them.

Because a user control can be used in a single project only, if you want to use a user control on two Web sites, you have to copy the control from the project that it was created in and paste it into the other project that it will be used in. This means that you will eventually end up with multiple copies of the same user control. When that happens you lose two of the benefits of components:

- **Standardization:** Inevitably, the multiple copies of the user control will start to diverge. Each version of the user control will be tweaked to work with the project that it's being used in. As a result, the functionality embedded in the user control will start to work differently in the different versions.
- **Productivity:** The first loss in productivity occurs because multiple developers continue to develop the different versions of the user control. The second loss occurs because developers will, eventually, have to take time to reconcile the different versions of the user control. For instance, when a bug is discovered, or a change is required because of changes in the organization, or the opportunity for an enhancement is recognized, developers will have to chase down all the versions of the control to make the change.

When to Use a Custom Control

Custom controls can do anything that a user control can do — it just takes longer to build them. (This makes custom controls an excellent choice if you are paid by the hour.) When building a custom control you may find that you have to write the server-side code that generates the client-side portion of your Web Part, including any HTML. This means that you give up the way that ASP.NET's standard controls automatically adapt their HTML to the client that requested them.

You can still use ASP.NET WebForm controls in your Web custom control, but you must write code to add those WebForm controls to your user interface rather than using drag-and-drop. The same is true of any client-side code that you add to your Web Part: The client-side code must be generated from your server-side code, rather than typed into the HTML view of a Web Page. Without the benefit of the Visual

Studio .NET designer, it's going to take much longer to lay out your user interface. And, without the benefit of Visual Studio .NET's IntelliSense support for writing client-side code, it's going to take longer to write bug-free client-side code, also.

You should use a custom control only if there is some compelling reason for not using a user control. In the days of the ASP.NET 1.0 and 1.1, there were several benefits to using custom controls compared to user controls — custom controls had a design-time interface and could be shared among projects, for instance. However, with ASP.NET 2.0, some of those differences have gone away. With ASP.NET 2.0, there are only three reasons that might cause you to consider using a custom control:

- You should use a custom control whenever the control will be used in more than one project.
- You should use a custom control when your HTML can't be generated by some combination of existing ASP.NET controls.
- You should use a custom control when you want to extend an existing ASP.NET control (rather than write all the functionality yourself). While you can extend an existing ASP.NET control by wrapping it inside a user control, it's often easier to extend an existing control by inheriting from the existing control and modifying it in some way.

Web custom controls do offer another benefit: they expose all the code involved in creating a control — a good thing in a book about creating your own controls.

In the book site example, a user control would be the best choice for the title bar because the title bar is limited to a single Web site and is built from existing Web server controls. The properties exposed by the title bar Web Part would allow the code behind a page to insert the text that the page needs. The listing control described in the case study would be best implemented through a custom control that extends the ASP.NET DataList control.

Web Parts in Action: Customization

But when should you use a Web Part? First, remember that any control can be used as a Web Part. When used as a Web Part, user controls and custom controls can be customized in several ways:

- The control can be added or removed from the page.
- The control's appearance can be modified.
- The control can be moved to a different location on the page.

Users will also be able to set the control's property values interactively at run time. However, if you build a control as a Web Part from the ground up, you can give your control even more features — the capability to pass data between other controls, for instance.

When considering how you can use Web Parts, ask yourself if it's necessary that you build every page in your application. Can you improve your productivity by letting your users build parts of the application for you? This section offers a few examples based on the bookstore application. Your users will certainly come up with many suggestions for customizing your application by using Web Parts.

When you build an application, you are faced with decisions on what user interface will work best for your users. For instance, the application's designers may have decided not to display book detail information on the same page as a book list. The site's designers may have thought the amount of information on a page with both a list and detailed book information would be overwhelming — for *most* (but not all) users. So, while users can generate a list of books with summary information, when the user wants to look at detail information he has to click a button and go to a new page. To continue to work through the list, users must click a button to return to the list. The result is that users "ping-pong" back and forth between the list and detail pages. For many users, this is the optimal design.

But there may be users out there who resent having to click an item in a book list in order to go to a new page that displays the detail information on a book. They would prefer to have the list display the detailed book information, rather than just the summary information. Given access to the controls already discussed, using those controls as Web Parts would let users build this detailed list page by dropping the detail book Web Part onto a page with the listing control. Look again at Figure 1-4: The top portion shows the standard book listing using the detailed book information Web Part, while the bottom portion illustrates the same listing, but now using the summary book information Web Part.

With Web Parts, any user can build a page to meet her unique needs, the only limits being the toolkit of Web Parts that you provide. For instance, the application probably has a page that displays all the books purchased by the current customer. The user just navigates to the page to see the books she's bought. However, it's not hard to imagine that customers might want to list all the books purchased by their company or some other buying entity that they have permission to view. To get this list by using one of the application's built-in lists, the customer has to navigate to the page, enter the name of the organization into the search criteria, and then generate the list. You could expand your application to hold the customer's various affiliations and automatically display books purchased by affiliated organizations — but where does this stop?

Instead, you could allow your users to build a dedicated search page. The first step would be to enhance the customer information control so that the user can set the properties on the control, including the customer name. A user could then drag the customer information control to a page and customize the control by setting the customer name to some buying entity that they are allowed access to. With that done, your user could drag the listing Web Part onto the page and connect it to the customized customer information Web Part. The listing Web Part would now display the books purchased by the entity entered in the customer Web Part. The user could redisplay the list just by navigating to the page.

As this example indicates, you may want to create Web Parts whose sole purpose is to support user customizations. For instance, the application has several places where users can enter search criteria for listing books. However, it may not make sense to build a separate control for entering search criteria or listing books because there's no opportunity for reuse. It may be that every search page supports a different set of criteria and each list has a unique format for displaying the books found in the search. In addition, this version of the application uses only the summary book information and detail book information Web Parts.

Even though there's no opportunity for reuse, it may still make sense to create controls just to support customization. To create opportunities for customization, you could create sets of Web Parts for:

- **Entering search criteria:** One control might provide a limited number of search criteria (just author and title), another control might provide an extensive list of options familiar to the general audience (author, title, publisher), while another control might offer options only of interest to collectors (allowing the user to specify particular editions or publication dates, for instance).

- **Listing books:** One control might provide a single column with limited options for sorting the list, another control could support complex sorting options, another control might format the user into a rigid grid format with a single line for each book, and yet another control might allow the list to "snake" through multiple columns, allowing more books to be listed on a page.
- **Displaying book information:** Different controls might vary in the amount of information displayed about a book or which information stands out. One control might be formatted so that information about book size and weight stands out for retail buyers concerned about reducing shipping costs — information that the typical reader isn't interested in.

With those controls created, you could add a page to your application that consists of two areas:

- One area at the top of the page to place one of the search criteria controls
- An area below that to put one of the controls for listing books

Users could draw from your toolkit of Web Parts to build the search page that they want. Users would be able to put the search criteria Web Part that most meets their needs at the top of the page and put the listing Web Part they want below that. To work with the listing control, they could add the book information Web Part that supports them best. This is a solution aimed purely at giving users the opportunity to create the application they need.

Providing for Personalization

In order to implement customization, you also need *personalization*. Your users won't be happy if they have to recreate their application each time that they return to your site, or if, when they return, they get some other user's customization. Customization is of no use unless the application remembers what changes a user has made and associates those changes with the user that made them. Fortunately, ASP.NET 2.0 comes with a personalization framework. The ASP.NET 2.0 personalization framework allows you to implement an application that tracks users and the choices they make so that when the users return to your application, they find their own customizations waiting for them. Each user is connected to his customized application after he logs on with little effort on your part.

This description makes personalization sound like a "nice-to-have" feature. In fact, personalization is really just the extension of identity-based security, which is essential in building an application. When users access your Web site, they are automatically logged on to your Web site's server. The logging in process assigns the user an identity, even if it's only the default "anonymous user" assigned by IIS. If you've turned off the capability to log on as the anonymous user, then the user may be silently logged on using whatever credentials are currently available (for instance, the user ID and password that the user logged on to his workstation with). If no valid credentials are available, the user may be asked to enter a user ID and password. After the user has logged on to your site's server, your application may have an additional level of security that requires the user to enter a user ID and password into your application's login page.

All of this work, both in the infrastructure that supports your Web application and in the application code behind your login page, has just one purpose: to establish who the user is (the user ID) and to authenticate that claim (the password). Once a user is authenticated, she is then authorized to perform specific activities.

Whatever mechanism is used to authenticate the user, when the process is completed successfully, the user has been assigned an identity. From this point of view, security is just the base level of personalization; security assigns an identity that is authorized to perform some activities (and forbidden to perform others). Personalization extends this security feature up from the ASP.NET infrastructure and into the application domain. Personalization allows you to manage your application on the basis of who the user is.

The identity you are assigned when you log onto the Web server is used just within the application. When your code accesses other services (for example, reading or writing a database), those accesses are normally performed by an identity that represents ASP.NET. (On Windows 2003, this identity is called NETWORK SERVICE; on other versions of Windows the identity is called ASPNET.) In your application's Web.Config file you can turn on impersonation, which causes the ASP.NET application to adopt the identity used to log on to the server: the anonymous user if anonymous access is enabled, the user's identity if anonymous access is not enabled.

Understanding the Personalization Framework

The good news is that the personalization framework will take care of itself—by and large you can just build on the personalization framework and count on it to work. However, there are some decisions that you will need to make as part of setting up a Web site (for example, selecting the correct provider for your site). In order to make those decisions you need to understand the components of the personalization framework.

The personalization framework has three main components:

- Login controls
- Membership providers
- Profile services and providers

The first components of the personalization framework that a user encounters are ASP.NET 2.0's new login and user controls. Rather than write all the code necessary to log in a user, you can simply drag and drop the new login controls to a Web page. These controls handle all the typical tasks associated with the log on process (including sending forgotten passwords to users). For personalization, these controls allow a user to be assigned an identity. Separate from this process, the site administrator has to register with the personalization datastore the identities that users can be assigned. Figure 1-6 illustrates the three elements of the personalization framework: login controls, membership providers, and profile services.

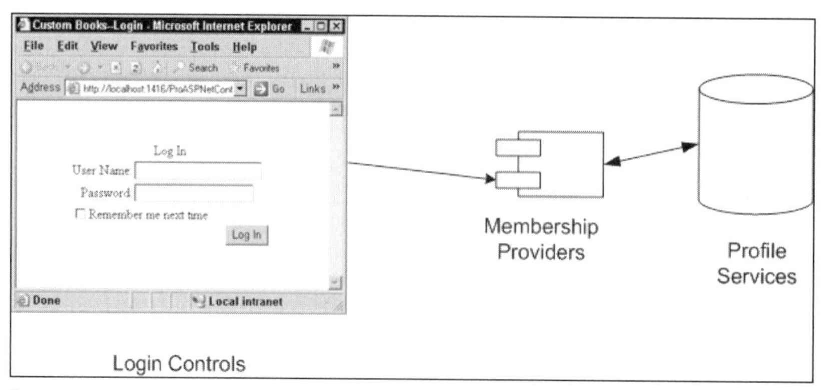

Figure 1-6

Within the area of user management, some other features of SharePoint have also migrated into ASP.NET 2.0. Within SharePoint, it's possible for authorized users to create new SharePoint sites, new users, new pages, and perform other administrative tasks.

In ASP.NET 2.0, as part of the personalization framework, it's possible to implement user management functions within the site itself (although you still can't create a whole new Web site from within an application). ASP.NET even comes with a set of pre-defined user administration pages that you can incorporate into your site.

Logging in is more than just assigning identities. For sites that have a small number of users, implementing personalization on an identity-by-identity basis is a viable choice. However, as the number of identities increases, the costs of maintaining personalized information increases. While costs increase with the number of identities, the benefits of personalization don't increase. In all likelihood, the customizations made for one identity will be applicable to other identities. In any user community, you can probably break your user community up into several groups. This can be handled by assigning individual users to roles and implementing customizations on a role-by-role (group) basis. As a result, you need a mechanism that not only assigns identities to users but also assigns users to roles.

The next component of the personalization framework, the membership provider, handles this. The membership provider is the glue that binds the site to the users that access the site and binds the site's functionality to the various user roles. Membership providers also handle all the tasks around storing user and role information. Two membership providers come with ASP.NET 2.0: one for storing information in Microsoft SQL Server and one for storing information in a Jet database. If you want, you can even build your own membership provider to connect to other data stores.

A provider is a component that extends or replaces some existing ASP.NET function. Any part of ASP.NET that is implemented through a provider model can be enhanced or replaced with a provider written by you (or some third party, such as IBM's Tivoli for transaction management). Once you have built a new provider, you plug it in to the list of available providers and select it when you build your application (which is why providers are said to be "pluggable"). The main requirement of a provider is that it has to reproduce the interface (methods, properties, events) for the provider that it extends or replaces. However, what happens behind that interface is up to the developer that creates the provider.

The final component of the personalization framework is the profile service. A profile is all the data associated with a specific identity. The profile service allows you to store and retrieve data for a particular identity or role. To access the profile service, you need a profile provider that handles all the data access for you. The profile service is very flexible: you can store any data from simple datatypes (for example, strings) right up to an object (provided that the object can be serialized). In addition, saving and restoring data from the profile is handled for you automatically.

The personalization framework allows you to store, as part of a profile, the Web Part customizations associated with some identity. The membership provider allows you to keep track of which identities are being used. The login controls assign identities to users.

Summary

In this chapter you've learned about the two types of controls that you can use in ASP.NET:

- **User controls:** A combination of content, static HTML, ASP.NET tags, and code, built using the same tools that you use to create Web pages.
- **Custom controls/WebParts:** A code-only solution, very similar to ASP.NET custom controls. Unlike custom controls, you cannot inherit from other controls when building a Web Part. These controls are the focus of this book.

By the end of this book you'll have learned how to build the more powerful and flexible custom controls. I also show you how to use these controls as Web Parts and how to extend custom controls to let users customize your site. Along the way, you'll also see how easy it is to build user controls — and both how to add custom control features to user controls and use them as Web Parts.

While it's good to know about controls, what's important to you is what you do with those controls. You've seen how these ASP.NET tools support two different scenarios:

- **Reusability:** Controls support reusability in the user interface (or presentation) layer rather than in the business rules layer. Like other reusability tools, controls enable you to provide a standardized set of services and improve your own productivity.
- **Customization:** Web Parts allow you to support customization to a degree that simply wasn't possible in earlier versions of ASP and ASP.NET. With Web Parts, you can allow your users to create customized versions of existing pages, or to create pages that were not intended to be included in the application. While this empowers your users, it also opens up a whole new set of challenges for the developer, both in determining what Web Parts the user community will need and ensuring that those Web Parts will work in all the different ways that users want.

Finally, in order to support customization, you also need personalization: the ability to keep track of a user's choices, remember those changes from one session to another, and connect the user to his customized pages. Personalization is the extension of identity-based security into application development. Over the rest of this book, you'll see how to build custom controls, user controls, and Web Parts.

2

Creating Customizable Pages

The capability to add customization to your Web application using Web Parts is completely new in ASP.NET 2.0. Before plunging in to the details of creating controls, it's worthwhile to take the time to understand what customization means to you and your users. Consider these four questions:

- How much work is required to enable customization? How do you turn it on?
- How do I take advantage of customization in my applications?
- Do I need to write a lot of specialized code to create customizable pages?
- What customization can the user expect to be able to do with a Web page?

This chapter shows you the detailed answers to all four of these questions, but here are the short answers: To turn on customization you just need to drag a single control onto our page. You can implement customization in your application just by dragging and dropping other standard ASP.NET controls to a page. And you don't have to write much code at all — two or three lines of code will allow your users to add and remove controls from the page, configure the appearance of the controls, and move controls from one part of your page to another.

From the more detailed answers in this chapter, you'll learn how to

- Create a customizable ASP.NET page
- Use the Web Part framework controls that come with ASP.NET
- Determine which parts of the page are available for customization
- Add standard ASP.NET server-side controls to let your users customize the page
- Customize a Web Part–enabled page

In this chapter, you use the standard server-side controls that come with ASP.NET 2.0 on a customizable page so that you can see that you don't need to create specialized Web Part controls to take advantage of customization. This is critical for your work as a developer creating controls: to create controls that support customization, you need to understand how the various tools that make up the Web Parts framework work together. These tools form the environment that your code will integrate with when you start creating your own controls.

Finally, you also get a glimpse of the kind of customizations that become available when you do add Web Part features to your own controls.

The Web Part Framework Controls

New to the Visual Studio 2005 Toolbox is a tab called WebParts. In this tab you find the dozen Web Part infrastructure controls that make up the Web Part framework. I refer to these as the *Web Part framework controls* (or just the *framework controls*) to distinguish them from the controls that you'll create or the standard ASP.NET controls that come with .NET. These framework controls include:

- **WebPartManager:** The control that enables a page for customization.
- **Zones:** These controls define the sections of a page that users can customize. Different kinds of WebPartZones support different kinds of Web Part controls, as follows:
    - **WebPartZone:** For holding controls (either standard ASP.NET controls or controls that you create).
    - **CatalogZone:** For holding Web Part framework controls that list the controls that you can add to WebPartZones.
    - **EditorZone:** For holding editors that allow you to modify controls on the page.
- **Editors:** The tools that allow the user to set properties on a control or otherwise modify a control.
    - **AppearanceEditorPart:** Allows the user to set the values of specific properties related to the way that a control is displayed.
    - **BehaviorEditorPart:** Allows the user to set the values of specific properties on a control in shared mode, which causes the changes to be made for all users instead of just for the user making the change.
    - **LayoutEditorPart:** Allows the user to move controls from one location on the page to another.
    - **PropertyGridEditorPart:** Allows the user to set any custom properties on a control (that is, those properties on a custom control that are not inherited from a base control).
- **Catalogs:** The tools that list the controls that can be added to the page, including:
    - **DeclarativeCatalogPart:** Lists controls that are declared in the HTML in the page but haven't yet been added to the page.
    - **PageCatalogPart:** Lists controls that are already added to the page but aren't visible to the user (controls that are closed).
    - **ImportCatalogPart:** Lists controls that can be added to the page by importing from files on your server.

- **ConnectionsZone:** Holds connection objects that represent connections between controls in a Web Part Zone.

Creating a Customizable Page

In Visual Studio 2005, you begin creating a customizable page for your application by dragging a WebPartManager from the toolbox and onto the page that you want to enable for customization. A WebPartManager control has no visible user interface at run time (at design time the WebPartManager appears as a plain gray box); the control is just there to support customization.

If you get the message "The operation could not be completed. Unspecified error" when dragging and dropping the WebPartManager, or if you're not working with Visual Studio .NET, you can add a WebPartManager to a page by putting this tag in your page right after the open <form> tag:

```
<asp:webpartmanager id="WebPartManager1" runat="server" />
```

> **You should add the WebPartManager control to any page where you want to use the other framework components *first*, before adding any other Web Part control. Attempting to use the other Web Part framework controls on a page without a WebPartManager just generates a run time error when you attempt to view the page in a browser. If you add a WebPartManager to a page after adding other Web Part framework controls, you must make sure that the WebPartManager is at the top of the page, before any of the other framework controls.**

Adding a WebPartManager not only supports customization on the page but also activates the necessary personalization support for your ASP.NET application, including creating a SQL Server (or SQL Server Express) database to hold your application's personalization information when you first debug your application.

> **Depending on the speed of your computer, it's possible that your Web application will time out before your personalization database is created the first time you test the page. If so, just restart your Web application and your database will be created by the time that you restart.**

The next time you start Visual Studio 2005, you'll see that the App_Data folder in Solution Explorer will have an entry for the ASPNETDB.MDF file. If the database doesn't appear in Solution Explorer, or you don't want to wait until you restart Visual Studio 2005, you can add the database to Solution Explorer manually:

1. Right-click on the App_Data entry in Solution Explorer.
2. Select Add Existing Item. The Add Existing Item dialog box opens.
3. Open the App_Data subdirectory. You should find the ASPNETDB.MDF directory there.

4. Click the ASPNETDB.MDF file to select it.
5. Click the Add button to add the file to Solution Explorer.

Clicking the plus sign beside the MDF file entry will let you explore the tables that hold personalization data as you would with any other database that you attach to your project.

Because the personalization data is held in a database on the server (rather than, for instance, cookies that are sent to the browser) a user's customizations are maintained even if the user accesses the site from different browsers or different computers.

While this is all that you need to get started with personalization and customization, in Chapter 10 you learn more about what you can with ASP.NET's personalization infrastructure (including how to specify which database management system will store your site's personalization data).

With the WebPartManager on the page, you must next set up the zones on the page where customization will be allowed. Because customization happens only within these zones, to protect parts of your page from customization simply make sure those parts of the page aren't in a zone.

In order to create a zone in Visual Studio 2005, you just drag a WebPartZone control onto your Web page. The samples used in this chapter are added to a page called CustomizablePage.ASPX. After the WebPartZone is on the page, you can control the position of the zone by selecting Layout ➪ Position ➪ Absolute from the Visual Studio menus and dragging the WebPartZone to where you want it. You can resize the WebPartZone by dragging its sides as you would with any other control. You can place as many WebPartZones onto a page as you want. Figure 2-1 shows a page with three WebPartZones.

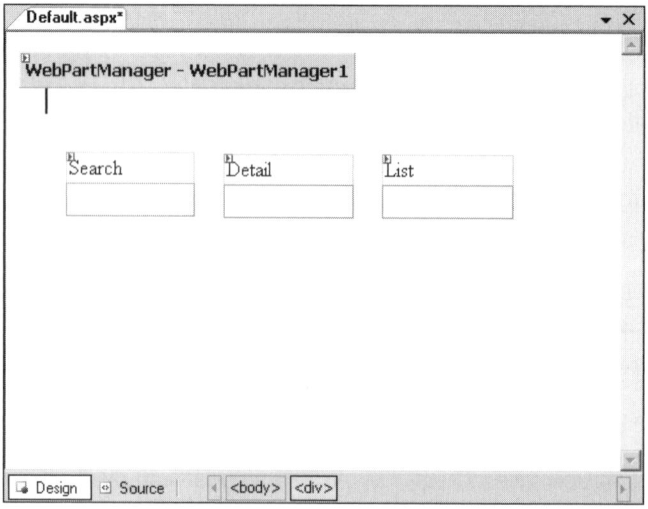

Figure 2-1

If you're working outside of Visual Studio 2005, you can add WebPartZones to your page using the asp:WebPartZone element. The following code shows the tags for the page shown in Figure 2-1:

```
<body>
    <form id="form1" runat="server">

    <div>

        <asp:WebPartZone ID="WebPartZone1"
            Style="z-index: 57; left: 10px; position: absolute;
                   top: 15px" Runat="server" Width="342px" Height="81px">
        </asp:WebPartZone>

        <asp:WebPartZone ID="WebPartZone2"
            Style="z-index: 56; left: 10px; position: absolute;
                   top: 96px" Runat="server" Width="126px" Height="318px">
        </asp:WebPartZone>

        <asp:WebPartZone ID="WebPartZone3"
            Style="z-index: 55; left: 136px; position: absolute;
                   top: 96px" Runat="server" Width="216px" Height="320px">
        </asp:WebPartZone>

    </div>

    </form>
</body>
```

Each WebPartZone consists of a header area and an area where controls can be added. The contents of the header can be set using the HeaderText property of the WebPartZone. In Figure 2-1, the HeaderText properties of the three zones have been set to Search, Detail, and List. In the figure, none of these controls has had any custom controls added, so the WebPartZone displays an empty area for you to drag your control to. You can modify the WebPartZone to display text in this area when no control is present (for example, "Drag a WebPart here") through the EmptyZoneText property of the WebPartZone. You can control the appearance of this "empty" area through the EmptyZoneTextStyle property.

A zone's HeaderText and EmptyPartText aren't displayed just at design time. As you'll see later in this chapter, the EmptyPartText can be visible to your users when they are customizing a page. So getting the EmptyPartText/EmptyZoneTextStyle and HeaderText/HeaderStyle correct can be an important design decision.

Adding Controls to a Zone

After you've added a WebPartZone to a page, in Visual Studio .NET you can add controls into the lower part of the zone by dragging them from the toolbox. Figure 2-2 shows a WebPartZone that has had a text box and a button dragged into it. The bad news is that after you drag a control into a zone, you can't position the control within the zone—controls are inserted either beside or underneath each other (this is controlled by the zone's LayoutOrganization property). You can't use absolute positioning within a zone.

In this chapter, only standard ASP.NET controls are used in a zone. However, you can put just about anything in a zone: HTML controls, plain text, custom controls, and (as you'll see) user controls.

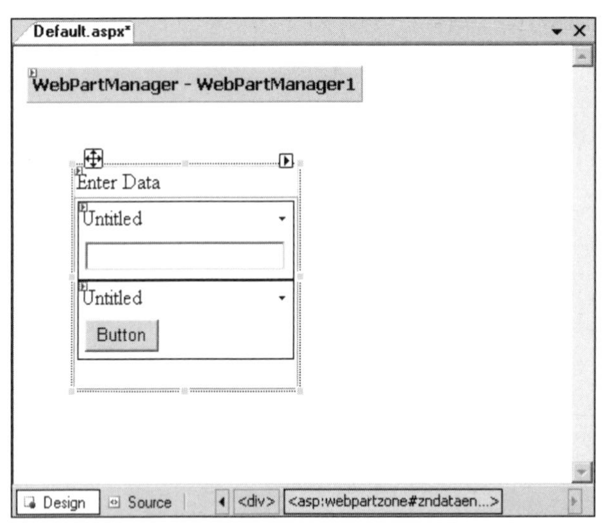

Figure 2-2

When you add a control to the WebPartZone it should appear as in Figure 2-2. However, if the control appears at the top of the WebPartZone, it means that the control has been added with absolute positioning. (In other words, the first option in the Position options dialog box reached through Layout ➪ Position ➪ AutoPosition Options has been set to Absolutely positioned.) To fix the problem in Visual Studio 2005, click the control and from the Layout ➪ Position menu, select the Not Set option (even if it's already selected). Or, switch to HTML view and delete "position: absolute;" from the control's Style attribute. You may have similar problems if you use relative positioning but the solution is the same: delete the position setting in your control's Style attribute.

To add the same controls outside of Visual Studio 2005's drag-and-drop environment, place the tags for the button and a text box inside a <ZoneTemplate> element inside the WebPartZone. As the following example shows, while WebPartZone elements use absolute positioning values in their style attribute, the controls within a WebPartZone don't:

```
<asp:WebPartZone ID="DataEntry" Runat="server"
     VerbButtonType="Link" HeaderText="Data Entry"
     style="z-index: 67; left: 72px; position: absolute; top: 88px">

     <ZoneTemplate>
          <asp:TextBox Runat="server" ID="TextBox1"></asp:TextBox>
          <asp:Button Runat="server" Text="Button" ID="Button1" />
     </ZoneTemplate>

</asp:WebPartZone>
```

Wrapping Controls in Web Parts

The ASP.NET Button and TextBox controls are not Web Parts so, at run time, these controls are programmatically wrapped inside of a GenericWebPart object. This gives a standard control the customization capabilities of a Web Part. Some of those characteristics show up in the visual display of the control in Visual Studio's Design view. For instance, as Figure 2-2 shows, the controls are each enclosed in a box and have a title bar that shows a small downward pointing arrow. Clicking the arrow displays a menu with two choices: Minimize and Close. The Minimize and Close options represent two of the customization actions that a user can perform on a control (these actions are referred to as *verbs*). By default, verbs are displayed as links but they can also be displayed as images and buttons, as controlled by the zone's TitleBarVerbButtonType property.

Technically speaking, what is in the WebPartZone is a Web Part (specifically, a GenericWebPart) which, in turn, contains a single ASP.NET control. What's the difference between a GenericWebPart with an ASP.NET control inside of it and an ASP.NET control? In the previous paragraph, it would have been more accurate to say that the Web Parts containing the ASP.NET controls have a menu that shows Minimize and Close actions.

At this point, there aren't many benefits in making the distinction between the control and the Web Part that the control is wrapped in. To begin with, there is a one-to-one relationship between controls and the Web Parts that are wrapped around them. In addition, the GenericWebPart wrapper for the control isn't generated until run time. One of the results of this delayed creation of the Web Part is that, when you click the control in the WebPartZone, the Property List in Visual Studio 2005 shows only the properties for the ASP.NET control that will end up inside the GenericWebPart. So, in this chapter, the controls in the zone are treated as if they were Web Parts rather than ASP.NET controls wrapped inside a Web Part.

Once you start creating your own Web Parts, you'll be able to create Web Parts that contain multiple ASP.NET controls. You'll also see how to access the methods and properties of Web Part objects even at design time.

Accessing Controls in a Zone

Initially, as shown in Figure 2-2, the title bar for a control contains the word "Untitled." For a generic control, you can't change this value from the Visual Studio Property List—but you can change the title from code. In code, individual controls inside a zone can be accessed through a zone's WebParts collection. The following Visual Basic 2005 code, for instance, sets the Title property of the first control in a WebPartZone called znDataEntry (the result is shown in Figure 2-3):

```
Me.znDataEntry.WebParts(0).Title = "Search"
```

In C#, the equivalent code looks like this:

```
this.znDataEntry.WebParts[0].Title = "Search";
```

You can also access the controls inside a zone through the zone's WebParts collection by using the Id property of the individual controls. This Visual Basic 2005 code sets the title for a control with the Id set to txtTopic in the zone znDataEntry:

```
Me.znDataEntry.WebParts("txtTopic").Title = "Search"
```

In C#:

```
this.znDataEntry.WebParts["txtTopic"].Title = "Search";
```

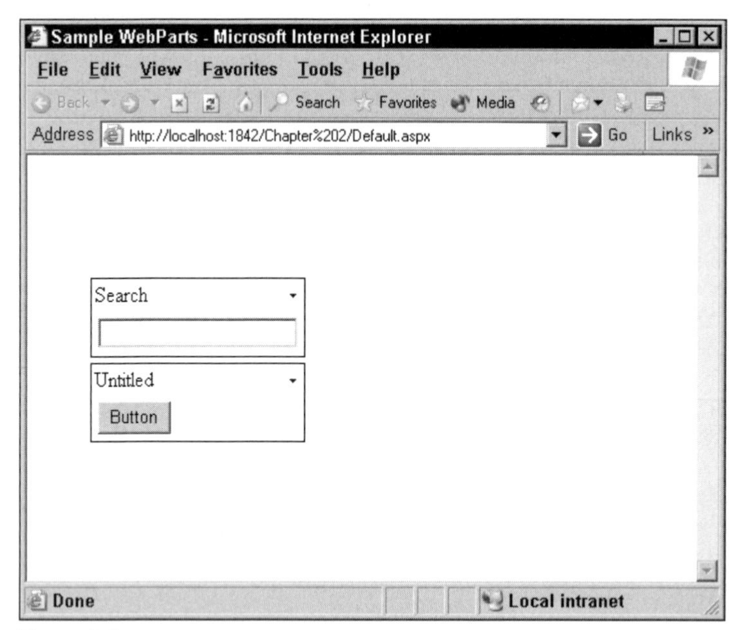

Figure 2-3

When a control is accessed through the WebParts collection, a WebPart object is returned. You can use this object to set properties relevant to a Web Part, as this Visual Basic 2005 code does by setting the Title property:

```
Dim wp As WebPart

wp = Me.znSearch.WebParts("TextBox1")
wp.Title = "Topic"
```

The same code in C# looks like this:

```
WebPart wp;

wp = this.znSearch.WebParts["TextBox1"];
wp.Title = "Topic";
```

You can also set the title of a control in a WebPartZone in the source view of your page by adding a title attribute to the control's tag. In this example, for instance, the TextBox control inside of the WebPartZone will be given the title "A textbox" instead of the default "Untitled":

```
<asp:WebPartZone ID="WebPartZone1" runat="server"
             style="z-index: 100; left: 282px; position: absolute; top: 76px" >
        <ZoneTemplate>
            <asp:TextBox runat="server" ID="TextBox1"
                                            title="A textbox"></asp:TextBox>
        </ZoneTemplate>
</asp:WebPartZone>
```

Adding a user control to a WebPartZone is handled the same way that you would add a user control to a WebForm. In Visual Studio .NET, you can just drag a user control from Solution Explorer into the WebPartZone. To add a user control outside of Visual Studio .NET, you must first add a Register directive for the user control after the Page directive:

```
<%@ Page Language="VB" AutoEventWireup="false" CompileWith="BookDetailList.aspx.vb"
                                ClassName="BookDetailList_aspx" %>
<%@ Register TagPrefix="uc1" TagName="WebUserControl"
                                Src="WebUserControl.ascx" %>
```

Once the user control has been registered, you can insert its tag inside a ZoneTemplate for a WebPartZone on a page that has a WebPartManager:

```
<asp:WebPartManager ID="WebPartManager1" Runat="server">
</asp:WebPartManager>

<asp:WebPartZone ID="znSearch" Runat="server" HeaderText="Search ">
   <ZoneTemplate>
       <uc1:WebUserControl Runat="server" ID="WebUserControl1" />
   </ZoneTemplate>
</asp:WebPartZone>
```

At this point, you have all that you need to create a basic, customizable page using standard ASP.NET controls. You can demonstrate this with a simple test:

1. Create a WebForm page in an ASP.NET 2.0 project.
2. Drag a WebPartManager control to the page.
3. Drag a WebPartZone control to the page.
4. Drag a WebForm TextBox into the WebPartZone. The page should look as it appears in Figure 2-4.
5. Browse the page in Internet Explorer by right-clicking on the page in Solution Explorer and selecting View in Browser.
6. Customize the page by selecting the Minimize action from the text box's menu (click on the small down arrow to display the menu). The text box disappears and the Minimize action changes to Restore. You have customized your page.
7. Shut down the browser.
8. View the page in Internet Explorer again. You will see that the text box is still minimized. ASP.NET has kept track of your customization.

This is a *very* simple customization application. Before you can take full advantage of the customization facilities in ASP.NET, you'll need to drill a little deeper into zones and controls and how Web Parts interact with them.

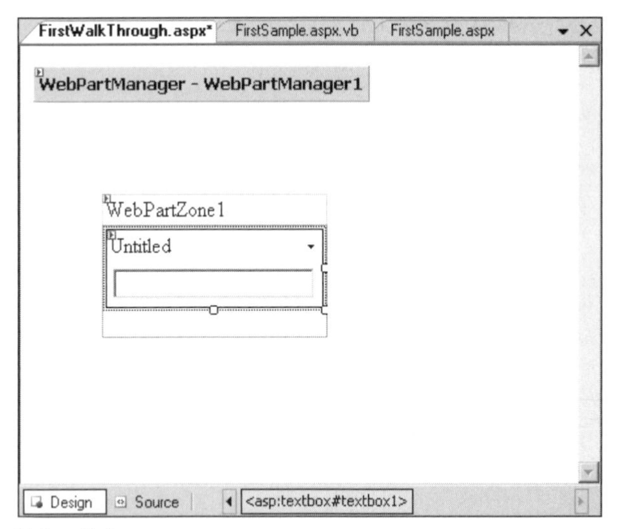

Figure 2-4

Configuring a Zone

WebPartZones support the standard properties for all WebForm controls (such as AccessKey, BackColor, and so on). However, there are several properties that are not only unique to the WebPartZone controls but are essential in understanding how the controls that you will create will work with a customizable page. Also critical, from the point of view of a Web Part developer, is ensuring that the settings are at the WebPartZone level that controls the behavior of the Web Parts in the zone.

Configuring Customization Verbs

The most important customization properties for a WebPartZone are the *verb properties: CloseVerb, ConnectVerb, DeleteVerb, EditVerb, ExportVerb, HelpVerb, MinimizeVerb, and RestoreVerb. These verbs represent the customization actions that can be performed on a control in a zone at run time, two of which (Minimize and Close) are included in the Web Part's menu by default:

- **Edit:** Allows the control to be edited.
- **Close:** Removes the control from the zone but leaves it on the page so that it can be added back later.
- **Delete:** Removes the control from the zone so that it can't be added back later.
- **Minimize:** Removes the control, visibly, from the zone. Also removes the Minimize verb from the menu and adds the Restore verb (which will re-display the control).
- **Restore:** Redisplays a minimized control and puts the Minimize option back on the Web Part's menu.
- **Help:** Shows the Help for the control.

- **Connect:** Allows the user to edit a control's connection.
- **Export:** Exports the control's personalization data.

Setting these properties at the zone level can be confusing because customization happens on a control-by-control basis. For instance, setting the MinimizeVerb properties controls how the Minimize action is displayed on each of the individual controls in the zone. However, setting the properties at the zone level ensures that all controls in the zone look and work alike.

Setting these properties on a WebPartZone also means that when a user drags a Web Part from one zone to another, the appearance of the Web Part may change if the two zones have different settings.

For any of these *verb properties, you can set four properties that will be applied to that verb for all the controls in the zone:

- **Description:** A description of the verb's action. When this description is displayed in the user interface, the name of the control currently selected is inserted into the description. The default is a string containing '{0}' (that is, the default Description for the ConnectVerb has the string "Edits the connections for '{0}'"). At run time the '{0}' is replaced with the name of the control.
- **Enabled:** When set to False, prevents the verb from being accessed.
- **Text:** Controls the text used to display the option on all controls.
- **Visible:** When set to False, prevents the verb from being displayed.

Figure 2-5 shows the results of setting the Text and Description properties for the MinimizeVerb. The Text property has been set to Min. so that "Min." displays instead of the default Minimize. The Description property has been set to Minimize '{0}''s display. Because the control's name is txtTopicName and the page is displaying in Internet Explorer, the tooltip displays as "Minimize *txtTopicName*'s Display."

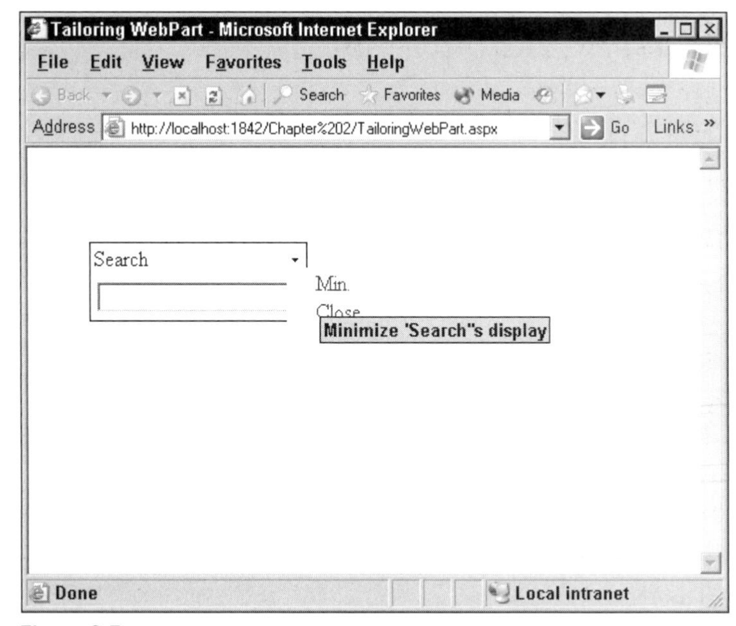

Figure 2-5

It's important to remember that, in the end, the display of the page is controlled by the browser. Different browsers may result in slightly different displays.

In addition to customizing the verbs that manage customization, you can turn off some of the customization's flexibility by setting the AllowLayoutChange property. When AllowLayoutChange is set to False, users can't add, remove, or move Web Parts in the zone (Web Parts in the zone can still be changed and modified).

Configuring the Verb Menu

The drop-down menu in the Web Part's title bar is called Verb Menu. The Verb Menu lists customization activities that can be performed on the control. By default, all that appears is a small down arrow; clicking the arrow causes the list of verbs for the control to be displayed.

In the zone, you can use the following properties to control how the Verb Menu is displayed:

- **MenuLabelText:** Sets the text displayed in the control's title bar before the menu is displayed.
- **MenuLabelStyle**, **MenuLabelHoverStyle:** Control the style to be applied to the menu label and the style to be used on the label when the user hovers the mouse pointer over it.
- **MenuVerbStyle**, **MenuVerbHoverStyle:** Control the style to be applied to the menu when the menu is displayed and the style to be used when the user hovers the mouse pointer over the menu.
- **MenuCheckImageURL**, **MenuCheckImageStyle:** The currently selected Verb in the menu is displayed with a checkmark beside it. These two properties control the image used for the checkmark and the style applied to it.
- **MenuPopupImageURL:** Sets the URLs for the image displayed as background for the menu.

Figure 2-6 shows a verb menu for a zone containing a custom Web Part with a single verb: Edit, appearing above the Minimize and Close command actions. The label for the Verb Menu has been set to the string Configuration using the MenuLabelText property.

In Chapter 5, you learn how to add your own verbs to the Web Parts that you build.

Styling the Zone

The zone also has a number of *style properties that control the appearance of both the zone and the controls within it. From the Property List you can:

- Control specific aspects of the appearance of the zone or control (for example, BackColor, BorderColor, Font).
- Apply a Class from a cascading stylesheet (using the CssClass property).

Some of the many parts of the zone that you can control the appearance for are:

- **HeaderStyle:** The header section
- **FooterStyle:** The optional footer

- **MenuVerbStyle:** The command actions (such as Close and Minimize)
- **PartStyle:** The box around each control
- **PartTitleStyle:** The title bar for each control
- **PartChromeStyle:** The border that frames controls
- **SelectedPartChromeStyle:** The border that frames the control that the user is currently interacting with

Two other properties control the appearance of the zone:

- The **ShowTitleIcons** property, when set to False, prevents controls from displaying their icons in their title bar.
- Like a Panel, a WebPartZone has a **BackImageURL,** which allows you to specify a URL for a graphic to be displayed within the zone.

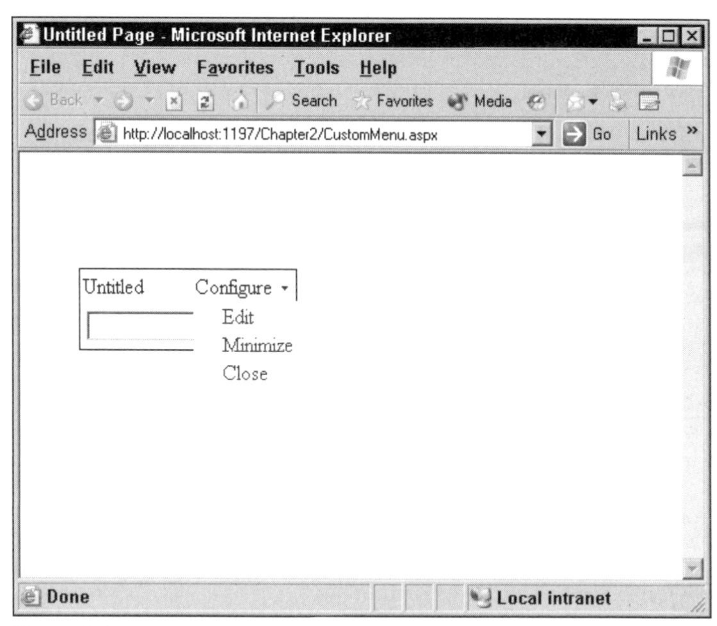

Figure 2-6

When you first add a WebPartZone to a page or when you click on a WebPartZone a small arrow appears in the upper-right corner of the WebPartZone. Clicking that arrow displays the WebPartZone Tasks Smart Tag (see Figure 2-7), which includes an Auto Format option. Selecting that option displays a list of predefined style options, or schemes (see Figure 2-8). Selecting one of the schemes sets a multitude of the zone's style options. After applying one of the Auto Format styles, you can remove it by selecting the Remove Formatting option from the list.

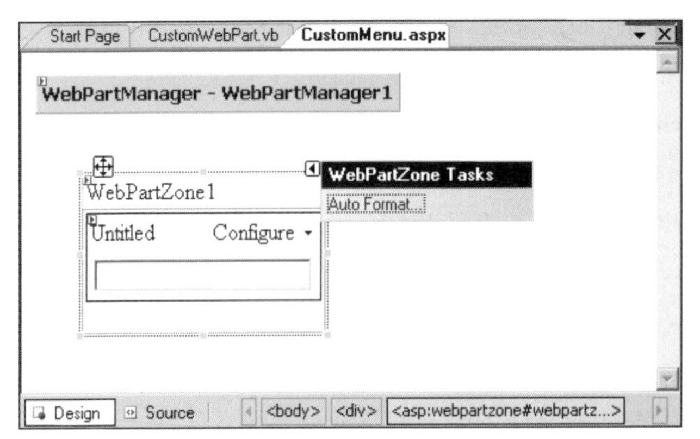

Figure 2-7

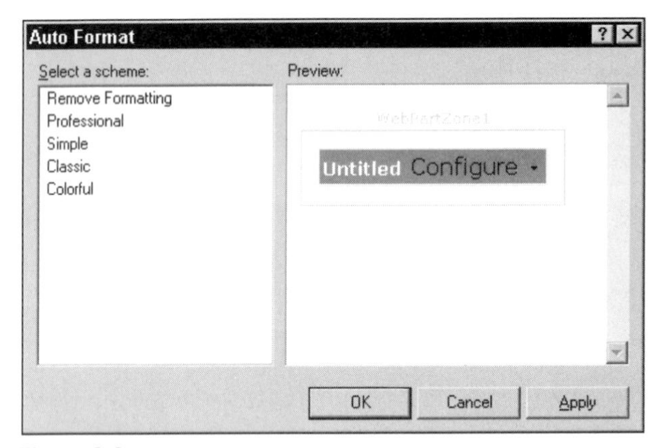

Figure 2-8

Turning on Customization

In its default mode, a page won't let a user do much more than minimize or close a control. In order to let the user take advantage of more advanced customizations, you must put the WebPartManager on the page into the appropriate mode. A WebPartManager can be in one of five standard modes:

- **Browse:** This is the default mode for a page and displays the contents of the page. Only the Close and Minimize actions can be performed.
- **Edit:** Displays any special editing controls and allows the user to edit the controls on the page.
- **Design:** Displays the zones themselves and allows users to drag controls inside a zone and between zones.
- **Catalog:** Displays any catalog type controls and allows users to add or remove controls from the page.
- **Connect:** Displays any special user interface elements related to connecting controls and allows the user to connect or disconnect parts.

When the WebPartManager is in any of these modes, all the WebPartZones on the page are affected. Once a WebPartManager has been put into any one of these modes, the WebPartManager will stay in that mode until the WebPartManager is explicitly put into another mode (no matter how many times the page is requested by the user).

> **Not all modes are available in all browsers. Only Internet Explorer can be counted on to support all five modes. Make sure that you test your application in all the browsers that you expect your users to access your site with.**

To change the WebPartManager's mode, you must set the WebPartManager's DisplayMode property to any one of five predefined values. They are:

- WebPartManger.BrowseDisplayMode
- WebPartManger.EditDisplayMode
- WebPartManger.CatalogDisplayMode
- WebPartManger.ConnectDisplayMode
- WebPartManger.DesignDisplayMode

The code to change a page to Edit mode looks like this in Visual Basic 2005:

```
Me.WebPartManager1.DisplayMode = WebPartManager.EditDisplayMode
```

In C#, the code is:

```
this.WebPartManager1.DisplayMode = WebPartManager.EditDisplayMode;
```

To perform some customizations, all that's necessary is to put the page into the right mode. For instance, putting the page into Design mode is all that you need to do to enable the user to drag controls between zones. For other customizations, putting the page into the right mode just enables the user to perform some customization. As an example, putting the page into Catalog mode displays any catalog editor controls that allow the users to add controls to the page. A user would still need to select a control from the list in the catalog and click the button in the catalog control that adds the selected control to the page.

Because some customization modes require specific framework controls to be present, it's not always possible to put a page into some modes. For instance, if all that you have on the page are WebPartZones, you can put the page only into Browse and Design modes (that is, the user can only view the page and perform simple actions such as minimizing and closing a control). The option to add Web Parts to the page (Catalog mode) appears only if there is a CatalogZone control on the page.

Follow these steps to try out the Design mode for a page by dragging controls between zones:

1. Drag a WebPartManager to a blank ASP.NET 2.0 WebForm.
2. Drag a WebForms button onto the page.

3. Add the following code to the Click event of the button that you added in the previous step:

   For Visual Basic 2005:

```
Me.WebPartManager1.DisplayMode = WebPartManager.DesignDisplayMode
```

   For C#:

```
this.WebPartManager1.DisplayMode = WebPartManger.DesignDisplayMode;
```

4. Drag two WebPartZones onto the page.
5. Drag a WebForms TextBox into one of the WebPartZones.
6. Drag a WebForms DropDownList into a different WebPartZone. Your page should look something like Figure 2-9.

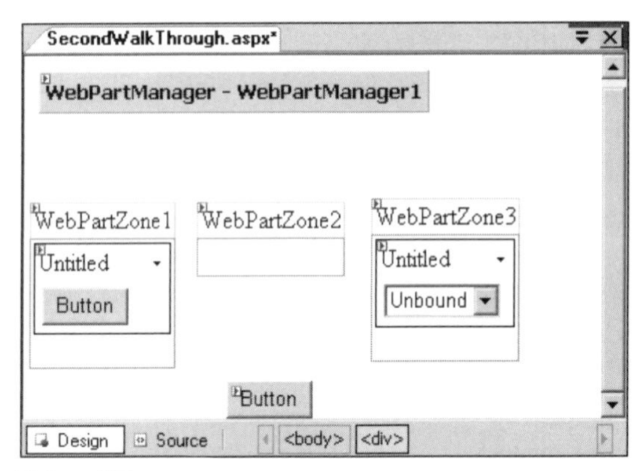

Figure 2-9

7. Display the page in Internet Explorer.
8. Click the button on the page to put the WebPartManager into Design mode. Your page should look like the page in Figure 2-10. The WebPartZones around the controls are visible as are the WebPartZones titles. The empty WebPartZone is also displayed with its EmptyZoneText.
9. You can now click the controls (in the upper-left corner) and drag the controls into different zones.
10. After you have moved one or more of the controls to a different zone, shut down Internet Explorer and return to Visual Studio 2005.
11. Display the page in Internet Explorer. You'll find that your site has remembered the customizations you made to the page and displays the controls in the zones where you last dragged them.

Now that you know how to work with WebPartManagers and WebPartZones you're ready to look at customizations more advanced than just minimizing and closing controls. These customizations include the capability to:

- Edit the properties for the control
- Change the appearance of the control

- Move controls between zones on the page
- Add new controls to the page from a catalog of controls

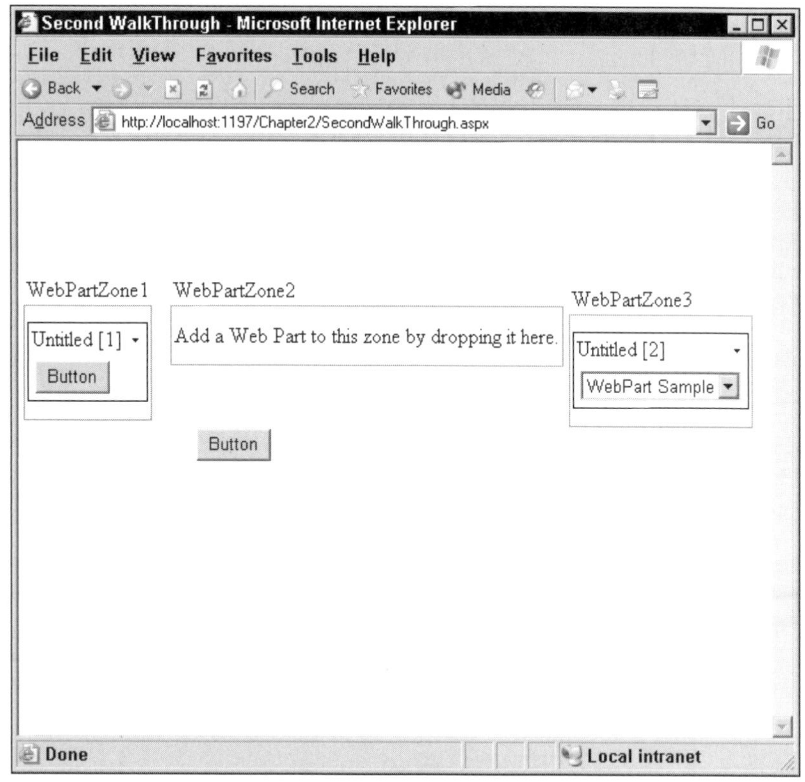

Figure 2-10

Not all of the customizable options that are available can be used with ASP.NET controls (for instance, you can update a property only at run time if the property has been set up to support that customization). The following section introduces the basics of customization and what can be done with the standard ASP.NET controls. In Chapter 5 you see how to create Web Parts that support more customizations than are possible with the standard ASP.NET controls.

Customization Tool Controls

In order to support more than just dragging controls between zones, you need to add additional controls to the page. Controls that are used to customize other controls are referred to as *parts*. Because this chapter uses just the standard ASP.NET controls, only a limited number of customizations are available.

Like Web Parts, the customization parts must be put inside zone controls. In addition, zones and parts are matched sets: Zone controls are customized to support a specific set of parts; parts can be added only to the zones that support those parts. For instance, the various editing parts (parts that allow users to customize the properties and appearance of controls) can be added only to an editing zone control.

You don't establish connections between the customization parts and the controls that they customize at design time. Instead, you make the tools available on the page and ASP.NET allows the user, at run time, to indicate what control she wants to customize with a particular part.

To demonstrate how customization works, the following sections look at two zones (the EditorZone and the CatalogZone) and some representative parts that can be used in those zones.

Editing the Controls with an EditorZone Control

ASP.NET comes with four parts for editing a control's properties at run time: AppearanceEditorPart, BehaviorEditorPart, LayoutEditorPart, and PropertyGridEditorPart. With the AppearanceEditorPart, for example, the user can customize a control's height, width, title, and other properties. Using this control, a user can increase the width of a text box if she finds that the text she wants to enter or display is longer than the default width of the text box.

In order to use any of these editing tools, you must first put an EditorZone control on your page. You can then add as many editing tools to the EditorZone as you want.

When an EditorZone is dragged to a page in Visual Studio 2005, it initially displays with a header and an area that tools can be dragged into. Figure 2-11 shows an AppearanceEditorPart in the EditorZone. You can drag editor controls such as the AppearanceEditorPart or LayOutEditorPart into the area under the header.

Figure 2-11

By clicking the arrow that appears in the upper-left corner of an EditorZone, you can display the EditorZone's Tasks Smart Tag (see Figure 2-12). Checking the View in Browse Mode option in the Tasks dialog box causes the EditorZone to display as a gray box — this gives you a better view of what your page will look like when the user isn't customizing the page.

Figure 2-12

Outside of Visual Studio 2005, you can add an EditorZone to a page by placing these tags in the page:

```
<asp:EditorZone ID="EditorZone1" Runat="server"
   Style="z-index: 39; left: 40px; position: absolute; top: 248px">
</asp:EditorZone>
```

To add a part to the EditorZone outside of Visual Studio 2005, you must insert a ZoneTemplate element inside of the EditorZone element, and then place the tags for the editing part inside of the ZoneTemplate element. This example shows an EditorZone with an AppearanceEditorPart inside of it:

```
<asp:EditorZone ID="EditorZone1" Runat="server"
   Style="z-index: 39; left: 40px; position: absolute; top: 248px">
   <ZoneTemplate>

     <asp:AppearanceEditorPart Runat="server" ID="AppearanceEditorPart1" />

   </ZoneTemplate>
</asp:EditorZone>
```

After an EditorZone is added to a page, you can put the WebPartManager on the page into Edit mode. Once the WebPartManager is in Edit mode, all the controls that can be edited will have their Verb Menu displayed.

It's easy for a user to miss the result of putting the page in Edit mode: the tiny down arrow in the title bar can easily be overlooked. It's a good idea to set the MenuLabelText and MenuLabelStyle to make the Verb Menu more obvious.

Figure 2-13 shows a page in Internet Explorer with the AppearanceEditorPart displayed inside of an EditorZone. When the user clicks a control's Verb Menu in the browser, a new option (Edit) has been added (see Figure 2-14). When the user selects that option, it causes the EditorZone (and whatever tools are in the EditorZone that can work with the control) to be displayed.

The controls that are displayed are also controlled by what controls are selected—an editor won't display unless the selected control can be manipulated by the editor. For instance, if a PropertyGridEditor is added to the EditorZone, setting the display mode to Edit won't cause the PropertyGridEditor to display unless the selected control has custom properties.

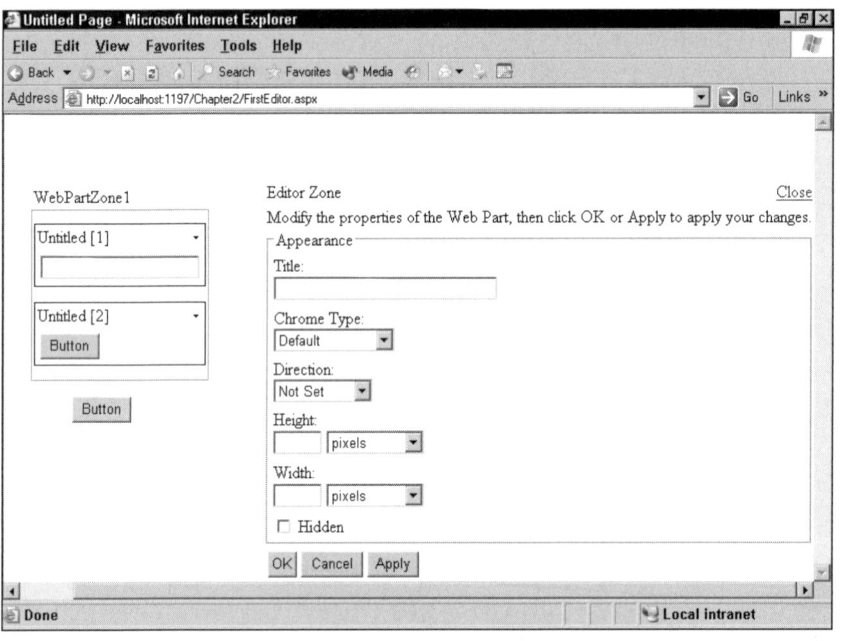

Figure 2-13

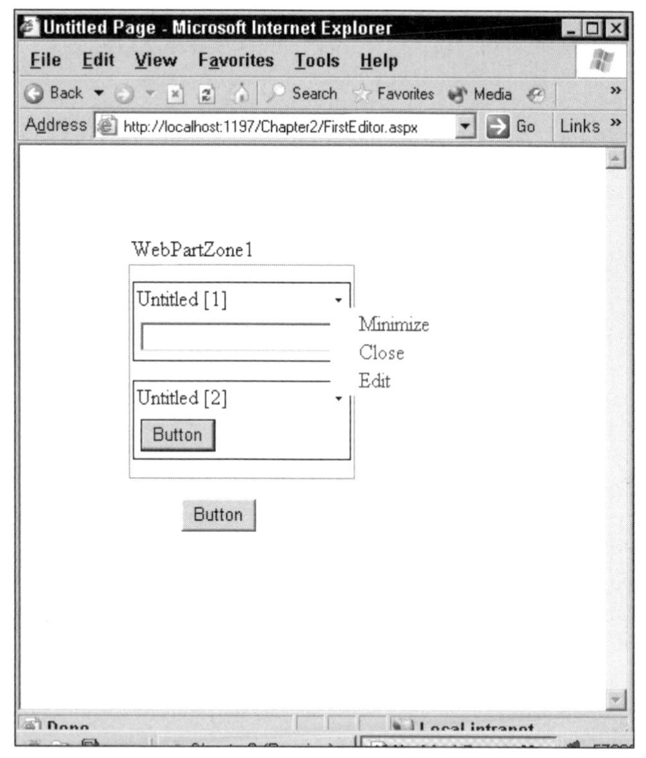

Figure 2-14

After a user has finished working with the tools in the EditorZone, she can select one of these four actions:

- **Close:** Removes the EditorZone from the page
- **OK:** Applies changes made in all the editor tools in the EditorZone to the control whose Edit action was selected and then closes the EditorZone
- **Apply:** Applies changes made in all the editor tools in the EditorZone to the control whose Edit action was selected
- **Cancel:** Abandons any changes in the editor tools in the EditorZone and closes the Editor zone

The Close action is displayed as a link in the header at the top of the zone. The other three actions are displayed at the bottom of the EditorZone. The page remains in Edit mode after all of these changes.

Adding New Controls with a CatalogZone Control

To enable users to add new parts to a page, you must put a CatalogZone control on the page and then add catalog tools to the CatalogZone. In Visual Studio 2005, you can just drag the CatalogZone onto the page from the Toolbox. Like the EditorZone control, the CatalogZone initially displays as a box with an area that catalog controls can be dragged into. Figure 2-15 shows a CatalogZone with a PageCatalogPart dragged into it.

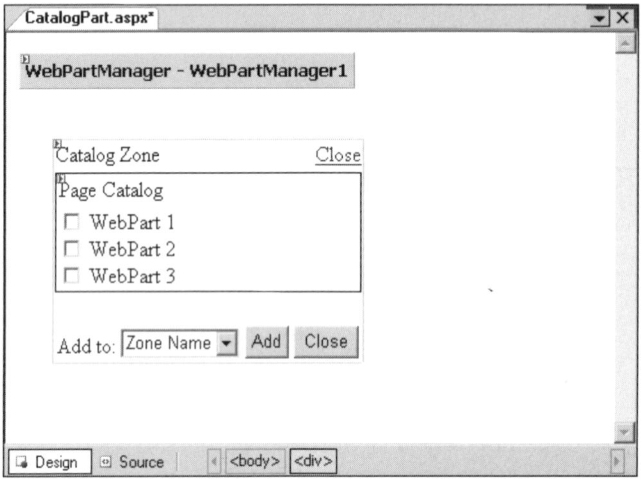

Figure 2-15

Outside of Visual Studio 2005, you can add a CatalogZone to the page with these tags:

```
<asp:CatalogZone ID="CatalogZone1" Runat="server"
    Style="z-index: 39; left: 112px; position: absolute; top: 256px">
</asp:CatalogZone>
```

If you click the arrow in the upper-right corner of the CatalogZone, a Smart Tag with the option View in Browse Mode appears. Like the EditorZone, checking that option switches the CatalogZone to a more compact view.

Outside of Visual Studio 2005, the tags for a catalog part can be added to a CatalogZone by placing the tags inside of a ZoneTemplate element, as in this example:

```
<asp:CatalogZone ID="CatalogZone1" Runat="server"
    Style="z-index: 39; left: 112px; position: absolute; top: 256px">

   <ZoneTemplate>
       <asp:PageCatalogPart Runat="server" ID="PageCatalogPart1" />
   </ZoneTemplate>

</asp:CatalogZone>
```

After you add a CatalogZone to a page, you can put the page into Catalog mode. In Catalog mode, any CatalogZone controls on the page are made visible, along with the catalog parts inside those zones. Users can then interact with the catalog parts to add controls to WebPartZones.

The CatalogZone control has two actions and a drop-down list:

- A Close action that closes the CatalogZone and returns the page to Browse mode.
- An Add button that moves the controls selected in the catalog tools to the WebPartZone listed in the WebPartZone selected in the drop-down list.
- A drop-down list displaying all of the WebPartZones on the page. The name displayed in this list is taken from the WebPartZone's title (in Catalog mode, all WebPartZones display with their titles).

The Close action appears twice in the CatalogZone control: once in the header at the top of the CatalogZone and again at the bottom of the CatalogZone.

ASP.NET comes with three CatalogPart tools:

- **DeclarativeCatalogPart:** At design time, you can add controls to a DeclarativeCatalogPart. At run time, the user can browse this list of controls and add the controls to a WebPartZone.
- **PageCatalogPart:** A page can hold controls that have been closed. These controls aren't visible on the page and can't be accessed by the user. The PageCatalogPart lists all the closed parts and lets the user add them back to the page in a WebPartZone.
- **ImportCatalogPart:** Allows the user to import Web Parts from WebPart files.

In the following sections, you learn how to use two of the catalog parts. (The ImportCatalogPart is discussed in Chapter 6 along with how to create a WebPart file.)

Using the PageCatalogPart

To use the PageCatalogPart, first drag a CatalogZone control onto the page and then drag a PageCatalogPart into the CatalogZone. Figure 2-16 shows a page in Design view with a PageCatalogPart and three WebPartZones with various controls.

It's helpful to assign titles to the controls on the page to see how the PageCatalogPart works (these titles are displayed in the PageCatalogPart when the user is looking at the list of available controls). The easiest way to do that is to put the title attribute on the controls in Source View. If you're working outside of Visual Studio 2005, you can update the tags directly as demonstrated in the following code, which shows the tags for the zone containing a button and a checkbox with the controls' Title properties set:

```
<asp:WebPartZone ID="WebPartZone1" runat="server">
  <ZoneTemplate>

        <asp:Button ID="Button1" runat="server" Text="Button" title="A button"/>
        <asp:CheckBox ID="CheckBox1" runat="server" title="A checkbox" />

  </ZoneTemplate>
</asp:CatalogZone>
```

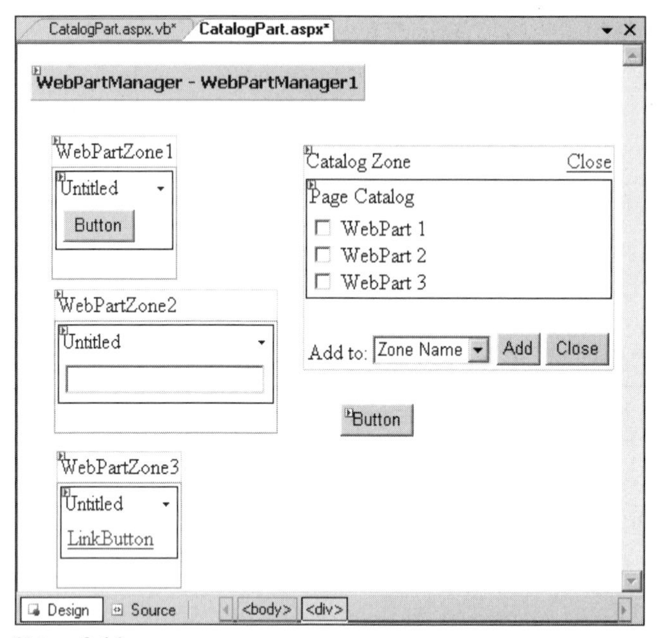

Figure 2-16

To make the CatalogZone visible at run time, some code will have to put the WebPartManager on the page into Catalog mode. This Visual Basic 2005 code in the Click event of a button on the page will do that:

```
Me.WebPartManager1.DisplayMode = WebPartManager.CatalogDisplayMode
```

In C#:

```
this.WebPartManager1.DisplayMode = WebPartManager.CatalogDisplayMode;
```

Figure 2-17 shows the result with both of the controls in the WebPartZones closed and the WebPartManager put into catalog mode. As the figure shows, PageCatalogPart now lists all the controls on the page that have been closed. The titles assigned to the controls are displayed in the PageCatalogPart. In the PageCatalogPart's list, the user can check the control(s) that he wants to add back to the page, select a WebPartZone from the drop-down list, and click the Add button to add the selected control(s) to the specified WebPartZone.

As controls are closed or dragged from one WebPartZone to another, you need to be careful when accessing controls through the WebParts collection of the WebPartZone. While WebParts(0) is valid as long as there is at least one control in the zone, if the user closes all the controls in a zone (or drags all the controls out of the zone) then WebParts(0) may no longer refer to a valid object.

Using the DeclarativeCatalogPart

To use the DeclarativeCatalogPart, you must (as with the PageCatalogPart) first drag a CatalogZone onto the page. You can then drag a DeclarativeCatalogPart into the zone after taking the CatalogZone out of Browse mode.

To add controls to the catalog, click the small arrow in the DeclarativeCatalogPart's upper-right corner to display the catalog's Smart Tag. Clicking the Edit Templates choice opens the catalog to display a WebPartsTemplate (see Figure 2-18). You can now drag controls out of the toolbox and into the WebPartsTemplate.

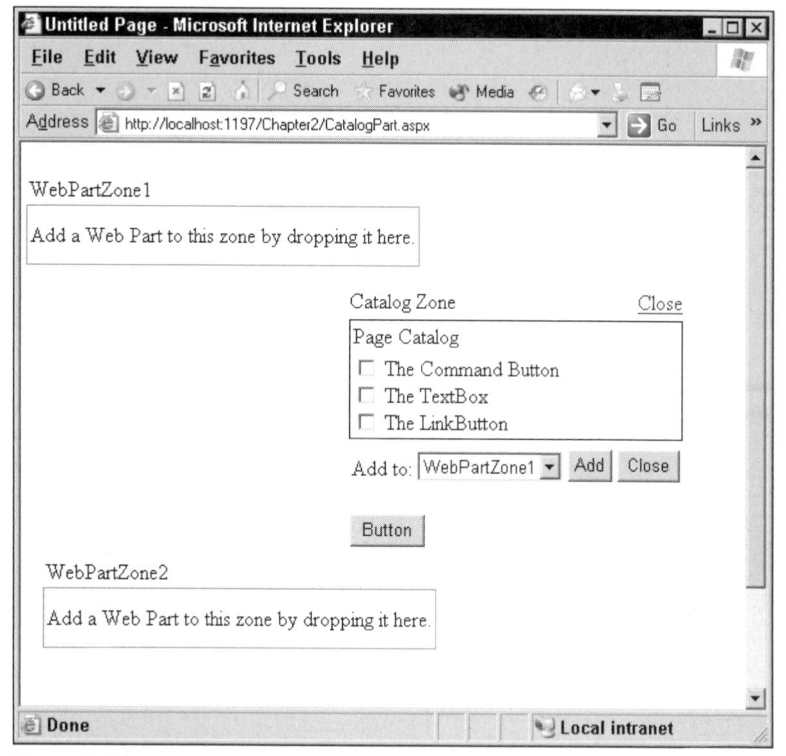

Figure 2-17

You do not need to add the user control to the page with the DeclarativeCatalogPart. You can also add controls to a DeclarativeCatalogPart by setting its WebPartsListUserControlPath to the name of a user control that has Web Parts on it (the Web Parts must be sitting directly on the user control and not in a WebPartZone). Effectively, this capability allows you to create user controls that act as a library of Web Parts that you can reference from other pages.

If you don't assign titles to the controls in the DeclarativeCatalogPart, the list of controls in the DeclarativeCatalogPart will display with "Untitled" as the name for each control. Again, this problem can be solved by adding title attributes to the tags for the controls.

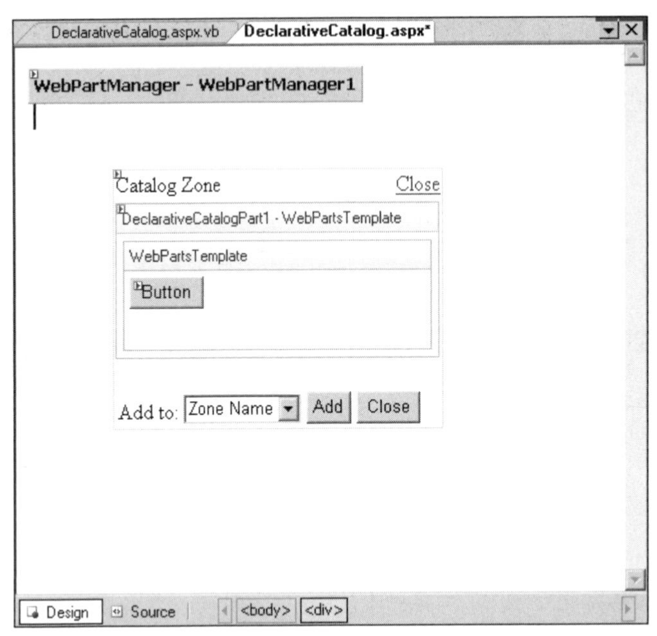

Figure 2-18

The following code shows the tags for a CatalogZone with a DeclarativeCatalogPart inside of it. The DeclarativeCatalogPart contains an ASP.NET button, checkbox, and text box. If you are working outside of Visual Studio 2005, you would use this code to set up a CatalogZone and DeclarativeCatalogPart:

```
<asp:CatalogZone ID="CatalogZone1" runat="server">
  <ZoneTemplate>

    <asp:DeclarativeCatalogPart runat="server" ID="DeclarativeCatalogPart1">
      <WebPartsTemplate>

        <asp:Button ID="Button1" runat="server" Text="Button" title="A button"/>
        <asp:CheckBox ID="CheckBox1" runat="server" title="A checkbox" />
        <asp:TextBox ID="TextBox2" runat="server" title="A textbox"/>

      </WebPartsTemplate>
    </asp:DeclarativeCatalogPart>

  </ZoneTemplate>
</asp:CatalogZone>
```

The result can be seen in Figure 2-19. Using a DeclarativeCatalogPart is similar to working with a PageCatalogPart.

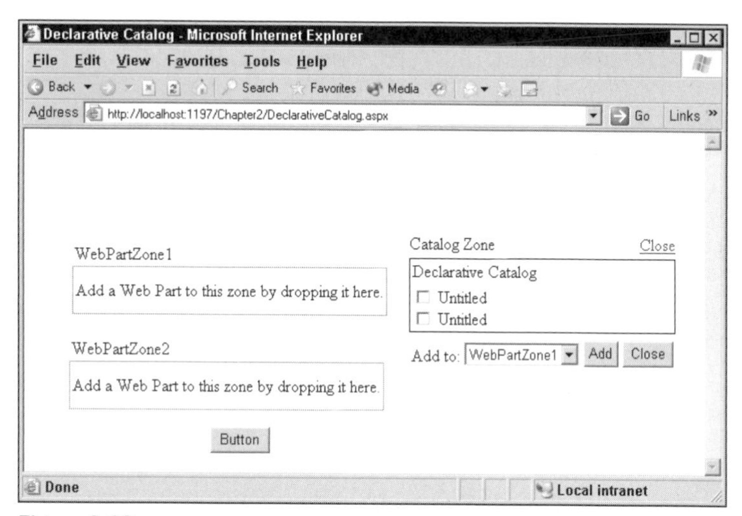

Figure 2-19

This chapter showed how to use standard ASP.NET controls as Web Parts. To take advantage of the capability to connect Web Parts or to export and import Web Parts, you must use full-fledged Web Part controls. The framework controls that support importing and exporting are covered in Chapter 11, as is how to create Web Parts that can work with the framework controls. Similarly, Web Parts that can use the framework controls to create connections between Web Parts (along with how create those Web Parts) are described in Chapter 10.

Configuring the Tool Zones

The various controls for holding tools tend to share a number of properties and work in a similar way. The EditorZone control is used here as an example of how you can configure an editing zone at design time.

At the bottom of a typical editor part in the EditorZone are three buttons: Apply, OK, and Cancel. As with WebPartZones, these buttons represent the verbs associated with the editor part and you can customize those verbs through *verb properties on the EditorZone:

- By default, the verbs are displayed as buttons, but you can display them as images or links by setting the VerbButtonType property.
- The way that the verbs are displayed can be set with the ApplyVerb, CancelVerb, and OKVerb. These properties let you set the text displayed on the buttons/links, whether the buttons/links are enabled or visible, and what tooltip is displayed for the button or link in Internet Explorer (by setting the Description property).
- The CCS style for these actions can be set with the VerbStyle property.

At the top of the EditorZone (in the zone's header) is a Close button that represents the Close verb for the EditorZone. You can customize the Close verb with these properties:

- The way that the action is displayed is set by the HeaderCloseVerb property, just like the ApplyVerb, CancelVerb, and OKVerb properties.
- The style for the header (with the Close action) is controlled by the HeaderVerbStyle.

You can set a common appearance for the editor parts in the EditorZone with these properties:

- The style for each editing part as a whole (such as background color or image) can be set with the PartStyle.
- The appearance for any UI components that accept input (such as text boxes or radio buttons) in all the editing parts is set with the EditUIStyle property.
- The appearance for all the labels in the editing parts is set with the LabelStyle property.
- The style for the borders around the tools can be set with the PartChromeStyle.
- The style for the editing parts' titles is controlled by the PartTitleStyle.

The EditorZone displays four different text messages:

- A title for the EditorZone at the top of the zone (this defaults to "Editor Zone")
- Instruction text that appears before any of the editor parts in the zone
- Text that appears in the zone before any editor parts are added to it
- A message to be displayed if there's an error when the Apply button is clicked on an editor part

You can set the text for these messages (and customize their appearance) with these properties:

- The title bar at the top of the EditorZone can be changed through the HeaderText property. The style applied to this text can be set through the HeaderStyle property.
- The text string that is displayed at the top of the EditorZone (before any of the editor tools) can be changed using the InstructionText property. You can control the text's appearance with the InstructionTextStyle.
- The text that displays when the EditorZone is empty can be set through the EmptyZoneText. You can control the style of the text using the EmptyZoneStyle.
- The error text that can be set using the ErrorText property. The style for that message is controlled by the ErrorStyle property.

The CatalogZone's properties are very similar to the EditorZone's — any difference just reflects the differences in the control. The catalog tools include a list of available controls, for instance, and so the CatalogZone's properties include a CatalogItemStyle that controls the style applied to each item in the list.

Summary

In this chapter you learned how to create a customizable page in ASP.NET 2.0, using the Web Part framework controls distributed with ASP.NET 2.0. You've seen how you can enable users to alter a control's properties or make a control invisible on the page. Using the Catalog controls, you can even enable the user to add or remove controls from a page.

More specifically, you learned to

- Use a WebPartManager to set up a page for customization
- Use WebPartZones to define areas for customization within a page
- Add standard controls to WebPartZones to allow users to customize them
- Change the WebPartManager's mode to let the user customize the page
- Support the various customization options using additional Web Part zones and parts

Creating a basic Web Part is covered in Chapter 5. Programming with WebPartZones and the other Web Part controls that ship with Visual Studio .NET is covered in more depth in Chapters 9, 10, and 11. However, this chapter has described the basic environment for the Web Parts and given you a better idea of what customization is available in ASP.NET. Because Web Parts are an extension of custom controls, in the next chapter you see how to create a custom control.

Part II
Creating Controls

3

Creating Custom Controls

In this chapter you learn how to create a custom control. As you'll see, you build a custom control by first inheriting from the WebControl object that comes with ASP.NET, so much of this chapter explores the methods and properties of the WebControl object that contains the utility code for implementing a custom control.

Working with custom controls requires you to think at several levels at once. For instance, a custom control can be added to a Web page, where the custom control behaves as a control within a container. In addition, a custom control can contain other controls — in this scenario, it's the custom control that's the container (the custom control is then called a *composite control*). So you need to think about the custom control both as a control within a container (the custom control's host page) and as a container for controls (the custom control's *constituent* controls).

Some terminology issues: Much of the documentation for custom controls uses the term "child controls" both for the controls contained within a custom control and for the controls on a Web page. In this book, the term "child controls" is used for the controls on a Web page with your custom control. This also avoids confusion with methods and properties that include the word "child." The term "constituent controls" is reserved for the child controls of the custom control. Figure 3-1 shows the relationships: A WebForm contains many controls, including a custom control; the custom control, in turn, contains other controls. In this book the controls on the WebForm are referred to as "child controls" while the controls inside the custom control will be referred to as the "constituent controls." Because the custom control contains other controls, it would be classed as a "composite control."

This multiple level of thinking continues when you consider how your custom control will be used by the page. The code in the host page for a custom control can manipulate the methods and properties of the WebControl object in order for the page to deliver functionality to the user. The code that you add to your custom control will also manipulate the methods and properties of the underlying WebControl object to add functionality to your custom control.

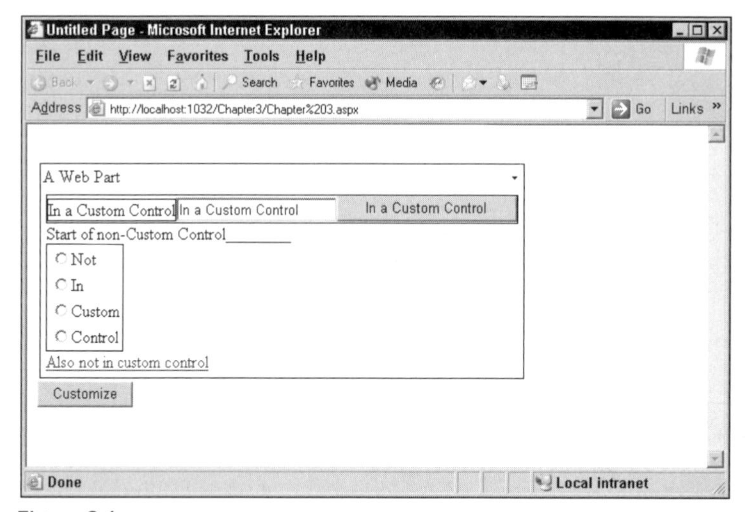

Figure 3-1

One last level of multiple-level thinking: In addition to calling the methods and properties of the WebControl object to implement your custom control, you can replace those methods and properties with your own code by overriding them. When you do override the methods and properties of the WebControl object, it will be your version of those methods and properties that is available to code on the host page. From within your custom control, you will sometimes be calling your version of these methods and properties, and sometimes be calling the base methods of the underlying WebControl object.

You need to be thinking about *all* of these levels as you design your custom control.

In this chapter, you learn to:

- Set up a Visual Studio solution to create a custom control library
- Control the HTML generated by a custom control
- Add constituent controls to your custom control
- Use and override the methods and properties of the WebControl object to create your own custom control
- Manage the appearance of your custom control on the Web page

Creating a Visual Studio Solution

There are several steps involved in creating a Visual Studio 2005 solution that will make it easy for you to create, test, and debug your Web Part:

1. Create a Visual Studio 2005 solution that contains the Web site that your control will be initially used on and your Web Control Library.
2. Configure the solution.
3. Set up the default custom control.

Starting a Custom Control Project

If you are using Visual Studio 2005 to create your custom control, you should always start by creating a new Class Library project to hold your custom controls. By creating your custom control in a separate Class Library you will be able to compile your project into a separate DLL and use your custom control in any application that needs it. However, you shouldn't create a solution that contains just your Class Library. Because you will be debugging your control in an ASP.NET application, you will need to have an ASP.NET application to use as a test bed for your control. Including an ASP.NET Web site in the same solution as your custom control makes debugging simpler.

Unless you're writing a book, the first time that you create a custom control will probably be to use it in a specific application. Adding your custom control project to the solution containing your Web application will let you test and debug your custom control in its intended application.

So, in Visual Studio 2005, your best option is to open the Web site solution that you are creating the application in and then, from the File menu, select Add ➪ New Project ➪ Visual Basic ➪ Windows ➪ Web Control Library or Add ➪ New Project ➪ Visual C# ➪ Windows ➪ Web Control Library to add the project where you will create your custom control. The result is a Visual Studio solution that contains both your site and your custom control.

Configuring the Solution

Once you've created a solution with both a Web site and your Web Control Library, you should set up the solution to make it easy to run your tests. Unfortunately, when you are working on the code in your custom control, pressing the F5 key to start debugging always results in an attempt to start the custom control — something that's not allowed. To ensure that pressing F5 will always start the Web page with your custom control, right-click your Web site project in Solution Explorer and select the Set as Startup Project option.

Now that you've created your Web Control Library, add a Web custom control to the project using Project ➪ Add New Item ➪ Web Custom Control, giving the control a meaningful name in the Add New Item dialog box before clicking the Add button. This adds a .cs (for C# projects) or .vb (for Visual Basic 2005) file to your project. This is where you will put the code for your custom control.

The sample code for this project uses a Web site called Booksite, a Web Control Library called MyWebControls, and an initial Web custom control called BookDetail.

Do not attempt to use the default control (called WebCustomControl1) that's inserted into a Web Control Library by Visual Studio 2005 as part of creating the project by renaming the control. Renaming changes the name only of the file that the control's code is held in — you'd still have to change the name of the class inside of the file in addition to other internal references to the file's original name. It's not only easier but safer to delete the default control and create a new one.

After you add your custom control file to your project, you need to modify the sample code that's included in the file to have it function as a custom control. The Class module has to inherit from the WebControl base class so you need to specify that as part of the Class declaration.

Inheriting from another object causes your object to automatically acquire all the methods, properties, and events of the object that you're inheriting from, along with the functionality of those methods and properties. Inheriting from the WebControl object gives your class all the support that it needs to function as an ASP.NET custom control—you just have to customize your object to do what you want.

The sample code that's included in the file is more of a hindrance than a help in creating a custom control, so the first thing that you should do is delete everything between the class declaration line and the end of the class. That leaves you with this code for Visual Basic 2005:

```
<DefaultProperty("Text"), _
ToolboxData("<{0}:BookDetail runat=server></{0}:BookDetail>")> _
Public Class BookDetail

End Class
```

In C#, your file should look like this:

```
using System;
using System.Collections.Generic;
using System.ComponentModel;
using System.Text;
using System.Web.UI;
using System.Web.UI.WebControls;

namespace MyWebControlsCS
{
 [DefaultProperty("Text")]
 [ToolboxData("<{0}:BookDetail runat=server></{0}:BookDetail>")]
 public class BookDetail : WebControl
 {
 }
}
```

The class declaration line in the default code also specifies the default property for your control as the Text property. Your custom control may not even have a property called Text and, even if it does, you may not want it to be your default property. The second step in configuring the custom control file is to delete the reference to Text as your default property. After all the modifications, your code file should look like this in Visual Basic 2005:

```
Imports System.ComponentModel
Imports System.Web.UI

<ToolboxData("<{0}:BookDetail runat=server></{0}:BookDetail>")> _
Public Class BookDetail
    Inherits System.Web.UI.WebControls.WebControls.WebControl
         Inherits System.Web.UI.WebControls.WebControl

End Class
```

The key line in this code is the Inherits line that references the WebControl object that you will build your custom control on.

In C#, the file should look like this after your changes:

```
using System;
using System.Collections.Generic;
using System.ComponentModel;
using System.Text;
using System.Web.UI;
using System.Web.UI.WebControls;

namespace MyWebControlsCS
{
    [ToolboxData("<{0}:BookDetail runat=server></{0}:BookDetail>")]
    public class BookDetail : System.Web.UI.WebControls.WebControl
    {
    }
}
```

The key line in this C# code is the class definition that references the WebControl class.

If you're working outside of Visual Studio 2005, these files are also the starting point for any custom control that you're creating.

You're now ready to compile your custom control by selecting Build ➪ Build *WebControlProjectName* from the Visual Studio Menu (or by running the .NET compile utilities from the command line if you're working outside of Visual Studio 2005).

If you're working in Visual Studio 2005, to use your custom control on your page, the control must appear in your Toolbox. Fortunately, this is very easy to do: Just compile your Web Control Library and, the next time that you view an ASPX page, your library with all of its controls will appear in the Toolbox (as shown in Figure 3-2). You can now test your custom control by dragging it from the Toolbox and onto the Web page you set up in your test Web site.

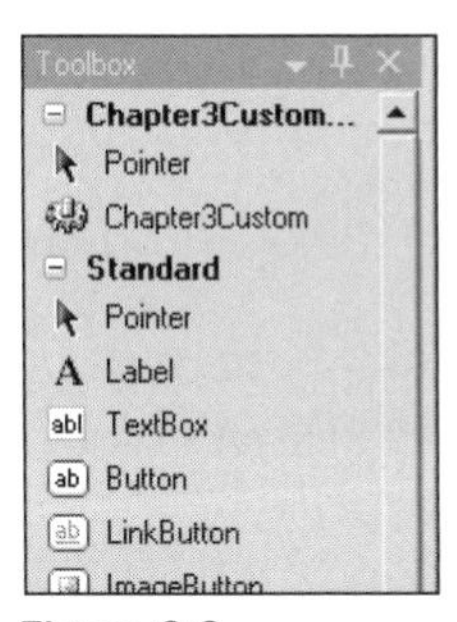

Figure 3-2

Staying in Sync

As your custom control becomes more complex, debugging and testing your custom control becomes more critical. It's essential, then, that you make sure that you are testing the most recent version of your code. The good news is that when you press the F5 key to start debugging, your control will be recompiled, your Web application be recompiled, and Internet Explorer will display your test page using the latest version of your custom control.

However, if you make a change to your custom control, the way that your control is displayed in Design view in Visual Studio 2005 isn't updated to reflect your change. Instead, your control's display reflects the last compiled version of your control at the time that you dragged the control onto the page. The same is true of dragging a control from the Toolbox onto the page: The display in Design view will reflect the last compiled version of your control and may not show your most recent changes.

You can end up with some discrepancies between the design time and the run time view of your custom control. For instance, imagine that you create a control that displays "Hello, World" and drag it onto your test page. On your page, in Design view the control displays "Hello, World." You now alter your custom control to say "Goodbye, World," recompile it, and drag a new copy onto the page. The first control will continue to display "Hello, World" while the second control will display "Goodbye, World." You go back to your control and alter it to say just "Hi." When you press F5 to test your page and your page is displayed in Internet Explorer, both of the controls will display "Hi." But when you shut down Internet Explorer and return to Visual Studio 2005, the first copy of the control continues to display "Hello, World" and the second copy of your control continues to display "Goodbye, World."

With Visual Studio 2005 you can resolve this issue in Design view by right-clicking the Web page and selecting Refresh from the pop-up menu. This updates the display of all copies of your control in Design view to reflect the last compiled version of your custom control. However, if you've made a change to your control and haven't rebuilt it, the display in Design view still may not be up to date relative to the code in your custom control.

To ensure that display of the custom control on your Web page at design time reflects your latest changes, you should:

1. Change your custom control's code.
2. Rebuild your custom control.
3. Switch to your test page.
4. Right-click on the page and select Refresh.

The easiest way to rebuild your control is to add the Build toolbar to the standard set of toolbars at the top of the Visual Studio 2005 window. With this toolbar, you can rebuild your custom control's DLL with a single mouse click (you could also use the Ctrl+Shift+B keyboard shortcut to rebuild the project, but that rebuilds all the projects in the solution).

Organizing Your Custom Controls

When you first create your project, you should start thinking about how you will present your custom controls to the developers who will be using them. The first level of organization is provided by the way that Visual Studio 2005 organizes your file and compiles your code. A second level of organization is provided by .NET namespaces.

Throughout this chapter (and the rest of the book) there are two potential "developers" that we are talking about. There is you, of course, developing a custom control. There is also, however, a second developer — the developer using your custom control to build a WebForm (in many cases, you'll be performing both roles). To distinguish between the developer building the control and the developer using the completed control, I use "you" when talking about the developer building the control and " the developer" or "the developer using your control" to talk about the developer who uses your control on a WebForm. You may, of course, be both of these people.

The first level of organization is the Visual Studio 2005 project that creates your custom control library. By default, all of the custom controls in this library will be compiled into a single DLL. As you consider how you will organize your custom controls, the first step is to decide whether all of your controls should go into one DLL or be divided up over several DLLs.

There are three terms in use here: "Visual Studio 2005 project," "custom control library," and "DLL." Let's add another term to the mix: In the Visual Studio Toolbox, your custom controls appear on a tab labeled "components." Rather than continue to juggle all these terms, this book uses "project" to refer to the source code that you work with in Visual Studio 2005 and "DLL" to refer to the results of compiling that source code.

There is one benefit to putting multiple custom controls in a single project so that they all compile into the same DLL: When an application requests one custom control in a DLL, the entire DLL is loaded, effectively "preloading" the rest of the custom controls in the DLL. As an example, for the sample book site in our case study it's likely that if one of the custom controls in the DLL will be used, others in the DLL will also be used. It makes sense, then, to put all of these custom controls into a single project so that they compile into a single DLL. So, looking only at the issue of what controls are used by an application, compiling all the controls into a single DLL is a good idea. While putting each class in its own project (and, as a result, in its own DLL) results in smaller DLLs that load faster, loading a DLL isn't free — an application that loads three DLLs in order to access three classes runs slower than an application that loads a single DLL containing all three classes.

In addition to looking at which custom controls are typically used together, there's another consideration in deciding when to put custom controls into the same DLL: Custom controls that share code should be in the same DLL. Code that is shared among custom controls can be placed in a class module within the project. As a result, when the application loads the custom controls' DLL, it also loads the custom controls' supporting classes.

Combining class modules into a single project has its costs. As classes are added to the project, the size of the resulting DLL grows. As a result, the DLL takes longer to load and occupies more room in memory. You may also run into locking problems where frequently used class modules share code. It makes sense to combine classes into a single DLL only if all of the classes in the DLL are likely to be used if any one of them is going to be used by the application. It doesn't make sense to put all of the classes that might ever be used by your application in a single DLL.

The project provides only a minimal level of organization: Each .cs or .vb file that you add to the project generates one custom control within the DLL that holds all of those custom controls. If you depend only upon the level of organization that the project provides, then in both the IntelliSense drop-down lists and the Object Browser, developers just see a series of undifferentiated custom controls within the project name. If you build multiple DLLs, developers won't be able to see any relationships between the custom controls in those DLLs.

You can insert multiple class definitions into a single .VB or .CS file. The result is that a single file generates multiple custom controls. However, there's no performance benefit to this practice and it reduces the transparency of your project—you can't determine what custom controls are in your project just by looking at the .cs or .vb files in the project. Also, combining classes in a single file makes it more difficult to distribute work among a team. The developer who signs out a file containing multiple classes in order to make a change to a single class prevents any other developer from working on any other of the classes in that file.

An Organization Case Study

As an example of providing a higher level of organization for your custom controls, consider the custom controls for the bookstore Web site. The custom controls described in Chapter 1 handle these tasks:

- Display detail book information
- Display summary book information
- Display specialized views of book information
- Search for books
- Accept and validate customer information
- Display customer information
- Display page-related title information

When developers think about the custom controls for the bookstore site, they would likely mentally divide the custom controls into three groups:

- Book information/searches
- Customer information
- Page information

It would be helpful, then, if the custom controls were presented to the developer in a way that reflects these functional groups rather than just as a list of custom controls in a DLL.

However, these custom controls reflect the requirements for a single site — the book site. It's not hard to imagine that the organization supporting the book site might also support sites selling music CDs, DVDs, and other entertainment products. Because these kinds of products have different information needs than books, these sites will use different custom controls to display product information and to search for products. Furthermore, a site that loads the DVD-enabled versions of the custom controls won't use the book-enabled versions. As a result, it makes sense to create separate DLLs for the DVD, CD, and book custom controls. This will result in separate projects for the book, CD, and DVD sites' custom controls, for instance.

The customer information custom control has different considerations, however. The customer information used on one site is the same for all the sites because customer information is defined at the organization level, rather than the site level. As a result, the customer custom control will be common to all of the sites. It makes sense then, to have the customer information custom control in a project by itself so that it will be compiled into its own DLL. With the custom information control in its own DLL, any of the sites can load the customer custom control without loading other custom controls that the site won't use.

As this case study suggests, you are always looking at the tradeoffs between keeping your DLLs small while ensuring that loading one DLL will also "pre-load" other custom controls that your application will likely be using.

While it would certainly be helpful if developers using your custom controls read your documentation (you did write the documentation, didn't you?), developers prefer to figure out how to use your custom controls by looking at the IntelliSense drop-down lists and the Object Browser. As you develop multiple DLLs, you need to start thinking about how you can organize the Web Parts when presenting them to developers in IntelliSense and the Object Browser.

Naming Conventions

The first step in providing a level of organization beyond the library level is to use a naming convention for your custom controls and their libraries that reflects the functions that are important to the control's users — the developers building Web pages. For the bookstore site, names that describe the function of the part (such as BookSearch, BookDetailDisplay, and CustomerSearch) are more useful to developers than, for instance, names that describe the order that the parts were developed in (FirstWebControl), how recent the custom control is (NewBookSearch), or the developer who created the custom control (MyWebControl — which is what's used in this book).

Having said that, the major benefit that you can pass on to your users is to be consistent in the way that you name your custom controls (for example, the descriptive names used earlier specified the type of data first, and then the activity performed). If you put out new versions of your custom controls, you should either create a new library or append version-related information to the end of the name (such as BookSearchV2).

Namespaces

The next step is to consider using namespaces, especially if you have (or expect to have) a project with many custom controls. Namespaces allow you to organize the custom controls within a project into meaningful groups — meaningful from the point of view of the developer using the custom controls. For the custom controls that support the bookstore Web site, namespaces that divide the custom controls into Book, Customer, and Site groups would reflect the way that developers think about the controls.

It may appear, in the IntelliSense lists, that your classes are organized into groups by the name of their project/DLL. That's an illusion. Classes are always organized by the namespaces that they belong to. By default, however, the namespace for each project is set to the name of the project. It is because of these default values for namespaces that it appears that controls are organized into groups by project name. By overriding the default namespace for a project you can provide a higher level of organization and group controls in different projects together.

You may want to have custom controls that have been created in different projects presented to the developer as a group. For instance, if there will be multiple projects to support the book, CD, and DVD store sites, a different way of organizing namespaces might make sense. Instead of dividing the custom controls into Book/Customer/Site namespaces, it might make more sense to divide the custom controls into Search/Information/Page namespaces with the Search custom controls from all the Web sites sharing a namespace. Within the Search namespace, the custom controls could be divided into Book/Music/DVD namespaces.

Dividing your custom controls among libraries is a technical *decision — you want to group the custom controls to reduce the number of DLLs that will be loaded at run time. The organization of your custom controls by Namespace is a* design *decision — you want to group your custom controls in a way that makes life easier for the developers using your custom controls. As with your naming convention, the namespace-based organization should reflect the way that developers think about using your custom controls.*

The number of possible conventions is large. One large conglomerate uses *CompanyName.ProjectArea .ComponentArea.ComponentSubArea.EntityName*. (For example, it assigns names like DVDSales .CustomerMgmt.UserInterface.Input.Address.) Other companies use naming conventions that help organize their source code in whatever source code repository they use. The company in the last example uses the parts of the control's name as subdirectories within SourceSafe. This means that the code for the Address custom control is found in a subdirectory nested five levels deep but it also means that the source code for any given control is easy to find — provided that developers understand the convention and follow it when naming their controls. It would be an exaggeration to say that the naming convention that you use doesn't matter (a good naming convention embeds key information about the control in the name), but the most important part of a convention is that it be used consistently.

The samples created for this book are in two namespaces: VB (for WebControls written in Visual Basic 2005) and CS (for the C# versions). This division reflects an important distinction for the audience of a .NET programming book: C# developers will want to use the versions of the custom controls written in C#; Visual Basic 2005 developers will want the Visual Basic 2005 versions. Coincidentally, this namespace division reflects the division of the libraries: The Visual Basic 2005 custom controls and the C# custom controls are in two different libraries. These two namespaces are nested within the PHVWebControls namespace, which causes the two libraries to be displayed together in the IntelliSense drop-down lists. This namespace represents the total audience, represented by the readers of this book.

To set the root namespace for a Visual Basic 2005 project in Visual Studio 2005:

1. Double-click the My Project entry in Solution Explorer to open the Property Pages for the project.
2. On the Application tab, set the Root namespace text box to the namespace you want to use for your project (see Figure 3-3).

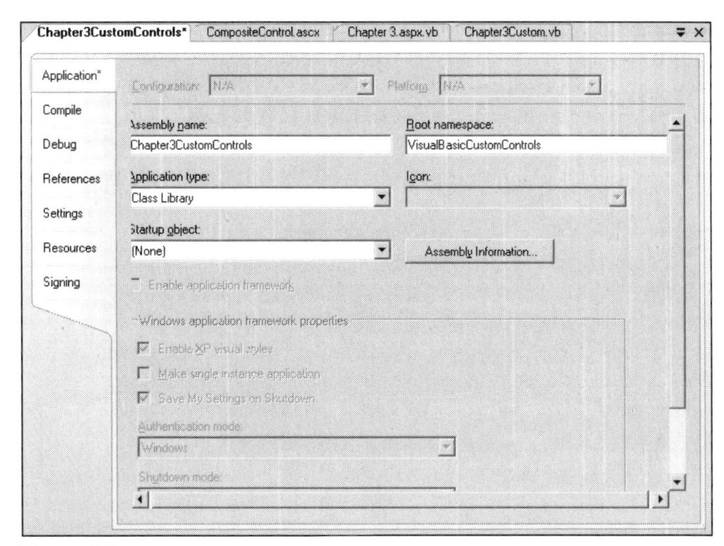

Figure 3-3

For C# projects:

1. Double-click the Properties entry in Solution Explorer to open the Property Pages for the project.
2. On the Application tab set the Default namespace you want for the project (see Figure 3-4).

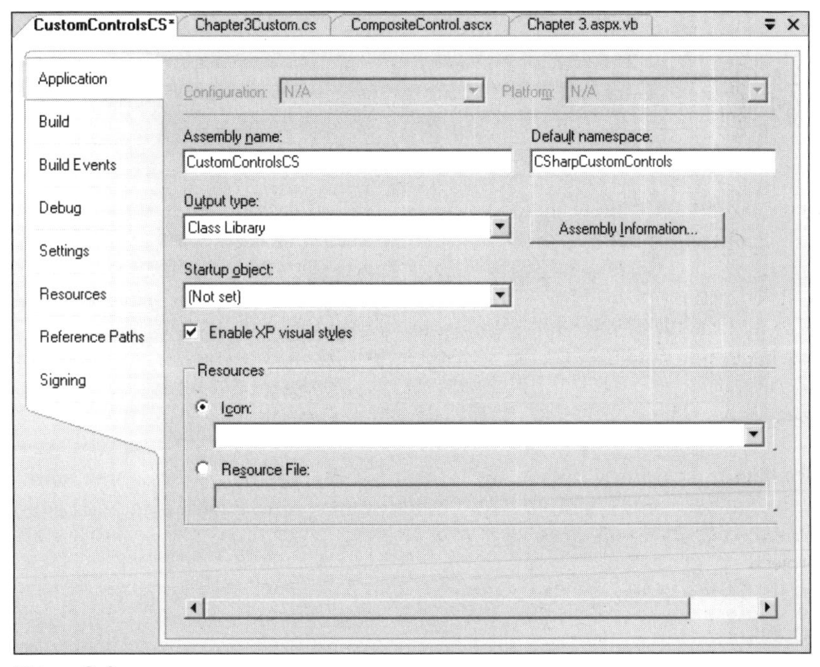

Figure 3-4

You can also get to these property pages by right-clicking the project (either Visual Basic 2005 or C#) and selecting Properties from the pop-up list.

Namespaces within the root namespace are set inside the code files for the custom control by using the Namespace keyword in Visual Basic 2005 and the namespace keyword in C#. The following Visual Basic 2005 code shows the definition of a namespace called VB within a Visual Basic 2005 class file:

```
Namespace VB

Public Class BookDetail
      Inherits System.Web.UI.WebControls.WebControl

End Class

End Namespace
```

For C#, the namespace is set like this:

```
namespace CS
{
public class BookDetail :  System.Web.UI.WebControls.WebControl
   {
   }
}
```

Extending Existing Controls

The rest of this chapter shows you how to build all the parts of a custom control. However, you don't always need to take on that level of complexity. Often what you want to do is change one or two features of an existing control, or just add a new method. For instance, if you haven't databound the ASP.NET list box, adding items to it can be awkward. As an example, this code adds some Canadian cities to a list box in Visual Basic 2005:

```
Me.ListBox1.Items.Add("Regina")
Me.ListBox1.Items.Add("Ottawa")
Me.ListBox1.Items.Add("Winipeg")
```

This isn't the most awkward code in the world, but it would be convenient to have a method that would add all of the items in a single statement, like this in Visual Basic 2005:

```
Me.PHVListBox1.AddList ("Regina,Ottawa,Winnipeg")
```

It's very easy to take an existing control and add a new method to it. Because this control is just modifying the existing list box control, simply have your custom control inherit from the ListBox object. That's what this Visual Basic 2005 code does:

```
<DefaultProperty("Text"), ToolboxData( _
         "<{0}:PHVListBox runat=server></{0}:PHVListBox>")> _
Public Class PHVListBox _
```

```
    Inherits System.Web.UI.WebControls.WebControl.ListBox

End Class
```

As does this C# code:

```
using System;
using System.Collections.Generic;
using System.ComponentModel;
using System.Text;
using System.Web.UI;
using System.Web.UI.WebControls;

namespace MyWebControlsCS
{
    [ToolboxData("<{0}:PHVListBox runat=server></{0}:PHVListBox>")]
    public class ListBox : System.Web.UI.WebControls.ListBox
    {
    }
}
```

This example demonstrates the power of inheritance. With no additional code, this custom control will have all the methods, properties, and events of a list box.

The next step is to extend the list box by adding the new LoadList method. As you write the code for this routine you can take advantage of all the methods of the base object that you've inherited from. This means that you can leverage your knowledge of the methods and properties of the base object in writing your new code. Adding the following Visual Basic 2005 to the class module creates a list box with all the features of the standard ASP.NET list box plus a new LoadList method. As you can see, the code just takes advantage of the Add method of the underlying list box's Items property:

```
Public Sub LoadList(strList As String)
Dim strValues() As String
Dim strValue As String

  strValues = strList.Split(",")
  For Each strValue in strValues
    MyBase.Items.Add(strValue.Trim)
  Next

End Sub
```

In C#, the code looks like this:

```
public void LoadList(string strList)
{string[] strValues;

strValues = strList.Split(',');
foreach (string strValue in strValues)
{
  base.Items.Add(strValue.Trim());
}
```

If you want to ensure that you call the base version of a method or a property, you must use the MyBase object in Visual Basic 2005 or the base object in C#. If you use the Me object (in Visual Basic 2005) or this object (in C#), you will call your overriding versions of these methods (if they exist).

Once the control is in your Toolbox and dragged onto the page where it is assigned the ID of BetterListBox1, the LoadList method can be called like this in Visual Basic 2005:

```
Me.BetterListBox1.LoadList("Regina,Ottawa,Winnipeg")
```

Or like this in C#:

```
this.BetterListBox1.LoadList("Regina,Ottawa,Winnipeg");
```

Creating a Complete Custom Control

While you are often able to create the control that you want by extending an existing control, sometimes there is no equivalent control for you to build on. Even if you don't intend to build a control from scratch, understanding all the options available to you in a custom control lets you do more when extending a custom control. These options include:

- Creating a control that consists of other ASP.NET controls
- Replacing existing methods and properties with your own versions
- Controlling all the HTML generated by your control
- Intermixing pure HTML and ASP.NET controls
- Controlling what your control does at design time in Visual Studio 2005
- Managing your control's style and appearance
- Extracting information about your control when it executes at run time

This section walks you through the first two of these tasks. The other tasks deserve sections of their own and are discussed later in this chapter.

There are two strategies you can follow when creating a custom control:

- **Leveraging existing ASP.NET controls:** In this strategy, you define your control by adding other controls (*constituent* controls) to it. Most of the HTML generated for your custom control will be produced by these other controls.
- **Generating all the HTML yourself:** Instead of counting on constituent controls to write out their HTML to create your control's UI, you write all of the code that generates all the HTML for your control.

Let's look at the constituent controls strategy first.

Adding Constituent Controls

One strategy for creating a useful custom control is to add constituent controls to your custom control. The customer information custom control, for instance, would contain several text boxes and labels. Even if all you want to add to your custom control is plain text and HTML tags, you can do so by adding HTML literal controls (although, as you'll see when we discuss the Render method, using controls for just text and HTML may not be the most efficient method).

The second strategy for creating a custom control, writing all the HTML yourself, is covered later in this chapter.

Using the CreateChildControls Method

Controls are typically added to the custom control in the CreateChildControls method. The CreateChildControls method is built into the WebControl object, but you should replace it with your own version of the method in order to add the controls you want to your custom control.

Most of this chapter deals with your custom control and the constituent controls as objects. While an object-oriented approach is a useful way to work with custom controls in code, the reality is that—in the end—your custom control will be turned into HTML and text in a Web page, and displayed in a browser. The process of converting your custom control object into HTML and text is referred to as "rendering." In this section, rendering is handled for you using methods built into the WebControl object and the constituent controls. Later in this chapter you'll see how you can take control of rendering your controls.

ASP.NET automatically calls your version of the custom control's CreateChildControls method. In the method you should add your constituent controls to the Controls collection provided by the WebControl object. The constituent controls will have their HTML automatically rendered to the host page by ASP.NET as part of rendering your custom control.

The process that you follow in the CreateChildControls method is simple:

1. Create an ASP.NET control.
2. Set any properties on the control.
3. Add the control to the WebControl object's Controls collection.

This Visual Basic 2005 code adds two HTML literal controls and a text box to the custom control. The HTML literal controls are used to add HTML breaks and text into the custom control's output, while the text box provides a fully functional ASP.NET server-side control with all of its methods and properties:

```
Protected Overrides Sub CreateChildControls()
Dim lt As LiteralControl
Dim txt As System.Web.UI.WebControls.TextBox

  lt = New LiteralControl("<b>Value: ")
  Me.Controls.Add(lt)

  txt = New System.Web.UI.WebControls.TextBox
  txt.Text = "Hello, World"
  txt.ID = "txtInput"
```

```
        Me.Controls.Add(txt)

        lt = New LiteralControl("</b>")
        Me.Controls.Add(lt)

    End Sub
```

In C#, you use this code:

```
protected override void CreateChildControls()
{
    LiteralControl lt;
    System.Web.UI.WebControls.TextBox txt;

    lt = new LiteralControl("<b>Value: ");
    this.Controls.Add(lt);

    txt = new System.Web.UI.WebControls.TextBox();
    txt.Text = "Hello, World";
    txt.ID = "txtInput";
    this.Controls.Add(txt);

    lt = new LiteralControl("</b>");
    this.Controls.Add(lt);
}
```

The resulting custom control, in a WebPartZone, is shown displayed in a browser in Figure 3-5.

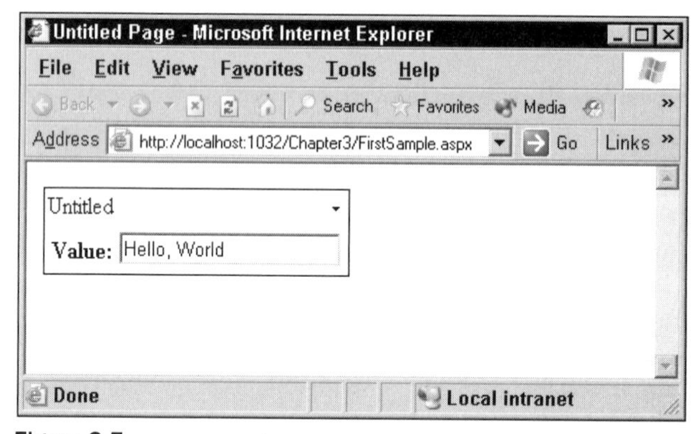

Figure 3-5

The presence of the Overrides keyword (in Visual Basic 2005) or the override keyword (in C#) in the method definition causes your method to be called in place of the base method provided by the WebControl object.

You can also use Shadows (in Visual Basic 2005) or new (in C#) instead of Overrides/override to create a new version of the base method. This allows your version of the routine to be different from the base routine (for instance, to replace a read-only property with a read/write property or change the datatype/number of parameters for a method). It's an unusual situation where you can replace a base method with a routine that has different characteristics and have your new method function effectively in the control framework.

In Visual Studio 2005, you can create a routine that overrides a method or a property by typing the word "overrides" (in Visual Basic 2005) or "override" (in C#). IntelliSense will then pop up a list of methods and properties that you can override. Pick the one that you want and Visual Studio 2005 writes out the skeleton of the routine for you.

You can also add controls to your Controls collection by using the WebPart's AddParsedSubObject method. This method, when passed a reference to a control, will add it to the Controls collection. This Visual Basic 2005 code adds a WebForm list box and text box to the Control's collection along with an HTML Button:

```
Protected Overrides Sub CreateChildControls()
Dim lb As New WebControls.ListBox
Dim tb As New WebControls.TextBox
Dim btn As New HtmlControls.HtmlButton

  Me.AddParsedSubObject(lb)
  Me.AddParsedSubObject(tb)
  Me.AddParsedSubObject(btn)

End Sub
```

In C#:

```
protected override void CreateChildControls()
{
  WebControls.ListBox lb = new WebControls.ListBox();
  WebControls.TextBox tb = new WebControls.TextBox();
  HtmlControls.HtmlButton btn = new HtmlControls.HtmlButton();

  this.AddParsedSubObject(lb);
  this.AddParsedSubObject(tb);
  this.AddParsedSubObject(btn);
}
```

You can access the controls in the Controls collection to set their properties.

Controlling the Display

When you drag your custom control onto a Web page, your constituent controls may not display. The CreateChildControls method is not automatically run at design time. Always check the display of the page with your custom control in the browser — that's the display that matters. To put it another way, the code that you write is primarily intended to control the run-time behavior of your control. The design-time behavior of your custom control won't always match the run-time behavior of your control.

To ensure that your constituent controls are displayed at design time, you can call the CreateChildControls method from methods or events that are run at design time. However, there are two potential problems:

- Your CreateChildControls method is automatically called by ASP.NET after you call the method, causing your controls to be added twice.
- Depending on when you call the CreateChildControls method, ASP.NET may already have called the method so that your call will add the constituent controls a second time.

There is a simple solution to this problem. First, at the end of the CreateChildControls method, set the ChildControlsCreated property to True. This is used by ASP.NET to signal that the CreateChildControls method has executed. If you set the property in the CreateChildControls method, you ensure that ASP.NET will not call the method a second time.

Second, you should never call the CreateChildControls method directly. Instead, you should call the WebControl object's EnsureChildControls method. This method first checks the ChildControlsCreated property and won't call the CreateChildControls method if the property is set to True.

This Visual Basic 2005 code calls the CreateChildControls method from the control's Init event (the Init event is called at design time). At the end of the CreateChildControls method, the ChildControlsCreated property is set to ensure that the method is not called a second time:

```
Private Sub BookDisplay_Init(ByVal sender As Object, _
                             ByVal e As System.EventArgs) Handles Me.Init
  Me.EnsureChildControls()
End Sub

Protected Overrides Sub CreateChildControls()
Dim txt As New WebControls.TextBox

  txt.ID = "fred"
  txt.Text = "Hello, World"
  Me.Controls.Add(txt)
  MyBase.CreateChildControls()

  Me.ChildControlsCreated = True

End Sub
```

This C# code does the same thing:

```
Private BookDisplay_Init(object sender, EventArgs e)
{
 this.EnsureChildControls();
}

protected override void CreateChildControls()
{
 WebControls.TextBox txt = new WebControls.TextBox();

 txt.ID = "fred";
```

```
    txt.Text = "Hello, World";
    this.Controls.Add(txt);
    base.CreateChildControls();

    this.ChildControlsCreated = true;
  }
```

If you don't like the way that the custom control's Controls collection behaves you can replace it with your own collection. To do this, override the WebControl object's CreateControlCollection with code to create your own collection object and return that object from the method.

Assigning Names to Controls

You can assign values to the Id property of your constituent controls. Assigning a value to the control's Id property allows you to retrieve a control from the Controls collection, using the FindControl method, as the following Visual Basic 2005 code does (because the FindControl method returns a generic control, the result must be converted to a text box before the text box's properties can be used):

```
Dim ct As System.Web.UI.Control
Dim txt As System.Web.UI.WebControls.TextBox

  ct = Me.FindControl("txtInput")
  txt = CType(ct, System.Web.UI.WebControls.TextBox)
```

This C# code does the same:

```
System.Web.UI.WebControls.TextBox txt;

txt = (System.Web.UI.WebControls.TextBox) this.FindControl("txtInput");
```

When the control is rendered to the page, the value in the Id property is automatically copied to the name and id attributes of the client-side HTML that is generated for the control. As a result, assigning values to the Id properties also makes it simpler to generate client-side code that manipulates the control (client-side code is covered in Chapter 9).

This Visual Basic 2005 code assigns a value to the Id property:

```
Dim btn As System.Web.UI.WebControls.Button

  btn = New System.Web.UI.WebControls.Button
  btn.Text = "Submit"
  btn.Id = "btnSubmit"
```

As does this C# code:

```
using System;

System.Web.UI.WebControls.Button btn;

  btn = new System.Web.UI.WebControls.Button();
  btn.Text = "Submit";
  btn.Id = "btnSubmit";
```

This is the resulting HTML:

```
<span id="BookDetail1" >
  <input type="submit" name="btnSubmit" id="btnSubmit" value="Submit" />
</span>
```

You can use the WebPart object's TagName property to retrieve the name of the tag that is used to enclose your constituent controls. The WebPart object's TagKey property returns the position of the TagName in the HTMLTextWriterTag enumeration.

However, if you set your constituent control's Id property, that value will be repeated for every copy of your Web control on a page. This means that any client-side code either generated by you or by the developer using your control will have to deal with multiple controls with identical names (though these controls will still be inside of span tags with unique identifiers). Here's an example:

```
<span id="BookDetail1" >
  <input type="submit" name="btnSubmit" id="btnSubmit" value="Submit" />
</span>
<span id="BookDetail2" >
  <input type="submit" name="btnSubmit" id="btnSubmit" value="Submit" />
</span>
```

Having multiple tags with the same name in your client-side HTML may not be a problem for at least three reasons. First, your control may be one that would never be used more than once on a page. Second, this affects your client-side code only. Even within your client-side code, the tags for your constituent controls are inside of uniquely named span tags (though you can override this, as discussed in the next paragraph). Third, it may even simplify your client-side code if all of these controls have the same name, as it will make it easier for client-side code to find all the "btnSubmit" controls and treat them as an array, for instance.

However, if you want to ensure that all your controls have unique names you can cause ASP.NET to automatically prefix your control's name with the name assigned to the custom control. The resulting HTML would look like this:

```
<span id="BookDetail1" >
  <input type="submit" name=" BookDetail1$btnSubmit"id=" BookDetail1_btnSubmit"
   value="Submit" />
</span>
<span id="BookDetail2" >
  <input type="submit" name=" BookDetail2$btnSubmit" id="BookDetail2_btnSubmit"
   value="Submit" />
</span>
```

To turn this functionality on, all you have to do is add the INamingContainer interface to your custom control. In Visual Basic 2005, the code looks like this:

```
Public Class BookDetail
    Inherits System.Web.UI.WebControls.WebControl
    Implements INamingContainer
```

In C#, the equivalent code is:

```
public class BookDetail : System.Web.UI.WebControls.WebControl, INamingContainer
{
}
```

The INamingContainer ensures that your control has a unique name within its container. For a custom control, the naming container is normally the page. However, if your custom control is on a user control, then the naming container is the user control, not the page that the user control is placed on. The WebPart object's NamingContainer property returns a reference to the control's naming container.

This gives you up to three properties of your custom control that can refer to the Page object that the control is on, depending on the situation: Page, NamingContainer, and Parent. For a control on a WebForm, the control's Parent, Page, and NamingContainer property all point to the same Page object. If the control is in a Panel, however, the custom control's NamingContainer and Page properties point to the page, while the Parent property points to the Panel. If the control is on a user control (that is, in turn, on a WebForm), the control's Parent and NamingContainer properties point to the user control while the control's Page property points to the Page. If the control is in a Panel on a user control, all three properties point to different objects: the Page property points to the Page object, the Panel property points to the Panel, and the NamingContainer points to the user control.

Interfaces in Object Development

If you're new to object development you may be wondering what an "interface" is. In application development, when you talk about a program's interface you are probably referring to the "user interface" — the face that the program presents to the user. In object development when you talk about the object's interface, you are talking about the face that the object presents to the developer: the collection of methods and properties that the object exposes. For instance, your custom control has an interface made up of the methods and properties that it exposes including the CreateChildControls method just discussed.

The .NET Framework has many sets of methods and properties that have been assigned names (the INamingContainer interface is one example). You can indicate to other programs that your custom control exposes a specific set of methods and properties by adding the interface that contains those methods and properties to your control (as the previous Visual Basic 2005 and C# code does by adding the INamingContainer interface). Many programs and objects look for specific methods and properties and will work with your control only if you have implemented the interface that has those methods and properties.

However, adding an interface to your control is also a contract: You are obliged to implement all the methods and properties specified by the interface. And, unlike inheriting from an object, you get no "free functionality" by adding an interface to your control: You have to write all the code for all the methods and properties specified by the interface.

The INamingContainer is a good interface to start with because it contains no methods or properties, making it a very easy interface to implement. An interface with no methods or properties is often referred to as a *marker interface*. The sole purpose of the INamingContainer interface is to flag ASP.NET that you want some special processing done when your control's HTML is generated.

At run time, when the HTML for your control is generated, the unique identifier for your control's client-side HTML is retrieved by reading your control's UniqueId property. You can, in theory, change the unique identifier used for your control by overriding the UniqueId property and returning your own value. However, as discussed in the following box text, it's hard to imagine any reason for doing that.

If you don't override the UniqueId property, the id attribute on the tag that encloses your custom control will automatically be set to the name assigned to your custom control's Id property (in other words, if the developer using your control sets your control's Id property to "EntryData" then, when the page is delivered to the browser, the constituent control will be enclosed in a tag that has its id attribute set to "EntryData").

If you do override the UniqueId property then all the instances of your control on a page will have the same id attribute even if you add the INamingContainer interface to your control. So if the developer puts two copies of your control on a page, even after the developer assigns them unique values in their respective Id properties, the span tags enclosing your custom controls will have the same id attribute. As a result, while it's possible to override the UniqueId property, it's hard to imagine why you would want to.

This Visual Basic 2005 example sets the UniqueId to "ui":

```
Public Overrides ReadOnly Property UniqueID() As String

  Get
    Return "ui"
  End Get

End Property
```

In C#:

```
public override string UniqueID()
 {
  get
  {
    return "ui";
  }
  }
```

The HTML that results from doing this, in conjunction with using the INamingContainer interface, looks like this when two copies of the BookDetail control are added to the page:

```
<span id="ui" >
  <input type="submit" name=" ui$btnSubmit" id="ui_btnSubmit"
   value="Submit" />
</span>
<span id="ui" >
  <input type="submit" name=" ui$btnSubmit" id="ui_btnSubmit"
   value="Submit" />
</span>
```

Another way to ensure that your constituent controls have unique names is to *not* set the Id property for your constituent controls. If you don't set the Id property then unique values are automatically generated for the name and id attributes of your constituent controls when your custom control is added to the page. However, these values are essentially random values, affected by what other controls on the page are also assigned automatic identifiers.

Here's an example of the HTML generated for a page that has two copies of a custom control called BookDetail that has two constituent controls (one control is a submit button, the other a reset button):

```
<span id="BookDetail1" >
  <input type="submit" name="ctl03" value="Submit" />
  <input type="reset" name="ctl04" value="Reset" />
</span>
<span id="BookDetail2">
  <input type="submit" name="ctl05" value="click here" />
  <input type="reset" name="ctl06" value="click here" />
</span>
```

You can retrieve the unique identifier that's assigned to a control after the control has been added to the Controls collection. You can then use that identifier when generating client-side code. This Visual Basic 2005 code retrieves the unique client-side identifier for a control:

```
Dim btn As System.Web.UI.WebControls.Button
Dim strId As String

  btn = New System.Web.UI.WebControls.Button
  btn.Text = "Submit"
  strId = btn.UniqueId
```

In C# the code looks like this:

```
using System;

System.Web.UI.WebControls.Button btn;
string strId;

  btn = new System.Web.UI.WebControls.Button();
  btn.Text = "Submit";
  strId = btn.UniqueId;
```

Writing HTML

The second strategy for creating a custom control is to write all the HTML yourself instead of using constituent controls to generate the HTML for your control. This allows you, at the cost of writing more code, to generate HTML without the overhead of creating more server-side objects to use as your constituent controls.

The simplest way to have your control generate HTML is to override the TagKey property of your custom control. This causes the control to write the tag specified by the TagKey property.

> **While the TagKey property is called by ASP.NET as part of building your control, the TagName property is not. Instead, the TagName property just reports on the value returned by the TagKey property and generates that value only when TagName is explicitly called.**

Most tags include attributes on their HTML in addition to the tag name. The WebControl object's base AddAttributesToRender method allows you to add attributes to the tag created for your control. If you do override the AddAttributesToRender method, you should also call the base method to make sure that any attributes required by the WebControl object are still written out.

The following Visual Basic 2005 code causes the custom control to generate an Input tag with two attributes: Name and Type. The Name attribute has its value set to the control's unique identifier while the Type attribute sets the tag to be a text box (an id attribute for the tag is generated automatically).

```
Protected Overrides ReadOnly Property TagKey() As System.Web.UI.HtmlTextWriterTag
  Get
    Return HtmlTextWriterTag.Input
  End Get
End Property

Protected Overrides Sub AddAttributesToRender( _
                      ByVal writer As System.Web.UI.HtmlTextWriter)

  MyBase.AddAttributesToRender(writer)
  writer.AddAttribute(HtmlTextWriterAttribute.Name, Me.UniqueID)
  writer.AddAttribute(HtmlTextWriterAttribute.Type, "text")

End Sub
```

In C#:

```
protected override System.Web.UI.HtmlTextWriterTag TagKey
{
 get
 {
  return HtmlTextWriterTag.Input;
 }
}

protected override void AddAttributesToRender(System.Web.UI.HtmlTextWriter writer)
```

```
{
 base.AddAttributesToRender(writer);
 writer.AddAttribute(HtmlTextWriterAttribute.Name, this.UniqueID);
 writer.AddAttribute(HtmlTextWriterAttribute.Type, "text");
}
```

The resulting HTML looks like this:

```
<input id="BookDisplay1" name="BookDisplay1" type="Text" />
```

Later in this chapter you see how to access the data that the user enters into the text box.

Writing Complex Tags

To create more complex HTML displays you can override the WebControl object's Render method. When ASP.NET needs your custom control's text, it calls the Render method — you just need to provide the right text. As you'll see, ASP.NET calls several different methods whose names begin with "Render": Render, RenderControl, RenderChildren. Those methods will be referred to as a group as the Render* methods.

Using the various Render methods, the TagKey property, and the CreateChildControls method are not mutually exclusive options. The Render method, for instance, is where controls added in the CreateChildControls method are converted into HTML. In this section you see how you can combine overriding the CreateChildControls method, the Render* methods, and the TagKey property to integrate your own HTML with the HTML generated by constituent controls.*

As an example, consider a custom control called BoldItalic that has a Text property whose value is to be displayed as both bold and italicized. Code that uses this custom control, outside of a WebPartZone, on an ASP.NET page looks like this in Visual Basic 2005:

```
Me.BoldItalic1.Text = "Hello, World"
```

In C#, the code looks like this:

```
this.BoldItalic1.Text = "Hello, World";
```

Unlike using the TagKey or adding constituent controls in CreateChildControls, using the Render method to generate HTML creates tags whose values you are not able to retrieve during server-side processing. In other words, if you write out a text box tag in the Render method, you are not able to access the data that the user enters into that text box when data is returned to the server.

The first step in creating the BoldItalic custom control is to define a Text property (Chapter 8 explains how to create properties). For this example, just assume that the code in the Text property updates an internal variable, called strText, which is used in the following examples.

The next step is, inside the Render method, to write out the HTML to be embedded in the page (this is an alternative to using a literal control in the CreateChildControls method). The Render method is passed an HtmlTextWriter object (called writer by default). You can use the HtmlTextWriter's Write method to write out the control's text.

When you use the Render method you don't have to take any additional action to ensure that your control is displayed correctly at design time: The Render method is automatically called by Visual Studio 2005.

The Render method for the BoldItalic control (which writes out the value of a variable called strText set elsewhere in the control) looks like this in Visual Basic 2005:

```
Protected Overrides Sub Render(ByVal writer As System.Web.UI.HtmlTextWriter)
   writer.Write("<b><i>" & strText & "</i></b>")
End Sub
```

In C#:

```
protected override void Render(System.Web.UI.HtmlTextWriter writer)
{
   writer.Write("<b><i>" + strText + "</i></b>");
}
```

The Write method has 17 overloaded versions. These include specialized versions that handle outputting various data types, accepting strings for formatting the output, and writing out the text representation of an array (or portions of an array).

ASP.NET ensures that the Render method is called at the appropriate moment to add the custom control's output to the page. Figure 3-6 shows the resulting page.

Figure 3-6

Don't expect the HTMLTextWriter's Write method to ensure that your tags are well formed— the Write method just transfers to the page whatever text you pass to it.

You can use the Render method to write out the HTML that would normally be generated by an ASP.NET HTML control. This allows you to add buttons and other controls to your page without incurring the overhead of creating the corresponding ASP.NET objects. However, as noted earlier, you cannot retrieve any data from these controls when the data is returned to the server after the user clicks the submit button on the page.

This Visual Basic 2005 code adds a submit button to the page:

```
Protected Overrides Sub Render(ByVal writer As System.Web.UI.HtmlTextWriter)
  writer.Write("<input type='submit' id='Button1' value='Click Me'/>")
End Sub
```

As does this C# code:

```
protected override void Render(System.Web.UI.HtmlTextWriter writer)
{
  writer.Write("<input type='submit' id='Button1' value='Click Me'/>");
}
```

The resulting HTML would look like this (the page can be seen in Figure 3-7):

```
<input type='submit' id='Button1'  value='Click Me'/>
```

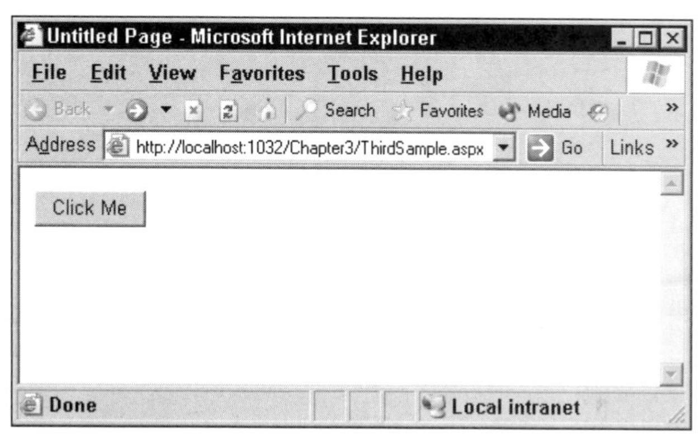

Figure 3-7

As you can see in this example, no additional HTML is generated for your control when you override the Render method. For instance, unlike a constituent control, no span tag is generated to enclose your HTML. And, because you're writing out your own HTML, ASP.NET has no chance to modify the id attribute of the resulting tags. This means that the id assigned to your control by the developer who adds it to a page and the unique identifier generated through the INamingContainter interface can't be applied to your tag's id attribute by ASP.NET.

Not having an id attribute for the tags generated by the Render method may not be a problem. The data in these tags isn't accessible from your server-side code so these id values are useful only to client-side code.

If you want to prevent multiple copies of your controls from having the same name, you need to generate a unique value for the id attribute yourself. You can retrieve the name of your control, including the ID assigned by the developer using the control, from the UniqueId property. This name is based on the name assigned to your control by the developer using the control and includes the prefix generated by the INamingContainer if you've added that interface to your control. If you are writing out multiple tags, you should consider adding text of your own to the id value to uniquely identify each tag within your control.

The following Visual Basic 2005 code writes out both a text box and an image tag, using the UniqueId property to create id attribute values for the tags. The code adds ':Image' to the image tag's id attribute value and ':Button' to the submit button id. It also encloses the two tags in a span tag (this will be useful later in this chapter when I show how you can support the developer who wants to apply styles to your control):

```
Protected Overrides Sub Render(ByVal writer As System.Web.UI.HtmlTextWriter)

 writer.Write("<span id='" & Me.UniqueID & "'>")
 writer.Write("<img id='" & Me.UniqueID & ":Image' src='MyPicture.gif'/>")
 writer.Write( _
   "<input type='submit' id='" & Me.UniqueID & ":Button'  value='Click Me'/>")
 writer.Write("</span>")

End Sub
```

In C#:

```
protected override void Render(System.Web.UI.HtmlTextWriter writer)
{
 writer.Write("<span id='" + this.UniqueID + "'>");
 writer.Write("<img id='" & this.UniqueID & ":Image' src='MyPicture.gif'/>");
 writer.Write(
    "<input type='submit' id='" + this.UniqueID + ":Button'  value='Click Me'/>");
 writer.Write("</span>");
}
```

The resulting HTML looks like this:

```
<span id='BookDisplay1'>
  <img id='BookDisplay1:Image' src='MyPicture.gif'/>
  <input type='submit' id='BookDisplay1:Button'  value='Click Me'/>
</span>
```

If you override the Render method, any values returned through the TagKey property won't be written out to the page. To use the Render method in conjunction with the TagKey property, you should call the base version of the Render method to ensure that the TagKey is written out (and that any other default processing by the Render method is done).

This Visual Basic 2005 example integrates the Render method HTML with the TagKey and AddAttributesToRender processing by calling the base version of the Render method inside the span tag, passing the HTMLTextWriter to the base Render method:

```
Protected Overrides Sub Render(ByVal writer As System.Web.UI.HtmlTextWriter)

  writer.Write("<span id='" + Me.UniqueID + "'>")
  MyBase.Render(writer)
  writer.Write("<img id='" & Me.UniqueID & ":Image' src='MyPicture.gif'/>")
  writer.Write(
    "<input type='submit' id='" & Me.UniqueID & ":Button' " & _
            " value='Click Me'/>")
  writer.Write("</span>")

End Sub
```

In C#:

```
protected override void Render(System.Web.UI.HtmlTextWriter writer)
{
  writer.Write("<span id='" + this.UniqueID + "'>");
  base.Render(writer);
  writer.Write("<img id='" & this.UniqueID & ":Image' src='MyPicture.gif'/>");
  writer.Write(
   "<input type='submit' id='" + this.UniqueID + ":Button'  value='Click Me'/>");
  writer.Write("</span>");
}
```

The resulting HTML looks like this:

```
<span id='BookDisplay1'>
  <input id="BookDisplay1" name="BookDisplay1" type="Text" />
  <img id='BookDisplay1:Image' src='MyPicture.gif'/>
  <input type='submit' id='BookDisplay1:Button'  value='Click Me'/>
</span>
```

Ensuring Well-Formed Elements

Within the Render method, you can call some additional methods to manage the creation of text. Using the HTMLTextWriter's RenderBeginTag method, for instance, helps ensures that a well-formed opening tag is created for whatever tag name is passed to it. The RenderEndTag creates a well-formed close tag for the last tag that was opened but is not yet closed, forming a complete HTML element.

As an example, the following Visual Basic 2005 code creates the text for the BoldItalic control by writing out an HTML bold tag (<b>), an italics tag (<i>) inside of the bold tag, and text inside of the italics tag. The first RenderBeginTag in the code opens the bold tag and the second RenderBeginTag opens the italics tag. The first RenderEndTag closes the italic tag while the second RenderEndTag closes the bold tag:

```
Protected Overrides Sub Render(ByVal writer As System.Web.UI.HtmlTextWriter)

 writer.RenderBeginTag("B")
   writer.RenderBeginTag("I")
      writer.Write(strText)
   writer.RenderEndTag()
 writer.RenderEndTag()

End Sub
```

The equivalent C# code looks like this:

```
protected override void Render(System.Web.UI.HtmlTextWriter writer)
{
 writer.RenderBeginTag("B");
   writer.RenderBeginTag("I");
      writer.Write(strText);
  writer.RenderEndTag();
 writer.RenderEndTag();
}
```

You can use the RenderBeginTag method to write out your own tags instead of the various HTML tags. However, the RenderBeginTag method automatically puts into lowercase any tag that it recognizes as an HTML tag. In the previous code examples, for instance, while the RenderBeginTag method was passed an uppercase B, the tag will be written out as a lowercase b (<b>) to match the HTML standard.

Ensuring Valid Tags

To ensure that only valid HTML is rendered, you can use the tags and character definitions that are part of the Web.UI namespace. The HTMLTextWriterTag set includes definitions for the standard HTML tags. Using the bold and italic tags from this set with the previous code would give this version in Visual Basic 2005:

```
Protected Overrides Sub Render(ByVal writer As System.Web.UI.HtmlTextWriter)

 writer.RenderBeginTag(HtmlTextWriterTag.B)
    writer.RenderBeginTag(HtmlTextWriterTag.I)
      writer.Write(strText)
    writer.RenderEndTag()
 writer.RenderEndTag()

End Sub
```

In C#:

```
protected override void Render(System.Web.UI.HtmlTextWriter writer)
{
  writer.RenderBeginTag(HtmlTextWriterTag.B);
   writer.RenderBeginTag(HtmlTextWriterTag.I);
     writer.Write(strText);
   writer.RenderEndTag();
 writer.RenderEndTag();
}
```

In addition, the HTMLTextWriter set includes the definitions for standard strings that are used in creating tags, including an equals sign with following double quotes (=") and the self-closing tag end (/>).

Writing Attributes

When writing tags that include attributes, you can use the AddAttribute method to ensure that the attributes on the tags that you create will be properly formatted. Any attribute created by the AddAttribute method is automatically added to the next tag that is written using the RenderBeginTag This Visual Basic 2005 code adds the href attribute (pointing to the PHVIS Web site) to an anchor tag:

```
Protected Overrides Sub Render(ByVal writer As System.Web.UI.HtmlTextWriter)

 writer.AddAttribute("href", "http://www.phvis.com")
 writer.RenderBeginTag(HtmlTextWriterTag.A)
    writer.Write("Click Here")
 writer.RenderEndTag()

End Sub
```

In C#, you use:

```
protected override void Render(System.Web.UI.HtmlTextWriter writer)
{
 writer.AddAttribute("href", "http://www.phvis.com");
 writer.RenderBeginTag(HtmlTextWriterTag.A);
   writer.Write("Click Here");
writer.RenderEndTag();
}
```

Combining Controls and HTML

It is possible to break your text generation down into finer parts by overriding the custom control's other Render* methods. These methods are automatically run by the base Render method in the WebControl object. By using these other methods you can combine writing text to the page with adding constituent controls.

Using the other Render* methods highlights a significant problem with overriding the Render method: When you override the Render method, you prevent the processing that takes place in the base Render method from executing. Overriding the Render method, for instance, prevented the tag defined in the TagKey property from being written out. In the same way, overriding the Render method prevents the controls that you've added to your WebControl object's Controls collection from being written. This is because the RenderChildren method that takes care of writing out the members of the Controls collection is called from the base Render method. If the Render method is overridden, the RenderChildren method won't execute, and controls in the Controls collection won't be added to the page.

Figure 3-8 shows the structure of the various Render* methods. Overriding a method at the top of the tree prevents methods from lower in the tree from executing automatically (you can still call these methods from your own version of the routine). For instance, if you override the Render method but still want the controls in the Controls collection to be written out, you can call the WebControl object's RenderChildren method from your version of the Render method. Or, better yet, call the EnsureChildControls method, which checks the ChildControlsRendered property before calling RenderChildControls. This allows you to intermix writing out text with creating constituent controls.

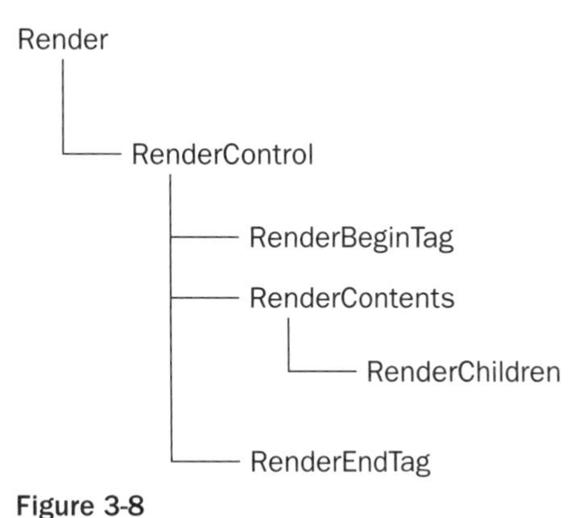

Figure 3-8

As an example, the following version of the Visual Basic 2005 Render method writes out a bold tag along with any controls in the Controls collection. In order to ensure that any constituent controls have been created, the EnsureChildControls method is called:

```
Protected Overrides Sub Render(ByVal writer As System.Web.UI.HtmlTextWriter)

  writer.RenderBeginTag("B")
    writer.Write(strText)
  writer.RenderEndTag()

  Me.EnsureChildControls()

End Sub
```

The C# version of this routine looks like this:

```
protected override void Render(System.Web.UI.HtmlTextWriter writer)
{
   writer.RenderBeginTag("B");
      writer.Write(strText);
   writer.RenderEndTag();

   this.EnsureChildControls();
}
```

Instead of calling the base RenderChildren method, you can use your own code to write any controls in the custom control's Controls collection to the host page. You may want to do this if you want to insert your own text in between the constituent controls (more efficient than using literal controls) or to selectively write out only some of the members of the Controls collection.

Each ASP.NET control has a RenderControl method that, when passed an HTMLTextWriter, writes out the control's text and HTML. Taking advantage of the RenderControl method, this Visual Basic 2005 code renders all the controls in your custom control's Controls collection (except buttons) and inserts a horizontal line between each control:

```
Protected Overrides Sub Render(ByVal writer As System.Web.UI.HtmlTextWriter)

Dim ct As System.Web.UI.WebControls.WebControl

 For Each ct In Me.Controls
  If ct.GetType.Name <> "Button" Then
    ct.RenderControl(writer)
    writer.Write("<hr/>")
 End If
Next
End Sub
```

In C#, the code looks like this:

```
protected override void Render(System.Web.UI.HtmlTextWriter writer)
{
 foreach(System.Web.UI.WebControls.WebControl ct in this.Controls)
```

```
{
  if (ct.GetType.Name != "Button")
  {
   ct.RenderControl(writer);
   writer.Write("<hr/>")
  }
 }
}
```

The resulting page, with two text boxes and a button in the Controls collection, is shown in Figure 3-9. As you can see, the button has not been rendered and a line has been inserted between each control.

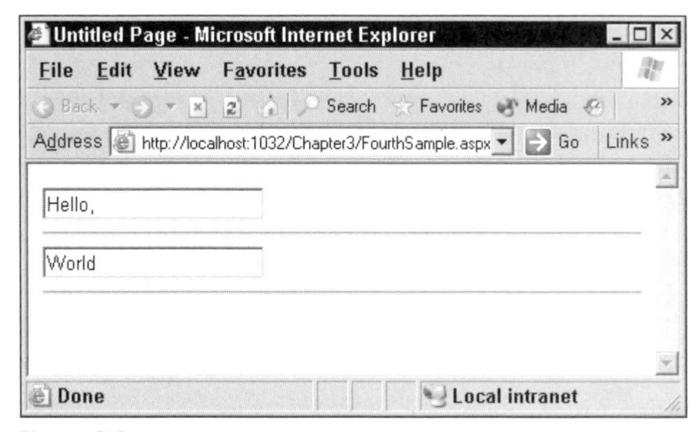

Figure 3-9

Don't use RenderControl on a control that isn't in your custom control's Controls collection. While the control will render to the page, the resulting objects aren't treated as constituent controls for your custom control.

Breaking up the Render Method

Putting all of your rendering code in the Render method can result in a single mass of unwieldy code. Rather than overriding the Render method, you may want to move your code from the Render method to the other Render* methods that are normally called from the base Render method. The most likely events that you would want to use to reduce the amount of code in the Render method are the RenderBeginTag, RenderContents, and RenderEndTag methods. Using these methods lets you divide the rendering of your custom control into three parts:

- Creating the opening tag for your custom control
- Creating the HTML inside your custom control (including any constituent controls)
- Creating your custom control's end tag

As an example, if you want to control the position of your constituent controls relative to each other, you might want to write out an HTML table as part of your custom control. You could break out the table creation into three parts:

- Writing out the initial <table> tags (creating the opening tag for your custom control)
- Rendering the constituent controls inside of table rows and cells (creating the HTML inside your custom control)
- Writing out the final </table> tag (creating your custom control's end tag)

Like the Render method, these methods are passed an HTMLTextWriter, which you can use to add text to the page.

The RenderBeginTag, RenderContents, and RenderEndTag methods are not called directly from the Render method. Instead, they are called from the RenderControl method, which is called from the Render method. So, in order to use these methods you must not override either the Render or RenderControl methods.

The RenderContents method calls the RenderChildren method, so if you do not override the RenderContents you could write a RenderChildren method of your own that would be called automatically. However, there is no benefit to using the RenderChildren method in place of the RenderContents method.

Supporting AutoPostback

You can give your control the capability to support AutoPostBack. In ASP.NET, AutoPostBack is implemented by adding some hidden fields and JavaScript code to your page. In addition, you must add some JavaScript client-side code to the control that is to trigger postback (adding custom client-side code is discussed in detail in Chapter 9). The GetPostBackEventReference method generates the JavaScript that you need. All you need to do is provide an AutoPostBack property that the developer using your control can set to turn on AutoPostBack, and then add the JavaScript code to your control.

At this point in the book you have to take some of the objects and code "as is." Adding client-side code, for instance, is discussed in detail in Chapter 9, while adding custom properties is covered in Chapter 8. However, giving your control AutoPostBack capability is a sufficiently common request so it's covered here.

Adding the AutoPostBack Property

An AutoPostBackProperty in Visual Basic 2005 looks like this:

```
Private AutoPostBackOn As Boolean

    Public Property AutoPostBack() As Boolean
        Get
            Return AutoPostBackOn
        End Get
        Set(ByVal value As Boolean)
```

```
            AutoPostBackOn = value
        End Set
    End Property
```

In C#:

```
bool AutoPostBackOn;

public bool AutoPostBack
{
 get
 {
        return AutoPostBackOn;
 }
 set
 {
        AutoPostBackOn = value;
 }
}
```

All this property does is enable the developer using your control to set or retrieve the value of the internal AutoPostBackOn variable. Later, in your code, you can check the value of this variable to determine if you should generate the AutoPostBack code.

Generating AutoPostBack Code

The GetPostBackEventReference method is found on the ClientScriptManager object, which can be retrieved from the Page object's ClientScript property. When you call the method, you must pass a reference to your control and an argument that will be returned to the server when the code is executed. This Visual Basic 2005 code generates the appropriate JavaScript code, passing a reference to the control and the string "MyControl":

```
Dim strPostBackCode As String
strPostBackCode = Me.Page.ClientScript.GetPostBackEventReference(Me, "MyControl")
```

In C#:

```
string strPostBackCode;
strPostBackCode =
              this.Page.ClientScript.GetPostBackEventReference(this, "MainText");
```

The argument passed as the second parameter is returned to the RaisePostBackEvent, discussed in Chapter 8.

This example, in a control with the ID TextAutoPostBack, generates this JavaScript code:

```
__doPostBack('AutoPostBack1','MyControl')
```

If you have constituent controls in your custom control, you can generate AutoPostBack code for them by passing a reference to that control when you call GetPostBackEventReference. This sample Visual Basic 2005 code generates the JavaScript code for a text box being used as a constituent control:

```
Protected Overrides Sub CreateChildControls()
Dim txt As New System.Web.UI.WebControls.TextBox
Dim strPostBackCode As String

  txt.ID = "MyTextBox"
  Me.Controls.Add(txt)

  If Me.AutoPostBack = True Then
   strPostBackCode = _
        Me.Page.ClientScript.GetPostBackEventReference(txt, "MainText")
  End If
End Sub
```

In C#:

```
protected override void CreateChildControls()
{
 System.Web.UI.WebControls.TextBox txt = new System.Web.UI.WebControls.TextBox();
 string strPostBackCode;

 txt.ID = "MyTextBox";
 this.Controls.Add(txt);

 if (this.AutoPostBack == true)
  {
   strPostBackCode =
          this.Page.ClientScript.GetPostBackEventReference(txt, "MyControl");
   }
}
```

For clarity, the test of the AutoPostBack property will be omitted in the following examples.

Because the text box has been given an idea of MyTextBox, the resulting JavaScript code refers to that control:

```
__doPostBack('MyTextBox','MyControl')
```

You can provide more control over the JavaScript code that is being generated by passing a PostBackOptions object to the GetPostBackEventReference. The PostBackOptions object has a number of properties that you can set in order to control what JavaScript code is created for you.

When you create a PostBackOptions object you must, at a minimum, pass a reference to a control (normally your custom control, but you could also pass a reference to a constituent control). After you've created your PostBackOptions object you can set any of these properties to control the JavaScript code that will, eventually, be generated by GetPostBackEventReference:

- **AutoPostBack:** When set to True, causes the page to be automatically posted back after a specified period of time has elapsed (the generated JavaScript code uses a client-side function called setTimeOut that is included with ASP.NET to implement the timeout).
- **ClientSubmit:** When set to False, the postback is not fired from the client-side code. You might use this option if you wanted to activate postback processing from your own client-side code by calling the _doPostBack method.

- **RequiresJavaScriptProtocol:** When set to True causes the prefix "javascript:" to be added to the start of the generated code (this is required for some browsers).
- **TrackFocus:** When set to True, when postback is completed, focus is returned to the control that triggered postback.
- **PerformValidation:** When set to True causes the control to trigger validation.
- **ValidationGroup:** If PerformValidation is set to True, you can use this property to control which Validators are fired (only Validators with a matching entry in their ValidationGroup execute).
- **Argument:** When you call the GetPostBackEventReference method and pass a reference to the custom control, you can pass a second argument to the method (this value will be returned to the server during postback). However, when you pass a PostBackOptions object to the method, you can't specify a second parameter. Setting this property allows you to specify an argument to be returned during postback.
- **ActionURL:** Typically, during postback, the page that triggers postback is requested. Setting the ActionURL to some other page's URL causes postback to request that page instead.
- **TargetControl:** Returns a reference to the control that the PostBackOptions referenced when the PostBackOption object was created. This property is read-only.

In this Visual Basic 2005 example, the PerformValidation and ValidationGroup are set before the PostBackOptions object is passed to the GetPostBackEventReference method to generate the JavaScript code. These settings cause validation controls that are part of the validation group UpdateItems to run before the form is posted back to the server. The AutoPostBack code is being generated for a text box that is a constituent control of the custom control:

```
Protected Overrides Sub CreateChildControls()
Dim txt As New System.Web.UI.WebControls.TextBox
Dim strPostBackCode As String
Dim pbo As PostBackOptions

  txt.ID = "MyTextBox"
  Me.Controls.Add(txt)

  pbo = New PostBackOptions(txt)
  pbo.PerformValidation = True
  pbo.ValidationGroup = "UpdateItems"

  strPostBackCode = Me.Page.ClientScript.GetPostBackEventReference(pbo)

End Sub
```

In C#:

```
protected override void CreateChildControls()
{
 System.Web.UI.WebControls.TextBox txt = new System.Web.UI.WebControls.TextBox();
 string strPostBackCode;
 PostBackOptions pbo;

 txt.ID = "MyTextBox";
```

```
    this.Controls.Add(txt);

    pbo = new PostBackOptions(txt);
    pbo.PerformValidation = true;
    pbo.ValidationGroup = "UpdateItems";

    strPostBackCode = this.Page.ClientScript.GetPostBackEventReference(pbo);
}
```

The resulting JavaScript code looks like this for a control called MyControl:

```
WebForm_DoPostBackWithOptions(new WebForm_PostBackOptions("MyControl", "",
                                   true, "UpdateItems", "", false, true))
```

Wiring Up AutoPostBack Code

The final step in the process is to attach the code to some client-side event on a control. The simplest way to do this is to use the Attributes collection of the control. This Visual Basic 2005 example associates the generated JavaScript code with the onBlur event of the control:

```
    strPostBackCode = Me.Page.ClientScript.GetPostBackEventReference(pbo)
    txt.Attributes("onBlur") = strPostBackCode
```

In C#:

```
    strPostBackCode = Me.Page.ClientScript.GetPostBackEventReference(pbo);
    txt.Attributes["onBlur"] = strPostBackCode;
```

Handling Returned Data

A Web page goes through a processing cycle that begins when the page is requested from a browser:

1. A user requests a page from the browser.
2. The request is received at the browser and rendered (as described throughout this chapter).
3. The user views the page in the browser and makes some changes to data in the page (for example, updating the value in a text box).
4. The user clicks the page's submit button and a new page is requested from the browser. Any data on the page is sent back to the server as part of this request.

In Step 4, ASP.NET pages normally request themselves. Effectively, then, the data from the browser is sent back to the original page on the server — a process known as *postback*. By implementing the IPostBackDataHandler interface and the one method that it contains, your custom control can capture and process its postback data.

If you add HTML to the page by overwriting the TagKey property and AddAttributesToRender method, then you must use postback to gather the data that is sent back to the server for your control. However, implementing this postback processing isn't necessary if you create a control using nothing but constituent controls (though you can still use postback processing). Data in constituent controls can be retrieved through their properties (for example, the Text property of a TextBox control) rather than through the postback interface.

To gather the data returned by the browser, you can implement the LoadPostData method. This method is called when the data is returned to the server and provides access to the data sent back from the browser. However, the LoadPostData method is called only if you let the Page object know that you will process posted data. You notify the page that you will be processing postback data by calling the Page's RegisterRequiresPostBack method, passing a reference to your custom control.

This Visual Basic 2005 code calls the RegisterRequiresPostBack method, passing a reference to the control. This could be used either with the previous code, which used the TagKey property to create the control's HTML, or with the CreateChildControls method, which added constituent controls to the Controls collection:

```
Private Sub BookDisplay_PreRender(ByVal sender As Object, _
                    ByVal e As System.EventArgs) Handles Me.PreRender
  Page.RegisterRequiresPostBack(Me)
End Sub
```

In C#:

```
private void BookDisplay_PreRender(object sender, System.EventArgs e)
{
 Page.RegisterRequiresPostBack(this);
}
```

Now that the control is registered for postback processing, you can add the IPostBackDataHandler interface to your control and implement the LoadPostData method. The LoadPostData method is passed two parameters: the name of your custom control on the page (the postDataKey parameter), and a collection of data from the page (the postCollection parameter).

This Visual Basic 2005 code would be used in a control that overrides the TagKey property so that you can retrieve the data posted back from the control (the class declaration is included to show the IPostBackDataHandler interface):

```
Public Class BookDisplay
    Inherits System.Web.UI.WebControls.WebControl
    Implements IPostBackDataHandler

Dim strTextBoxData As String

Public Function LoadPostData(ByVal postDataKey As String, _
        ByVal postCollection As Collections.Specialized.NameValueCollection) _
```

```
        As Boolean Implements IPostBackDataHandler.LoadPostData

    strTextBoxData = postCollection.Item(postDataKey)

  End Function

  End Class
```

In C#:

```
  public class BookDisplay : System.Web.UI.WebControls.WebControl,
                             IPostBackDataHandler
  {
    string strTextBoxData;

   public bool LoadPostData (
                  string postDataKey,
                  System.Collections.Specialized.NameValueCollection postCollection)
   {

    strTextBoxData = postCollection (postDataKey);
   }
```

At the very least, you want to retrieve this data so that it can be used when the page is rendered and sent back to the user. Tags that are generated through the TagKey method do not have their data automatically copied to the page that is sent back to the user. In other words, if you don't set the value attribute of an input tag generated through the TagKey, the user's data will be lost when the page is re-rendered.

In the previous example, the data was retrieved into a module-level variable called strTextBoxData. That variable should be used in the AddAttributesToRender method to cause the user's input to be displayed in the text box when the page goes back to the browser, as this Visual Basic 2005 code does:

```
  Protected Overrides ReadOnly Property TagKey() As System.Web.UI.HtmlTextWriterTag
    Get
      Return HtmlTextWriterTag.Input
    End Get
  End Property

  Protected Overrides Sub AddAttributesToRender( _
                        ByVal writer As System.Web.UI.HtmlTextWriter)

    MyBase.AddAttributesToRender(writer)
    writer.AddAttribute(HtmlTextWriterAttribute.Name, Me.UniqueID)
    writer.AddAttribute(HtmlTextWriterAttribute.Type, "text")
    writer.AddAttribute(HtmlTextWriterAttribute.Value, strTextBoxData)

  End Sub
```

In C#:

```
  protected override System.Web.UI.HtmlTextWriterTag TagKey
  {
   get
```

```
    {
      return HtmlTextWriterTag.Input;
    }
   }

   protected override void AddAttributesToRender(System.Web.UI.HtmlTextWriter writer)
   {
    base.AddAttributesToRender(writer);
    writer.AddAttribute(HtmlTextWriterAttribute.Name, this.UniqueID);
    writer.AddAttribute(HtmlTextWriterAttribute.Type, "text");
    writer.AddAttribute(HtmlTextWriterAttribute.Value, strTextBoxData);
   }
```

However, for a control that contains constituent controls, you will want to retrieve the value of your constituent controls. Those values are also in the data collection and can be retrieved by using the name of the constituent controls. Unfortunately, the Controls collection of your custom control isn't loaded at the time that the LoadPostData method is called, so you can't retrieve the constituent control ids from that collection (the LoadPostData method is called after the Init event and before the CreateChildControls method when the Controls collection is re-built). Instead you must provide the name of the constituent control concatenated with the custom control's UniqueId and IdSeparator properties.

The following Visual Basic 2005 code builds on the previous CreateChildControls method to process the data for the TextBox constituent control after it is returned from the browser. The code uses the same id assigned to the TextBox in the CreateChildControls method to retrieve the browser data from the data from the postCollection collection:

```
Dim strTextBoxData As String

Public Function LoadPostData(ByVal postDataKey As String, _
        ByVal postCollection As
Collections.Specialized.NameValueCollection) _
         As Boolean Implements IPostBackDataHandler.LoadPostData

   strTextBoxData = postCollection.Item(postCollection[Me.UniqueID &
 Me.IdSeparator & "MyTextBox")

End Function
```

In C#:

```
string strTextBoxData;

public bool LoadPostData (
                string postDataKey,
                 System.Collections.Specialized.NameValueCollection
postCollection)
  {
   strTextBoxData = postCollection[this.UniqueID + this.IdSeparator +
"MyTextBox"];
  }
```

You can fire events as part of your postback processing to signal to server code in the page that some condition has occurred in your custom control. Raising custom events is discussed in Chapter 8.

Controlling Related HTML

Regardless of which strategy you follow for creating custom controls, managing the HTML for your control is obviously a key part of creating a custom control. The HTML that is generated by your custom control *is* your control when it finally appears in the browser. In addition, if you intend to write client-side code that interacts with your custom control (discussed in Chapter 9), you need to be familiar with the HTML generated for your custom control. This section walks you through the HTML and gives you some additional ways of controlling the HTML generated for your custom control.

In addition to the tags and text generated *within* your custom control, there are two other sets of tags and text that you need to consider:

- The tags that are added to your Web page at design time when a developer wants to use your control.
- The HTML generated *around* your custom control at run time. When ASP.NET renders your custom control, it encloses the control that you render with some additional HTML to manage your control on the page. (For instance, by enclosing your control in a <span> tag, ASP.NET can assign style properties to the <span> tag that will control the appearance of your custom control's HTML in your browser.)

In addition, you can specify some of the HTML to be used with your custom control as part of defining the class for your custom control.

Design-Time HTML

When a custom control is dragged to the page, two tags may be added to the page:

- **The tag for the control itself:** This tag is always added.
- **A Register directive:** This tag is added the first time that a custom control from a particular DLL is added to the page. Subsequent controls from the same DLL will be based on the first Register directive.

The Tag for the Control

Handling the tag used for the control at design time is straightforward: You just use the ToolboxData attribute on the class module for your control. The ToolboxData attribute lets you specify the design time tag generated for the control when a developer drags your custom control from the toolbox and onto the page:

```
<ToolboxData("<{0}:BookDetail runat=server></{0}:BookDetail>")> _
  Public Class BookDetail
        Inherits System.Web.UI.WebControls.WebParts.WebControl
```

This C# code does the same:

```
using System;

[ToolboxData("<{0}:BookDetail runat=server></{0}:BookDetail>")]
public class BookDetail : System.Web.UI.WebControls.WebParts.WebControl
```

At run time, the {0} is replaced with the namespace prefix for the control (the namespace for the control is discussed in the next section). For instance, the resulting design time tag might look like this, assuming that "cc1" is used as the prefix for the custom control:

```
<cc1:BookDetail runat=server><cc1:BookDetail>
```

At run time, this tag is replaced with the HTML generated by your custom control (along with whatever HTML ASP.NET wraps around your custom control).

The Register Directive

The Register directive is added at the top of the page and defines the namespace and prefix to be used with all the custom controls from the DLL. By default, if no namespaces have been specified in the project, the namespace will be the name of the project. The prefix used with the tags defaults to "cc" and some numeric value to distinguish the custom controls drawn from different libraries. As an example, this is the Register directive that is generated when a control from the MyWebParts project is dragged to the page from the toolbox (and is the first Register directive added):

```
<%@ Register TagPrefix="cc1" Namespace="MyWebParts" Assembly="MyWebParts" %>
```

The tag generated at design time for a custom control called BookDetail from the MyWebParts project looks like this:

```
<cc1:BookDetail ID="BookDetail1" runat="server" />
```

By using the TagPrefix attribute you can control the prefix used when the Register directive for your custom control is generated. The TagPrefix attribute appears before the class definition for your control and accepts two parameters: the namespace (which must match the namespace set in the code for your control) and the prefix. This Visual Basic 2005 example applies the prefix myc to a custom control whose root namespace is set to MyControls:

```
<assembly: TagPrefix("MyControls", "myc")> _
Public Class BookDetail

End Class
```

In C#:

```
[assembly: TagPrefix("MyControls", "myc")]
public class WebCustomControl1 : WebControl
 {
 }
```

The Register tag and the tag for the custom control that is generated by Visual Studio 2005 when the control is dragged to the page look like this:

```
<%@ Register Assembly="ControlsVB3" Namespace="MyControls" TagPrefix="myc" %>
<myc:BookDisplay ID="BookDisplay1" runat="server" />
```

Run-Time HTML

The ToolboxData attribute also allows you to control what HTML will be placed in the page at run time. For instance, this Visual Basic 2005 example causes the HTML to create a red border, 1 pixel wide around the control:

```
<ToolboxData( _
  "<{0}:BookDetail runat=server
            BorderStyle=Solid BorderWidth=1 BorderColor=red></{0}:BookDetail>")> _
Public Class BookDetail
```

In C#:

```
using System;

[ToolboxData("<{0}:BookDetail runat=server
              BorderStyle=Solid BorderWidth=1 BorderColor=red ></{0}:BookDetail>")]
public class BookDetail : System.Web.UI.WebControls.WebParts.WebControl
```

The resulting HTML in the page delivered to the browser looks like this:

```
<cc1:BookDetail runat=server BorderStyle=Solid BorderWidth=1 BorderColor=red>

</cc1:BookDetail>
```

Setting Attributes

If the constituent controls for your custom control were written out by the default Render method, they will be enclosed by a <span> tag:

```
<span>
  ...constituent controls...
<span>
```

The WebControl object gives you two ways to alter the attributes on the <span> tag that encloses your custom control's constituent controls and on the constituent controls themselves: the Attributes property and the AddAttributesToRender method.

Many of the attributes generated at run time can be managed through property settings on the controls. However, not all the attributes that are available in the HTML specification are available as properties on your custom control or its constituent controls. The techniques that are described in this section enable you to go beyond the properties exposed by the ASP.NET controls.

The simplest method for adding attributes is to use the Attributes property on the WebControl object, which allows you to add arbitrary attributes to the <span> tag for a custom control that uses the default Render method.

Modifying the <span> tag allows you to control the way that all the constituent controls within the custom control are handled by the browser. For instance, the HTML generated for the book detail control, when it's displayed in the browser, looks like this:

```
<span id="MyBookDetail">
 <input type="submit"...
 ...tags for other constituent controls...
</span>
```

This Visual Basic 2005 code in your WebControl adds the lang attribute to the custom control and sets it to support U.S. English:

```
Me.Attributes("lang") = "en-us"
```

In C#:

```
this.Attributes["lang"] = "en-us";
```

The result is this HTML being rendered to the page:

```
<span id="MyBookDetail" lang="en-us">
<input type="submit" ...
...tags for other constituent controls...
</span>
```

Extending Control over Attributes

While the Attributes method is very simple to use, overriding the AddAttributesToRender method allows you more control over the attributes that you add to your custom control's <span> tag. The HTMLTextWriter object that is passed to the AddAttributesToRender method has several methods that give you more control over the way your attributes are written.

Unlike the Attributes property, this method can't be used with the constituent controls to add attributes to them.

The code for overriding the AddAttributesToRender method to add the lang attribute used in the previous example and to write out any default attributes looks like this in Visual Basic 2005:

```
Protected Overrides Sub AddAttributesToRender( _
       ByVal writer As System.Web.UI.HtmlTextWriter)

writer.AddAttribute("lang", "en-br")
MyBase.AddAttributesToRender(writer)

End Sub
```

In C#, the code looks like this:

```
protected override void AddAttributesToRender(System.Web.UI.HtmlTextWriter writer)
{
   writer.AddAttribute("lang", "en-br");
   base.AddAttributesToRender(writer);
}
```

So far, the AddAttributesToRender method has just duplicated what was done with the Attributes property. However, the AddAttribute method of the HTMLTextWriter gives you access to features that the Attributes property does not. For instance, one of the four versions of the AddAttribute method of the HTMLTextWriter supports encoding. As another example, the HTMLTextWriter also supports using predefined constants for defining attributes. This Visual Basic 2005 example adds an Href attribute set to the value "http://phvis.com/Logo.Gif" with encoding:

```
Protected Overrides Sub AddAttributesToRender( _
                              ByVal writer As System.Web.UI.HtmlTextWriter)

  writer.AddAttribute(HtmlTextWriterAttribute.Href, _
                           "http://phvis.com/Logo.Gif", True)

End Sub
```

In C#:

```
protected override void AddAttributesToRender(System.Web.UI.HtmlTextWriter writer)
{
   writer.AddAttribute(HtmlTextWriterAttribute.Href, _
                             "http://phvis.com/Logo.Gif",True)
}
```

The HTMLTextWriter's AddStyleAttribute is another useful tool for managing your custom control's appearance and is discussed later in this chapter.

If you do override both the Render method and the AddAttributesToRender method, you should make sure that your version of the Render method calls your version of the AddAttributesToRender method: In the Render method, don't use the MyBase or base objects when calling AddAttributesToRender. Instead, use me or this. If you use MyBase or base, your version of the AddAttributesToRender render won't be called. Instead the version in the base WebControl object is called.

As with the AddAttribute method and the Attributes collection, using AddAttributesToRender allows you to update attributes already on the <span> tag in addition to adding new attributes.

Managing Attributes for Constituent Controls

As mentioned earlier, you can also use the Attributes collection with the constituent controls you add to your custom control. Often, if you add attributes to a single constituent control, you want to add those same attributes to all the constituent controls within the custom control in order to ensure consistency. Fortunately, it doesn't require a lot of code to keep attributes consistent across several constituent controls: You can add the attributes you want to a single control and then copy those attributes to another control using the CopyBaseAttributes method of the constituent control you want the attributes copied to.

Style-related attributes are not copied by the CopyBaseAttribute. Style-related attributes include the style attribute itself along with assorted other attributes that control appearance. Basically, any attribute represented by a property on the Style object won't be copied by CopyBaseAttributes. Managing style-related attributes is discussed in the section "Managing Your Custom Control's Style" later in this chapter.

The following Visual Basic 2005 code, used in the CreateChildControls method, adds the lang attribute to the first text box in the custom control and then copies that attribute (and any others on the text box) to a second text box:

```
Dim txt1 As System.Web.UI.WebControls.TextBox
Dim txt2 As System.Web.UI.WebControls.TextBox

  txt1 = New System.Web.UI.WebControls.TextBox
  txt1.Id = "Text1"
  txt1.Attributes("lang") = "en-us"
  Me.Controls.Add(txt1)

  txt2 = New System.Web.UI.WebControls.TextBox
  txt2.Id = "Text2"
  txt2.CopyBaseAttributes(txt1)
  Me.Controls.Add(txt2)
```

In C#:

```
System.Web.UI.WebControls.TextBox txt1;
System.Web.UI.WebControls.TextBox txt2;

  txt1 = new System.Web.UI.WebControls.TextBox();
  txt1.Id = "Text1";
  txt1.Attributes["lang"] = "en-us";
  this.Controls.Add(txt1);

  txt2 = new System.Web.UI.WebControls.TextBox();
  txt2.CopyBaseAttributes(txt1);
  txt2.Id = "Text2";
  this.Controls.Add(txt2);
```

The resulting HTML looks like this:

```
<input name="Text1" type="text" value=" " lang="en-us" />
<input name="Text2" type="text" value=" " lang="en-us" />
```

Extracting and Controlling WebControl Properties

Within your code, you can determine a great deal about your own custom control from properties on the WebControl object, including values set at design time by the developer when adding your custom control to a Web page. If you override these properties you can control the changes that the developer makes through these properties.

Server-Side Properties

The following list shows those properties that are available from code within the custom control (not all of these properties are available to client-side code on the host page):

- **ToolTip:** Returns the value of the ToolTip set for the control. If you set this property in your custom control's code, the value will be displayed in the Property List for the custom control when the custom control is used in Visual Studio 2005 and as a tooltip in some browsers.
- **Enabled:** When False, the custom control is currently disabled. The IsEnabled property returns the same value but is available only from code within the custom control, while the Enabled property is available to the code in the host page that is manipulating your control. If you intend to take control of the custom control's Enabled state (for example, to prevent the custom control from being disabled) you should override the Enabled property and use the IsEnabled property from your code within your control to determine whether your control is enabled.
- **Visible:** When True, the HTML for the custom control is not sent to the browser. This can be used only when the custom control is not in a WebPartZone. For custom controls in a WebPartZone, use the Hidden property to prevent the control from being displayed in the browser without closing it.
- **IsLiteralContent:** When True, indicates that the custom control contains only a single literal control. You can take advantage of this feature by designing your control to contain a single literal control (with some combination of text and HTML) when it's in a particular state. In other states your control can contain no constituent controls, multiple literal controls, or controls other than literal controls. For instance, the control might contain a single literal control displaying "Error" when something goes wrong, but hold multiple controls when everything goes well. A developer using your control can check for the Error state by checking the IsLiteralContent property.
- **HasAttributes:** When True, indicates that the <span> tag surrounding the custom control's constituent controls has had attributes added to it.
- **HasControls:** When True, indicates that the custom control has controls in its Controls collection.

Determining the Tag

Because the namespace is set in the Register directive (which can be altered by the developer), you won't necessarily know the full name of your control's tag when you are writing the control. Specifically, while you can use the ToolBoxData attribute to control the tag name, the prefix applied to the tag when the tag is dragged from the Toolbox isn't set until the control is added to the page. However, by adding the ConstructorNeedsTag attribute to the class, you can cause ASP.NET to pass the full tag name generated for your control in Visual Studio 2005 to the constructor for your custom control. This technique lets you determine the prefix used with your control's tag at design time.

For instance, in this Visual Basic 2005 example, the ConstructorNeedsTag attribute has been applied to the class and the New method modified to accept a single parameter:

```
<ConstructorNeedsTag(True)> Public Class BookDetail
        Inherits System.Web.UI.WebControls.WebParts.WebPart
Dim strTag As String

Public Sub New(ByVal strFullTagName As String)
```

```
    strTag = strFullTagName
End Sub
```

In C#

```
[ConstructorNeedsTag(true)]
public class BookDetail : System.Web.UI.WebControls.WebParts.WebPart
{
 string strTag;

 public BookDetail(string strFullTagName)
  {
    strTag = strFullTagName;
  }
```

For a tag called <BookDetail> with a namespace of "cc1" the result of this code is that strTag is set to "cc1:BookDetail".

Managing Your Custom Control's Style

As part of creating your custom control, you may want to manage both the style of your custom control and of the constituent controls within the custom control. The WebControl object provides a number of methods and properties for setting style-related attributes on the HTML generated for your custom control.

Before using these methods and properties, you should first consider which, if any, of these methods and properties you should take control of. In most cases, you will want your custom control to integrate with whatever style is being used on the host page. As a consequence, you may want to leave the setting of the custom control's styles up to the developer using your custom control.

Having said that, there are still some style-related activities that you will want to take control of:

- When the developer sets style properties for your custom control, you may want to propagate those settings to your custom control's constituent controls. At design time, the developer has access only to the style properties for your custom control and cannot directly address the style properties for the constituent controls. At run time, to set style properties for the constituent controls, the developer is obliged to cycle through your custom control's Controls collection to set those properties. You'll see how to propagate those settings later in this section.
- Even if you are allowing the developer to set style properties on your custom control, there may be some settings that you don't want to allow the developer to change. For instance, you might have a label on your custom control that displays errors, and you want to ensure that error messages are always displayed with red text on a white background. You can meet this goal by overriding the WebControl properties described in this section.
- You may want to set properties for your custom control to determine how the custom control is initially displayed when it is dragged onto a design surface in an editor. While you may expect the developer to override those settings (either at design time or run time) you may want to provide an initial set of values so that your custom control looks like a professional product when it's added to the design environment. In this case, you want to make sure that your settings won't prevent the developer from changing the settings. To meet this goal, you'll need to understand how to save your custom control information, which is described in Chapter 6.

Themes and Skins

ASP.NET supports using themes (themes are re-usable collections of styles and graphics). Themes are organized into skins, specific to controls, which can be applied to user interface components. In general, you'll want to leave themes to the developer using your custom control.

While you usually leave themes up to the developer, you may want to determine from your code how themes are applied to your custom control. There are three properties that you can use to access information about how themes are being used with your custom control:

- **EnableTheming/IsThemeEnabled:** When the EnableTheming property is set to True, themes may be applied to the custom control (and its constituent controls), at least from *the custom control's point of view*. However, the EnableTheming property depends on the IsThemeEnabled property, which indicates whether the page supports theming. When the IsThemeEnabled property is set to True, it indicates that themes may be applied to the custom control (and its constituent controls) from *the host page's point of view*. A control may have EnableTheming set to True but have IsThemeEnabled set to False if, for instance, the host page doesn't have EnableTheming turned on. In that case, while the custom control is enabled for themes, the page level setting prevents themes from being applied to the custom control.
- **SkinId:** When themes are applied to the control, this property returns the identifier for the skin applied. Setting this property changes the skin applied to the custom control or raises an error if the skin isn't available in the theme or if the skin is of the wrong type.

To prevent themes from being applied to your custom control, you can override the EnableTheming property with a version of your own and set the underlying version of this property on the WebControl object to False.

Using Cascading Stylesheet Classes

The CssClass property on the custom control and constituent controls allows you to assign a Cascading Stylesheet class to the object. This Visual Basic 2005 code assigns a class called WebControlSample to a text box and a button:

```
Dim txt As System.Web.UI.WebControls.TextBox
Dim btn As System.Web.UI.WebControls.Button

txt = New System.Web.UI.WebControls.TextBox
txt.CssClass = "WebControlSample"

btn = New System.Web.UI.WebControls.Button
btn.CssClass = "WebControlSample"
```

In C#:

```
System.Web.UI.WebControls.TextBox txt;
System.Web.UI.WebControls.Button btn;

txt = new System.Web.UI.WebControls.TextBox();
txt.CssClass = "WebControlSample";

btn = new System.Web.UI.WebControls.Button();
btn.CssClass = "WebControlSample";
```

Updating the Style

The major problem with using classes from a stylesheet is that, as a custom control developer, you don't have a lot of control over what stylesheet is being used with your custom control at run time. Typically, the stylesheet is assigned at the level of the Web page, rather than assigned on a control-by-control (or custom control–by–custom control) basis. Even if you were to insert a style tag into your custom control to ensure that the stylesheet that your CSS class is drawn from is referenced by the page, you can't be assured that the stylesheet will be available to the project using your custom control.

The moral of this story is that if you want to establish a specific style for your custom control, you should work with the style attribute on the custom control and on any constituent controls.

The WebControl object provides you with several ways to control the style of your custom control and its constituent controls. You can work with

- The style attribute directly through the AddAttributesToRender method
- The Style property on the control
- A Style object

Using the Style object allows you to create a custom control that integrates with styles set on the host page while still maintaining some distinctive elements. If you are going to write much code to deal with style, your best choice is to use the Style object, which gives you a central point of control for all style-related activities.

In the end, however, whether you work with the Style object or use the other ways described later in this section, the result is that attributes on the HTML tags delivered to the browser (principally, the style attribute) are going to be updated. Working with the style attribute directly gives you better performance than working with the Style object, at the cost of more complexity in your code. You should consider using the Style property or the AddAttributesToRender method only if you aren't doing much around managing your control's appearance.

Using the Style Property

An HTML tag has a style attribute, which consists of a concatenated list of key/value pairs, separated by semicolons. While you can update this attribute using the Attributes collection of the WebControl object or your custom control's constituent controls, you would have to update the whole style attribute rather than individual key/value pairs. Rather than do that, you should use the Style property of your custom control (and its constituent controls). The Style property contains a collection of key/value pairs that lets you add or update individual elements of the style attribute. Adding or updating keys in the Style collection of your WebControl objects sets the style attribute on the <span> tag that encloses your custom control.

This Visual Basic 2005 code, for instance, adds the position key (set to the value "absolute"), the top key (set to " 20px"), and left (set to " 30px"):

```
Me.Style("position") = "absolute"
Me.Style("top") = "20px"
Me.Style("left") = "30px"
```

In C#:

```
this.Style["position"] = "absolute";
this.Style["top"] = "20px";
this.Style["left"] = "30px";
```

The resulting HTML looks like this:

```
<span style="position:absolute;top:20px;right:30px">
```

> **Using absolute positioning on your constituent controls makes it impossible for developers to use your controls as Web Parts.**

Updating the Style Attributes in AddAttributesToRender

You can also set the style attribute for the custom control itself by overriding the WebControl object's AddAttributesToRender method and then taking advantage of the AddStyleAttribute method of the HTMLTextWriter that's passed to the method. The AddStyleAttribute method accepts a style key and value and incorporates them into the style attribute string for the custom control's <span> tag. This sample Visual Basic adds values to control the border color and border width to the <span> tag's style attribute (you should also call the base AddAttributesToRender method first to make sure that any default attributes are written):

```
Protected Overrides Sub AddAttributesToRender( _
       ByVal writer As System.Web.UI.HtmlTextWriter)

  MyBase.AddAttributesToRender()
  writer.AddStyleAttribute("border-color", "Black")
  writer.AddStyleAttribute("border-width", "1px")

End Sub
```

In C#:

```
protected override void AddAttributesToRender(System.Web.UI.HtmlTextWriter writer)
{
  base.AddAttributesToRender();
  writer.AddStyleAttribute("border-color", "Black");
  writer.AddStyleAttribute("border-width", "1px");
}
```

The resulting HTML looks like this:

```
<span style="border-color:Black;border-width:1px;">

...constituent controls...

</span>
```

You can also use this method to update values already in the style attribute.

Managing Styles

If you are planning to do more than the simplest changes to your control's style, you should use a Style object. A Style object can provide you with a single point of control for all of your style-related activities.

The place to begin is by overriding the WebControl's CreateControlStyle method. The CreateControlStyle method is called automatically by ASP.NET to get the Style object that will be used for your control. By overriding the CreateControlStyle method you can customize this object to provide the base style characteristics for your control. This Visual Basic 2005 example creates a Style object, sets some properties on the object, and then returns it:

```
Protected Overrides Function CreateControlStyle() As _
                                        System.Web.UI.WebControls.Style
Dim st As WebControls.Style

  st = New WebControls.Style

  st.Font.Bold = True
  st.Font.Name = "Arial"
  Return st

End Function
```

In C#:

```
protected override System.Web.UI.WebControls.Style CreateControlStyle()
{
 WebControls.Style st;

 st = new WebControls.Style();

 st.Font.Bold = true;
 st.Font.Name = "Arial";
 return st;
}
```

In addition to the general purpose Style object, .NET supports style objects tailored to specific objects including TableSectionStyle and a TableItemStyle objects. If your control uses a table to position your constituent controls, you may want to return a table-based Style object from your CreateControlStyle method.

You can also create a Style object outside of the CreateControlStyle method. For instance, you might want to create a single Style object that is to be used to manage the styles for your constituent controls (if you do set the style for one of your custom control's constituent controls, it's likely that you'll want to use that style for all the constituent controls). After creating a Style object you can then apply that Style object to your constituent controls using the controls' MergeStyle or ApplyStyle methods.

This sample Visual Basic 2005 code, in the CreateChildControls method, creates a Style object and sets several properties on it. With the Style object created, the style is applied to two text boxes being added to the Controls collection using the ApplyStyle method:

```
Dim txt1 As System.Web.UI.WebControls.TextBox
Dim txt2 As System.Web.UI.WebControls.TextBox
Dim stl As New System.Web.UI.WebControls.Style

stl = New System.Web.UI.WebControls.Style
stl.ForeColor = Drawing.Color.Red
stl.Font.Bold = True
stl.BorderWidth = 12

txt1 = New System.Web.UI.WebControls.TextBox
txt1.Id = "Text1"
txt1.ApplyStyle(stl)
txt1.Text = "Hello"
Me.Controls.Add(txt1)

txt2 = New System.Web.UI.WebControls.TextBox
txt2.Id = "Text2"
txt2.Text = "World"
txt2.ApplyStyle(stl)
Me.Controls.Add(txt2)
```

In C#:

```
System.Web.UI.WebControls.TextBox txt1;
System.Web.UI.WebControls.TextBox txt2;
System.Web.UI.WebControls.Style stl;

stl = new System.Web.UI.WebControls.Style();
stl.ForeColor = Drawing.Color.Red;
stl.Font.Bold = true;
stl.BorderWidth = 12;

txt1 = new System.Web.UI.WebControls.TextBox();
txt1.Id = "Text1";
txt1.Text = "Hello";
txt1.ApplyStyle(stl);
this.Controls.Add(txt1);

txt2 = new System.Web.UI.WebControls.TextBox();
txt2.Id = "Text2";
txt2.Text = "World";
txt2.ApplyStyle(stl);
this.Controls.Add(txt2);
```

The (very unattractive) results can be seen in Figure 3-10.

If style values have already been set on a control, the MergeStyle method integrates the Style object's properties with the already existing style settings. Settings in the Style object will *not* override the style settings already on the control. This makes the MergeStyle method a very useful tool for integrating style settings made by the developer with style settings that you want to maintain as part of your custom control's design.

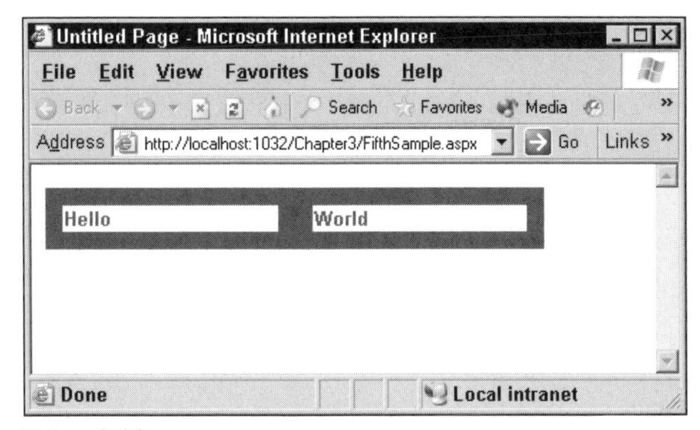

Figure 3-10

This Visual Basic 2005 code retrieves the control's Style object using the ControlStyle method. The code then sets the BorderStyle property of the Style object to Inset and sets the ForeColor property on a TextBox and a Button object. Finally, the code uses the Style object with the constituent controls through the MergeStyle method to apply the style to the text box without overriding their individual ForeColor settings. Only controls that don't have an explicit ForeColor setting will pick up the new ForeColor:

```
Dim txt As System.Web.UI.WebControls.TextBox
Dim btn As System.Web.UI.WebControls.Button
Dim stl As System.Web.UI.WebControls.Style

  stl = Me.ControlStyle()
  stl.BorderStyle = System.Web.UI.WebControls.BorderStyle.Inset

  txt = New System.Web.UI.WebControls.TextBox
  txt.ID = "Text1"
  txt.ForeColor = Drawing.Color.Red
  txt.MergeStyle(stl)
  Me.Controls.Add(txt)

  btn = New System.Web.UI.WebControls.Button
  btn.ForeColor = Drawing.Color.Green
  btn.ID = "Button1"
  btn.MergeStyle(stl)
  Me.Controls.Add(btn)
```

In C#

```
System.Web.UI.WebControls.TextBox txt;
System.Web.UI.WebControls.Button btn;
System.Web.UI.WebControls.Style stl;

  txt = new System.Web.UI.WebControls.TextBox();
  btn = new System.Web.UI.WebControls.Button();

  stl = this.ControlStyle;
```

```
    stl.BorderStyle = System.Web.UI.WebControls.BorderStyle.Inset;

    txt.ID = "Text1";
    txt.ForeColor = Drawing.Color.Red;
    txt.MergeStyle(stl);
    this.Controls.Add(txt);

    btn.ID = "Button1";
    btn.ForeColor = Drawing.Color.Green;
    btn.MergeStyle(stl);
    this.Controls.Add(btn);
```

Recycling Styles

You can retrieve a Style object from an existing control by accessing the control's ControlStyle property. This Visual Basic 2005 code extracts a Style object from an existing text box and then uses it with another constituent control:

```
Dim stl As System.Web.UI.WebControls.Style
Dim txtNew As New System.Web.UI.WebControls.TextBox

stl = New System.Web.UI.WebControls.Style
stl = txtName.ControlStyle
txtNew.MergeStyle(stl)
```

In C#:

```
System.Web.UI.WebControls.Style stl;
System.Web.UI.WebControls.TextBox txtNew = new System.Web.UI.WebControls.TextBox();

stl = System.Web.UI.WebControls.Style();
stl = txtName.ControlStyle;
txtNew.MergeStyle(stl);
```

You can extract the style for your custom control using the WebControl object's ControlStyle property. By retrieving the Style object from the ControlStyle property, you can access the Style object created in the CreateControlStyle routine from other routines without having to declare your Style object at the class level. If the Style object for your control has not yet been created, reading the ControlStyle property causes your CreateControlStyle method to run.

This Visual Basic 2005 code retrieves the Style object from the custom control and then uses it with two constituent controls:

```
Dim txt As System.Web.UI.WebControls.TextBox
Dim btn As System.Web.UI.WebControls.Button
Dim stl As System.Web.UI.WebControls.Style

stl = Me.ControlStyle()

txt = New System.Web.UI.WebControls.TextBox
txt.Id = "Text1"
txt.MergeStyle(stl)
```

```
    Me.Controls.Add(txt)

    btn = New System.Web.UI.WebControls.Button
    btn.Id = "Button1"
    btn.MergeStyle(stl)
    Me.Controls.Add(btn)
```

In C#:

```
System.Web.UI.WebControls.TextBox txt;
System.Web.UI.WebControls.Button btn;
System.Web.UI.WebControls.Style stl;

stl = this.ControlStyle();

txt = new System.Web.UI.WebControls.TextBox();
txt.Id = "Text1";
txt.MergeStyle(stl);
this.Controls.Add(txt);

btn = new System.Web.UI.WebControls.Button();
btn.Id = "Button2";
btn.MergeStyle(stl);
this.Controls.Add(btn);
```

If you extract the Style object from the ControlStyle property of your custom control, any changes that you make to the Style object's properties will be reflected in the HTML for your custom control, provided they are made before your control's Render method is called.

If you do override the default Render method with your own version, remember that you suppress any default processing that occurs. For instance, overriding the Render method prevents the default RenderBeginTag method from executing, and this is where the information from the Style object is added to your control's HTML.

You can ensure that the default rendering does take place by calling the base Render* methods from your version of the Render method and passing those methods the HTMLTextWriter object passed to the Render method. This Visual Basic 2005 code modifies the Style object drawn from the ControlStyle method and ensures that the Style information is added to the resulting HTML by calling the default RenderBeginTag and RenderEndTag methods through the MyBase object:

```
Protected Overrides Sub Render(ByVal writer As System.Web.UI.HtmlTextWriter)
Dim stl As System.Web.UI.WebControls.Style

    stl = Me.ControlStyle
    stl.ForeColor = Drawing.Color.Red
    MyBase.RenderBeginTag(writer)
    writer.Write(strText)
    MyBase.RenderEndTag(writer)

End Sub
```

In C#, the code looks similar but uses the base object to access the default RenderBeginTag and RenderEndTag methods:

```
protected override void Render(System.Web.UI.HtmlTextWriter writer)
{
  System.Web.UI.WebControls.Style stl;

  stl = this.ControlStyle;
  stl.ForeColor = Drawing.Color.Red;
  base.RenderBeginTag(writer);
  writer.Write(strText);
  base.RenderEndTag(writer);
}
```

Another solution in using the Style object when overriding the Render method is to take advantage of the Style object's AddAttributesToRender method. This method accepts an HTMLTextWriter object and creates a set of attributes that will be added to the next tag written by the HTMLTextWriter. The following Visual Basic 2005 code retrieves the control's Style object from the ControlStyle method, sets properties on the Style object, and then uses the Style object's AddAttributesToRender with the control's RenderMethod to apply the style to the control:

```
Protected Overrides Sub Render(ByVal writer As System.Web.UI.HtmlTextWriter)
Dim stl As System.Web.UI.WebControls.Style
Dim txt As System.Web.UI.WebControls.TextBox

  stl = Me.ControlStyle
  stl.ForeColor = Drawing.Color.Red
  stl.AddAttributesToRender(writer)

  txt = New System.Web.UI.WebControls.TextBox
  txt.Text = "hello, world"
  txt.RenderControl(writer)
End Sub
```

In C#

```
protected override void Render(System.Web.UI.HtmlTextWriter writer)
{
 WebControls.Style stl;
 WebControls.TextBox txt;

  stl = new System.Web.UI.WebControls.Style();
  stl = this.ControlStyle;
  stl.ForeColor = Drawing.Color.Red;
  stl.AddAttributesToRender(writer);

  txt = new WebControls.TextBox();
  txt.Text = "hello, world";
  txt.RenderControl(writer);
}
```

Dealing with Design Mode

While the primary purpose of adding code to a custom control is to control how the custom control displays at run time when displayed in a browser, you must also consider how your custom control will behave in the design environment. This section shows you:

- How to check to see if you're in Design mode so that you can make the appropriate adjustments to your code
- Attributes that you can add to your control to integrate with the Visual Studio 2005 environment

Managing Code at Design Time

Your custom control is just as active in Visual Studio 2005 as it is in a browser. Any code that renders the HTML to display your custom control will execute in the editor as it will in the browser, and as the developer sets your custom control's properties in Design mode, the code behind those properties executes as the code will when those properties are set from code in the host page. At design time some events won't execute (the Load event, for instance) while others will (Init). The same is true of the methods in your custom control. As already discussed, your CreateCustomControls method won't be called at design time, but your custom control's constructor will. You want to make sure that when your code does execute in the design environment that the control behaves properly. It's your responsibility to manage your control's execution not only at run time but also at design time—another example of the multiple levels of thinking required when creating a custom control.

The WebControl object has a DesignMode property that allows you to determine whether or not your custom control is being used in design mode or being displayed on a page in a browser. The property returns False when your custom control is being displayed in the browser and True when the control is being used during a design session, allowing you to control what code executes in your custom control at design time.

Because most of the custom control's events don't normally execute in the design environment, often the best way to handle the design time environment is to put "design-unfriendly" code into your custom control's event routines (this is covered in more depth in Chapter 8).

There are several cases when, in Design mode, you need to override your custom control's standard rendering. If your custom control supports databinding, you won't want to attempt to access a data source when your custom control is being used in Design mode. Instead, you'll want to display some standard text in the databound controls. This Visual Basic 2005 code sets the Text property of a text box to a dummy value when DesignMode is True:

```
Dim ct As System.Web.UI.WebControls.Control
Dim txt As System.Web.UI.WebControls.TextBox

If Me.DesignMode = True Then
   ct = Me.FindControl("txtInput")
   txt = Ctype(ct, WebControls.TextBox)
   txt.Text = "#databound"
Else
    ...databinding support
End If
```

In C# the code looks like this:

```
System.Web.UI.WebControls.Control txt;

if (this.DesignMode == true)
{
   txt = (System.Web.UI.WebControls.TextBox) this.FindControl("txtInput");
   txt.Text = "#databound";
}
else
 {
      ...databinding support
}
```

Databinding is covered in Chapter 9.

Other reasons that you want to control what code executes at design time include the following:

- Some custom controls (especially databound controls) display multiple rows at run time—one row for each data item. At design time, rather than retrieve the data and display all the rows, you may want to always display exactly three rows.
- Some controls depend on other controls to do their work. For instance, all WebParts require a WebPartManager, and some WebParts communicate with other WebParts to do their work. At design time you may want to use dummy values in place of the values that will be supplied by these other controls at run time. This can be especially important at design time to avoid forcing the user to add interrelated controls in a specific order.

Controlling How Visual Studio Handles Your Control

While the focus for your custom control is how the control will behave in the browser at run time, there are some easy changes you can implement to make your control easier to work with for developers at design time. Primarily, these are several attributes that you can apply to your custom control behavior in Visual Studio 2005 at design time:

- **DefaultProperty:** This attribute, applied to the Class declaration, allows you to specify which property will have the focus in Visual Studio 2005's IntelliSense Lists when the list is initially displayed for your control.

The best property to choose for your default property is the one developers using your control will (a) always want to change, and (b) want to change most often.

- **DefaultEvent:** This attribute allows you to control what event routine is automatically generated by Visual Studio 2005 when a developer double-clicks your control in Visual Studio 2005. This Visual Basic 2005 example makes Category the default property and the InvalidValue event the default event:

```
<DefaultProperty("Category"), DefaultEvent("InvalidValue")> _
    Public Class BookDetail
```

In C#:

```
[DefaultProperty("Category"), DefaultEvent("InvalidValue")]
    public class BookDetail
```

The DefaultProperty is also useful when supporting databinding, as discussed in Chapter 9.

- **Category:** This attribute allows you to control in which group a property appears in Visual Studio 2005's Property List when the list is sorted by categories. This Visual Basic 2005 example puts the property in the Appearance category:

```
<Category("Appearance")> Property StyleType As String
```

In C#:

```
[Category("Appearance")] public string StyleType
```

- **ToolboxItem:** If, for some reason, you don't want your control to display in the Toolbox, you can add the ToolBoxItem attribute to your Class declaration and pass it a False value. In Visual Basic 2005:

```
<ToolBoxItem(False), ToolboxData( _
                    "<{0}:BookDetail runat=server></{0}:BookDetail>")> _
Public Class BookDetail
```

In C#:

```
using System;

[ToolBoxItem(False), ToolboxData(
                    "<{0}:BookDetail runat=server></{0}:BookDetail>")]
public class BookDetail : System.Web.UI.WebControls.WebParts.WebControl
```

Summary

In this chapter you learned how to:

- Create a custom control
- Set up Visual Studio 2005 to create a custom control project efficiently
- Add constituent controls to your custom control
- Handle your control's behavior at design time
- Extract information about your control
- Manage all the HTML rendered for your custom control

You got a start on the multiple levels of thinking required when creating a custom control: moving from the host page to the custom control to the constituent controls, and moving from design time to run time. You've seen the role that the WebControl object fulfills in creating a custom control. The

WebControl object provides the utility code for implementing a custom control and an infrastructure where you can override existing methods and properties in order to add functionality to your custom control.

Now you can create custom controls that have all the functionality of the standard ASP.NET server-side controls. You can create a custom control that contains plain HTML or constituent controls (including both HTML controls and server-side ASP.NET controls).

In the next chapter, you learn how to create a user control. In Chapter 5, you'll learn how to extend your custom control to include the additional functionality available to a full-fledged Web Part.

Building User Controls

This is the shortest chapter in this book—and for good reason: As an ASP.NET developer, you already know most of what you need to know to create a user control. As you will see, creating a user control is very much like creating a Web page. If you have experience building Web applications and want to get started with creating reusable components, user controls are a great place to start. You will also see, however, that the features described in the previous chapter on creating custom controls can be incorporated into user controls.

In this chapter you learn how to:

- Understand the differences between user controls, WebForms, and custom controls
- Create a static user control by dragging and dropping constituent controls at design time
- Take advantage of the features discussed in the chapter on custom controls to dynamically add constituent controls at run time to your user control
- Access custom properties, methods, and events built into your user control
- Give your user control a constructor

User Controls, WebForms, Custom Controls

A user control is much like a WebForm. It consists of a user interface file (holding HTML, ASP.NET tags, and client-side code) and a related file of server-side code written in some .NET language.

As with WebForms, you can create user controls either in a single file model (with HTML, aspx tags, and code held in the .aspx file) or with the two-file model (with your code held in a separate language file). The code used in this chapter will work in either model, but the sample code uses the two-file model throughout.

As with a WebForm, in Visual Studio 2005 a user control (like an ASP.NET page) normally appears as a single item in Solution Explorer (in Figure 4-1 the user control is called CustInfo.ascx). As you do in a WebForm, you add constituent controls to the user control by dragging controls from your Toolbox onto the design surface; you add code by writing it in the event routines in the user control's codebehind file.

Figure 4-1

The major difference between creating a custom control (as explained in Chapter 3) and a user control is that custom controls have no design surface for adding constituent controls. The impact is equally obvious: The absence of a design surface makes creating custom controls very coding-intensive. User controls, on the other hand, provide you with an opportunity to balance building your control's user interface graphically and implementing the user interface with code. As this chapter demonstrates, most of the features available to you when you are creating a custom control are available to you when you are creating a user control.

So why create a custom control if user controls have so many benefits? There are two major disadvantages to creating a user control, as opposed to creating a custom control. Unlike custom controls:

- User controls can't be shared among projects.
- User controls can't be extended to acquire the code-based features of a full-fledged Web Part (without converting the user control to a custom control).

There are other, less important differences between a user control, a custom control, and a WebForm. For instance, one of the differences between a user control and a custom control is that when developers are building a page using your controls, they will drag user controls onto their page from Solution Explorer and drag custom controls from the Toolbox.

The major difference between WebForms and user controls is that you can't, from a browser, request a user control — user controls can be sent down to the browser only as part of a WebForm. Unlike a WebForm, the file extension for a user control is .ascx rather than .aspx.

And that's about it.

Starting a User Control

A typical example for a user control is a control for displaying and entering customer information. As shown in Figure 4-2, this control displays customer address information to the user and allows the user to enter information. This control has a large number of constituent controls, so the user control's support for a drag-and-drop user interface design will save time when building the control. The user interface might not be completely static: When used as part of a data entry form, this control's user interface might include buttons for triggering validation or data retrieval, some text boxes might be replaced with drop-down lists, and space might be left for displaying error messages resulting from bad data being entered (see Figure 4-3).

Figure 4-2

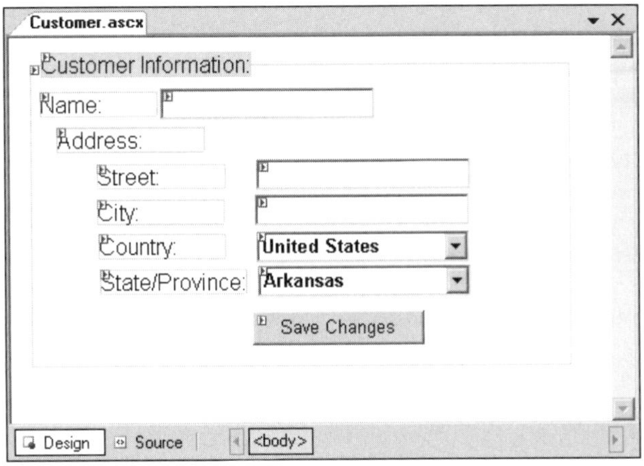

Figure 4-3

These dynamic changes to the user control's user interface can be handled in at least three ways:

- A control can be placed on the design surface and have its Visible property set to False. At run time, the control could be made to appear by setting its Visible property to True.
- Panel and PlaceHolder controls can be added to the design surface, and controls can be loaded into them at run time.
- Constituent controls can be dynamically added to the user control's Controls collection in the CreateChildControls method, as described in Chapter 3.

If you're working with Visual Studio 2005, you can create a user control by selecting Website ➪ Add New Item ➪ Web User Control. If you're working outside of ASP.NET, you need to create a text file with the extension .ascx and a Control directive at the top of the file:

```
<%@ Control %>
```

Because a user control looks much like a WebForm, the attributes that you can use with the Control directive for a user control look much like the directive for a Web page. These attributes (all of which are used in the Control directive at the top of the ascx file) are explained in the following lists.

Two attributes specify the relationship between your ascx file and its class module:

- **Inherits:** This attribute specifies the class module for ASP.NET to load at run time. For the two-file model (that is, when using a codebehind file) this is the class name specified in the Class line of the codebehind file. If the Inherits attribute, for instance, is set to CustInfo_ascx, the Class declaration should look like this in Visual Basic 2005:

```
Partial Public Class CustInfo_ascx
        Inherits System.Web.UI.UserControl
```

  In C#:

```
public partial class CustInfo : System.Web.UI.UserControl
```

- **ClassName:** If you are using the single-file model for programming your server-side control, this attribute lets you specify the name of the class for the code in the file. If you omit this attribute, a class name is generated automatically at run time, which really means that you are taking a chance on what name is used for the object behind your user control. By using this attribute in the single-file model you control that name. In the two-file model, this name will override the name specified in the class line of your codebehind file.

Four options specify how your user control is compiled:

- **CompilerOptions:** Allows you to set switches to be used by the compiler.
- **WarningLevel:** Can be set to a value of 0 to 4, indicating at what level of compiler warnings the compilation should be abandoned. A setting of 0 (the default) causes all warnings to be ignored; a setting of 4 causes any warning (such as an unused variable) to terminate the compilation.
- **Debug:** When set to true, causes the code to be compiled in debug mode (debug mode causes the debug information file — the pdb file — to be regenerated and some code optimizations to be skipped). The default is true.
- **LinePragmas:** When set to true causes meta information about lines of code to be generated at compile time.

Two attributes specify how the control is recompiled at run time:

- **Src:** The path to the file that contains the source code when your control is dynamically compiled at run time.

- **CompilationMode:** This attribute controls when the user control should be dynamically compiled at run time. It can be set to one of three values:
    - **Always:** The user control is compiled whenever it is used.
    - **Never:** The user control is never recompiled at run time.
    - **Auto:** The user control is compiled only if no compiled version of the code is available to ASP.NET. The default is Auto.

Two options are relevant when writing Visual Basic 2005 in the single-file model:

- **Explicit:** When set to true, requires that all variables used in the code in this file be declared.
- **Strict:** When set to true, requires that most type conversions performed in the code in this file be explicit.

One option is relevant when using the single-file model, regardless of the language:

- **Language:** This is used to specify the server-side language used in the ascx file. If you are working in the single-file model and adding server-side code to the ascx file along with your tags, the language that you use in the ascx is specified here. This has no effect on the language used in the codebehind file in the two-file model.

If you are using the two-file model you should specify this attribute:

- **CodeFile:** The file containing your source code.

The other attributes that you can use are:

- **AutoEventWireup:** When set to true, it causes ASP.NET to tie events to your code routines by the name of the routine instead of through event handlers (for example, with this attribute set to true, when a button called btnSubmit fires a Click event, ASP.NET will look for a routine called btnSubmit_Click to execute).
- **Description:** A text string description of the user control.
- **EnableTheming:** When set to true, allows themes to be used with the user control.
- **EnableViewState:** When set to false, disables the ViewState for the user control.

Here are two examples, both of which assume that you won't want to compile your source code dynamically at run time:

- Assuming that you're using the two-file model in Visual Studio with event handlers to associate your routines with events fired by your constituent controls, you want to set the following attributes and let the other attributes remain at their default values:

```
<%@ Control AutoEventWireup="false" Inherits="AClass" CodeFile="AClass.ascx.vb"
CompilationMode="Never" %>
```

    - **AutoEventWireup** to false (the default is true)
    - **Inherits** to the name of the class module in the codebehind file

    - **CodeFile** to the name of the file holding your source code
    - **CompilationMode** to Never to prevent recompiling at run time
- Assuming that you're using the single-file model with C# with event handlers associated with your routines by name, you want to set the following attributes and let the other attributes remain at their default values:

```
<%@ Control ClassName="MyClass" Language="CS" Inherits="AClass" %>
```

    - **ClassName** to the name that you want to assign to the class associated with your control
    - **Inherits** to the name in the ClassName attribute
    - **Language** to CS to use C#

After the Control directive at the top of the file, you can add almost any of the tags that you would use in a Web page. The three exceptions are the tags that define a page to HTML: the <html>, <head>, and <body> tags. Those tags will be supplied by the host page for the control.

If you are using Visual Studio 2005, the Debug, Explicit, and Strict attributes (which apply only to Visual Basic 2005) can be set from the Property List; the Language attribute can be read from the Property List but cannot be changed. The other attributes must be set directly in HTML view of the ascx file.

Writing Code for Your Control

Along with your ASCX file, assuming that you're using the two-file model, you'll need a codebehind file. If you're working in Visual Studio 2005, the codebehind file is created automatically when you add your user control to your project. If you're working outside of Visual Studio 2005, you need to create a Visual Basic 2005 file like this:

```
Partial Class CustInfo
    Inherits System.Web.UI.UserControl

End Class
```

In C#, the file looks like this:

```
public partial class CustInfo : System.Web.UI.UserControl
{

}
```

If you're working outside of Visual Studio 2005, remember to set the CodeFile attribute in the ASCX file to the name of your codebehind file and to set the Inherits attribute to the name of the class in your code.

Adding server-side code to your codebehind file is much like writing code for a standard Web form. For instance, in the CustInfo control discussed earlier in the chapter, you could put the code to retrieve the user information in the PreRender event of the user control. That code would look something like the following Visual Basic 2005 (this code assumes that the variables strCustId and strConnection have been set earlier in the control's life cycle, presumably through custom properties, as discussed in Chapter 8):

```
Protected Sub Page_PreRender(ByVal sender As Object, _
                             ByVal e As System.EventArgs) Handles Me.PreRender
Dim con As System.Data.SqlClient.SqlConnection
Dim cmd As System.Data.SqlClient.SqlCommand
Dim dr As System.Data.SqlClient.SqlDataReader

  con = New System.Data.SqlClient.SqlConnection(strConnection)
  cmd = New System.Data.SqlClient.SqlCommand( _
        "Select CustFName, CustLName From Customers Where CustId = '" & _
        strCustId & ";", con)
  dr = cmd.ExecuteReader(CommandBehavior.SingleRow)
  dr.Read()

  Me.txtCustFirstName.Text = dr.GetString(0)
  Me.txtCustLastName.Text = dr.GetString(1)

  dr.Close
  con.Close

End Sub
```

In C#:

```
protected void Page_PreRender(object sender, System.EventArgs e)
{
  System.Data.SqlClient.SqlConnection con;
  System.Data.SqlClient.SqlCommand cmd;
  System.Data.SqlClient.SqlDataReader dr;

  con = new System.Data.SqlClient.SqlConnection(strConnection);
  cmd = new System.Data.SqlClient.SqlCommand(
          "Select CustFName, CustLName From Customers Where CustId = '" +
          strCustId + ";", con);
  dr = cmd.ExecuteReader(CommandBehavior.SingleRow);
  dr.Read();

  this.txtCustFirstName.Text = dr.GetString(0);
  this.txtCustLastName.Text = dr.GetString(1);

  dr.Close();
  con.Close();
}
```

Simulating a Constructor

Unlike a custom control, a user control doesn't have a constructor. This means that the first opportunity to have any of your server-side code execute is during the Init event. The Init event, however, doesn't execute until after the host page's Init event rather than at the moment that the control is actually created. For instance, if the developer using your user control is using the LoadControl method to dynamically add your control to the page, no code in your user control will run when your control is created (the LoadControl method is discussed in the following section, "Dynamic Interfaces").

You can execute code before the Init event of the user control by overriding the Construct method of the underlying UserControl object. If a developer then loads your user control using the LoadControl method, the Construct method will fire immediately after the LoadControl method executes.

Here's the declaration for a Construct method in Visual Basic 2005 code:

```
Protected Overrides Sub Construct()

End Sub
```

In C#:

```
protected override void Construct()
{

}
```

After you create a constructor for your user control, you can use the ConstructorNeedsTag attribute (as described in Chapter 3) to have the constructor passed the tag that encloses your user control.

Dynamic Interfaces

Even though you are creating a *user* control you can use many of the methods and properties discussed in the previous chapter on creating a *custom* control. Taking advantage of these methods significantly increases the flexibility of the user control. Many scenarios require controls that have dynamic interfaces—for instance, a control that lists data items needs to add new controls dynamically, depending on the number of items to be listed. Many developers avoid creating user controls when they need a dynamic interface because they believe, incorrectly, that the drag-and-drop interface used when creating a user control prevents them from creating the kind of dynamic interface that a listing control requires.

Because user controls support the same CreateChildControls method and Controls collection that a custom control does, you can add constituent controls dynamically to a user control. This allows you to, for instance, drag and drop the static header at the top of a control that lists records while using the CreateChildControls method to dynamically add labels or controls that display individual records.

At design time, for a user control, the CreateChildControls method is not automatically invoked. As a result, controls that you add to the user interface for your user control in the CreateChildControls method do not appear in the Visual Studio 2005 editor window either when you're creating your user control or when you drag the user control onto a page. Don't panic! The controls appear on your WebForm when it is displayed in the Web browser.

If you combine adding controls using drag-and-drop with adding controls in your code, remember that the Controls collection will contain both sets of controls. In a custom control, you could assume that the only controls in the Controls collection were the ones added in the code. With a user control, however, the controls added through drag-and-drop will already be in the Controls collection before you add your first control from your code.

However, there's also one thing that you can do with constituent controls in a user control that you can't do with a custom control: Constituent controls for a user control can include both user controls and custom controls (custom controls can't have user controls as a constituent control).

When a user control is added to a host page, it functions as a constituent control to the host page. To add a constituent user control at design time, just drag the user control from Solution Explorer to the host page. On the other hand, to add a constituent user control to the host page at run time, you must use the LoadControl method of the host page. The LoadControl method must be passed the name of your constituent user control. You can then add that returned result to your host user control's Controls collection.

The following Visual Basic 2005 code loads a user control called CountryInfo dynamically by using the host's LoadControl method and passing the path to the user control. Once the control is loaded, it's added to the hosting user control's Controls collection:

```
Dim uc As System.Web.UI.Control

uc = Me.LoadControl("CountryInfo.ascx")
Me.Controls.Add(uc)
```

In C# the same work looks like this:

```
System.Web.UI.Control uc;

uc = this.LoadControl("CountryInfo.ascx");
this.Controls.Add(uc);
```

Simply using the LoadControl method to load your user control isn't enough to cause the user control to be rendered — you must add the User Control to the Controls collection of some containing control (including Panels or PlaceHolders) or another User Control (you can't add a User Control directly to the Controls collection of a form).

Also, to ensure that your user control's events fire correctly, you must load the user control in the host page's Init event or in the CreateChildControls method. If the user control is loaded later in the user control's life cycle, the user control's events may not fire, and data entered at the browser may not be displayed in the User Control when the page is regenerated.

Using Web Parts

In addition to dragging standard ASP.NET controls onto a user control, you can also drag WebPartZones, WebPartsEditors, and Web Parts onto the control. You could also drag a WebPartManager onto your user control — but it's not a good idea. ASP.NET allows only one WebPartManager on a page. As a result, if you add a WebPartManager to a user control, your user control cannot be used on a page that already has a WebPartManager (or on a page that has another copy of your user control or on a page that has any other user control with a WebPartManager). Furthermore, a WebPartManager must precede any other Web Parts on the page. So, if your user control contains a WebPartManager, you severely limit where your user control can be placed.

As a result, even if your user control requires a WebPartManager, it's a good practice not to place the WebPartManager on your user control. Instead, the developer using your user control should add a WebPartManager to the host page to support your user control. In your user control, you can access the WebPartManager for the host page for your user control by calling the WebPartManager's GetCurrentWebPartManager method and passing a reference to the host page. The

GetCurrentWebPartManager method is a static method of the WebPartManager object, which means that the method can be called even if a WebPartManager instance isn't available. You can retrieve the reference to the host page that you must pass to the method from the user control's Page property.

The following Visual Basic 2005 code retrieves a reference to the WebPartManager on the host page and sets its display mode:

```
Dim wpm As System.Web.UI.WebControls.WebParts.WebPartManager

wpm = WebPartManager.GetCurrentWebPartManager(Me.Page)
wpm.DisplayMode = WebPartManager.DesignDisplayMode
```

In C#:

```
System.Web.UI.WebControls.WebParts.WebPartManager wpm;

wpm = System.Web.UI.WebControls.WebParts.WebPartManager.GetCurrentWebPartManager(
                 this.Page);
wpm.DisplayMode = WebPartManager.DesignDisplayMode;
```

When you change the display mode for the page's WebPartManager from within a user control, all WebPartZones, WebPartEditors, and Web Parts on the page are affected — not just the ones in your user control.

ASP.NET makes no effort to reconcile names for the zones, editors, or Web Parts on your user control and zones, editors, or Web Parts on the hosting page. As a result, you should make sure that you give your user control's constituent controls names that are unlikely to duplicate the names of controls — otherwise a page with your user control may get errors the first time that it is called, complaining about controls with duplicate names. One strategy is to use your user control's name as a prefix for all controls on your user control — for example, UserControl_wpCustomerName.

Working with a User Control

After you drag a user control to a host page, the user control's constituent controls will be displayed, along with a green arrow in the upper-left corner that represents the user control as a whole. Clicking the green arrow (i.e., the "smart tag") on the box displays the common tasks list for the user control (see Figure 4-4). This list has two tasks:

- **Edit UserControl:** Opens the user control in design mode.
- **Refresh Contents:** Updates the user control on the host page with the current version of the user control (use this to update the host page after making changes to the user control without having to close and re-open the host page).

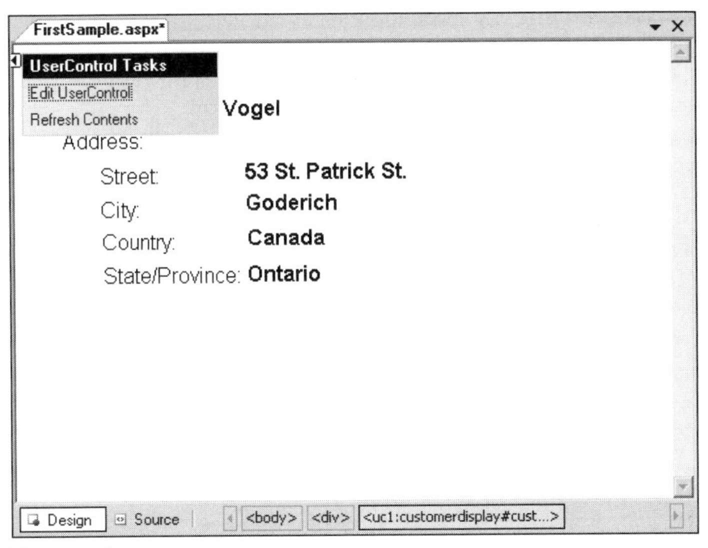

Figure 4-4

Clicking on the box or on any of the constituent controls will display the properties for the user control in the Visual Studio 2005 Property List. Three properties can be set from the Property List: EnableViewState, Runat, and Visible.

To add a user control to your page if you're working outside of Visual Studio 2005 you must insert two tags to your ASPX file:

- A Register directive that provides ASP.NET with the information to find the user control at run time
- A tag that actually places the user control in the page

The Register directive must be placed at the start of the page:

```
<%@ Register TagPrefix="uc1" TagName="CustInfo" Src="CustInfo.ascx" %>
```

This directive provides all the information that ASP.NET needs to retrieve the control at run time. The TagPrefix and TagName specify the parts of the tag (or tags) used to add your user control to the host page. By default, the TagPrefix is set to "uc" (user control) followed by a numeral; the TagName is the filename for the file holding the user control. You can change these to anything you want. The Src attribute is the path name to the file containing the user control.

Because a user control must be part of the project, the Src attribute must point to a location in your Web site. You can, however, use the tilde (~) to indicate that a URL begins at the root of your Web site (~/MySite/MyControl.ascx would point to a user control called MyControl.ascx in the MySite directory of the Web site).

The second tag actually adds the user control to the page:

```
<uc1:CustInfo id="CustInfo1" runat="server"></uc1:CustInfo>
```

The tag prefix and tag name must match the values from the TagPrefix and TagName attributes for the Register tag that holds the path name to the ASCX file. The id attribute provides the name for this copy of the control as a constituent control of the host page.

When the host page is sent to the browser, the user control isn't treated as a separate component. Instead, ASP.NET simply adds the HTML rendered by the user control to the HTML rendered by the host page. If, for instance, you have placed a constituent control (such as a text box) 400 pixels from the top of the user control, that text box is going to be 400 pixels from the top of the host page when it shows up in the browser. (Make sure your user control and your host page don't put two HTML objects in the same place.)

If you do want to manage the position of the user control on the page, you can use a container control (like a Panel or a WebPartZone) to hold the user control at either design time or run time. At design time just drag a Panel onto your page where you want the user control to appear, and then drag the user control into the Panel. When a user control is inside a panel, all distances are calculated from the Panel's top and left sides (so the text box from my previous example will be 400 pixels from the top of the Panel).

If you're working outside of Visual Studio 2005, you can place the tag for the user control inside the tags of the containing control. This set of tags puts the user control inside a Panel control:

```
<asp:Panel Style="z-index: 100; left: 104px; position: absolute; top: 73px"
           ID="Panel1" runat="server" Height="50px" Width="125px">
    <uc1:CustAddress ID="CustAddress1" runat="server" />
</asp:Panel>
```

You can also add your user control to the Panel at run time. To do this, place a Panel control on the host page as before, and then use the following Visual Basic 2005 code in your host page to load your user control. The code uses the host's LoadControl method to create a reference to the user control and then uses the Panel Controls collection's Add method to place the user control on the page:

```
Dim uc As System.Web.UI.Control
uc = Me.LoadControl("CustInfo.ascx")
Me.Panel1.Controls.Add(uc)
```

The equivalent C# looks like this:

```
System.Web.UI.Control CustInfo1;
CustInfo1 = this.LoadControl("CustInfo.ascx");
this.Panel1.Controls.Add(CustInfo1);
```

While you can add a user control directly to the Controls collection of a hosting user control, as noted briefly earlier you can't add a user control directly to the Controls collection of a hosting WebForm — this generates a message of the type "control must be inside <form> tags." When dynamically loading a user control to a WebForm, you must add the user control to the Controls collection of some containing control (such as a Panel or a PlaceHolder).

Accessing the Control

Earlier in this chapter, you saw how to load the control using the LoadControl method. However, the LoadControl method returns only a standard WebControls.WebControl object, which means that you are able to use only the standard methods, properties, and events for the Control you just loaded. If you've added any custom methods or properties to your user control, they will be unavailable to the code in the host.

To solve this problem, you need to declare a variable that references your user control's class using either the name given in the class declaration in the codebehind file or the default name given to the user control. Typically, the default name is the name of the user control with _ascx appended to it. For a user control called CountryInfo that hasn't used the ClassName attribute, the default name would be CountryInfo_ascx. Your user control's class can be found in the ASP namespace.

Using the ClassName attribute on the Control directive in the ascx file lets you specify the name used for your user control's object at run time.

To be able to declare a variable that references your user control's class name, you must still add the Register tag to the host page. For the CountryInfo ascx control, that would look like this:

```
<%@ Register TagPrefix="uc1" TagName="CountryInfo" Src="CountryInfo" %>
```

Because you are loading the user control dynamically, you don't need to add the tag for the control itself.

With the Register tag in place, you can now declare a variable in the host that references the class for your user control, as this Visual Basic 2005 code does:

```
Dim uc As ASP.CountryInfo_ascx
```

In C#:

```
ASP.CountryInfo_ascx uc;
```

You can also declare the variable without the ASP namespace and the _ascx suffix, like this:

```
Dim uc As CountryInfo
```

In C#:

```
CountryInfo uc;
```

You can now load your control using the LoadControl method. Because the LoadControl method returns a reference of type Control, you have to convert the reference to your user control's type as seen in this Visual Basic 2005 code:

```
uc = CType(Me.LoadControl("CountryInfo.ascx"), ASP.CountryInfo_ascx)
```

In C#:

```
uc = (ASP.CountryInfo_ascx) this.LoadControl("CountryInfo.ascx");
```

You could now use the uc variable to call any custom methods or properties you've written for the CountryInfo user control.

User Control HTML

As noted earlier, the user control has no actual presence in the HTML for the host page. Instead, the HTML for the user control's constituent controls is simply merged into the HTML for the host page. A user control that consisted of two buttons (with their Id properties set to Button1 and Button2), would cause this HTML to be added to the host page:

```
<input type="submit" name="ctl02$Button1" value="Button" id="ctl02_Button1"
        style="z-index: 100; left: 119px; position: absolute; top: 63px" />
<input type="submit" name="ctl02$Button2" value="Button" id="ctl02_Button2"
        style="z-index: 102; left: 227px; position: absolute; top: 148px" />
```

As you can see, the constituent controls for the user control are distinguished from the rest of the page's child controls by having a prefix added to the constituent controls' id and name attributes. If you are generating client-side code to interact with these controls, you can determine what prefix is being applied to the user control's constituent controls by reading the user control's UniqueId property.

For more discussion of the UniqueId property and how client-side names are generated, see the material in Chapter 3 on the UniqueId.

Summary

As an experienced ASP.NET developer, you already know much of what's required to build a user control. This chapter has filled in the gaps between user controls and WebForms:

- Starting a user control
- Defining the tags
- Simulating a constructor
- Building a dynamic interface

More important, you're familiar with the differences between a custom control and a user control so that you can make an informed decision as to which is the best choice for any problem that you face. To take full advantage of your user control, though, you should consider reviewing the material on custom controls in Chapter 3.

In Chapter 5, you learn how to build the third type of component covered in this book: Web Parts.

5

Building Web Parts

In Chapter 2 you learned how a standard ASP.NET control can be used as a Web Part by dragging the control into a WebPartZone. In Chapters 3 and 4 you learned how to build custom controls and user controls. Those controls can also be used as Web Parts, simply by dragging them into WebPartZones. However, those controls don't support all the functionality of the Web Part framework. In this chapter you learn to:

- Set up properties in a custom controls and user controls to integrate with the Web Parts framework
- Create a full-fledged Web Part using many of the same tools and techniques that you used to create a custom control

As you'll see, any custom control or user control can integrate its properties into the Web Parts framework. However, while any control can be used as a Web Part, in order to take full advantage of the Web Parts framework, you have to build your control as a Web Part from the beginning. The good news is that building a Web Part is just like building a custom control with a few more features that are covered in this chapter.

In the same way that a custom control can be given personalization functionality, a Web Part can be used as a custom control. In fact, because Web Parts can do anything that a custom control can do, you might want to consider building all your custom controls as Web Parts, even if you don't intend to take advantage of the extended features of a Web Part. Remember: A developer can always use a Web Part as an ordinary custom control by dragging the Web Part onto the page instead of into a WebPartZone.

If, when building a Web Part, you implement the specialized features of a Web Part, those features lie dormant when your Web Part is used as a custom control. But, if a developer drags your Web Part into a WebPartZone, the specialized Web Part features that you've built into your control become available to the developer.

This chapter covers the basics of adding personalization to a custom control and creating a Web Part. However, when you use a Web Part in conjunction with the other Web Part framework controls, you can enable features not discussed here. For example, if you want to see how to connect two Web Parts, look at Chapter 10. Chapter 11 shows how to work with the personalization system that Web Parts integrate with.

I begin by discussing how to add personalization support to a custom control or a Web Part. Following that, you'll see how to create a full-fledged Web Part.

Enabling Personalization for Control Properties

One feature of the Web Part framework is that users can add editors to a page that let the user update the values of properties of the Web Part controls on the page. You can make any property on a custom control or a user control available to be customized by a user at run time through these editors by adding two attributes to any custom properties in your control (custom properties are covered in depth in Chapter 8):

- **WebBrowsable:** To make a property available to be changed when the user is customizing the page in the browser, you add the WebBrowsable attribute to the property and pass the attribute a value of True.
- **Personalizable:** To cause the customizations to be remembered, you add the Personalizable attribute to a property and pass it a value of True. The Personalizable attribute also allows you to control whether customizations are remembered only for the user making the change or are applied for all users.

Turning on Customization

As an example of enabling a property for customization, this Visual Basic 2005 code shows a custom property with the WebBrowsable attribute on it and set to True:

```
<WebControls.WebParts.WebBrowsable(True)> _
Property BookTitle As String

End Property
```

In C#, the property looks like this:

```
[WebControls.WebParts.WebBrowsable(true)]
public string BookTitle
{
}
```

Because the WebBrowsable attribute has been added to the BookTitle property, when the PropertyGridEditorPart is added to the page, the BookTitle property appears in the editor as an editable item when the WebPartManager is put into EditDesignMode and Edit is selected from the Web Part's Verb menu. (See Figure 5-1.)

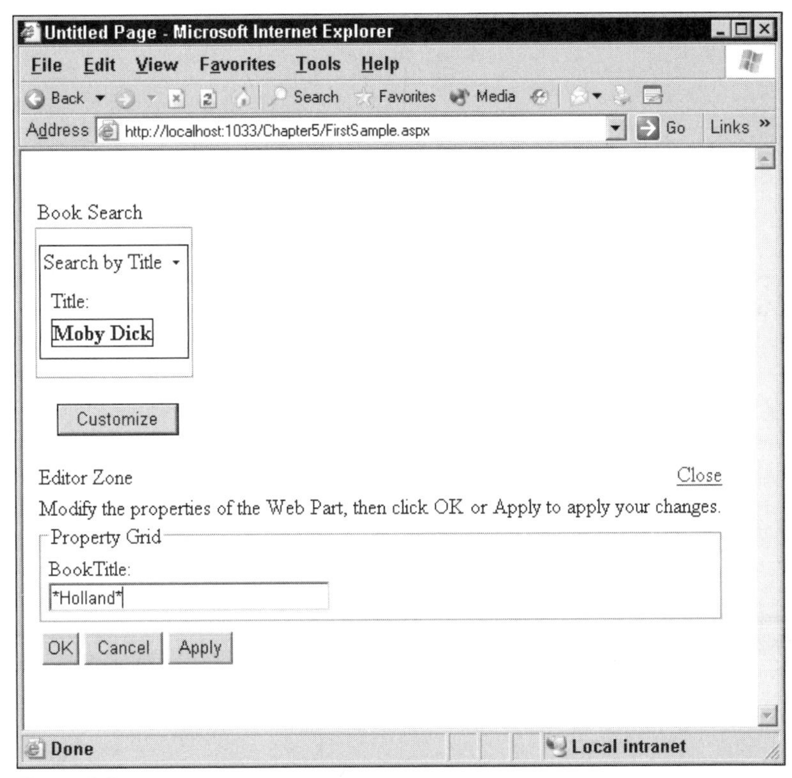

Figure 5-1

Preserving Customization

However, while the WebBrowsable attribute makes properties available for customization, it doesn't preserve the property's settings past the user's current session with the page. In other words, the property has been enabled for customization, but not for personalization. To have the property remember the user's customization from one session to another, you need to add the Personalizable attribute to the property and pass it True as a parameter. This Visual Basic 2005 code shows both attributes in place:

```
<WebControls.WebParts.Personalizable(True),
  WebControls.WebParts.WebBrowsable(True)> _
Property BookTitle() As String

End Property
```

In C#:

```
[System.Web.UI.WebControls.WebParts.Personalizable(true),
 System.Web.UI.WebControls.WebParts.WebBrowsable(true)]
public string BookTitle
{
}
```

Sharing Customizations

If you turn on personalization with the Personalizable attribute by passing a single parameter, the changes made by a user will be applied to the page only when the page is requested by that user. If, instead of passing True, you pass one of the Personalizable constants, you can not only turn on personalization, but cause changes made to the page to be applied for all users:

- **Webcontrols.WebParts.PersonalizationScope.User:** Customized values for the property are applied only to the current user (this is the default).
- **Webcontrols.WebParts.PersonalizationScope.Shared:** Customized values for the property are applied to all users.

This Visual Basic 2005 code turns on personalization and causes any changes made by a user to be made for all users:

```
<WebControls.WebParts.Personalizable( _
        WebControls.WebParts.PersonalizationScope.Shared),
 WebControls.WebParts.WebBrowsable(True)> _
Property BookTitle() As String

End Property
```

In C#:

```
[System.Web.UI.WebControls.WebParts.Personalizable(
    System.Web.UI.WebControls.WebParts.PersonalizationScope.Shared),
 System.Web.UI.WebControls.WebParts.WebBrowsable(true)]
public string BookTitle
{
}
```

When using the scope settings with the Personalizable attribute, you can pass a second parameter, the IsSensitive parameter. This parameter controls under what conditions the property's values will be exported (exporting Web Parts is discussed in Chapter 11).

As you start working with Personalization, you may find your page "remembering" changes that you'd rather the page forgot (for example, when you close a Web Part that you want to continue to work with). To get back to your "pre-customization state," open the database containing your personalization data and delete all the records in the tables PagePersonalizationAllUsers and PagePersonalizationPerUser. If you've just taken the defaults for turning on personalization (as described in Chapter 2), the personalization data is being managed by SQL Server and kept in a file called ASPNetDB.MDF. You can see the database file in Solution Explorer in your project's App_Data folder (if the database isn't visible, close your project and re-open it) and browse it from your Database Explorer window.

Enabling Customization for Inherited Properties

While the previous examples showed enabling personalization and customization for custom properties, you can also enable customization for the base properties of the underlying object. All you have to do is override the base property with a new routine that updates and returns the value from the base object. This Visual Basic 2005 code overrides the AccessKey property and makes it customizable:

```
<WebControls.WebParts.Personalizable(True),
 WebControls.WebParts.WebBrowsable(True)> _
Public Overrides Property AccessKey() As String
  Get
    Return MyBase.AccessKey
  End Get

  Set(ByVal value As String)
    MyBase.AccessKey = value
  End Set

End Property
```

In C#:

```
[System.Web.UI.WebControls.WebParts.Personalizable(true),
 System.Web.UI.WebControls.WebParts.WebBrowsable(true)]
public override string AccessKey
{
 get
 {
   return base.AccessKey;
 }

 set
 {
   base.AccessKey = value;
 }
}
```

Omitting the Personalization and WebBrowsable attributes causes them to default to False. While you can pass the attribute a value of False to turn off Personalization and Customization, omitting the attribute has the same effect.

Documenting Properties

Two other attributes can be applied to a customizable property:

- **System.Web.UI.WebControls.WebParts.WebDescription:** Accepts a single string parameter that can be used to document the property.
- **System.Web.UI.WebControls.WebParts.WebDisplayName:** Accepts a single string parameter. This name is used in the UI of the Web Part editors to provide a user-friendly name when users are customizing a control in the browser.

Creating a Full-Fledged Web Part

The rest of this chapter addresses Web Part features that you can take advantage of only if you build your custom control as a Web Part from the very beginning. However, if you've read Chapter 3 on custom controls, you already know 90 percent of what's required to build a Web Part. Basically, a Web Part is just a custom control with a few more properties and methods to support the special features of a Web Part.

The rest of this chapter covers the Web Part–specific features:

- Checking for the kind of personalization data that's been saved
- Adding additional verbs to the control's Verb menu
- Understanding the HTML that results when your control is used in a WebPartZone
- Exploring additional properties for configuring the appearance of your Web Part and how it behaves in Visual Studio 2005
- Preventing your user from making some customizations

The first step in creating a full-featured Web Part is to have your custom control inherit from the WebPart object instead of the WebControl object. This Visual Basic 2005 code is the base from which you should start creating your Web Part:

```
Imports System.ComponentModel
Imports System.Web.UI

<ToolboxData("<{0}:BookDetail runat=server></{0}:BookDetail>")> _
Public Class BookDetail
    Inherits System.Web.UI.WebControls.WebControls.WebParts.WebPart

End Class
```

The key line that lets you build a full-featured Web Part is the Inherits line, which references the WebPart class.

In C#, the base file should look like this:

```
using System;
using System.Collections.Generic;
using System.ComponentModel;
using System.Text;
using System.Web.UI;
using System.Web.UI.WebControls;

namespace MyWebControlsCS
{
    [ToolboxData("<{0}:BookDetail runat=server></{0}:BookDetail>")]
    public class BookDetail : System.Web.UI.WebControls.WebParts.WebPart
    {
    }
}
```

The key line in this C# code is the class definition, which inherits the WebPart class.

Because there is so much overlap between the WebControl object and the WebPart object you can often convert a custom control into a full-featured Web Part just by changing the object that your control inherits from. However, you can't convert a user control to a full-featured Web Part without, effectively, starting over — there's too much difference between the two development models. You would, for instance, have to add a CreateChildControls method to your User Control that recreates, in code, the user interface that you generated by dragging and dropping constituent controls onto the User Control's design surface.

Checking Personalizable Data

As with a custom control or a user control, you enable customization for properties by adding the Personalizable and WebBrowsable attributes to the property. In a Web Part you can determine whether shared or user customizations exist by checking the Web Part's HasSharedData or HasUserData properties. Because some properties can have their Personalizable attribute set to share customizations while other properties are set to save customizations on a user-by-user basis, a single custom control can have both kinds of customizations. In that case, the user's experience will be a combination of both the shared and user customizations, and both the HasSharedData and HasUserData properties will be true.

Accessing Attributes

At some point, you may want to determine from your code what the attribute settings are for one of the subroutines or a function you've written as part of your control. To determine the value for an attribute you must:

- Retrieve the collection of attributes for the class, property, method, or event.
- Find the attribute that you want.
- Examine the properties of the attributes.

In the following example, the code retrieves the toolbox data settings for the control. The code first defines an attribute collection (called atts in the example) to hold the retrieved attributes. The code then declares a variable (called ts) to hold a ToolboxData attribute.

In order to discover information about the object that your code is executing in, you use the methods of the TypeDescriptor class. The GetAttributes method, for example, returns all the attributes on the Class declaration if you pass the method a reference to the class (that is, using me in Visual Basic 2005 or this in C#). Because the toolbox data is set on the class's declaration, the code must retrieve information about the class that the code is in.

Once you have the collection of attributes, you can retrieve any particular attribute by using the attribute's data type. The simplest way to retrieve a data type is to use the GetType function, passing the data type that you want. In the following Visual Basic 2005 code, the GetType function is used with the ToolboxDataAttribute type to retrieve the right attribute out of the attributes collection:

```
Dim atts As System.ComponentModel.AttributeCollection
Dim ts As ToolboxDataAttribute
Dim strData As String

  atts = TypeDescriptor.GetAttributes(Me)
  ts = atts(GetType(ToolboxDataAttribute))
  strData = ts.Data
```

In C#:

```
System.ComponentModel.AttributeCollection atts;
ToolboxDataAttribute ts;
string strData;

atts = TypeDescriptor.GetAttributes(this);
ts = atts(GetType(ToolboxDataAttribute));
strData = ts.Data;
```

In order to retrieve the attributes set on a particular property, you must first use the GetProperties method of the TypeDescriptor class to get a collection of descriptors for all the properties in the class. Once you have the collection of properties, you can retrieve the description for a particular property by using the property's name. Once you've retrieved a property's description, you can retrieve the attributes for the property. This code retrieves the attributes for a property called Text:

```
Dim pd As PropertyDescriptorCollection

  pd = TypeDescriptor.GetProperties(ts)
  atts = pd("Text").Attributes
```

In C#:

```
PropertyDescriptorCollection pd;

pd = TypeDescriptor.GetProperties(ts);
atts = pd("Text").Attributes;
```

To retrieve a collection of all the event descriptions, use the GetEvents method of the TypeDescriptor.

As an example of when you might find retrieving attributes useful, this Visual Code .NET code allows you to determine if a property is going to be personalized for all users or just the current user:

```
Dim atts As System.ComponentModel.AttributeCollection
Dim ps As WebControls.WebParts.PersonalizableAttribute
Dim strData As String

  atts = TypeDescriptor.GetAttributes(Me)
  ps = atts(GetType(WebControls.WebParts.PersonalizableAttribute))

  If ps.Scope = WebControls.WebParts.PersonalizationScope.Shared Then
      ...warn the user that customizations will be shared...
  End If
```

In C#:

```
System.ComponentModel.AttributeCollection atts;
System.Web.UI.WebControls.WebParts.PersonalizableAttribute ps;

atts = TypeDescriptor.GetAttributes(this);
ps = atts(GetType(System.Web.UI.WebControls.WebParts.PersonalizableAttribute));

if(ps.Scope == System.Web.UI.WebControls.WebParts.PersonalizationScope.Shared)
{
   ...warn the user that customizations will be shared...
}
```

Adding New Verbs

While you can add additional methods to your Web Part (as described in Chapter 8), those new methods are accessible only from the code in the host page—not to the users working with your Web Part in the page. You can also extend your Web Part by adding new verbs to your Web Part's Verb menu. Users are then able to execute these extended functions when your Web Part is in a WebPartZone by selecting the verbs from the Web Part's Verb menu.

Only full-fledged Web Parts can add verbs to their own Verb menu. User controls and custom controls can't add new verbs to their Verb menu. However, both custom controls and user controls, when used as Web Parts, can have new verbs added to their Verb menu by ASP.NET when editors are on the same Web page as the Web Part. For example, if there's an AppearanceEditorPart on the page and enabled, then a user control being used as a Web Part will have an Edit item automatically added to its Verb menu.

Creating a Verb List

To add verbs to your Verb menu you must override the default Verbs property provided in the WebPart object. This is a read-only property, so you have to provide only a Get part.

ASP.NET reads the Verbs collection when necessary and expects the property to return a WebPart-VerbCollection. A WebPartVerbCollection is created from an array of WebPartVerb objects. Each item in the WebPartVerb array represents an entry in the Verb menu for the Web Part.

The first step, then, in updating the Verb menu is to override the Verbs property and open the Get section:

```
Public Overrides ReadOnly Property Verbs() As _
                    WebControls.WebParts.WebPartVerbCollection

  Get
```

In C#:

```
public override System.Web.UI.WebControls.WebParts.WebPartVerbCollection Verbs
{
  get
  {
```

The next step is to define some WebPartVerb objects (one for each item that you want to add to the Web Part's Verb menu). When the user selects a verb from the Web Part's Verb menu, some subroutine in the Web Part must run. The easiest way to assign a subroutine to the Verb is to pass the address of the subroutine to the WebPartVerb as the second parameter to the constructor when the WebPartVerb is created, as shown in this Visual Basic 2005 code (the first parameter is the ID for the verb):

```
Dim vrbEnglish As New WebControls.WebParts.WebPartVerb( _
                            "EnglishSetting", AddressOf Me.SetEnglish)
Dim vrbFrench As New WebControls.WebParts.WebPartVerb( _
                            "FrenchSetting", AddressOf Me.SetFrench)
```

In C#:

```
System.Web.UI.WebControls.WebParts.WebPartVerb vrbEnglish = new
 System.Web.UI.WebControls.WebParts.WebPartVerb("EnglishSetting", this.SetEnglish);

System.Web.UI.WebControls.WebParts.WebPartVerb vrbFrench = new
 System.Web.UI.WebControls.WebParts.WebPartVerb("FrenchSetting", this.SetFrench);
```

The constructor for the WebPartVerb accepts a third parameter for linking the verb to client-side code, as discussed in Chapter 9.

A number of properties can be set on a WebPartVerb, but, for now, we'll just set the Text property. The Text property controls what is displayed for each verb in the Web Part's Verb menu. This Visual Basic 2005 code sets the two verbs just created to display "English" and "French":

```
vrbEnglish.Text = "English"
vrbFrench.Text = "French"
```

In C#:

```
vrbEnglish.Text = "English";
vrbFrench.Text = "French";
```

With the verbs configured, they can be added to an array of WebPartVerbs. This Visual Basic 2005 code defines an array with two positions and puts the verbs in the first and second position:

```
Dim vrbsLanguage(1) As WebControls.WebParts.WebPartVerb
vrbsLanguage(0) = vrbFrench
vrbsLanguage(1) = vrbEnglish
```

In C#:

```
System.Web.UI.WebControls.WebParts.WebPartVerb[] vrbsLanguage =
                new System.Web.UI.WebControls.WebParts.WebPartVerb[2];

vrbsLanguage[0] = vrbFrench;
vrbsLanguage[1] = vrbEnglish;
```

Finally, the last step is to create the WebPartVerbCollection object from the array and return it from the Get section of the Verbs property, as this Visual Basic 2005 code does:

```
        Dim vrbs As WebControls.WebParts.WebPartVerbCollection
        vrbs = New WebControls.WebParts.WebPartVerbCollection(vrbsLanguage)

        Return vrbs

    End Get

End Property
```

In C#:

```
        System.Web.UI.WebControls.WebParts.WebPartVerbCollection vrbs;
        vrbs = new
            System.Web.UI.WebControls.WebParts.WebPartVerbCollection(vrbsLanguage);

        return vrbs;
    }
}
```

The result can be seen in Figure 5-2, which shows a Web Part with its Verb menu displayed.

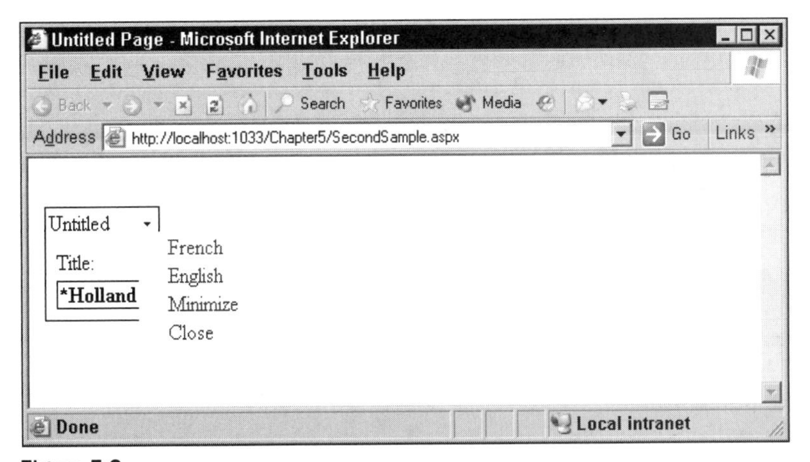

Figure 5-2

Any verbs required by the Web Part infrastructure (for example, the Edit verb, which allows a Web Part to be edited by the Appearance Editor) are automatically added to the Verb List even if you override the Verbs property.

Sharing Routines

In addition to associating a verb with a routine when it's created, you can also associate a verb with a routine in your Web Part by using a WebPartEventHandler. This technique can be useful if you have a single subroutine that is to be called by several verbs; you can set up a single WebPartEventHandler and then associate that routine with as many verbs as you want.

As you did with the WebPartVerb, when you create a WebPartEventHandler, you pass it the address of the routine to be called. You can then create the WebPartVerb, this time passing the WebPartEventHandler instead of the address of a routine. This Visual Basic 2005 code demonstrates the technique:

```
wevLang = New _
   System.Web.UI.WebControls.WebParts.WebPartEventHandler(AddressOf Me.SetLanguage)

vrbEnglish = New System.Web.UI.WebControls.WebParts.WebPartVerb( _
                                               "LanguageMgr", wevLang)
```

In C#:

```
System.Web.UI.WebControls.WebParts.WebPartEventHandler wevLang =
      new System.Web.UI.WebControls.WebParts.WebPartEventHandler(this.SetLanguage);

System.Web.UI.WebControls.WebParts.WebPartVerb vrbEnglish =
      new System.Web.UI.WebControls.WebParts.WebPartVerb("LanguageMgr", wevLang);
```

Each WebPartVerb object has a ServerClickHandler property that points to the subroutine associated with the WebPartVerb and is set using the techniques just described. This provides you with a technique for ensuring that a number of verbs use the same routine as a particular verb. First, create one verb and then use the WebPartVerb's ServerClickHandler property to retrieve a reference to the subroutine associated with the WebPartVerb. Then use that reference when creating other verbs to link those new verbs to the same routine as the original verb. This Visual Basic 2005 code uses the ServerClickHandler to retrieve the subroutine associated with the verb and uses that reference with another verb:

```
vrbFrench = New _
  System.Web.UI.WebControls.WebParts.WebPartVerb( _
                         "LanguageMgr", vrbEnglish.ServerClickHandler)
```

In C#:

```
System.Web.UI.WebControls.WebParts.WebPartVerb vrbFrench = new
     System.Web.UI.WebControls.WebParts.WebPartVerb(
                           "LanguageMgr", vrbEnglish.ServerClickHandler);
```

What you are actually retrieving from the ServerClickHandler is a delegate that points to the routine to be called when a user selects the verb.

Creating a Verb Routine

A routine that is associated with a verb follows the typical .NET Framework pattern for an event routine by having two parameters:

- The first parameter is declared as an Object. This parameter is passed a reference to the object that fired the event (in this case, the WebPartVerb).
- The second parameter is a WebPartEventArgs object. The Verbs property of this object provides a reference to the Verbs collection that the verb is part of.

This Visual Basic 2005 routine could be called from the routine associated with a verb. The code checks to see which Web Part it's called from before determining what action to take:

```
Private Sub SetLanguage(ByVal sender As Object, _
                ByVal e As System.Web.UI.WebControls.WebParts.WebPartEventArgs)
Dim wp As System.Web.UI.WebControls.WebParts.WebPart

    wp = CType(sender, System.Web.UI.WebControls.WebParts.WebPart)
    Select Case wp.ID
      Case "wpBookSearchDetail"
        ...processing...
      Case "wpBookSearchSummary"
        ...processing...
    End Select

End Sub
```

In C#:

```
private void SetLanguage(object sender,
                System.Web.UI.WebControls.WebParts.WebPartEventArgs e)
{
  System.Web.UI.WebControls.WebParts.WebPart wp;

  wp = (System.Web.UI.WebControls.WebParts.WebPart) sender
  switch(wp.ID)
  {
   case "wpBookSearchDetail":
        ...processing...
        break;

   case "wpBookSearchDetail":
           ...processing...;
  };
}
```

If a user selects one of your verbs from the Verb menu, that routine is called before the Verbs property is read or the CreateChildControls method is called. As a result, if your verb routine sets properties on constituent controls, those changes are typically overwritten by the code in the CreateChildControls method.

Configuring the Verb

You can set some additional properties on the WebPartVerb objects:

- **Checked:** When set to True, causes the verb to display with a checkmark beside the verb.
- **Description:** Provides tooltip text for the verb.
- **ImageURL:** The URL for an image to be displayed by the verb in the Verb menu.

- **Enabled:** When set to False, the verb displays in the menu but cannot be used.
- **Visible:** When set to False, the verb does not display in the menu.

In this sample Visual Basic 2005 code, The vrbEnglish verb has its Checked property set to True. The vrbFrench verb has had its ImageURL property set to display a GIF image and its Enabled property set to False:

```
Dim vrbEnglish As New _
 System.Web.UI.WebControls.WebParts.WebPartVerb("English", AddressOf Me.SetEnglish)
Dim vrbFrench As New _
 System.Web.UI.WebControls.WebParts.WebPartVerb("French", AddressOf Me.SetFrench)

  vrbEnglish.Checked = True

  vrbFrench.ImageUrl = "Book.Gif"
  vrbFrench.Enabled = False
```

In C#

```
System.Web.UI.WebControls.WebParts.WebPartVerb vrbEnglish =
     new System.Web.UI.WebControls.WebParts.WebPartVerb("English", this.SetEnglish)
System.Web.UI.WebControls.WebParts.WebPartVerb vrbFrench =
     new System.Web.UI.WebControls.WebParts.WebPartVerb("French", this.SetFrench)

  vrbEnglish.Checked = true;

  vrbFrench.ImageUrl = "Book.Gif";
  vrbFrench.Enabled = false;
```

Figure 5-3 shows the result. The first verb in the Verb menu has a graphic displayed beside it and is grayed out because its Enabled property is set to False. The second verb has a checkmark displayed beside it.

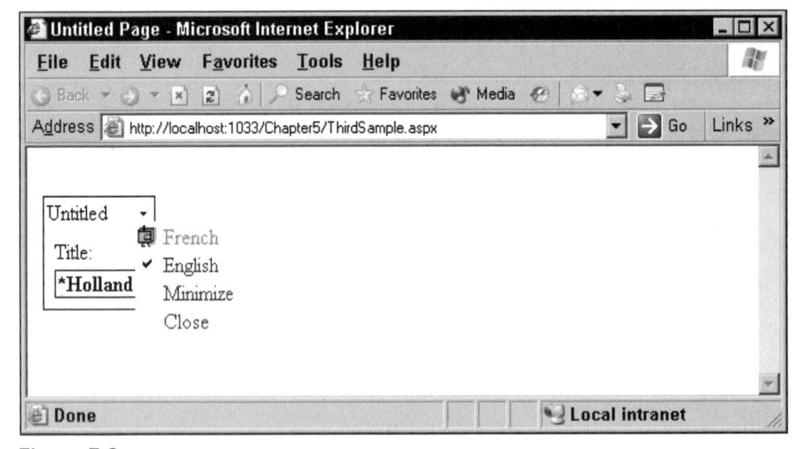

Figure 5-3

HTML for Web Parts

As you saw in Chapter 3, your custom control generates the HTML that represents the custom control on the page when the page is delivered to the browser. A Web Part, when delivered to the browser, looks very similar to a custom control — a set of tags representing the text or constituent controls generated in the various Render* methods, surrounded by a <span> tag. The id and name attributes for a Web Part follow the format for a standard custom control. This example shows a custom control with an id of MyBookDetail that has a single submit button as its constituent control (the button's ID property was set to btnSubmit):

```
<span id="MyBookDetail" style="border-style:Inset;">
  <input type="submit" name="MyBookDetail$btnSubmit" id="MyBookDetail_btnSubmit"
                                                    value="Submit" />
</span>
```

As you saw in Chapter 2, your custom controls can be used as Web Parts whenever a developer drags your control into a WebPartZone. When a custom control is used as a Web Part, a lot of additional HTML is generated, in addition to the text produced by the custom control's Render method. This additional HTML is required to represent the custom control as a WebPartZone in the browser.

Overall, the structure for the WebPartZone's HTML is a set of tables nested within tables, like a set of Russian dolls. As a result, the best way to describe the resulting HTML is one level at a time.

In the early days of programming in high-level languages, developers still needed some knowledge of the actual machine language generated by their language's compiler. While the ASP.NET objects do a wonderful job of distancing developers from the ugly details of writing HTML, we're not yet at the point in Web development where you can ignore the HTML that is generated by your custom controls.

It's not unusual for developers to find that their Web page looks great in one browser and unfortunate in another. Diagnosing the problem involves decoding the HTML that's ending up in the page and understanding how that HTML is generated by the ASP.NET objects that are used on the page. At the very least, if you intend to add client-side code to your controls (as discussed in Chapter 9), you need to be familiar with the identifiers assigned to the tags used in your page — and which tags they're attached to.

A warning: The HTML generated by ASP.NET controls is what's referred to as "an implementation detail." Basically, that means that the HTML generated is likely to change from one version of ASP.NET to another — or, possibly, even from one build to another. The following description of Web Part HTML may vary in some details with your particular version of ASP.NET.

Top Level: The WebPartZone

At the highest level is the HTML that's generated for a WebPartZone: a set of nested HTML tables. The id attribute for this table is set to the value of the ID property of the WebPartZone. Within the table representing the WebPartZone is another table that holds the controls within the WebPartZone (there's one row for each control). A final, empty row closes off the table.

This sample HTML shows the WebPartZone table schematically:

```
<table cellspacing="0" cellpadding="0" border="0" id="WebPartZone1">
  <tr>
    <td style="height:100%;">
      <table cellspacing="0" cellpadding="2" border="0"
                style="width:100%;height:100%;">
        <tr>
          <td>
            ...first control...
          </td>
        </tr>
        <tr>
          <td>
            ...next control...
          </td>
        </tr>
        <tr>
          <td>
            ...etc....
          </td>
        </tr>
        <tr>
          <td style="padding:0;height:100%;" />
        </tr>
      </table>
    </td>
  <tr>
</table>
```

Middle Level: Web Parts

Within the table representing the WebPartZone, each Web Part is implemented by a nested table, the first row of which contains yet another table that holds the title bar for the control and the control. The id attribute for this table is taken from the value assigned to ID property by the developer when she added the control to the page. The text "WebPart_" is added to the front of the name, so a typical name would be WebPart_MyBookDetail if the Web Part's ID property were set to MyBookDetail.

The first row of the table representing the WebPart contains the title bar for the Web Part while the second row contains the HTML generated by the control itself (as you'll see, this is where the <div> tag for the Web Part appears). This sample shows schematically the HTML for the table containing the Web Part and its title bar:

```
<table id="WebPart_MyBookDetail" class="aspnet_s0"
              cellspacing="0" cellpadding="1" border="0" style="width:100%;">
  <tr>
    <td>
      ...title bar...
    </td>
  </tr>
  <tr>
    <td>
```

```
        ...control...
      </td>
    </tr>
  </table
```

Because each Web Part consists of a single control (although that control may have many constituent controls), this table always has only two rows.

Bottom Level: Title Bar

The title bar is held in yet another table — but this table consists of a single row with two cells. The first cell in the row holds the Web Part's title (inside a span tag) and the second cell holds the Verb menu. The id attribute for the cell with the title is set to the Web Part's ID property with the text "WebPartTitle_" prefixed to it. An example would be WebPartTitle_MybookDetail.

The second cell in the title bar row containing the Verb menu contains a <span> tag that holds all the rest of the contents of the cell and sets formatting for the menu as a whole. The id attribute for this span tag is taken from the ID property for the control with WebPart_ prefixed to it and Verbs added to the end of it (for example, WebPart_MyBookDetailVerbs).

The first element within that <span> tag is another span tag that contains the small down arrow that opens the menu (actually the letter *u* in the Marlett font). Its id attribute is the control's ID property with WebPart_ prefixed to it and VerbsPopup added to the end (for example, WebPart_MyBookDetailVerbsPopup). Following the span tag with the down arrow is a <div> tag containing the HTML for the individual verbs on the menu. Its id attribute is the control's ID property with WebPart_ prefixed to it and VerbsMenu added to the end (for example, WebPart_MyBookDetailVerbsMenu). These <span> and <div> tags are used to control the appearance of the tags inside the <span> and <div> tags.

This sample shows the title bar row with the Web Part title ("Untitled") but with the detail HTML for the verbs omitted:

```
  <table cellspacing="0" cellpadding="0" border="0" style="width:100%;">
    <tr>
      <td id="WebPartTitle_MyBookDetail"
                     style="width:100%;white-space:nowrap;">
        <span title="Untitled_">Untitled_</span> 
       </td>
       <td style="white-space:nowrap;">
         <span id="WebPart_MyBookDetailVerbs"
                     style="cursor:hand;display:inline-block;padding:1px;
                            text-decoration:none;">
           <span id="WebPart_MyBookDetailVerbsPopup"
                            style="font-family:Marlett;font-size:8pt;">u</span>
           </span>
           <div id="WebPart_MyBookDetailVerbsMenu" style="display:none;">
              ...verb menu item's HTML...
           </div>
       </td>
    </tr>
  </table>
```

At this point, you probably aren't surprised to find that the Verb menu is represented as a table. None of the tags in the Verb menu have id attributes, so it's more difficult to access these tags from client-side code. Each verb has a separate row that contains a single cell. Within the cell, the verb is represented by some text and an image, enclosed by an anchor tag (the image tag's href property is what is set by Verb's ImageUrl property). Some utility JavaScript code is attached to the image and the anchor to implement the verb's action.

Here's an example of the HTML for a verb, showing the Minimize verb:

```
<table cellspacing="0" cellpadding="1"
                      style="border-collapse:collapse;width:100%;">
  <tr>
    <td style="white-space:nowrap;">
      <div>
        <a title="Minimizes 'Untitled _[1]_'"
                      href="javascript:void(0)" class="menuItem"
                      onclick="document.body.__wpm.SubmitPage('WebPartZone1',
                          'minimize:WebCustomControl1_1');" >
          <img alt="Minimizes 'Untitled _[1]_'" width="16" height="16"
                          src="/TestCC/WebResource.axd?a=s&r=Spacer.gif&t=63239"
                          style="border-style:none;vertical-align:middle;" />
             
            Minimize
             
          </a>
      </div>
      <div>
        ...next verb...
      </div>
      <div>
        ...etc....
      </div>
    </td>
  </tr>
</table>
```

Bottom Level 2: Web Part

The second row of the Web Part's table holds the HTML and text generated by your Web Part. The id attribute for the <div> tag that encloses the control is formed from the ID property of the WebPartManager and the ID property for the control. This sample HTML shows what would be generated for a Web Part called MyBookDetail with a single constituent control (a submit button with an ID value of btnSubmit):

```
<div id="WebPartManager1_MyBookDetail" style="border-style:Inset;">
  <input type="submit" id="WebPartManager1_MyBookDetail_btnSubmit"
          name="WebPartManager1$MyBookDetail$btnSubmit" value="Submit" />
</div>
```

Constituent Control Name and id Attributes

As you've seen, the id and name attributes for the constituent control's HTML are generated at run time. Knowing these values is critical to generating client-side code that will access these controls. Here's a typical example of the HTML rendered for a submit button:

```
<input type="submit"
  name="WebPartManager1$BookDetail1$btnSubmit"
  value="Hello, World"
  id="WebPartManager1_BookDetail1_btnSubmit" />
```

The name and id attributes are formed by adding prefixes to the value of the constituent control's ID property. The control's ClientId property returns the full value of the client-side id attribute (for example, WebPartManager1_BookDetail1_btnSubmit). You can retrieve just the prefix to be applied to the Id property from the WebControl object's ClientId property — normally this will be:

- The value of the Id property of the WebPartManager (for example, WebPartManager1)
- An underscore (_)
- The value of the Id property of the Web Part (BookDetail1)
- Another underscore (_)

> **You can't change the prefix used by ASP.NET. While you can override the ClientId property to return a different value and even set the WebControl object's ClientId property to a different value, it doesn't change the value used when ASP.NET generates the HTML.**

For example: WebPartManager1_BookDetail1_.

You can also retrieve a reference to the WebPartManager that's managing the page from the WebControl object's WebPartManager property. You might be tempted to use that reference to retrieve the value of the ID property of the WebPartManager, but this will generate a design-time error when using your Web Part. If you plan on accessing the page's WebPartManager from your code, you should check the DesignMode property first and work with the WebPartManager only when DesignMode is False.

The name attribute for the constituent controls is also generated at run time. For this attribute, however, the various components of the name are separated by a dollar sign. The full value of the client-side name for a control can be retrieved from the constituent control's UniqueId property. This is referred to as the "hierarchically qualified name" for the control because it includes the identifiers for all the objects that the constituent control is nested inside. You can retrieve just the prefix for the name attribute from your underlying WebPart's UniqueId property.

The value being used as a separator can be retrieved from the WebControl object's IdSeparator property. This Visual Basic 2005 code uses that property to dynamically build an identifier to be used with a literal control:

```
Dim strClientId As String

  strClientId = Me.UniqueId & Me.IdSeparator & "spnText"
  output.Write("<span id='" & strClientId & "'>Book Information</span>")
```

In C#:

```
string strClientId;

  strClientId = this.UniqueId + this.IdSeparator + "btnSubmit";
  output.Write("<span id='" & strClientId & "'>Book Information</span>");
```

All constituent controls have a name attribute as part of their HTML. However, if a constituent control's ID property isn't assigned an explicit value, then the HTML generated for the control won't have an id attribute either.

Configuring the Web Part

While a Web Part has all the properties of a custom control, the Web Part has some additional properties that give you additional control over your Web Part. These other properties let you control the way that your Web Part is displayed in the browser, find out information about your Web Part, and selectively turn off the ability to perform customizations on the Web Part.

Controlling Your Web Part's User Interface

As part of creating a Web Part, you want to define how it is displayed to users. The various techniques for working with the Style object discussed in Chapter 3 also apply to Web Parts. This section discusses handling those parts of your user interface that are relevant only to Web Parts. Primarily, this involves setting the text in the Web Part's title, but Web Parts have four additional properties that are related to controlling the Web Part's user interface, covered in the following sections.

Working with the Title Bar

You can change the text in your Web Part's title bar by setting the Title property of the Web Part object. In addition, you can append text to the Title by using the WebControl object's Subtitle property. The Subtitle property is a read-only property, so the only way to set it is to override the property. To dynamically change the value of the subtitle, you have to use a module-level variable, as in this Visual Basic 2005 sample:

```
Private strSubtitle As String

Public Sub New()
   strSubtitle = "As of "& Now.ToString
End Sub

Public Overrides ReadOnly Property Subtitle() As String
 Get
     Return strSubtitle
 End Get
End Property
```

In C#:

```
string strSubtitle;

public void BookDetail()
{
   strSubtitle = "As of " + System.DateTime.Now.ToString();
}

public override string Subtitle
{
   get
   {
      return strSubtitle;
   }
}
```

Figure 5-4 shows the results.

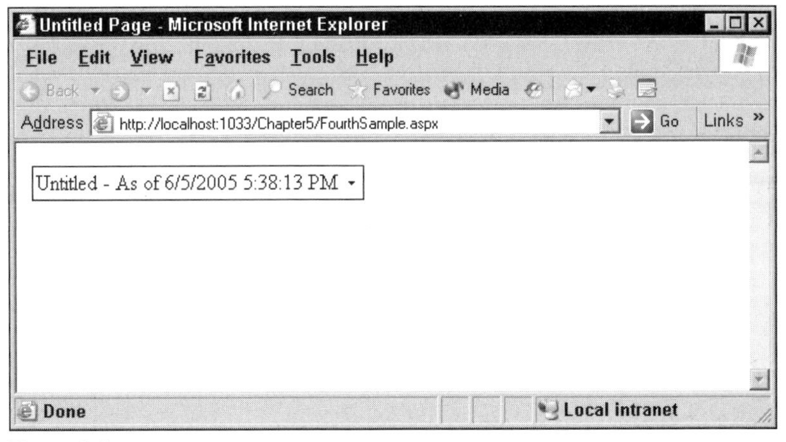

Figure 5-4

> *A Web Part always displays some text in the title bar. If you set the Title property to a zero-length string, the Web Part displays the literal "Untitled" in the title bar.*

You can also add an icon to your Web Part's title bar by setting the WebControl object's TitleIconImageUrl property to the icon's URL. The icon displays to the left of the Web Part's title in the title bar, as shown in Figure 5-5.

> **In order for your icon to be displayed, you must set the TitleIconImageURL property before the Render method (for instance, in the CreateChildControls method or the Init event). You must also make sure that ShowTitleIcons in the PartTitleStyle property is set to True (this is the default for ShowTitleIcons).**

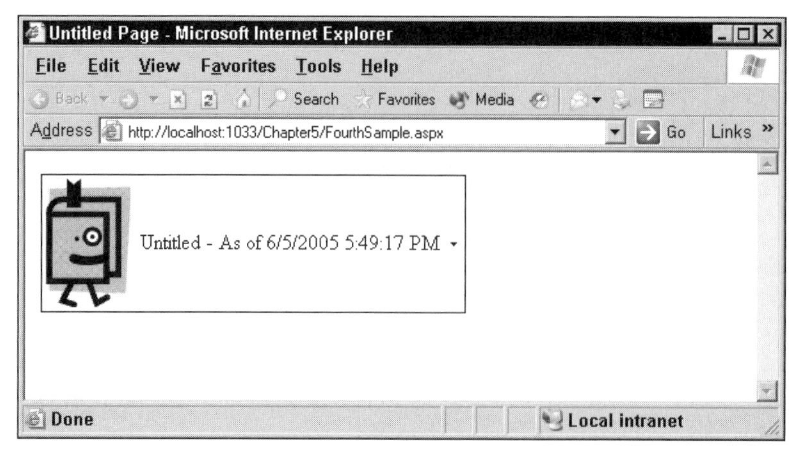

Figure 5-5

You can convert your Web Part's title into a link to another page by setting the WebControl object's TitleUrl property to a URL. This URL is treated as a relative address unless you explicitly make it an absolute URL. For instance, if the URL is set to /MyPage.aspx, when the user clicks the hyperlink, a page called MyPage.aspx in the same directory as the Web Part is requested by the browser. To set an absolute path for the URL, you should use a full URL beginning with http://.

This Visual Basic 2005 code sets the TitleUrl to (presumably) a help page for using the Web Part:

```
Me.TitleUrl = "BookDetailHelp.html"
```

In C#:

```
this.TitleUrl = "BookDetailHelp.html";
```

Additional Properties

Besides the title bar, Web Parts have four other properties that other types of controls don't have that help define your user interface. They are:

- **Description:** You can set this property to a text string. This string is displayed in the tooltip for the Web Part when the page is in one of the customization modes. The text also appears in the title attribute of the <span> tag around the Web Part's title.
- **CatalogIconImageUrl:** Set this property to a URL for an image to have that image displayed when the part is listed in a catalog editor.
- **ChromeState:** Setting this property to Minimized causes the border around the Web Part to be minimized (you can also read this property to determine what the current state of the border is).
- **ChromeType:** You can use this property to control what part of the Web Part is enclosed in a border (title, control, title and control, neither, or take the default).

While it is a property of the WebPartZone, the WebPartVerbRenderMode property also controls how your WebPart is displayed. The WebPartVerbRenderMode defaults to WebPartVerbRenderMode.Menu, which turns your Verb menu into a drop-down list. However, if the property is set to WebPartVerbRenderMode.

TitleBar, then all the verbs in your Verb menu display in the title bar as hyperlinks. Because the Verb menu always includes the Web Part default verbs (e.g., Close Minimize), setting WebPartVerbRenderMode to TitleBar can give you a very long title bar and a very wide Web Part.

Finding out about Your Web Part

There are many aspects of your Web Part that you won't be able to determine at design time. For example, the developer that adds your Web Part to a page will set the Web Part's name. Web Parts have a number of properties that let you determine what those settings are at run time. They are:

- **DisplayTitle:** The title as currently displayed on the page reflecting the value of the Title property plus any modification, changes, or personalizations. This property is read-only.
- **Hidden:** When True, indicates that the part is not visible in a WebPartZone when the page is being displayed in the browser. You can't use the Visible property to suppress the display of a Web Part when the Web Part is in a WebPartZone. You can, however, use the Hidden property to suppress the Web Part's display when the Web Part is in a WebPartZone (setting the Hidden property in a Web Part that's not in a WebPartZone has no effect on the Web Part). Effectively, this property provides another state for a Web Part in addition to the closed, minimized, and browse states available through the Verb menu. A hidden custom control does not appear on the page, is not minimized (when a Web Part is hidden, the title bar for the custom control is not displayed, unlike a minimized control), and is not closed (the Web Part does not appear in the catalog for the page). When the page is viewed in one of the customization modes, the text "(Hidden)" appears in the title bar to indicate the part's state.
- **IsClosed:** True when your Web Part is closed.
- **IsShared, IsStandalone:** If a WebPart is in a WebPartZone (that is, when a WebPart can be customized) then IsShared is True if the Web Part is visible to all the users of the page; IsStandalone is True when the Web Part is visible only to a single user.

  For instance, a Web Part added to a WebPartZone at design time has its IsShared property set to True and IsStandalone set to False because it is visible to all users. On the other hand, a Web Part that a user imported into the page as part of a user's customizations will have its IsShared property set to False and IsStandalone set to True because it is visible only to the user who imported it. When a WebPart is not in a WebPartZone (that is, when it cannot be customized), IsStandalone is True and IsShared is False.
- **IsStatic:** True if the Web Part has been added to the page declaratively (that is, the Web Part's tag was added to the page at design time rather than the Web Part being loaded dynamically at run time).
- **SetPersonalizationDirty:** If you make customization changes to the Web Part's properties from your code, your changes may not be recognized by the personalization framework and, as a result, not saved. Calling the SetPersonalizationDirty method ensures that your changes are saved.
- **Zone:** Returns a reference to the WebPartZone that your Web Part is inside. If the Web Part is not in a WebPartZone, Zone returns Nothing.
- **ZoneIndex:** Returns the position of your control inside the WebPartZone (if your control is the first Web Part in the zone or if your control is not in a WebPartZone, ZoneIndex returns 0).

Web Parts also inherit many of the properties of the Panel control (for example, Direction, DefaultButton, HorizontalAlignment), so if you're familiar with these properties from working with the Panel control, you can also use them in the Web Part.

Turning off Personalization

Several properties on the WebControl and WebPart objects allow you to turn off customization options (all customization options are available by default). These properties, when set to False, prevent the WebPart from performing some action:

- **AllowClose:** The Web Part cannot be closed in the browser. This prevents the user from losing your control by closing it.
- **AllowConnect:** The Web Part cannot be connected to other controls.
- **AllowEdit:** The Web Part cannot have its properties set in the browser.
- **AllowHide:** The Web Part cannot be hidden.
- **AllowMinimize:** The Web Part cannot be minimized in the browser.
- **AllowZoneChange:** The Web Part cannot be moved to a different WebPartZone. This allows you to control where on the page a Web Part can be dragged.

While you can set these properties in your Web Part's code, nothing prevents the developer from setting the properties back to some other value (unless, of course, you set these properties in the Render* methods when it's too late for the host page code to change the value back). A better strategy for controlling these properties is to override the properties to ensure that they remain set to whatever value you want. The following Visual Basic 2005 code, for example, overrides the AllowClose property to keep the property set to False. When code in the host page reads the property, the code returns False; when the code attempts to set the property to any other value, the code sets the WebPart's version of the property to False (it might be a good idea to raise an error when the user attempts to set the property).

```
Public Overrides Property AllowClose() As Boolean

  Get
     AllowClose = False
  End Get

  Set(ByVal value As Boolean)
     MyBase.AllowClose = False
  End Set

End Property
```

In C#:

```
public override bool AllowClose
{
  get
  {
   AllowClose = false;
```

```
    }

    set
    {
     base.AllowClose = false;
    }
  }
```

Providing Help

Two properties allow you to provide your users with help at run time: HelpMode and HelpURL. The HelpUrl property specifies the start page for help information on your Web Part. When the HelpUrl property is set to a string, a Help verb is added to the control's Verb menu at run time (see Figure 5-6). You can let the developer using your control set the HelpUrl property, or you can set it from within your Web Part's code. This Visual Basic 2005 code sets the HelpURL property in the Init event of the Web Part:

```
Private Sub BookDisplay_Init(ByVal sender As Object, _
  ByVal e As System.EventArgs) Handles Me.Init
    MyBase.HelpUrl = "http://www.phvis.com/Booksite.htm"
End Sub
```

As does this C# code:

```
private void BookDisplay_Init(object sender, System.EventArgs e)
{
  base.HelpUrl = "http://www.phvis.com/Booksite.htm";
}
```

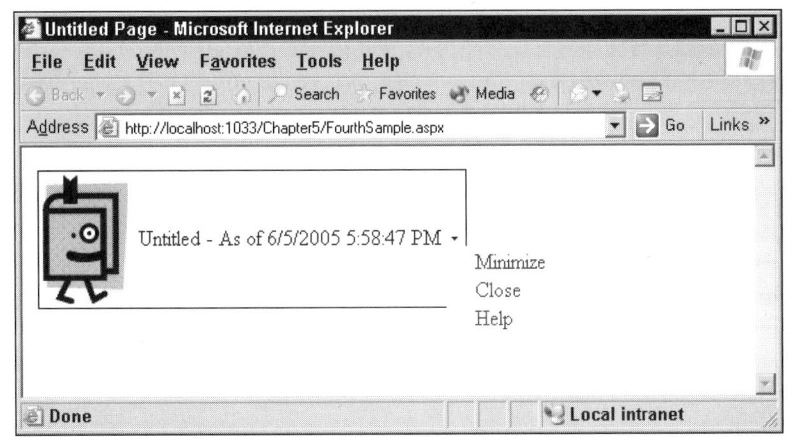

Figure 5-6

By default, the HelpUrl property is treated as a relative URL to a location somewhere on the site where your control is being used. To have the URL used as an absolute URL that points, for instance, to a location on your Web site, you must begin the URL with http://.

If you do set the HelpUrl property from within your code, you should override the HelpUrl property of the WebPart object with a ReadOnly version. This will help send a message to a developer using your control that he won't be able change the HelpURL in the Property List. This Visual Basic 2005 code is an example of a replacement HelpURL property:

```
Public Shadows ReadOnly Property HelpUrl() As String

  Get
     Return MyBase.HelpUrl
  End Get

End Property
```

In C#:

```
public override string HelpUrl
{
 get
 {
  return base.HelpUrl;
 }
}
```

The HelpMode property controls how your Help page is displayed when the user clicks the Help verb. You can set HelpMode to one of the three values:

- **System.Web.UI.WebControls.WebParts.WebPartHelpMode.Modalless:** Opens the Help page in a new instance of the browser. The user can switch back to the page with your Web Part or close the copy of Internet Explorer displaying the Help page.
- **System.Web.UI.WebControls.WebParts.WebPartHelpMode.Modal:** Opens the Help page in a dialog box that prevents the user from returning to the browser. The user has to close the dialog box to return to the page with your Web Part.
- **System.Web.UI.WebControls.WebParts.WebPartHelpMode.Navigate:** Opens the Help page in the same instance as the page with the Web Part. The user can return to the page with the Web Part by using the browser's Back button.

The result of setting the HelpMode varies from one browser to another. The behavior described here is what you get with Internet Explorer.

Summary

In this chapter you have learned a few important skills:

- First, the chapter has shown you both how to create a Web Part and how to give user controls or custom controls more functionality when used as Web Parts. Any custom control or user control can have its properties made both customizable (that is, able to be changed by a Web Part editor at run time) and personalizable (that is, having its customizations saved). You make both your custom properties (described in Chapter 8) and base properties from the underlying class customizable and personalizable.
- The bulk of the chapter, however, showed you how the WebPart class provides additional features for your control in the Web Part environment—provided that you're willing to build a custom control. You saw, for example, how you can add additional verbs to your Verb menu and manage the appearance of your control. You also saw the HTML generated for your Web Part when it is used inside of a WebPartZone.

In Chapter 8, you see how to add business logic to your Web Parts, custom controls, and user controls. However, there's more to say about the special features of Web Parts. In Chapter 10, you see how to give your Web Parts the capability to communicate with each other. In Chapter 11 you get more details on the ASP.NET 2.0 personalization framework. That chapter focuses on the code that you put in your host page to manipulate the Web Part framework controls and how to configure your Web site to take advantage of the Web Parts that were built in this chapter.

6

Maintaining State with the ViewState

One of the essential problems in creating Web applications is state management. Each page, after it's been sent back to the user, is removed from memory and all of its internal data discarded. The next time the same user requests the page, the page will have suffered the worst kind of short-term memory loss — everything about the previous request has been lost. And, of course, what applies to the page as a whole applies to your control: If you want to carry information from one page request over to another request of the same page by the same user then you're going to have to write some code to make that happen.

Fortunately, ASP.NET provides a set of tools for managing state: State can be managed at the page level (ViewState), the user level (the Session object), and at the application level (the Application object and the ASP.NET Cache).

When you're building a control you can use those same tools. However, managing state from a control does have some special problems, and some tools for solving them.

This chapter shows you the tools and techniques for managing state from a custom control or user control. You see how to:

- Access the ViewState from your control's code to efficiently handle large blocks of data
- Deal with situations where the developer using your control has disabled the ViewState
- Take advantage of the ASP.NET 2.0's control state portion of the ViewState
- Use the ASP.NET Cache to reduce the size of the ViewState
- Use type converters to improve the efficiency of your data storage

Using the ViewState

The ViewState for your page provides a simple mechanism for maintaining information from one request of a page to another. The ASP.NET control framework gives you three mechanisms for storing data in the ViewState:

- **Access the ViewState directly:** This is the simplest (but least efficient way) of saving state, with all data saved as key/value pairs.
- **Override the default control methods:** This mechanism allows you to add (and retrieve) large blocks of data in the ViewState as efficiently as possible (both in terms of execution time and amount of data put in the ViewState).
- **Use the area of the ViewState reserved for controls:** This mechanism allows you to separate state information that you must manage for your control to function from the state information that the developer should control.

One of the attractive features of these mechanisms is that they all work equally well in user controls, custom controls, and Web Parts.

Accessing the ViewState Directly

Accessing the ViewState from a custom control or a user control is handled the same way as you would from your Web Page. As you do in your Web pages, to add data to the ViewState you provide a key and set it to a value.

To reduce the footprint of the ViewState, ASP.NET stores only updated values in the ViewState. In order to implement this facility, ASP.NET tracks changes to entries in the ViewState and saves only changes that the tracking process flags. You need to be aware of this because the tracking process is not started as soon as your control is loaded. This allows ASP.NET to update your control's properties with values that were set at design time without having to add to the size of the ViewState.

If you are storing values in the ViewState during events that occur early in the control's life cycle (for example, in the Init event), there is the possibility that your changes will be lost. To be sure that your changes are kept you should call the WebControl's TrackViewState method, as this Visual Basic 2005 code does:

```
Me.TrackViewState()
Me.ViewState("custId") = "A123"
```

In C#:

```
this.TrackViewState();
this.ViewState["custId"] = "A123";
```

Regardless of whether the state of the ViewState is being tracked, if the ViewState for your control is not enabled, your changes to the ViewState will be discarded. You can determine whether it's worthwhile to update the ViewState by checking your control's IsViewStateEnabled, as this Visual Basic 2005 code does:

```
If Me.IsViewStateEnabled = True Then
   Me.ViewState("StateData") = strData
End If
```

In C#:

```
if(this.IsViewStateEnabled == true)
{
 this.ViewState["StateData"] = strData;
}
```

Figure 6-1 shows the relationship of the host page, your control, and the ViewState.

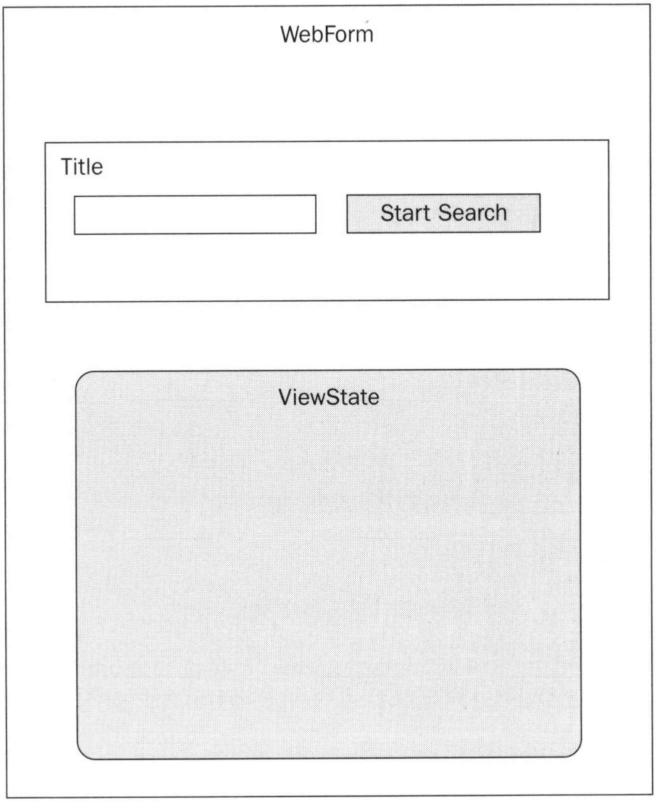

Figure 6-1

Unfortunately, checking your control's IsViewStateEnabled property tells you only whether the ViewState has been enabled for your control. If your control is in a panel or a WebPartZone that has had the ViewState turned off, you won't be able to determine if the ViewState for all of your control's potential parents have their ViewState turned off. It's not impossible that your control might be used in a Panel on a user control that is being used in another Panel on a host page.

ASP.NET 2.0 provides a solution to this problem: an area of the ViewState that can't be turned off that is intended to be used by control (referred to as the *ControlState* in this book). This doesn't mean that you shouldn't use the ViewState—as I discuss later, you will often want to use both the ViewState and the ControlState. Regardless of whether you're using the ViewState or just the portion set aside for controls, you need to understand how to use the ViewState.

Managing ViewState Efficiently

The problem with using the ViewState property is that, while it's easy to use, it can result in very large amounts of data being transmitted to the browser.

At the very least, storing multiple pieces of data in the ViewState requires setting up multiple key/value pairs in the ViewState. If you have large amounts of data to store it makes more sense to build a custom object or structure and store that object or structure as a single unit by overriding the LoadViewState and the SaveViewState methods.

The LoadViewState and SaveViewState methods are called automatically during processing of your control. In brief:

- **The SaveViewState is a function.** Anything that you return from this function is saved in the ViewState.
- **The LoadViewState is a subroutine.** A copy of the data saved in the SaveViewState method is passed to the single parameter that this method accepts.

> **If you do use LoadViewState and SaveViewState methods, you can't access the ViewState directly—using the SaveViewState method overwrites the key/value pairs saved through the ViewState property.**

When a page is first requested, the LoadViewState method is not called because the page does not yet have a ViewState to load data from. The SaveViewState method is called, however, just before the control's Render method, allowing you to save data to the ViewState.

When the page is requested on postback, the Page object loaded back into memory and the ViewState information is recovered from the data sent back to the server. The LoadViewState is called early in the control's life cycle, after the Page's PreRender event and before the CreateChildControls method. This allows you to use data retrieved in the LoadViewState method as part of re-creating your control in the CreateChildControls and Render routines.

The SaveControlState will run, as it did when the page is first requested, before the control's Render method. Figure 6-2 shows the process.

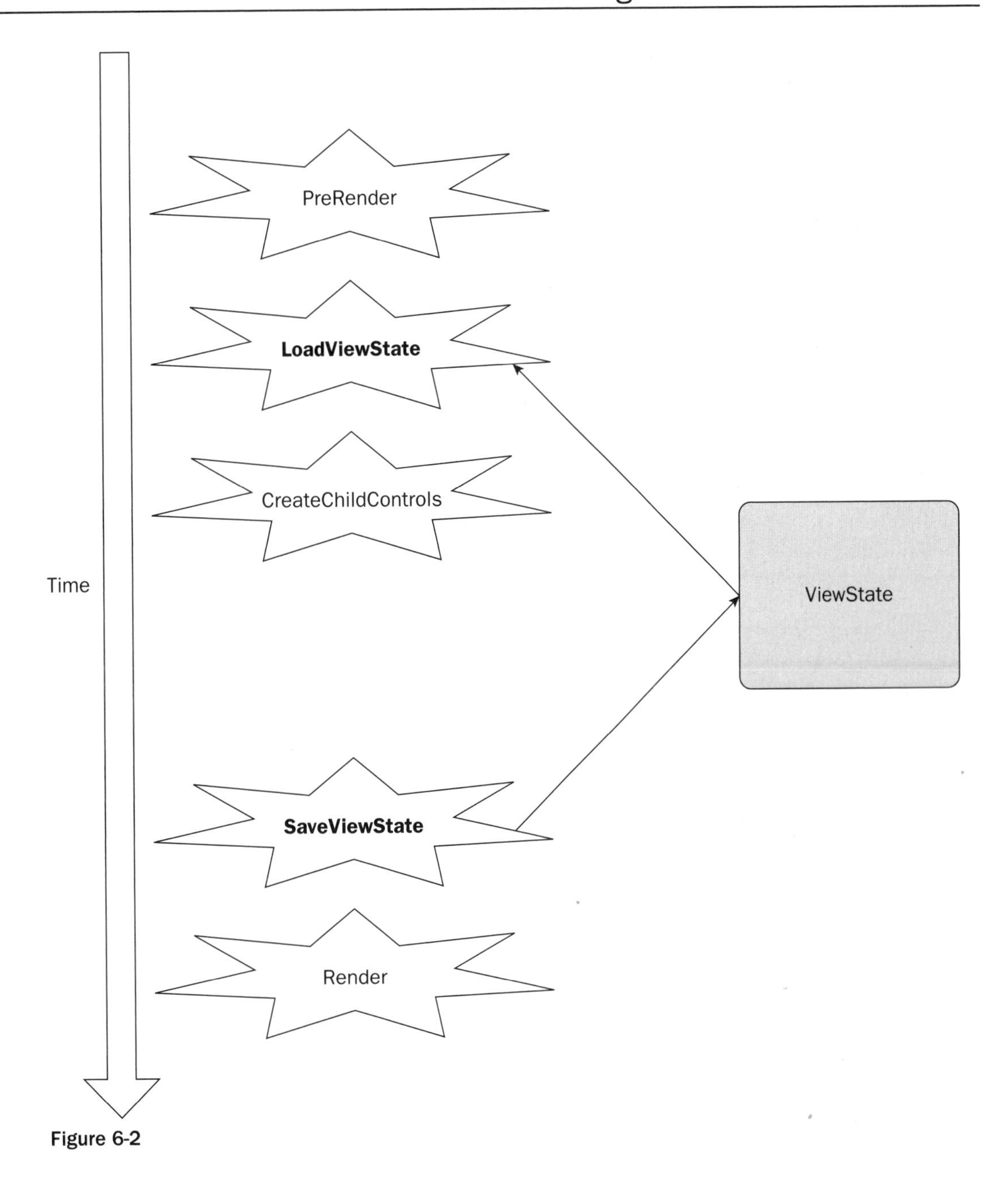
PreRender
LoadViewState
CreateChildControls
Time
ViewState
SaveViewState
Render

Figure 6-2

Because the SaveViewState is called before the Render method, you don't want your code in the Render event to change data in your controls (or for control data to be changed in any methods that run after the Render method). Any changes made to control data in the methods that run after SaveViewState are lost when the host page is removed from memory.

Similarly, you don't want to use the information that is retrieved from the ViewState before the LoadViewState method runs. This means, for instance, that you can't use the information from the ViewState in your control's Init or Load events.

Both of these restrictions emphasize why it's so important to know the order of events in the control's life cycle.

There is another wrinkle in using the ViewState: Not everything that you store in the ViewState will necessarily be saved in the ViewState. In order to save space, only changed items are stored in the ViewState. However, the ViewState doesn't start tracking changes at the start of the Page's life cycle. If you make a change to the ViewState before tracking is turned on, your changes will be lost. In the Init related events (Init, PreInit, etc.) you should always check the Page's IsTrackingViewState property before saving data to the ViewState. When IsTrackingViewState is False, you can turn on ViewState tracking by calling the Page's TrackViewState method, as this Visual Basic 2005 code does:

```
If Me.IsTrackingViewState = False Then
    Me.TrackViewState()
    Me.ViewState("StateData") = strStateData
End If
```

In C#:

```
if (this.IsTrackingViewState == false) {
    this.TrackViewState();
    this.ViewState["StateData"] = strStateData;
}
```

In many cases, you need to store more than a single piece of data. Because the SaveViewState method can return only a single value and LoadViewState is passed only one parameter, you must put all of your data into a single entity. You can handle this either by creating an object or a structure.

The best strategy is to take the data you need to track your control's state and store it in a structure (you'll need to mark the structure with the Serializable attribute to make it compatible with the ViewState). This strategy also lets you control how much data goes into the ViewState so that you can keep the amount of data going down to the browser to a minimum.

This Visual Basic 2005 example creates a data structure called StateData and returns that in the SaveViewState method. The LoadViewState method accepts the parameter (called savedState) holding the control's ViewState data, converts the data to the StateData structure's datatype, and retrieves the data:

```
<Serializable()> _
Private Structure StateData
  Dim strCustNumber As String
  Dim intCustStatus As Integer
```

```
End Structure

Private sData As StateData

Protected Overrides Function SaveViewState() As Object

  sData.intCustStatus = 9
  sData.strCustNumber = "A49K72"
  Return sData

End Function


Protected Overrides Sub LoadViewState(ByVal savedState As Object)

  sData = CType(savedState, StateData)

End Sub
```

This is the equivalent C# code:

```
[Serializable()]
public struct StateData
 {
   public string strCustNumber;
   public int intCustStatus;
}

StateData sData;
protected override object SaveViewState()
 {

   sData.intCustStatus = 9;
   sData.strCustNumber = "A49K72";
   return sData;
}

protected override void LoadViewState(object savedState)
 {
  sData = (StateData) savedState;
 }
```

If the developer using your control has set the control's EnableViewState property to False, these methods are not called. However, if your control is in a panel or a WebPartZone that has its ViewState disabled, then these methods are still called and successfully write and read data to the ViewState. Initially this may strike you as a good thing: The *ViewState methods, if called, always work. However, it also means that a developer who disables ViewState for a panel that encloses your control will not successfully turn off the ViewState for your control (if you're using the *ViewState methods). It's good for you and bad for the developer.

Writing code that would check all the parents of your control would be time-consuming and the code would potentially be error prone. As a result, if you're using the *ViewState methods, it's worthwhile to advise developers in your documentation that setting the EnableViewState property on a panel that holds your control won't suppress your control's ViewState. You could also provide a custom property (discussed in Chapter 8) on your control that allows developers to suppress your ViewState.

Managing State for Controls

Why would a developer want to turn off the ViewState for your control? The typical scenario is that the host page is putting a great deal of information in your control and doing that every time the page is requested.

Because the host page is loading your control with data every time the page is requested, there's no need to enable ViewState. And, because the host page is loading a great deal of data, there are real benefits in lowering the size of the ViewState by disabling the ViewState for your control. Unfortunately, if you are storing state information in the ViewState and the developer disables the ViewState for your control, then she is also disabling your control's ability to keep track of its internal state, perhaps crippling your control's functionality.

In ASP.NET 1.x, you can see the how disabling the ViewState affects a control by experimenting with a text box. Once the ViewState is disabled, the text box fires its TextChanged event whenever the text box holds a value that's different from the value set for the text box at design time. Typically, this isn't what you want: You want the TextChanged event to fire whenever the value is different from the last value in the text box at run time.

As an example, consider a text box whose Text property at design time is set to nothing. With ViewState turned off, if the user changes the text box from its original value to (for instance) "Hello, World," the TextChanged event fires the next time the page's data is sent to the browser. The TextChanged event also continues on every page request after that because "Hello, World" doesn't match the text box's original value. It also means that if the user erases the text "Hello, World," which restores the Text property to its design time value of nothing, no TextChanged event fires because the control's content now matches its original value of nothing.

ASP.NET 2.0 gives you access to a separate area of the ViewState reserved for control state information, the *ControlState*. Controls can now store their state information in the ControlState area, separate from the data that ASP.NET stores in the ViewState. If a developer disables ViewState for your control, it won't affect your ability to manage your control's state, provided that you have stored any essential state information in the ControlState.

This doesn't mean that you should abandon the SaveViewState and LoadViewState methods or using the ViewState property. It does mean that you should distinguish between two kinds of state management:

- ❑ Data that you're willing to let the developer disable in order to improve efficiency
- ❑ Data that you don't want to lose under any circumstances

For instance, if your control consists of several text boxes, you might store the text data in your control in the ViewState so that developers can reduce the data in the page's ViewState by turning it off. However, you might store in the ControlState some compacted hashed value of all of the text in your text boxes. When the control's data is returned to the server, you could generate a new hash value for the returned data, compare it to the hash value you stored in the ControlState, and (if they're different) fire an event to notify the host page that data was changed by the user while the page was displayed in the browser. (Firing events is covered in Chapter 8.)

To use the ControlState you must override two methods that look very much like the *ViewState methods just discussed: LoadControlState and SaveControlState. In your control's life cycle, the *ControlState methods "bracket" the equivalent *ViewState methods: The LoadControlState method is called just before the LoadViewState method and the SaveControlState method is called after the SaveViewState method. Figure 6-3 shows the complete process for both the *ViewState and *ControlState methods.

While the ControlState is treated as a different area from the Page object's ViewState, in practice both the ControlState data and the ViewState data end up in the same hidden field in the HTML page.

The first step in using the ControlState is to notify the host page that your control has ControlState information to save. You do this by calling the RegisterRequiresControlState method of the Page object that represents your control's host page (your control's Page property gives you access to the Page object for the host page). Typically, you want to notify the Page object as early in your control's life cycle as possible, so the Init event of your control is the best place to signal this to the host page. You must pass the RegisterRequiresControlState a reference to the control whose state is being saved (use *Me* in Visual Basic 2005 code and *this* in C# code). Here's a typical example in Visual Basic 2005:

```
Private Sub WebCustomControl1_Init(ByVal sender As Object, _
                                   ByVal e As System.EventArgs) Handles Me.Init

    Me.Page.RegisterRequiresControlState(Me)

End Sub
```

In C#, the equivalent Init event looks like this:

```
private void WebCustomControl1_Init(object sender, System.EventArgs e)
{
 this.Page.RegisterRequiresControlState(this);
}
```

Presumably you could pass the RegisterRequiresControlState a reference to some other control — a constituent control that you add to your control's Controls collection. However, it's difficult to imagine a scenario where a control would use the ControlState but leave the registration to the hosting control.

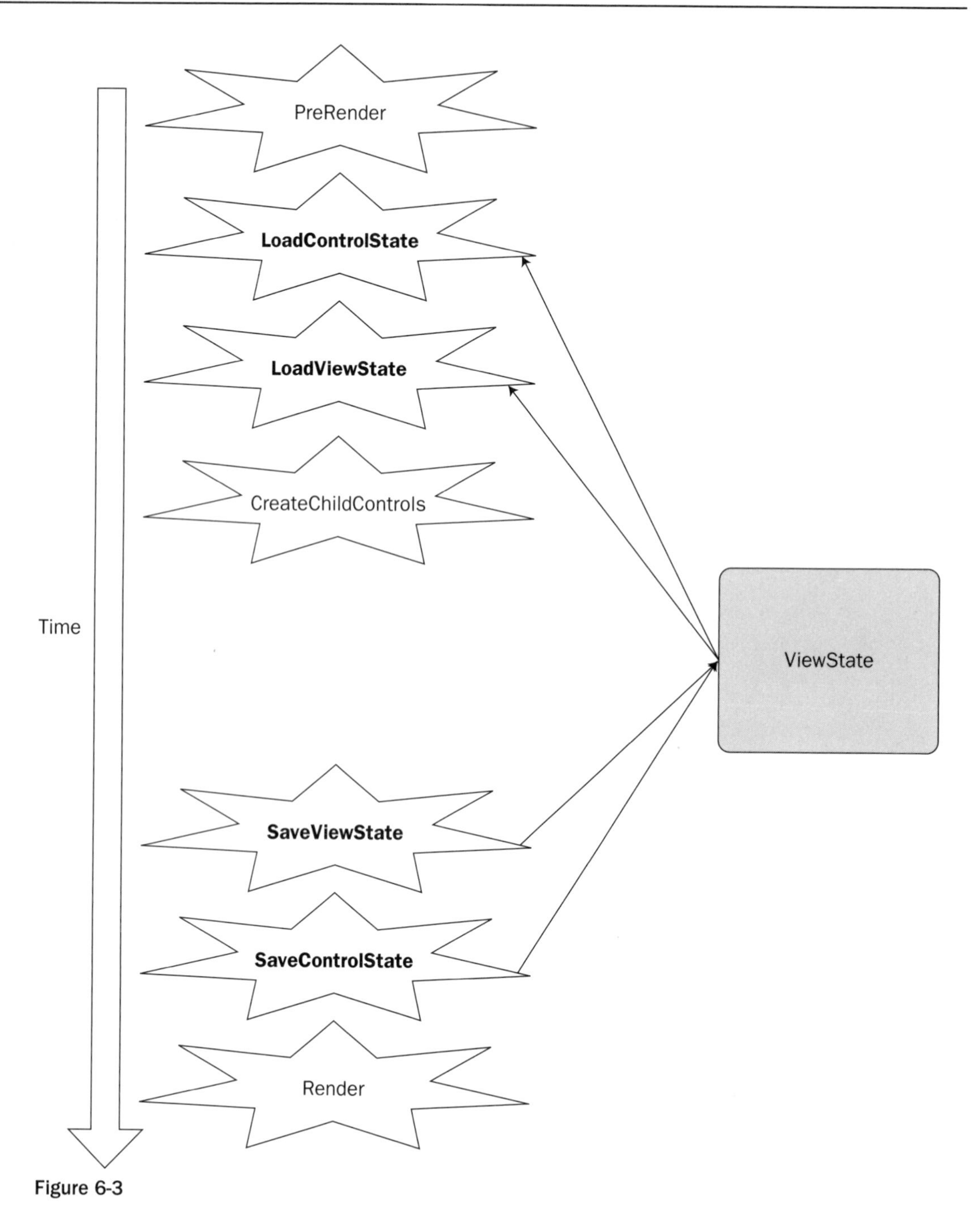
PreRender
LoadControlState
LoadViewState
CreateChildControls
Time
ViewState
SaveViewState
SaveControlState
Render

Figure 6-3

Once you've registered your control with the host page, the SaveControlState and LoadControlState methods are called automatically. The two routines work like the equivalent *ViewState methods:

- **SaveControlState is a function:** Any values that you return from this function are saved in the ControlState.
- **LoadControlState is a subroutine:** This routine is passed a single parameter (named savedState), which is the data that was placed in the ControlState by the SaveControlState routine.

Code for the *ControlState methods is almost identical to code for the *ViewState methods, as this Visual Basic 2005 example shows:

```
Dim sData As New StateData

Protected Overrides Function SaveControlState() As Object

  sData.intData = 9
  sData.strData = "A94K34"
  Return sData

End Function


Protected Overrides Sub LoadControlState(ByVal savedState As Object)

   sData = CType(savedState, StateData)

End Sub
```

In C#:

```
protected override object SaveControlState()
 {

    sData.intCustStatus = 9;
    sData.strCustNumber = "A49K72";
    return sData;
}

protected override void LoadControlState(object savedState)
 {
  sData = (StateData) savedState;
 }
```

You should think very carefully about what data you want to put in the ControlState. By using the ControlState you deprive developers of the ability to manage their page's payload because the developers using your control cannot disable the ControlState. Generally speaking, information related to the user interface or the data that the host page puts in the control should stay in the ViewState so that the developer can turn it off if desired. And when you do use the ControlState, you should keep very little data in it.

You can check to see if your control has enabled ControlState tracking by calling the host Page object's RequiresControlState method and passing a reference to your control. If the method returns True, the page will call your *ControlState methods. Here's an example in Visual Basic 2005:

```
If Me.Page.RequiresControlState(Me) = False Then
   Me.Page.RegisterRequiresControlState(Me)
End If
```

In C#:

```
if(this.Page.RequiresControlState(this) == false)
{
 this.Page.RegisterRequiresControlState(this);
}
```

*Unlike the *ViewState methods, using the *ControlState methods does not interfere with using the ViewState property. Further, the ability of your control to use the ControlState method is independent of any other control's use of the ControlState—even if your control is used as a constituent control in another custom control, user control, or Web Part. One of the reasons that the RegisterRequiresControlState method is passed a reference to your control is to ensure that ControlState management is enabled only for that control.*

Clearing State

Sometimes it's necessary to get rid of ViewState information. For instance, your control's constituent controls are probably actively using the host page's ViewState. As you update and manipulate these controls, you can't be guaranteed that the constituent controls will update their ViewState information correctly. The simplest solution is to call the control's ClearChildState method, which causes all information placed in the ViewState by any child controls to be discarded. You can also selectively discard just the constituent control's ControlState information with the ClearChildControlState method, and just the ViewState information with ClearChildViewState method.

You can check to see if your constituent controls have saved ViewState information with the HasChildViewState. For ControlState information, you can use the IsChildControlStateCleared property. Putting this together, this Visual Basic 2005 code checks for ViewState and ControlState information for constituent controls and deletes it, if present, while always doing the minimum amount of work:

```
If Me.HasChildViewState = True And _
   Me.IsChildControlStateCleared = False Then
   Me.ClearChildState()
ElseIf Me.HasChildViewState = True Then
   Me.ClearChildViewState()
```

```
ElseIf Me.IsChildControlStateCleared = False Then
   Me.clearChildControlState()
End If
```

In C#:

```
if (this.HasChildViewState == true &&
    this.IsChildControlStateCleared == false)
  {
   this.ClearChildState();
  }
  else if (this.HasChildViewState == true)
  {
   this.ClearChildViewState();
  }
  else if (this.IsChildControlStateCleared == false)
  {
   this.ClearChildControlState();
  }
```

*Because the ViewState isn't processed until after the control's Init event, you shouldn't check the HasChildViewState or the IsChildControlState properties or use the Clear*State methods until your control's Load event. No error occurs if you use these methods and properties before the Load event, but nothing is accomplished, either.*

Creating Case-Sensitive Keys

By default, the ViewState is case-insensitive. This means that if you store an item in the ViewState using a key called "CAT" and follow that by storing a different value under the key "cat" then the second value will overwrite the first value. You can check this setting by reading the control's ViewStateIgnoresCase property.

If you want the capability to keep keys with the same characters but with different casing separate, you need to override the ViewStateIgnoresCase property and have it return False, as this Visual Basic 2005 code does:

```
Overrides Protected ReadOnly Property ViewStateIgnoresCase As Boolean

  Get
    Return False
  End Get

End Property
```

In C#:

```
protected override bool ViewStateIgnoresCase
{
 get
 {
   return false;
 }
}
```

Integrating with the Cache

While storing data in the ViewState is relatively convenient, the more data that you put in the ViewState, the larger the payload that goes from the server to the browser and back again.

In ASP.NET 2.0, saying that the ViewState data goes from the server to the browser and back again is a simplification. In ASP.NET 2.0 you can specify that your data be persisted at the Server in the Session object. However, it's important to recognize that picking your location is moving the location of the problem. For instance, if you put a large amount of data in the ViewState and store it in the Session object, you avoid the time it takes to send the data down to the browser and back. However, you now have to consider the amount of memory that the ViewState is consuming on the server: Wherever you store your ViewState, you want to store as little as possible.

You can decrease your dependence on the ViewState by integrating the ViewState with the ASP.NET Cache. The goal is to store the bulk of your information in the Cache and use the ViewState to hold just enough information to re-create that cached information.

The Cache object, as used here, shouldn't be confused with PartialCaching. PartialCaching allows someone using your user control to decide when the user control's content is to be refreshed at run time.

The Cache is an adaptive data store. As the server runs out of memory, items are automatically removed from the Cache, freeing memory. Of course, if you want to use that data and it has been removed from memory, you'll have to re-create the missing data. This may seem pointless, but there are several key points here:

- ❑ As long as you have enough memory to support your data, your data is kept in memory where you can retrieve it quickly.
- ❑ If there isn't enough memory to hold your data, your data is automatically removed without any work on your part. Yes, you have to re-create your data but you are no worse off than if you hadn't stored the data in the Cache.
- ❑ If your data is removed from memory, it is re-created only if you actually need it. If, in the course of processing, you never need that data again, the data is never re-created.

Cache Limitations

There is a major limitation to using the Cache. Cache information is kept in memory on the server. In a Web farm, this means that each server in the farm has its own separate cache. A user who has a request processed on the first server in the farm and has subsequent requests processed on some other server will not have access to the Cache on the first server.

However, Cache data is always at risk of being removed because of memory constraints. You need to provide some mechanism to add data back to the Cache, whether because ASP.NET has removed the data or because the user's request has been routed to a different server in a Web farm.

If your control updates a Cache object in a server farm environment and doesn't persist the data back to some central location, your control may not have access to the updated Cache object if the user is routed to another server in the farm.

> Even if the application isn't running on a Web farm, it may be running on a computer with multiple processors. Because each processor in the computer will get its own copy of the ASP.NET process, each CPU has its own separate Cache. Here again, data needs to be persisted back to some central location.

Storing objects becomes easier if you take advantage of the Cache. You can hold an object in memory by using the Cache and store, in the ControlState or the ViewState, only the information required to re-create the object. Much of the time, all that needs to go in the ControlState or ViewState is the data to pass to the object's constructor and/or properties that are no longer set to their default values.

An example will help make clear how useful the Cache is. In the book site case study, a Book object that holds all the information for a book is a useful object. However, between tracking biographical information for all the authors and holding graphics of the book's front and back covers, a Book object is both very large and difficult to store in the ViewState. Rather than store the Book object in the ViewState, you can store the object in the Cache.

There are a couple of problems to address here:

- The Cache is application-level in scope — anything stored in the Cache is shared among all users on the site.
- Objects can be removed from the Cache by ASP.NET when memory is tight.

Handling the second problem is the easiest: If the object is missing from the Cache, you re-create it and add it back to the Cache. As a result, if memory runs short, the Book object is removed from the Cache and is added back only if the application needs it again. In order to re-create the Book object, you need some piece of information that retrieves the necessary data. Because all books are assigned a unique identifier (the ISBN), all that you need to store in the ViewState is the book's ISBN, less than a dozen characters. In the sample code you see later in this section, I assume that the Book object's constructor accepts an ISBN and uses that to retrieve the book's data from the company database.

Handling the first problem (keeping the Book objects separate for other data) is only slightly more complicated. All that's necessary is a unique key for the Book information that can be used when the book is added to the Cache. If you assume that a book's information is the same for all users on the site, a Book object can be stored in the Cache using just the book's ISBN as the key for the Cache. This also ensures that if any one user is using the information for a book, any other users that need the book will find that book's information already in the Cache.

For the purposes of this discussion (and to make the example more interesting), assume that the application stores some customer-specific information in the Book object (for instance, the customer's rating). To keep the customer's customized copy of the Book object separate from other customers' versions of the Book object, the key used when placing the Book object in the Cache also needs to include some customer-specific piece of data. You could use the customer's logon information for this (for example, a user id). However, ASP.NET provides an alternative: the Session object's SessionId. Because the SessionId is unique for each user currently accessing the site, using the SessionId as part of the key keeps each user's information separate.

Using the SessionId to tie an object in the Cache to a specific user emphasizes an often overlooked feature of the Session object: Even if you don't use the Session object for its intended purpose (storing data), the automatically generated SessionId can be useful.

To make sure that the combination of the ISBN and the SessionId doesn't duplicate the value of some other key, it's a good idea to put a purpose-specific prefix on the key. As a result, a good key might consist of the string "Book" plus the book's ISBN plus the SessionId.

The final decision to be made is how long a Book object should be left in the Cache. One answer is not to place any time limits on the book's duration in the Cache. If the Book object's Cache priority is set to normal, the Book object is removed from the Cache automatically when there is no longer enough memory to support it. Because the Cache object removes objects that haven't been used for the longest period of time, Book objects that aren't being used any longer are the first to be removed.

In the following code, however, a sliding expiration date is set on the Book object when the object is placed in the Cache. A sliding expiration date causes the object to be removed from the Cache if it hasn't been used for a specified period of time (in the sample code, the time period is 20 minutes). This ensures that the Cache is kept small while still keeping currently used information in memory.

The following code represents a function used to manage a Book object in the Cache. The routine first assembles the Book object's key. Using the key, the code then checks to see if the object is in the Cache. One of two scenarios now occurs:

- If the object isn't in the Cache (either because the object hasn't been created or has been removed from the Cache because of memory shortages) the code creates a new instance of the Book object using the ISBN passed to the function. Once created, the Book object is put in the Cache and the ISBN is put in the ViewState where the application can access it as required.
- If the object is in the Cache, the object is retrieved.

This code won't be identical in a custom control, a Web Part, and a user control:

- In a custom control or Web Part, the Session object and the Cache can be accessed through the host page's Page object as, for instance, Me.Page.Session or this.Page.Session.
- In a user control, you can access the Session object and the Cache object from properties on the control. So, in a user control, you can use either Me.Session or this.Session instead of Me.Page.Session/this.Page.Session.

Here's the Visual Basic 2005 code that would be used in a custom control:

```
Private bk As Book

Public Function GetBook(strISBN As String) As Book
Dim TwentyMinutes As TimeSpan
Dim strBookKey As String
Dim bk As Book

  strBookKey = "Book" & strISBN & Me.Session.SessionId

  If Me.Page.Cache(strBookKey) Is Nothing Then
    bk = New Book(strISBN)
    TwentyMinutes = New TimeSpan(0, 20, 0)
```

```
    Me.Page.Cache.Add(strBookKey, bk, Nothing, DateTime.MaxValue, TwentyMinutes, _
       Web.Caching.CacheItemPriority.Normal, Nothing)
    Me.Page.ViewState("BookKey") = strISBN
  Else
    bk = Me.Page.Cache(strBookKey)
  End If
  Return bk

End Function
```

Here's the equivalent C# code:

```
private Book bk;

public Book GetBook(string strISBN)
{
 TimeSpan TwentyMinutes;
 string strBookKey;
 Book bk;

 strBookKey = "Book" + strISBN + this.Session.SessionId;

 if (this.Page.Cache(strBookKey) == null)
 {
  bk = new Book(strISBN);
  TwentyMinutes = new TimeSpan(0, 20, 0);
  this.Page.Cache.Add(strBookKey, bk, null, DateTime.MaxValue, TwentyMinutes,
                    Web.Caching.CacheItemPriority.Normal, null);
  this.Page.ViewState["BookKey"] = strISBN;
 }
 else
 {
  bk = (Book) this.Page.Cache(strBookKey);
 }
 return bk;
}
```

If your goal is to hold on to your object across more than one page, you can keep the minimal information required to re-create the object in the Session or Application object.

Serializing Objects Efficiently

If you're going to save data in the ViewState, you should consider how your code will handle the necessary conversions. Fundamentally, strings work best with the ViewState. While you can build the appropriate serialization mechanisms into any object you create, you can't do the same with objects that you don't build. In addition, even if you are building an object yourself, you may want to customize which parts of the object are serialized so that you can store different information in different scenarios.

If you have a property that has a complex datatype (something other than the base datatypes of string, integer, Boolean, and the like) you may also want to create a TypeConverter. Without a TypeConverter assigned to the property, the developer using your control won't be able to update the property at design time using the Property List. This is covered in Chapter 8, where you learn how to add custom properties to your control.

The solution to serializing objects that you haven't created and serializing different parts of an object at different times is to build a TypeConverter. A TypeConverter accepts an object, extracts just the information that you specify, and returns a string that can be used in the ViewState. If this is an object that you're creating and the TypeConverter you create is the one that you always want used with the object, you can associate the TypeConverter with your class. Associating a specific TypeConverter with a class makes it easier to use.

TypeConverters built into the .NET framework handle conversions between the existing framework datatypes.

A TypeConverter can do a great many things for you, but this chapter covers just the basic functionality required to handle serializing an object. Only three steps are required to create a TypeConverter to handle the basic serializing/deserializing that support saving a specific object to the ViewState:

1. Add a new Class module to your control project and have it inherit from System. ComponentModel.TypeConverter.
2. Override the TypeConverter's ConvertFrom method. In this method, put the code that converts from your object to your serializable format (typically a string).
3. Override the TypeConverter's ConvertTo method. In this method put the code that converts from a string back into your object.

For this example, I create a TypeConverter called BookToString that extracts two properties from the Book object (Title and Description) and returns them as a string.

The first step is to define a class that inherits from TypeConverter, as this Visual Basic 2005 code does:

```
Public Class BookToString
   Inherits System.ComponentModel.TypeConverter
```

The C# code looks like this:

```
public class BookToString : System.ComponentModel.TypeConverter
```

The ConvertFrom method handles the actual conversion. In this very basic version of a TypeConverter, of the three parameters passed to the ConvertFrom method, I'm interested only in the third one (called value), which holds the item to be converted (be sure to check that the item is of the right type). The following Visual Basic 2005 code extracts the values of the ISBN and CustomerRating properties and concatenates them into a string with some arbitrary text between them to make it easier to pull the values back out:

```
Public Overrides Function ConvertFrom( _
        ByVal context As System.ComponentModel.ITypeDescriptorContext, _
        ByVal culture As System.Globalization.CultureInfo, _
        ByVal value As Object) As Object
Dim strBookSerialized As String

   bk = CType(value, Book)
   strBookSerialized = bk.ISBN & "*" & bk.CustomerRating & "*"

   Return strBookSerialized

End Function
```

In C#:

```
public override object ConvertFrom(
    System.ComponentModel.ITypeDescriptorContext context,
    System.Globalization.CultureInfo culture, object value)
{
string strBookSerialized;

 bk = (Book) value;
 strBookSerialized = bk.ISBN + "*" + bk.CustomerRating + "*";

 return strBookSerialized;
}
```

The ConvertTo method handles the reverse conversion. The following Visual Basic 2005 code uses the Split function to divide the string at the arbitrary text inserted between the data components and place the results in an array (called strProps). The routine then creates a Book object using the ISBN and sets the CustomerRating property using the data in the strProps array. The Book object is then returned from the routine:

```
Public Overrides Function ConvertTo( _
          ByVal context As System.ComponentModel.ITypeDescriptorContext, _
          ByVal culture As System.Globalization.CultureInfo, _
          ByVal value As Object, _
          ByVal destinationType As System.Type) As Object
Dim bk As Book
Dim strValue As String
Dim strProps() As String

   strValue = CType(value, String)
   strProps = Split(strValue, "*")
   bk = New Book(strProps(0))
   bk.CustomerRating = strProps(1)

   Return bk

End Function
```

In C#:

```
public override object ConvertTo(
   System.ComponentModel.ITypeDescriptorContext context,
   System.Globalization.CultureInfo culture,
   object value, System.Type destinationType)
 {
 Book bk;
  string strValue;
  string [] strProps;

  strValue = (string) value;
  strProps = value.Split(new char[] {"*"});
```

```
    bk = new Book(strProps[0]);
    bk.Description = strProps[1];

    return bk;
  }
```

Using Your TypeConverter

Now that you've created your type converter, you can use it to handle conversions. The following Visual Basic 2005 example uses the BookToString TypeConverter in the SaveViewState method to serialize the Book object. While the ConvertTo method has to be passed three parameters, the only parameter that matters to our TypeConverter is the third one, which must contain the object to be serialized (this code assumes that the variable bk represents a book object declared at the class level):

```
Protected Overrides Function SaveViewState() As Object
Dim tcv As New BookToString
Dim strSerializedBook As String

  strSerializedBook = tcv.ConvertFrom(Nothing, Nothing, bk)
  Return strSerializedBook

End Function
```

In C#:

```
protected override object SaveViewState()
{
 BookToString tcv = new BookToString;
 string strSerializedBook;

 strSerializedBook = (string) tcv.ConvertFrom(null, null, bk);
 return strSerializedBook;
}
```

For the LoadViewState method, shown in the following Visual Basic 2005 code, you call the ConvertTo method, which takes four parameters. The key parameter for this method is also the third parameter, which must be passed the savedState data passed into the LoadViewState routine. The savedState parameter holds the data to be deserialized into a Book object. Because the ConvertTo method returns an Object, the result must be converted to a Book object:

```
Protected Overrides Sub LoadViewState(ByVal savedState As Object)
Dim tcv As BookToString
Dim objDeserialized As Object

  tcv = New BookToString
  objDeserialized = tcv.ConvertTo(Nothing, Nothing, savedState, Nothing)
  bk = Ctype(objDeserialized, Book)

End Sub
```

In C#:

```
protected override void LoadViewState(object savedState)
{
 BookToString tcv;
 object objDeserialized;

 tcv = new BookToString();
 objDeserialized = tcv.ConvertTo(null, null, savedState, null);
 bk = (Book) objDeserialized;
}
```

Associating a TypeConverter with a Class

Now that you've created your TypeConverter you can associate it with the class that it's to be used with. By making this association, you make the code that uses the TypeConverter more general because it no longer has to know what converter to use. Instead, the code can extract the converter from the class's definition.

You can associate a type converter with a class only if you're writing the class yourself. However, if you're working with someone else's object, this is the technique you would use to retrieve the TypeConverter associated with the object.

The first step is to use the TypeConverter attribute on the Class declaration of the object to attach the TypeConverter to the Class, as this Visual Basic 2005 code does:

```
<System.ComponentModel.TypeConverter(GetType(BookToString))> _
Public Class Book
```

In C#:

```
[System.ComponentModel.TypeConverter(GetType(BookToString))]
public class Book
```

Now, in your *ViewState methods, you can use the GetConverter method of the TypeDescriptor object to determine which TypeConverter is to be used when serializing and deserializing your object. This Visual Basic 2005 code defines a variable to work with any TypeConverter object and then uses the GetConstructor method to retrieve the TypeConverter from a Book object. The code then uses the retrieved TypeConverter to serialize the object:

```
Protected Overrides Function SaveViewState() As Object
Dim tcv As System.ComponentModel.TypeConverter
Dim strSerialized As String

  tcv = TypeDescriptor.GetConverter(bk)
  strSerialized = tcv.ConvertFrom(Nothing, Nothing, bk)
  Return strSerialized

End Function
```

In C#:

```
protected override object SaveViewState()
{
 System.ComponentModel.TypeConverter tcv;
 string strSerialized;

 tcv = TypeDescriptor.GetConverter(bk);
 strSerialized = (string) tcv.ConvertFrom(null, null, bk);
 return strSerialized;
}
```

Summary

It's critical that all Web components, including custom controls, Web Parts, and user controls, have some mechanism for managing state. In addition to being able to use the same tools as a Web page, your control has a special option: the ViewState of the host page. In this chapter you've seen how to:

- Use the ViewState property to update the host page's ViewState
- Use the LoadViewState and SaveViewState methods to update the ViewState more efficiently
- Use the LoadControlState and SaveControlState methods to separate state information that is required for your control to function correctly and the data that a developer using your control should control

In order to manage the ViewState information effectively, this chapter also outlined two other methods for handling state information efficiently:

- You can take advantage of the adaptive store of the ASP.NET Cache to store large amounts of data.
- You can handle the serialization and deserialization of objects by writing your own type converters.

In Chapters 1 and 2, you saw how custom controls, user controls, and Web Parts are used in a Web application. In Chapters 3 through 5 you learned how to create your own controls. This chapter also gave you the solutions for handling state—a major issue in creating Web applications. Chapter 7 gives you the tools to distribute and update your controls (and explains how to license your control). If you're creating Web Parts, Chapter 7 also shows you how to manage the personalization system that Web Parts depend upon.

7

Developer Tools

At this point you've seen how to use and create both custom and user controls, and how to extend custom controls to take advantage of the Web Parts framework. In the next section, you learn how to add custom business functionality to your controls and how to handle various specialized environments (such as creating Validator custom controls). However, before we wrap up this part of the book on creating controls, you need a few additional tools. This chapter covers what you need to know after you've finished writing your code.

In this chapter you learn to:

- Debug your control while it is running in Visual Studio 2005
- Distribute your controls to work with a single site and to be shared across sites
- License your controls so that you can sell them to third parties and have them used by ISPs
- Update your controls without redeploying your Web site
- Manage the personalization system used by Web Parts

Debugging Your Controls at Design Time

As you've probably realized, much of the code in your controls executes while your control is being displayed in Visual Studio 2005. (You may already have encountered the "Error Creating Control" message that indicates an error with your design-time code when you dragged a control onto a form at design time.) Fortunately, you can debug your custom controls and Web Parts at design time by starting another copy of Visual Studio 2005. You can also debug user controls, but the process is more awkward, as described later in this section.

The first step in creating an environment for debugging your controls at design time is to set up a new "debugging Web site" to be used for testing design-time code. Because you have to debug your code's design-time behavior in a separate copy of Visual Studio 2005, you should also create a second Web site to open in that copy of Visual Studio 2005.

You don't need to open a second Web site in the new copy of Visual Studio 2005: You could have the second copy of Visual Studio 2005 open whatever Web site you're using in your solution. However, it's easier to manage the debugging process if you have a second, simpler site for testing the design-time behavior of your controls.

After you've created that second Web site, you need to add your custom controls to the Toolbox so that you can use them on your new site. Open an ASPX page in Design view, right-click the Toolbox, and pick Choose items from the popup menu. In the Choose Toolbox Items dialog box that displays, click the Browse button, and in the Open dialog box that appears, navigate to the DLL for your controls and select it. Now close all the dialog boxes to add your controls to the Toolbox for your new Web site.

For a user control, every time that you want to debug you must open a second copy of Visual Studio 2005 and then copy your user control from the project where you've created it into the new project. Unfortunately, because user controls are not shared between projects, you have to copy your user control to your new project each time that you want to debug it. The good news is that it's relatively unusual to need to debug a user control at design time. Because so much of the user control is defined in the ASCX file, most of the user control's code executes at run time only. However, if you add properties to your user control and want to test the code at design time, you may find yourself needing to debug your user control at design time.

The final steps are to set up the debugging options for your custom control project so that pressing F5 (or starting debugging in any way) opens a second copy of Visual Studio 2005 and loads your debugging Web site into that copy. In Solution Explorer, double-click either the My Project entry (for Visual Basic 2005 projects) or the Properties entry (for C# projects). In the Properties window, select the Debug tab (shown in Figure 7-1).

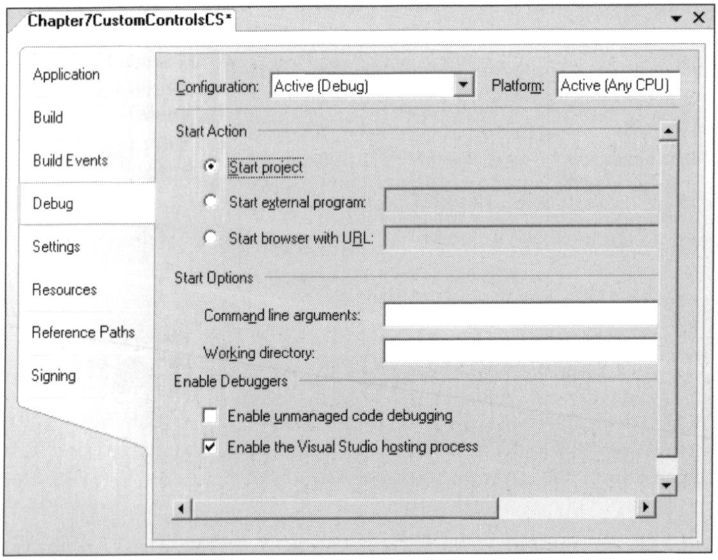

Figure 7-1

One warning: Making these settings in a custom control project will override the settings recommended in Chapter 3 that caused the ASPX page where you're testing your control to launch. After making these settings, starting debugging in a custom control project causes a second copy of Visual Studio to open.

To start a second copy of Visual Studio 2005, in the Debug settings window select the Start external program option and type the name of the Visual Studio 2005 executable (devenv.exe) into the text box.

It may be necessary to enter the full path name to devenv.exe. If so, the simplest method is to click the builder button (the button with the three dots) by the Start external program entry and navigate to devenv.exe.

Now you can set the command-line arguments that will open your debugging Web site in the second copy of Visual Studio 2005. In the Command line arguments text box, enter the following line (where *DebugSite.sln* is the name of the solution file in your Web site project):

```
/Command File.OpenWebsite DebugSite.sln
```

The final step is to enter the full path name of the directory for your solution file in the Working directory text box.

Deploying Controls

The good news is that if you are deploying controls as part of deploying a Web site using Visual Studio 2005, you have virtually nothing to do in order to deploy the controls used on the site. If you reference a control library (including either custom controls or Web Parts), that library will be included in the deployment package along with any other components referenced by your project. Deploying user controls is equally pain-free: Any user controls in your application will be deployed with your WebForm pages.

The .NET environment provides several different ways for you to distribute your Web site. For this chapter, to simplify the discussion, I use just two techniques for distributing Web applications:

- The Publish Web Site option on the Build menu in Visual Studio .NET
- Copying files to an already existing ASP.NET Web site

These two techniques enable me to discuss all the issues in distributing Web applications with custom controls, Web Parts, and user controls. In addition, these techniques are simple to work with in a test environment, allowing you to put the samples in this section to the test. However, the best practice for distributing production ASP.NET applications is to create a setup and deployment package (an msi file) that can be executed on the server where the application is to be deployed. I'll duplicate the results of using a deployment package by using the Publish Web site menu option.

While there's nothing new that you need to do to distribute your controls as part of deploying your Web site, once the site is deployed you may want to update your controls without redeploying your whole Web site. There are three different formats for a deployed ASP.NET Web site. Depending on which format your Web site uses, you will have different options for updating your site.

Deployed Web Site Formats

The three formats for a deployed Web site, in terms of how your user controls will be deployed, are:

- **Source code only:** All the source code for your user controls is on the Web site (that is, the source code for both your codebehind file and your ASCX file). In Visual Studio 2005, you can get this result by using the Copy Web Site tool.
- **Compile code only:** The codebehind file for your user control is compiled into a DLL and placed on the Web site with the source code for your ASCX file. This is one of the two options available if you pick Publish from the Visual Studio 2005 Build menu.
- **Compile all:** Compiled versions of both your ASCX file and its codebehind file are placed on the Web site. This is the other option available if you pick the Publish option from the Visual Studio 2005 Build menu.

Typically, you will create custom controls and Web Parts in a separate project from your Web site so that the controls can be compiled independently of the Web site and shared among several Web sites. In this scenario, the source code for the custom control is never copied to the Web site. Only the compiled DLL for the controls is deployed to the site. However, if you add a custom control or Web Part to a Web site project, the code for your custom control or Web Part will be treated like the codebehind file for an ASPX page and treated as just described.

In addition, you can choose to assign a strong name to your application when you deploy it, which also affects your ability to update your controls without re-deploying the whole site, as described later in this section.

The easiest way to deploy your project is to use the first option and copy the source files to the Web site. In Visual Studio 2005, using the Copy Web tool, shown in Figure 7-2, lets you copy all or some of the site files to the Web site. Because you've only moved source code to your Web site, ASP.NET will have to compile your source code when someone uses a page with your controls on it, which will affect the site's initial performance. Also, anyone who can gain access to the files on your Web site will be able to read your code.

Therefore, for any site where security or performance matters, you should precompile your application before distributing it. Compiling your site improves performance by eliminating the need to compile your application when a page is requested and also hides your code from prying eyes.

Precompiling Your Site with Visual Studio 2005

When you select the Publish option from the Build menu, Visual Studio 2005 compiles the files that contain program code into DLLs and moves the DLLs to a folder called bin on your Web site.

If you put both the source code and the compiled DLL for your user control on your site then ASP.NET uses either the compiled version of the code or generates an error. Either way, making changes to the source code files on your Web site has no effect.

When you choose to publish your Web site, you can choose to have the files with your user interface (the ASPX and ASCX files) compiled along with your program files. This choice is made in the Publish Web Site dialog box by checking the "Allow this precompiled site to be updateable" option, as shown in Figure 7-3. Sites marked as updateable have only their program code files compiled. In terms of developing controls, this option is relevant only for user controls because, while user controls have a code file and an ASCX file, custom controls consist only of code. When you pick the updateable option, the ASCX files for your user control are copied unchanged to the Web site, while the codebehind file is compiled to a DLL and put in the bin folder on the Web site. A user control called MyControl.ascx will have its codebehind file compiled to a DLL with a name similar to App_Web_MyControl.ascx.cdcab7d2.dll.

The precompile process is an intelligent process: Only changed files are recompiled.

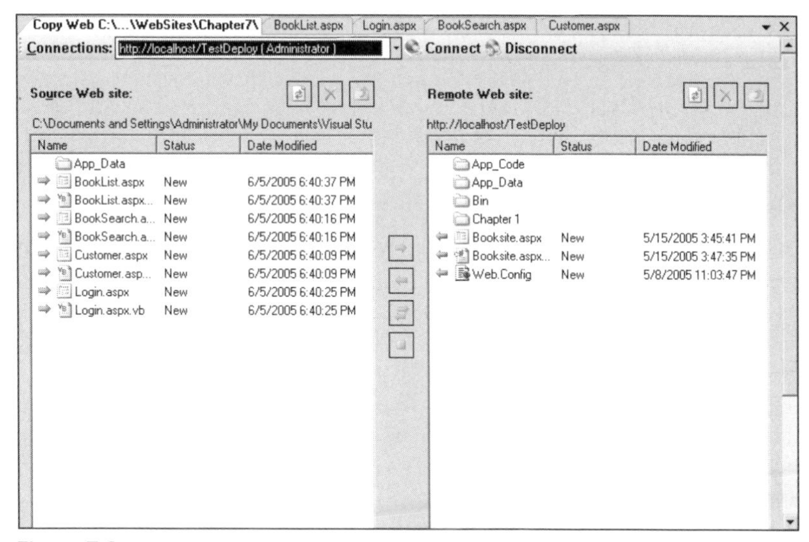

Figure 7-2

Figure 7-3

If you *don't* select the updateable option when using the Publish option, your ASCX file is compiled into the DLL with your codebehind file. In other words, the compiler adds code to the DLL file to dynamically generate the tags and text that are defined in your ASCX file. This process also adds a new file to the site's bin directory with the file extension *.compiled* (e.g., compiling a user control called MyControl without the updateable option will generate a file with a name similar to mycontrol.ascx.cdcab7d2.compiled). No ASCX file will be placed on the Web site.

The absence of the ASCX file is one of the differences between a user control and a WebForm. Even with the update ability turned off, publishing a WebForm to a site still generates an ASPX file. That ASPX file is, however, just a placeholder. The placeholder ASPX file is added to your site so that when users request some page by using the page's URL (such as http://www.myserver.com/MySite/default.aspx) some file exists to be the target of the request. Because ASCX files are not permitted to be requested from a browser, there's no need to generate a placeholder file for them.

Precompiling Your Site without Visual Studio 2005

If you are working outside of Visual Studio 2005, you can precompile your Web site by following these steps:

1. Change to the .NET Framework directory (typically C:\Windows\Microsoft.NET\Framework\2.0.*buildnumber*).
2. Call the ASP.NET compiler using the p option to specify the path to your Web site project, the v option (with a slash) to indicate that you want to precompile your application, and the destination to put the resulting precompiled site:

```
aspnet_compiler -p ProjectPath -v / destinationLocation
```

If you want to precompile your site but leave your ASCX files uncompiled (what Visual Studio 2005 refers to as having an updateable site), add the u option:

```
aspnet_compiler -p ProjectPath -v / destinationLocation -u
```

This example compiles the project in the C:\MyProjects\WebSites\MySite directory, places it in the C:\MyCompiledProjects\MySite directory, and makes it updateable:

```
aspnet_compiler -p C:\MyProjects\WebSites\MySite -v / C:\MyCompiledProjects\
MySite -u
```

Updating User Controls

If you pick the Copy Web site option to deploy your application, all of your user controls' source code will be available on your Web site. This format lets you update your user interface (in the ASCX file) and your program code (in the codebehind file) just by opening the files in Notepad (or any text editor), making your changes, and saving the result back to the Web site. The next time a page with your user control on it is requested, the new version of the code is used and your code is recompiled.

If you use the Publish menu choice and select the updateable option, a copy of the ASCX file is placed on the Web site and only your codebehind file is precompiled. Because your ASCX file is on the Web site as source code, you can still update the user interface for your control by opening the file in a text editor and changing it. However, because the codebehind file's source code has been compiled you have to use some development tool to update your user control's business logic.

There are limits to the changes that you can make to the ASCX file and still have it work successfully with the compiled code in the user control's DLL. For instance, deleting the tags that represent some object used by the code in the codebehind file will cause your WebForm to fail (for example, if you remove the <asp:TextBox> tags that define a TextBox object then your page will fail the next time that code in the codebehind file attempts to use that TextBox object).

Even if your Web site is deployed only with DLLs (for example, by publishing the Web site without the updateable option), you can still make changes to your user control without replacing the whole application. The updateable option refers only to the ability to make changes to the ASCX file in a text editor on the Web site. After you have published your site, you can still use Xcopy deployment to update your user controls. That is, you can still copy new versions of your ASCX file and DLLs to the Web site, replacing the existing versions. You can choose to replace the ASCX file, the codebehind file, the compiled DLL, or any combination of these, depending on how your site has been deployed.

As an example, you might have deployed your Web site with both the ASCX file and the codebehind file compiled into a DLL. You then discover that one of the user controls is displaying the company name spelled incorrectly. In this control, the company's name is set in an attribute in the ASCX file. Even though the user control is compiled into a single DLL, you can fix this problem without redeploying the whole site. You just need to fix the error in Visual Studio 2005, precompile the control, and then copy the precompiled DLL to the bin folder on the Web site, replacing the original version. Your new change will take effect the next time that a page with your user control is requested.

The precompiled versions of the files can be found in the folder specified in the MSBuild section of your project's Property Pages or in the Target location text box in the Publish Web Site dialog box.

If the Web site has been published with the updateable option (that is, a copy of the ASCX file and the codebehind file compiled as a DLL moved to the Web site), then, when you discover the company's name is incorrect, you have two ways to fix the problem:

- Open the ASCX file on the Web site with Notepad, correct the spelling, and save the ASCX file to the Web site.
- In Visual Studio 2005, open the ASCX file in the original project, make your change, and then copy the fixed version of the ASCX file to the Web site, replacing the original version.

But what if the company name is being set in the user control's codebehind file, which is compiled as a DLL? In that case, you have to fix the problem in the codebehind file, precompile the user control, and then copy the new version of the DLL to the bin folder on the Web site, replacing the original version.

Updating Custom Controls and Web Parts

The process of distributing and updating custom controls and Web Parts that are developed in a separate project from the Web site is simpler than distributing user controls simply because you have fewer options. Custom controls and Web Parts in a separate project must be compiled to a DLL before being distributed and the DLL must be placed in the Web site's bin folder.

For this section, I use the term "custom control" to refer to both custom controls and Web Parts.

When you add a reference to a custom control to your Web project, the DLL for the custom control is automatically copied to your project's directory. In addition to copying the DLL for the custom control, some additional files may also be added to your project (for example, an RESX file containing resources for the control, or a PDB file containing debugging information for the control). As Figure 7-4 shows, adding the custom control to the project in the figure results in at least two files — a DLL file and a PDB file — being added to the project (an XML file may also be added).

Figure 7-4

If you deploy your project by using the copy the Web site option, you don't need to copy all of the files that were added to your Web project when you added the custom control's reference to your project. For instance, you probably don't need to copy the PDB file containing debugging information for the control to the Web site. Only if the control uses resource files will you to need to copy those files — check the control's documentation to be sure. You will, of course, always need to copy the control's DLL.

Unfortunately, the Publish menu choice copies all of the custom control's files to the Web site. As a result, if you use the Publish option you may want to go to the Web site's bin folder after the site has been published and delete those files that aren't required. If you use the Copy Web Site option, you can choose which files you copy.

Updating a custom control on the Web site is straightforward:

- If the problem is with the control's code, replace the custom control's DLL file with a new version.
- If the problem is with one of the control's resource files, replace the resource file that has the problem.

If you create a deployment package that includes a custom control, you can select which files are distributed as part of the deployment package. Selecting the project's Primary Output adds just the control's DLL file to the deployment package.

Sharing Custom Controls and Web Parts

But what if you're creating a custom control that you want to share among several sites? In the case study introduced in Chapter 1, the company managed several sites (one for selling books, one for selling CDs, and so on). However, the customer information gathered on each site was the same. Rather than install a custom control for each site, it makes sense to install just a single copy of the control on the server to be used on all sites. To share a control among sites you must install it to the .NET Global Assembly Cache (GAC). There are a number of ways to do this, but the simplest is to create a setup and deployment project in Visual Studio 2005 and generate an MSI file that will install the control to the GAC.

User controls cannot be installed into the GAC.

Using a Setup and Deployment Project with Visual Studio 2005

To create a Setup and Deployment project in Visual Studio, select File ➪ Add ➪ New Project. In the Add Project dialog box that appears, open the Other Project Types section and select Setup and Deployment. From the list of projects, select Setup Project (see Figure 7-5).

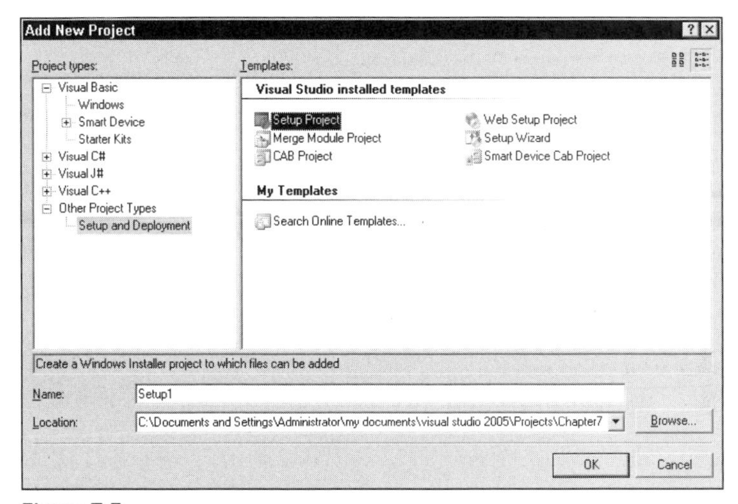

Figure 7-5

When your setup project is loaded, the first editor that displays shows a tree view of selected folders on the computer where the control is installed (see Figure 7-6).

To install your control into the GAC on the target computer you must add the GAC folder to the list of selected folders. To add the GAC folder to the list:

1. Right-click the line File System on Target Machine in the left-hand pane.
2. Highlight Add Special Folder on the pop-up menu (see Figure 7-7).
3. Select Global Assembly Cache Folder from the list that's displayed.

The GAC is added to the list of folders.

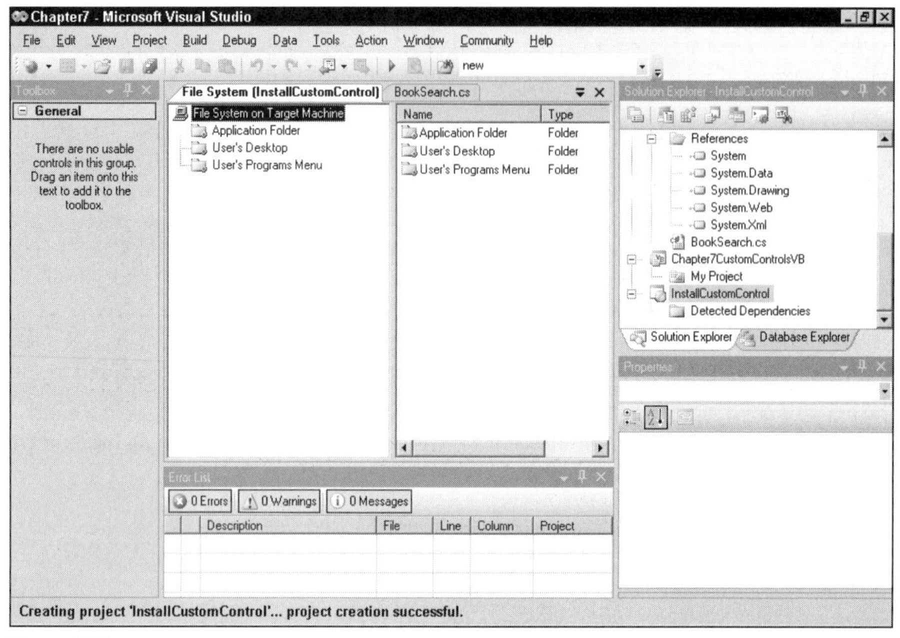

Figure 7-6

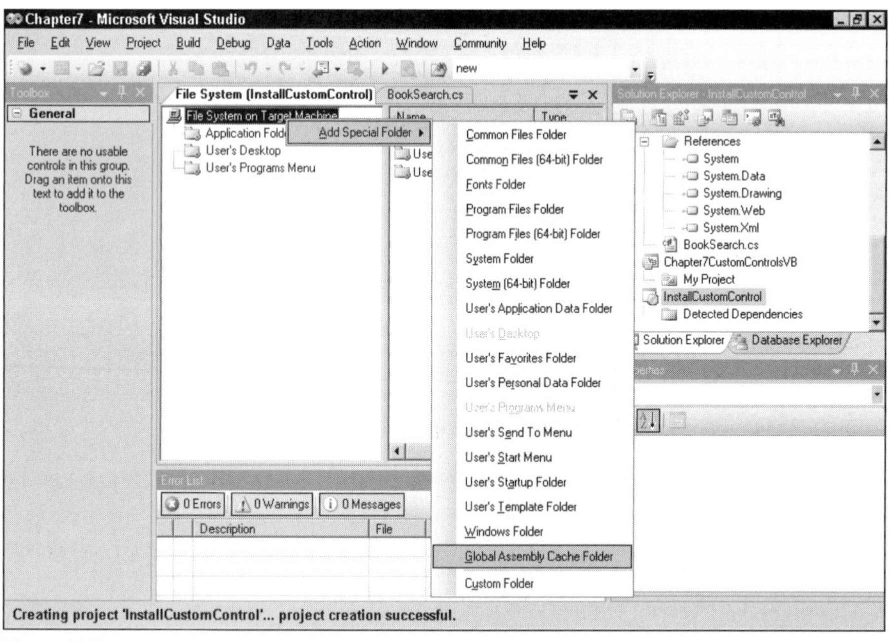

Figure 7-7

The target machine isn't just the Web server that your application will be running on. The target machine is also the computer of any other developer who might want to use your control to build her Web application.

With the GAC specified in your Setup project, you can add your control to the folder:

1. In Solution Explorer, right-click your setup project's name.
2. Select Add ➪ Project output from the popup menu. The Add Project Output Group dialog box appears.
3. In the drop-down list at the top of the dialog box, select your custom control project. (If your custom control project is the only other project in the solution, it will already be selected.)
4. From the list of items that you can install, select Primary output and click OK (see Figure 7-8).

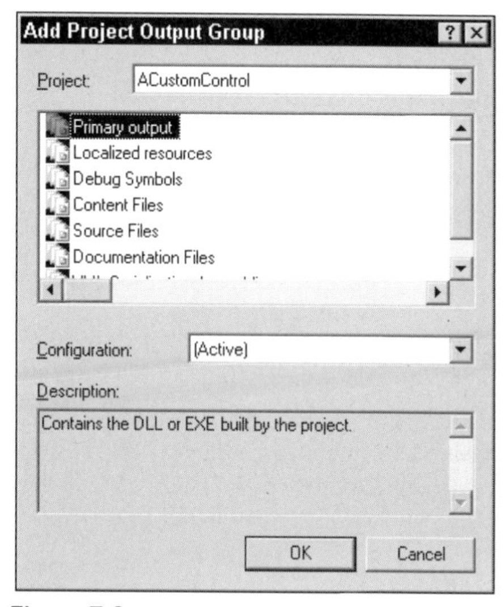

Figure 7-8

As discussed earlier in this chapter, you may need to select other options in this list. If, for instance, your custom control uses resource files, you'll need to add those resource files to your setup project also.

5. In Solution Explorer, select the entry Primary Output from *name of your custom control project.*
6. In the Property List for the Primary Output, click the Folder entry, which causes a builder button to appear in the property entry.
7. Clicking this button lets you select the Global Assembly Cache Folder you just added to your list of folders (see Figure 7-9).

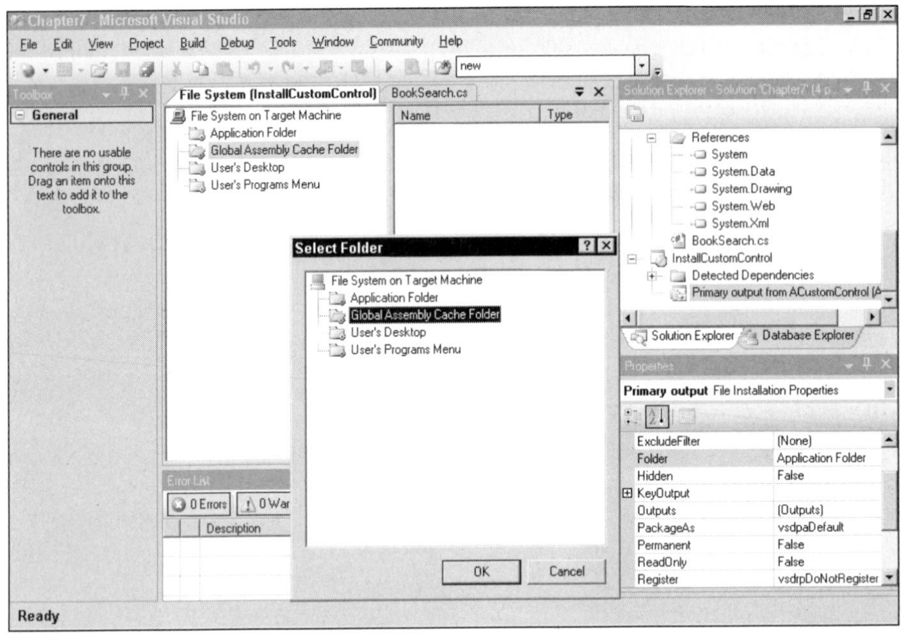

Figure 7-9

8. Click OK to return to Visual Studio 2005.

You can now select Build from the Build menu, and the MSI file for your setup project is generated. Developers who want to use your custom control can copy the MSI file to their computers and just double-click the file to install your control into their GAC. When developers right-click on their Toolbox and select Choose Items, they will find your control listed in the first tab of the Choose Toolbox Items: .NET Framework Components.

Using the gacutil Utility without Visual Studio 2005

If you're working without Visual Studio 2005, you can install your application in the GAC by using the gacutil utility. After compiling your application, open the Visual Studio command window or navigate to directory containing gactutil.exe. Then call the gacutil utility, passing any options that you need and the full path name to your DLL file. Using the /if option installs your control, overwriting any previous versions already in the GAC. This example installs MyControl.dll to the GAC:

```
gacutil /if MyControl.dll
```

Strong Names

You can also choose to precompile your Web site with a strong name by providing a key file containing a public/private key pair. Assigning a strong name to your compiled Web site ensures that the files cannot be changed by anyone who doesn't have access to the key you used to compile the file. Using strong naming doesn't prevent you from updating user controls on your site. However, the files that you use to update your user controls have been precompiled with the same key as the files already on the site. So, if you do assign a strong name to your Web site, you must make sure that anyone who is going to update the site has access to the key that you used (so that they can assign the same strong name to their updates). Alternatively, you must establish a process which ensures that the final compile of any updates to the site is made on a computer that has a copy of the key that you used.

There are a number of ways to create keys to use with your control. For this discussion, let's assume that you've generated a public/private key into a single file as described in the sidebar "Key Files."

Files that aren't precompiled (for example, the ASCX file of a user control when the site is published with the updateable option) aren't assigned strong names.

Compiling Your Web Site with a Strong Name

In Visual Studio 2005 you can precompile your Web site with a strong name by selecting the Enable strong naming option in the Publish Web Site dialog box and providing a key (the default is to precompile without a strong key). You also can change the default settings for strong naming for your Web site to compile your site with a strong name:

1. In Solution Explorer, right-click the Web site project name.
2. Select Property Pages from the pop-up menu.
3. Go to the MSBuild Options section.
4. Set your strong name options.

Compiling Controls with a Strong Name

If you precompile your Web site with a strong name, any custom controls used with the Web site must also be compiled with a strong name. You can add a strong name key file to your controls in the Property Pages for the control project, in the Signing section. At the bottom of the Signing page, check the Sign the assembly option, and browse to the key file using the <Browse. . .> option in the drop-down list. Figure 7-10 shows a project set to use the key file c:\MyKeys.snk.

You can also assign a key file using the AssemblyKeyFile attribute at the top of your code file. However, this attribute is deprecated in .NET 2.0 (in C#, using this attribute generates a design-time warning) and is supported in .NET 2.0 primarily for backward compatibility with earlier versions of C# and Visual Basic 2005. The AssemblyKeyFile attribute is being deprecated for a number of reasons, one of which relates to security: Using AssemblyKeyFile embedded the path name to the key file in the compiled DLL, which can make it easier for your key file to be found and copied.

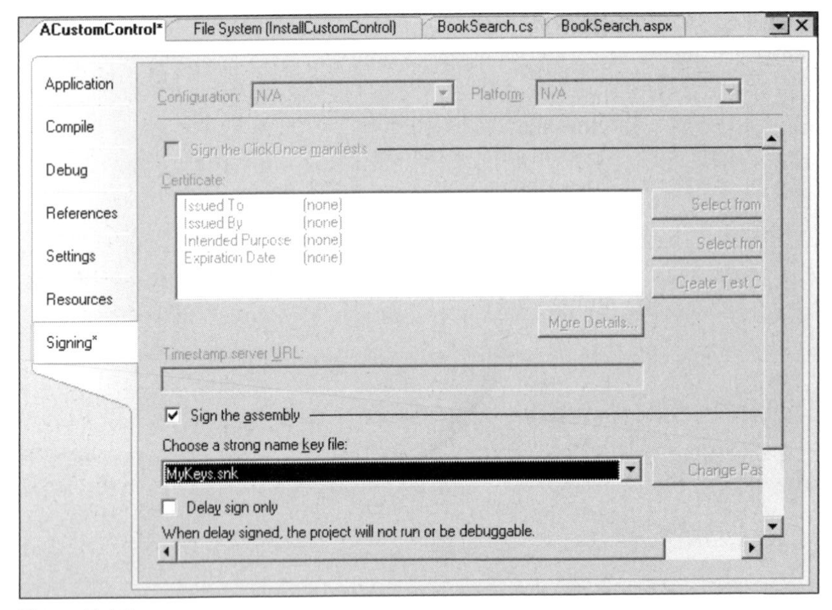

Figure 7-10

If you update a custom control file that has been compiled with a strong name, you must replace the file with a control that was compiled with the same key file.

Key Files

One way to use a strong name is to generate a key file containing both a public and private key. To generate a key file you have to step outside of Visual Studio 2005 and run a utility from the Windows command prompt. To do this:

1. Open the Visual Studio 2005 Command Prompt.
2. When the command window opens, use this command to create a key file called MyKey.snk with both a private and a public key:

   sn -k MyKeys.snk

3. Optionally, you can create a file with just the public key to distribute to others. This command pulls the public key from MyKeys.snk and puts it into a file called MyKey.snk:

   Sn -p MyKeys.snk MyKey.snk

4. Copy MyKey.snk to some location where you can find it again or add it to your project.

Managing Key Files Centrally

In some environments, key files are not distributed to individual programmers. Instead, key files are stored in a central location. In these environments, the programmer specifies which key file to use as part of creating the control, specifies that the key will be supplied later, and then compiles the control. Later in the release process, the person (or persons) responsible for the key files actually insert the key file into the compiled output as described later in this section.

For a custom control, you can delay inserting the key file by checking the Delay sign only option that appears below the text box for the key file name in the Signing section of the project's Property Pages. For a Web site, you can defer signing your Web site (and its user controls) by checking the Delay signing option in the Publish Web Site dialog box or in the Signing section of the Property Pages.

However, a problem remains: If you defer inserting keys into your custom control, then your compiled custom control doesn't have a key. By default, a Web site with a strong key successfully compiles only if all the custom controls have their key files inserted (checking the Delay signing option in the Web site's Publish Web Site dialog box doesn't affect this). If you attempt to precompile your Web site with a strong key and the Web site uses a custom control with a deferred key, the precompile fails. To compile a signed Web site with controls that have delayed signing, you must turn off the signature verification by passing the –Vr option to the compiler.

Because a site with delayed signing cannot be used — or tested — you shouldn't assign keys to your components until you're ready to release the site.

Before you can deploy or test your site the person responsible for managing the key files will have to insert the key into the compiled DLLs. This must also be done outside of Visual Studio 2005, using the sn utility with the -R option. This command inserts the keys in the MyKey.snk file into MyControl.dll:

```
sn -R MyControl.dll MyKey.snk
```

Using Strong Names Outside of Visual Studio 2005

If you are working outside of Visual Studio 2005, you use two options with aspnet_compiler to manage strong naming:

- **keyfile:** The physical path to a file containing a file containing your keys.
- **delaysign:** If present, this option delays key signing.

Licensing Your Control

If you intend to distribute your custom control to other developers, you may want to license your control. Licensing a control helps ensure that developers cannot use your control unless they also have a license from you for that control. Typically, a license prevents developers from using your control at design time. If a developer can successfully build a page with your control, he is automatically allowed to use it at run time. Licensing is not only a commercial matter (ensuring that you get paid for your work) but also a matter of liability. By managing licenses you are in a position to ensure that the people who use your control are using it for the purpose that you intended.

The licensing infrastructure in the .NET Framework does not make it impossible for someone to use your control without a license. It does, however, make it more difficult for someone to use your licensed control. The point of using a licensed control is to ensure that anyone who uses the control without your permission cannot do so accidentally. Someone using a licensed control without obtaining a license through whatever process you offer must make a conscious effort to circumvent your license.

The first step in licensing is to create a License object to handle the validation function. A License object inherits from System.ComponentModel.License and returns a string value from its LicenseKey property. It's up to you to decide how that LicenseKey is generated. (Reading the value from some text file that developers must have on their computer is one option; accessing a Web Service is another.) The License object must also implement a Dispose method, as this Visual Basic 2005 example does:

```
Public Class SampleLicense
    Inherits System.ComponentModel.License

   Public Overrides ReadOnly Property LicenseKey() As String
     Get
         Return "OK"
     End Get
   End Property

   Public Overrides Sub Dispose()

   End Sub

End Class
```

In C#:

```
public class SampleLicense : System.ComponentModel.License
{
 public override string LicenseKey
 {
   get
   {
    return "OK";
   }
 }

 public override void Dispose()
 {

 }
}
```

The next step is to create a LicenseProvider. This is a class that inherits from System.ComponentModel .LicenseProvider and implements the GetLicense method. This method must return your License object or throw a LicenseException error. The following Visual Basic 2005 code creates the License object just described and returns it. If the LicenseKey property doesn't have the correct value, the LicenseProvider throws a LicenseException error:

```
Public Class MyLicensingProvider
      Inherits System.ComponentModel.LicenseProvider

Public Overrides Function GetLicense( _
   ByVal context As System.ComponentModel.LicenseContext, _
   ByVal type As System.Type, _
   ByVal instance As Object, _
   ByVal allowExceptions As Boolean) As System.ComponentModel.License

Dim lic As New SampleLicense

  If lic.LicenseKey = "OK" Then
    Return lic
  Else
    If allowExceptions Then
        Throw New System.ComponentModel.LicenseException(type)
    End If
  End If

End Function

End Class
```

In C#, this minimal license provider looks like this:

```
public class MyLicensingProvider : System.ComponentModel.LicenseProvider
{
  public override System.ComponentModel.License
 GetLicense(System.ComponentModel.LicenseContext context,
            System.Type type,
            object instance,
            bool allowExceptions)
 {
  SampleLicense lic = new SampleLicense();

  if(lic.LicenseKey == "OK")
  {
   return lic;
  }
  else
  {
   if(allowExceptions)
   {
      throw new System.ComponentModel.LicenseException(type);
   }
  }
 }
```

The LicenseProvider is passed a number of parameters:

- **context:** This object provides information about the environment that the control is executing in. The UsageMode property in this object, for instance, allows you to check whether the control is in design or run time mode.
- **type:** The datatype of the control.
- **instance:** A reference to the control.
- **allowExceptions:** When set to True, it indicates that a LicenseException is to be thrown if licensing fails.

Now that your license and license provider are built, you need to attach the license provider to your custom control. Follow these steps:

1. Add the LicenseProviderAttribute to your class declaration and pass the attribute a reference to your license provider. This Visual Basic 2005 example uses the license provider created in the previous section:

```
<LicenseProvider(GetType(MyLicensingProvider)), _
  ToolboxData("<{0}:MyControl1 runat=server></{0}:MyControl1>")> _
Public Class MyControl
```

   In C#:

```
[LicenseProvider(typeof(MyLicensingProvider))]
[ToolboxData("<{0}:MyControl1 runat=server></{0}:MyControl1>")]
 public class MyControl
 {
```

2. In your control's constructor, your control should call the Validate method of the LicenseManager object (the LicenseManager automatically references the LicenseProvider referenced by the attribute on the class). If the licensing fails, a LicenseException error is raised, terminating the control's processing. This Visual Basic 2005 code demonstrates how the Validate method is used:

```
Dim lic As System.ComponentModel.License

Public Sub New()
  lic = LicenseManager.Validate(GetType(MyControl), Me)
End Sub
```

   In C#:

```
public class MyControl
{
 System.ComponentModel.License lic;

 public MyControl()
 {
   lic = LicenseManager.Validate(typeof(MyControl), this);
 }
}
```

3. In the Dispose method of your control, call the Dispose method of any license that you retrieved in your control's constructor and haven't already disposed:

```
Public Overloads Overrides Sub Dispose()
  If lic IsNot Nothing Then
    lic.Dispose()
    lic = Nothing
  End If
End Sub
```

In C#:

```
public override void Dispose()
 {
  if(lic != null)
  {
   lic.Dispose();
   lic = null;
  }
 }
```

In Step 2, instead of using the Validate method, you can call the IsValid method, passing the type of the custom control. The IsValid method doesn't throw an exception but returns False if licensing fails. This is a Visual Basic 2005 example of the IsValid property:

```
Public Sub New()

  If LicenseManager.IsValid(GetType(CustomControl1)) = False Then
    Throw New System.Exception("Licensing failed.")
  End If

End Sub
```

In C#:

```
public MyControl()
 {
  if(LicenseManager.IsValid(GetType(CustomControl1)) == false)
  {
   throw new System.Exception("Licensing failed.");
  }
 }
```

The LicenseManager object that you call from your control is created for you automatically, and handles calling the GetLicense method of your License provider either through the LicenseManager's Validate or IsValid method.

This is just the bare bones of implementing licensing. You can have your License object check the licensing source (a text file, a Web Service) for any set of conditions. You might specify usage counts in your licensing, or list which functions on the control are to be enabled. In your license provider, you can add additional methods or properties that interact with the license object to check for these conditions. Finally, in your custom control, you can call these methods and properties to determine what your control is allowed to do.

Rather than writing your own licensing provider, you can use the LicFileLicenseProvider, which is part of the .NET framework. You can create a licensing provider by inheriting from LicFileLicenseProvider and implementing only the functions that you want to override. If you have worked with licensing in COM applications, you'll find that the LicFileLicenseProvider supports the same functionality as ActiveX licensing.

Managing the Personalization Subsystem

When you deploy your Web Parts they will take advantage of the membership subsystem that is part of ASP.NET. The membership subsystem is automatically activated and a membership data store is set up in SQL Server Express the first time you add a WebPartManager to a Web page in Visual Studio 2005. However, to take full advantage of personalization, you need to provide a method for users to identify themselves so that the personalizations that users make are applied to them.

In addition, ASP.NET provides a mechanism for you to control where your personalization data is stored and allows you to switch between data stores from within your code. As you'll see, there are many aspects of personalization that you can control from your code. You can even set up your page so that changes made by one user (the system administrator, for instance) are applied to all users.

This all boils down to these three topics:

- Allowing users to identify themselves to the application
- Setting up personalization providers
- Managing personalization for your page

Identifying the User

ASP.NET 2.0 comes with a set of login controls that you can add to a Web page to create a login page. The key component is the Login control, which adds text boxes for entering the username and password, a button for logging in, and a checkbox for setting up a cookie that will let the user be remembered by the login process. Using these controls allows a user to log on to the site with a specific identity and be assigned the customizations that he has made.

In order for users to log on to the membership system, you need to set up those user identities for the site. You can add new users to your site from Visual Studio 2005 with these simple steps:

1. Select ASP.NET Configuration from the Website menu.
2. When the Web site administration page is displayed (see Figure 7-11), click the Security tab.
3. Click the Create user link to display the Create User form.

   If your Web site is using Windows authentication, you won't be able to create users and the Create User link won't appear. To stop using Windows authentication, click the Select authentication type link (see Figure 7-12), and then select the From the Internet option and click Done.
4. Enter the information required by the form and click the Create User button to create the user.

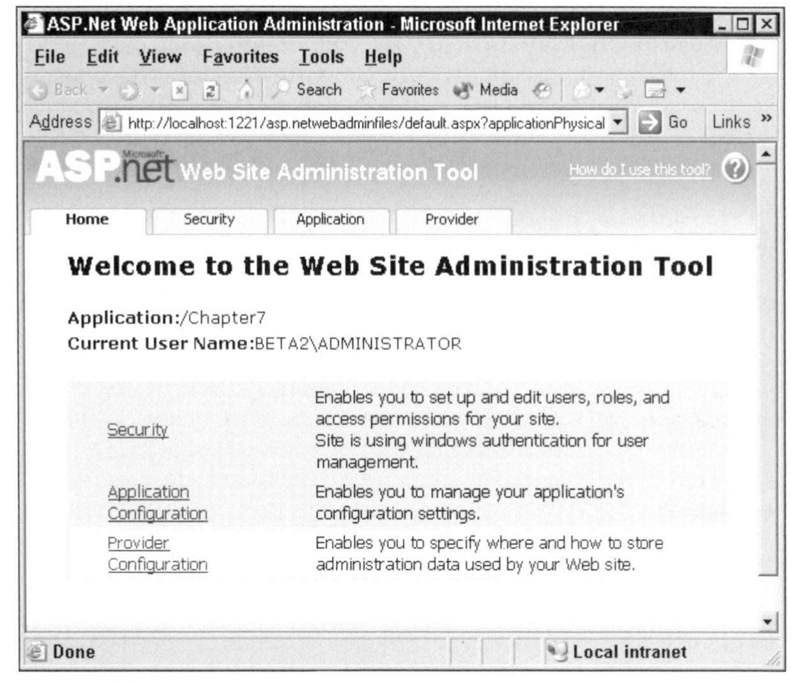

Figure 7-11

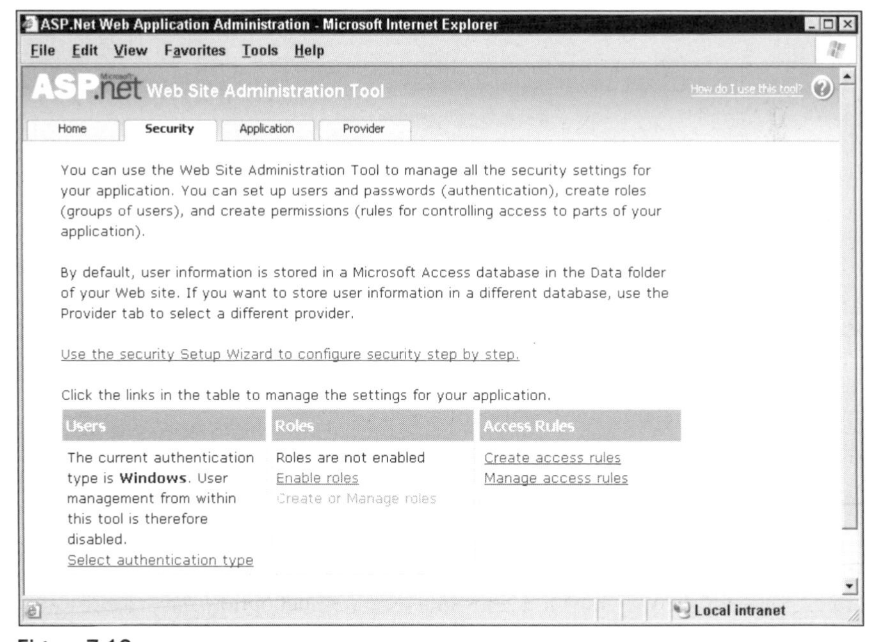

Figure 7-12

In most cases, you probably already have a list of users with usernames and passwords stored in some datastore (such as a database or Active Directory repository). In these situations, it makes more sense to create code that will read users from your datastore and add them to your site's membership system.

To create a user from your code, you can use the CreateUser method of the Membership object. This method can accept a number of parameters that set the user's name, password, e-mail address, and other items required on the Create User page of the administration pages. Some of the CreateUser methods accept a MembershipCreateStatus object while others do not. If you use one of the methods that doesn't accept a MembershipCreateStatus object, if the user isn't successfully created, a MembershipCreateUserException error is raised. On the other hand, if you use one of the methods that *does* accept a MembershipCreateStatus object, no error is thrown if the user isn't successfully created. Instead, the MembershipCreateStatus object passed as a parameter is updated with the result from attempting to create the user.

The following Visual Basic 2005 code uses one of the versions of the CreateUser methods that accepts a MembershipCreateStatus object. After calling the CreateUser method, the code tests the Membership-CreateStatus's value using one of the MembershipCreateStatus enumerated values to see if the attempt to create a user succeeded.

```
Dim nu As System.Web.Security.MembershipUser
Dim stat As System.Web.Security.MembershipCreateStatus

  nu = System.Web.Security.Membership.CreateUser("PeterVogel", "CMingus", _
       "peter.vogel@phvis.com", "Who is a bassist", "Charlie", True, stat)

  If stat <> MembershipCreateStatus.Success Then
    Me.txtError.Text = "User creation failed."
  End If
```

In C#:

```
System.Web.Security.MembershipUser nu;
System.Web.Security.MembershipCreateStatus stat;

  nu = System.Web.Security.Membership.CreateUser("PeterVogel", "CMingus",
       "peter.vogel@phvis.com", "Who is a bassist", "Charlie", true, out stat);

  if (stat != MembershipCreateStatus.Success){
    this.txtError.Text = "User creation failed.";
  }
```

While administering your users from Visual Studio 2005 makes sense for your test site, you will want to use a more sophisticated tool on your production Web site. You can:

- Add the ASP.NET user creation controls to your pages to give you (or your users) the ability to create users.
- Administer users with the Web administration pages for your Web site by selecting ASP.NET Configuration from the Website menu from within Visual Studio 2005. From outside Visual Studio 2005 or on a deployed site, use http:/hostname/sitename/WebAdmin.axd.
- Build user management pages with the Membership objects.

However, to test and develop your Web site, Visual Studio 2005 provides you with all the functionality that you need through the Website Administration tool.

Setting up Personalization Providers

The connection between your application, your personalization information, and the membership system is handled through personalization providers. Two personalization providers ship with the .NET Framework: one for working with Access (AspNetAccessPersonalizationProvider) and one for SQL Server (AspNetSqlPersonalizationProvider).

The provider being used is specified in the web.config file in the NET directory using <add> tags within the <personalization> element inside the <webParts> element. In the <add> tag you must specify the type of the provider, a name to refer to the provider, and a connection string to the provider. The web.config file for the computer is kept in the .NET directory and, by default is set to use the SQL Server provider.

In this example, the SQL Server provider is being used and the connection string is defined inside the connectionstrings element, which is also in the web.config file:

```
<connectionStrings>
  <add name="LocalSqlServer"
       connectionString="data source=.\SQLEXPRESS;Integrated Security=SSPI;
                 AttachDBFilename=|DataDirectory|aspnetdb.mdf;User Instance=true"
       providerName="System.Data.SqlClient"/>
</connectionStrings>
<system.web>
 <webParts>
  <personalization>
    <providers>
      <add name="AspNetSqlPersonalizationProvider"
           connectionStringName="LocalSqlServer"
           type="System.Web.UI.WebControls.WebParts.SqlPersonalizationProvider,
                 System.Web, Version=2.0.0.0, Culture=neutral,
                 PublicKeyToken=b03f5f7f11d50a3a" />
    </providers>
```

You can change this setting to use the AspNetAccessPersonalizationProvider for the computer that the web.config file is installed on with these tags:

```
  <add name="AspNetAccessPersonalizationProvider"
       connectionStringName="AccessDBpath"
       type="System.Web.UI.WebControls.WebParts.AccessPersonalizationProvider"/>
```

Inserting these tags in your application's web.config file allows you to set the personalization provider used just for your application.

You can also set up multiple providers within the <providers> tag. The defaultProvider attribute on the personalization element lets you specify which provider should be used automatically (later in this section you'll see how to switch between providers dynamically). This example defines both the Access and SQL providers but sets the Access provider as the default provider:

```
<personalization defaultProvider="AspNetAccessPersonalizationProvider">
  <providers>
    <add name="AspNetSqlPersonalizationProvider"
         connectionStringName="LocalSqlServer"
         type="System.Web.UI.WebControls.WebParts.SqlPersonalizationProvider,
                System.Web, Version=2.0.0.0, Culture=neutral,
                PublicKeyToken=b03f5f7f11d50a3a" />
    <add name="AspNetAccessPersonalizationProvider"
         connectionStringName="AccessDBpath"
         type="System.Web.UI.WebControls.WebParts.AccessPersonalizationProvider"/>
  </providers>
```

You can also set up several providers of the same type but with different connection strings. This enables you to switch between different SQL Server personalization datastores.

In Chapter 11, you see how you can manage personalization options from your code (including changing providers at run time).

Summary

This chapter covered the essential issues that appear after you've created your custom control. You learned how to:

- Configure your control project to support design time debugging
- Update user controls, custom controls, and Web Parts after you've deployed your Web site
- License your control to ensure that only developers you have provided a license to can use your control
- Manage the personalization and membership system that supports Web Parts

At this point, you're ready to write and deploy controls with all of the functionality of a custom control. However, you won't create a control for the fun of it—you want to use the control to support your application. So the next step is to look at how you can incorporate business functionality into your controls, which is the topic of the next chapter.

Part III

Extending Controls

8

Adding Business Functionality

Creating a custom control or a Web Part (or even a user control) isn't an end in itself—you create these components to have them perform some business functionality. As discussed in Chapter 1, the reason that you create a control is to build a reusable component containing logic that belongs in your application's user interface. At this point in the book, you can create a custom control or a Web Part and deploy it. You can use any of these controls on a page, as part of another user control, or as a Web Part. Now you want to go beyond simply implementing a control and add business-specific functionality: the methods, properties, and events that will support your application.

This chapter gives you the tools to extend your controls by adding code to support your application. Specifically, you can add code to perform these tasks:

- Associate code with the events fired by your constituent controls
- Add new methods and properties with business-specific logic
- Have your control fire events that allow developers to integrate their processing with your own code
- Trigger events that normally execute only at run time to also execute at design time
- Control what happens as new constituent controls are added or removed from your custom control

You've probably realized that you have many places to put your application code: the events for your control (such as Init and Load); methods and properties of the underlying object that you can override; custom methods and properties that you add to your control; and your control's constructor. So one of the decisions that you have to make is how to divide up all of the code that you want to put in your custom control, a process known as *factoring*.

The tools and code in this chapter can be used not only in custom controls and Web Parts but also in user controls.

Factoring Your Code

This chapter addresses three kinds of procedures that may seem very much alike:

- The methods discussed in previous chapters that were called automatically by ASP.NET (such as CreateChildControls, the control's constructor)
- The events that you're already familiar with from creating Web pages: Init, Load, PreRender
- The custom methods that you learn to create in this chapter

What are the differences between these three types of routines? What kind of code should you put in each type of routine? How do you decide what to put where? To put you in a position to factor your code, let's consider the problem in stages.

Any discussion of methods in the following section applies equally to properties, as you'll see in the section "Methods versus Properties."

Methods and Events

What are the differences between the two kinds of methods — the custom methods you'll see how to create in this chapter and the methods discussed in the previous chapters? The most important difference is what causes the methods to run:

- Your custom methods that you create are run only when called by some other set of code (this is also true of any custom properties that you create).
- The .NET Framework methods discussed in the previous chapters are called automatically by ASP.NET.

This distinction makes a difference to the kind of code that you should put in each kind of method.

The code that goes in the custom methods that you create should be code that the developer wants control over. Typically, this means the code that supports the *business functionality* implemented by your custom control. The developer using these methods wants to be able to control when they're run and in what order. On the other hand, the code that goes in the .NET Framework methods will be called automatically by .NET and, so, the developer can't decide whether to invoke those methods.

The Framework methods covered in the previous chapters are where you should put any code that you want to make sure actually executes. Further, those methods are designed to support specific purposes in creating a custom control. Think of these procedures as the utility code that makes your custom control work properly. The developer using your control needs these methods to run in order to have a usable control.

However, if these utility methods are run automatically, aren't events also just procedures that are run automatically? The answer, of course, is yes—code in events and code in the utility methods of the base object are both executed automatically. So that leads to the second question: What's the difference between the automatically run methods (such as CreateChildControls, Render, and so on) and the automatically triggered events (such as Init, Load, and so on)?

In many ways they are alike: Events fire at specific points in ASP.NET processing, causing the code in those events to execute; the methods described in the last chapter are invoked at specific points in ASP.NET processing, causing the code in those methods to execute. Like the utility methods that are called automatically, the events are where you should put code that the developer wants to run every time.

There is, however, an important *technical* distinction: Many event routines are not normally called in the design environment. Most of the utility methods discussed previously are called both at design time and run time. So the events are where you should place code that should run every time at run time but not at design time.

> *There are exceptions to the rule that in the design environment events won't execute, while the .NET Framework methods do execute. The Init event is invoked in the design environment, for instance, although the other events such as Load and PreRender are not; the CreateChildControls method is not always run in the design environment while other methods (for example, Render) are.*
>
> *In addition, in .NET events are often implemented as an overridable method that holds the code that raises the event. The convention in .NET is to have each event raised in a dedicated method. The naming convention for this method is the name of the event with "On" as a prefix.*
>
> *For instance, a control that fires an Init event will have an overridable method called OnInit. Rather than embed the code to raise an event in the midst of other processing code, the code to raise the event is segregated into the OnInit event. The control will, in the course of its processing, call the OnInit method to raise the event.*
>
> *Another convention is that the method that raises the event is passed a single parameter: the EventArgs object that the event then passes as one of its parameters. Going back to my original example, before raising the Init event the control's code would create an EventArgs object and then call the OnInit method passing the EventArgs object. The code in the OnInit event would raise the Init event, passing a reference to the control and the EventArgs object to whatever client was catching the Init event.*
>
> *In practical terms this means that you have a choice when you want to attach code to a particular event. You can, of course, put your code in an event handler as you do when catching a WebForm's Load or PreRender events. However, you can also override the On* method that raises the event and put your code in that routine. For instance, if you wanted to attach code to the Init event of the previous example, you could override the OnInit method. If you still wanted the Init method to fire you could then call the base object's OnInit method.*
>
> *You can also call the On* methods to trigger these events in the control. For our example, calling the control's OnInit method will cause the control to fire its Init event.*

There's also a key *conceptual* distinction between the control's events and the framework methods: The Framework methods described in the previous chapters should contain just the utility code necessary to generate your custom control's output both at design time and run time; the event routines are where you should put the logic related to supporting the application functionality. As examples of application processing, the event routines such as Init, Load, and the like are the places where you should put code that analyzes and responds to user input, that reads data from the database, or that responds to the changing environment of the host page. On the other hand, Framework methods (such as

CreateChildControls) should be used for the utility functions needed to support the control functioning on the page rather than for business-specific functionality. Many of the Framework methods (again, such as CreateChildControls) have names that suggest what the method should be used for — moving beyond that purpose may cause unexpected results.

In short, you should put your application code in the control events and put utility code in the Framework methods. However, that gives you two places to put application code. How do you decide between the two? The most important distinction between events and custom methods is one I made earlier: Events are run automatically at run time while your custom methods are called only when the host page calls them.

So you should divide your business application code between the code that must run on every page request, and the code that needs to run only when the host page needs it. The "must run" code goes into your events; the rest of the code goes into your custom methods.

To sum up: You have two rules to use when dividing your application code between the automatically run methods, the custom methods that you create, and events:

- Application code that you don't want to execute at design time goes into events and custom methods. At design time there is, for instance, no user input to analyze and the database that your custom control accesses may not be available, so attempting to perform those activities will cause your custom control to generate an error.
- Application code that you want to execute every time should go into events and the utility Framework methods. Code that the developer using your control will want to control should go into your custom methods. The code that should execute every time the page is requested should go in the control's events.

What ends up in the custom control events like Init, Load, and PreRender is the application code at the intersection of the previous two rules: Code that is intended to execute only at run time and that must execute every time.

The events that are built into your custom control (Init, Load, and so on) also mark where in the series of control events you should put your application code. For instance, developers expect that in the PreRender event of the host page they will have an opportunity to affect the output of their page — and the output of your custom control. If your custom control performs significant formatting activities after the PreRender event (such as in the Render method), developers lose control of their ability to control their page's appearance. The Render method should just output your control's HTML based on input from the developer made in the events leading up to the PreRender event. This is discussed in more detail later in this chapter in the section "The Life Cycle of a Custom Control."

The distinction between your custom control's "application code" and "utility code" doesn't follow any hard and fast rules: What one developer calls utility code, another may call application code. Just because reasonable people can disagree on the division doesn't mean that you shouldn't attempt to make the distinction. Much of this decision will be driven by how you expect developers to use your custom control.

Methods versus Properties

So how do you decide which of your code should go in a method and which should go in a property? The first thing to realize is that methods and properties perform essentially the same function: They package code up in your control so that developers can take advantage of that functionality. From the point of view of a developer creating a control, it really doesn't make much difference if that code is executed by calling a method, or by setting and reading a property. In many ways, it doesn't make that much difference to the developer using your control, either. The developer can as easily invoke the functionality of your control by calling methods or reading/setting those properties (unlike code in the control's events such as Init, which executes every time the page is requested).

As a result, deciding whether to put code in a property or a method is a design decision rather than a technical decision. The code to implement some particular functionality is roughly the same, whether it is in a method that passes parameters and returns values or is in a property that has its value set or read. When deciding between a method and a property, the question to ask is "What makes sense to the developer using the object?"

As an example, a Car object could have a property called Go that could be set to the name of the city that the car is to drive to. While that could be done, it probably wouldn't make much sense to a developer using this Car object. To help developers better understand the Car object, the object would be better designed if the functionality is either in a *method* called Go (that would be passed the name of the city) or in a *property* called Destination (that would be set to the name of the city to go to).

Three other rules for deciding between methods and properties are worth mentioning.

While you can create properties that accept multiple parameters, generally speaking developers are more comfortable using methods with multiple parameters than they are with using properties with multiple parameters.

Again, generally speaking, if the name of the routine is a noun, it should be implemented as a property; if the name of the routine is a verb, it should be implemented as a method. The reverse is also true: If you implement some functionality as a property, the routine should have a noun as its name; if you implement it as a method, the routine should use a verb as its name.

If you want to make functionality available at design time to the developer using your control, implementing the functionality as a property enables the user to access it through the Property List.

Adding properties and events is handled in custom controls and user controls as it is in other objects. So if you're familiar with these techniques, you can skip over the discussion of those topics later in this chapter.

The Role of Events

Events function differently than methods and properties. Methods and properties enable code in the host page to communicate with the control: The host page's code calls a method (or sets/gets a property) and some piece of code in your control executes. Events work in the other direction — they allow the control to communicate with the host page by causing some code in the host page to execute. Events are a way for your control to send messages to the host page.

In most classes used in the ASP.NET environment, events are less important than methods and properties because most objects execute only when some application calls some method or property on the object. When a method finishes executing, the method can return a value (if the method is implemented as a function) or update one of the method's parameters. Code can retrieve data from a property just by reading the property.

When an event executes as part of the host page calling a method or working with a property, the event can provide a service that returning a value or setting a parameter cannot. Events provide a way for:

- The code in the control to notify the host page that some condition has occurred and pass information about that condition
- The host page to determine how the condition is to be handled

As an example of when events can be useful, consider a method or property on a control that accesses a database. When the code in the control finds that the database is closed (or is unable to connect to the database for some other reason), the code can raise an event. The host page can catch that event in order to have some host-page code execute when the database is found to be closed.

For this scenario, you have some options other than raising an event. For instance, if the method is a function, your method could return a condition code that describes what happened while the routine was executing. If the method is defined as a subroutine, you can still return the condition code by placing the condition code in one of the routine's parameters. Another option is to raise an error that the host page can catch.

All of these options have a significant limitation: The method in your control has to stop executing and return processing to the host page in order to communicate the condition (database closed, for instance). The method in your control cannot accept input from the host page and use that to continue processing.

This highlights what events can do that your other options cannot: Events allow the host page to integrate its processing with the routine. Processing looks like this:

1. The host page calls the method (or sets or reads the property).
2. The routine finds that the database is closed.
3. The routine fires an event, passing whatever data seems appropriate in the second parameter of the event. As an example, the routine might return the connection string it was using to open the database.
4. The host page's event routine starts executing.
5. The host page can take whatever action seems appropriate based on the data passed from the event. The host page can even modify the data sent as part of the event to return a value that indicates how the method should handle the problem.
6. The host page's event routine finishes.
7. The code in the control resumes executing immediately after the line of code that raised the event. The code in the control can examine the data set by the host page and use that to decide what to do next.

To put it another way: events are .NET's way for a control to initiate a conversation with its host page.

Effectively, events give the host page an opportunity to affect how the method handles the condition. In the case of the closed database, the event that is fired might pass the current connection string to the host page as part of the event. The host page can then take one of three actions:

- Update the connection string with a new connection string, effectively telling the control to try another database
- Leave the connection string alone, telling the control to try the database again
- Set the connection string to nothing, telling the control to terminate database access

By using an event, you provide more flexibility to developers using your control.

When designing events, you need to recognize that the host page is not obliged to write code to respond to the events that you fire. When designing an event, you should consider how you will deal with a situation in which the host page doesn't handle your event. In the previous example, for instance, the event is written so that if the connection string is unchanged after firing the event, the control should attempt the open the database again. If the host page doesn't handle the event, the connection string will be unchanged after the event fires and the control will attempt to open the database again. Since nothing has changed since the first, failed attempt, this is wasted time. A better design might be to have the host page set a condition code that indicates what the control should do rather than try to use the state of the connection code as a signaling device.

Using Events in the Web Environment

In the Web environment, events have a special purpose that isn't duplicated in other environments: Events provide a way for your control to notify the server-side host of changes that were made in the browser. Non–Web development environments (such as Windows forms applications) don't need this facility because the code continuously interacts with the user. In the Web environment, however, the user interacts with a page in the Web browser, which is inaccessible to the server-side code. Code in your control, however, can check for changes made in the browser and report those changes to the host page's server-side code.

After the host page finishes calling events and setting or reading properties in a control, the control's HTML and text is added to the page and the page is sent to the browser. Eventually, the browser requests the host page and data from the page returned to the browser. Your control can then analyze the data within its constituent controls and determine what changes took place in the browser while the page was displayed to the user. If your control added client-side code to the page, that client-side code may have executed and generated important data that was returned to the server.

You could communicate the results of your code's analysis of its data by creating properties whose values change, depending on what happened in the browser. However, this forces the developer to write code that checks those properties to determine what happened in the browser. If nothing else, this code is inefficient because the host page's code must execute even when no change took place in the browser.

For instance, a control that accepted customer address information could have properties called IsStreetChanged, IsPostalCodeChanged, IsCityChanged, and so on. The host page's code would have to check all of those properties on every request to determine which data had changed.

However, if your control's code determines that something has changed you can use an event to signal to the host page code that something has happened. The host page can then, in its event handling code, check any relevant properties on your control to get the information returned from the browser. In this scenario, events are used to report to the host page that something took place in the browser, based on the information returned from the browser.

This kind of analysis is exactly what happens when a text box fires a TextChanged event or a button fires a Click event: by analyzing the data returned from the browser, controls notify the host page (by raising events) that something has changed.

Events are supported in custom controls as they are in other objects but with a new ability: You can bubble events from constituent controls up to your custom controls, as discussed later in this chapter.

The Life Cycle of a Custom Control

Knowing what the events are in the life cycle of your custom control, the host page, and the constituent controls is critical to deciding where you should put your application code. You also need to know what resources are available at each event and when those events fire relative to each other. This section shows you how these three sets of events integrate.

The Custom Control's Events

The events in the life cycle of the custom control, in the order that they fire, are:

- **Init:** Indicates that the custom control has been loaded but no ASP.NET processing has taken place. For instance, at the Init event, controls will not have been loaded with the values sent back to the server from the client.
- **Load:** Initial processing of the host page has taken place. For instance, any values sent back to the server from the client will have been loaded into the custom control's constituent controls by the time this event fires. In addition, property values for the custom control and the constituent controls will have been set to their default values or to values stored in the ViewState. If, during the Init event, you had set any properties for any constituent controls, those changes may have been overwritten by post–Init processing.
- **PreRender:** This event is fired just before ASP.NET prepares the custom control to be returned to the browser. After this event, ASP.NET calls the Render* methods on your custom control.
- **Unload:** Indicates that the custom control has been sent to the browser and that ASP.NET is about to complete processing of the custom control.
- **Disposed:** The custom control is about to be removed from memory. This occurs during .NET garbage collection and, as a result, may happen some time after the Unload event has fired. Because of the uncertainty of when this event will execute, it should generally be avoided and will be ignored for the rest of this book.

The Host Page's Events

The custom control's events fit within the life cycle of the host page. The host page's events are fired by the Page object that contains your control instance. The Page object in ASP.NET 2.0 has several more events than a custom control does: What is one event in the custom control can be several events in the Page. For instance, while the custom control has an Init event, the Page has a PreInit event, an Init event, and an InitComplete event. In these cases, the custom control's equivalent event happens in between the related multiple events for the page. For instance, the custom control's Render event happens between the Page's PreRender and PreRenderComplete events.

At the start of the host page's life cycle are the PreInit, Init, and InitComplete events. Changes made to the controls on the page (including changes to the custom control) during the invocation of these events may be overwritten by the ASP.NET standard processing. For instance, in the PreInit event, code on the host page will have access to the WebPartZone but not to the custom controls within the zone.

At the end of the host page's life cycle, the custom control's Render method executes *after* the host page's PreRender and PreRenderComplete events. The sequence of the Render events is

- Page PreRender
- Page PreRenderComplete
- Control Render

This sequence gives code in the host page's PreRender event a last chance to manipulate the methods and properties of your custom control before your custom control renders itself.

Constituent Control Events

Constituent controls in the custom control fire the same events that the custom control does (Init, Load, and so on). These events are triggered by the creation of the constituent controls. While not an event, the control's constructor is also part of this process and executes before any of the constituent control's events.

A constituent control's Init event is called when the control is created by the custom control.

Normally, the constituent control's Load event fires when the constituent control is added to the custom control's Controls collection. Therefore, assuming that you create your constituent controls in the custom control's CreateChildControls method, the constituent control's constructor, Init, and Load events will execute during the custom control's CreateChildControls method. Here's a typical CreateChildControls method in Visual Basic 2005 with the constituent control's events marked:

```
Dim btn As System.Web.UI.WebControls.Button
Dim txt As System.Web.UI.WebControls.TextBox

btn = New System.Web.UI.WebControls.Button     'Button's constructor runs
                                               'Button's Init event fires
txt = New System.Web.UI.WebControls.TextBox    'TextBox's constructor runs
                                               'TextBox's Init event fires

Me.Controls.Add(btn)                           'Button's Load event fires

Me.Controls.Add(txt)                           'TextBox's Load event fires
```

In C#:

```
System.Web.UI.WebControls.Button btn;
System.Web.UI.WebControls.TextBox txt;

btn = new System.Web.UI.WebControls.Button();  //Button's constructor runs
                                                //Button's Init event runs
txt = new System.Web.UI.WebControls.TextBox(); //TextBox's constructor runs
                                                //TextBox's Init event runs

this.Controls.Add(btn);                         //Button's Load event runs

this.Controls.Add(txt);                         //TextBox's Load event runs
```

After a control is added to the Controls collection of the host control, ASP.NET keeps the events for the constituent controls synchronized with the host control. ASP.NET's goal is to have the host control and the constituent controls all at the same point in their event life cycle. For instance, at the moment when the constituent control is added to the host control's Controls collection, if the *host* control has fired its Init, Load, and PreRender events, then ASP.NET fires the *constituent* control's Init, Load, and PreRender events one after the other.

The exception to this pattern is when a page is requested because of some action inside the custom control (such as the user clicking a submit button that's a constituent control of the custom control). In that scenario, the constituent control's Load event fires later in the sequence, *after* the host control's Load event.

In addition to the standard events, a constituent control may fire what are referred to as *client-side notification events*. Client-side notification events are fired at the server when the user has performed some activity with the control when it was displayed in the browser. Common examples include the Click event for a button (indicating the user clicked the button when the page was displayed in the browser to submit the page's data to the server) and the TextChanged event for a text box (indicating that the text sent back to the server was different from the text sent to the browser). These client-side notification events fire at the server between the custom control's Load and the Page's LoadComplete events. This means that you can assume that constituent controls have performed all of their processing, except for any PreRender processing, by the time that the host page finishes loading.

Your custom control may also include, as constituent controls, Validator controls for editing user input. While the Validator controls don't fire server-side events, validation does execute at a specific point in the custom control's life cycle: just before the Click event of the button that triggered sending data back to the server, regardless of whether the button is in the custom control (a constituent control) or on the host page (a child control). If no button was clicked to trigger processing (for example, if the page was submitted through client-side code), validation is performed before the Page's PreRender event. This timing is important because you can't check a Validator control's IsValid property until after validation has occurred.

If you want to check the Validator control's IsValid property before validation normally occurs, you can force validation to occur by calling the Validator's Validate method.

Handling Events

Because of the lack of user intervention, server-side processing is really a kind of batch processing: ASP.NET processes all the events one after another. From that point of view, there are only a few key facts to remember about the custom control's life cycle:

- Information entered by the user into controls in the browser isn't available until the Load event.
- Code that is intended to change the appearance of the page must be in either the PreRender event or one of the events that precedes it.
- Values updated prior to the DataBinding event may be overwritten by the results of DataBinding.
- Client-side notification events cannot be assumed to fire in any particular order.

As a result, barring some compelling reason to put the code elsewhere (for instance, the code is part of creating constituent controls and should go in the CreateChildControls method, or the code should not be run automatically and should go in a custom method), you should put your custom control's code in the PreRender event. In the PreRender event, you are guaranteed that all user input is present, that the results of DataBinding are complete, and that the IsValid property on any validators has been updated. As an example of an exception to this rule, any code required to initialize the custom control and its constituent controls (and that should execute only at run time) should go in the custom control's Load event or CreateChildControls method.

Because the host page's PreRender method runs before the custom control's Render method, code in your custom control's Render method can overwrite changes made by host page code in the host page's PreRender event. It's your responsibility as a custom control developer to make sure that your Render method propagates, rather than steamrolls over, the work done by code in the host page's PreRender event.

The lack of a guaranteed position in the event sequence for the DataBinding event means that if, for instance, you update a constituent control in the custom control's Load event and the DataBinding event fires after your Load event, your changes may be overwritten by the DataBinding process.

Approaching the problem from the other direction, if you update some control in the control's Load event, you may be overwriting the results of a DataBinding event that occurred before the Load event. To handle this problem, you should set a Boolean variable in the DataBinding event to indicate that databinding has occurred. As discussed in Chapter 9, specific methods are provided by the WebControl class to support databinding. However, you may have code related to or dependent on databinding that you don't want to put in that event. For instance, displaying default values when databinding doesn't occur is one example of databinding-related code. Because this code should execute only when databinding *doesn't* occur, you can't put that code in the custom control's databinding methods. You can use one of two tactics for dealing with your databinding-related code:

- Put databinding-related code in the DataBinding event, making the code independent of any other event. You must then check the Boolean variable set in the DataBinding event in any other routine to make sure that you don't overwrite the results of the DataBinding event.
- Put your databinding-related code in the PreRender event but execute the code only if the Boolean variable has been set, indicating that the DataBinding event was actually called. With all of your code in the PreRender event, you can now control the order that your event-related code executes in.

Following the first strategy gives you a code structure like this in Visual Basic 2005:

```
Private bolDataBound As Boolean = False

Public Sub Page_Load()
   If bolDataBound = False Then 'only process if databinding hasn't loaded data
       ...initialization code...
 End if
End Sub

Public Sub Page_DataBind(...)
   bolDataBound = True
End Sub

Public Sub Page_PreRender (...)

   If bolDataBound = False Then 'only process if databinding hasn't loaded data
       ...most of the custom control code...
   End if

End Sub
```

In C#, the equivalent code looks like this:

```
Boolean bolDataBound = false;

public sub Page_Load()
   {
    if (bolDataBound = false) //only process if databinding hasn't loaded data
  {
           ...initialization code...
  }
  }

public sub Page_DataBind(...)
   {
    bolDataBound = True
}

public sub Page_PreRender (...)
{
   if (bolDataBound = False) //only process if databinding hasn't loaded data
   {
   }
  }
```

Running Events at Design Time

By calling the OnInit, OnDataBinding, OnPreRender, and OnUnload methods, you can trigger the custom control's Init, DataBinding, PreRender, and Unload events. For instance, calling the OnPreRender method causes your custom control's PreRender routine to run even at design time. At run time, even if the PreRender event is run in response to calling the OnPreRender method, the PreRender event will still run as it would in the normal sequence of events, so the result of calling the OnPreRender method at run time is to cause the PreRender event to run twice.

The On* methods must be passed an EventArgs object so the relevant Visual Basic .NET code to call the OnPreRender method to trigger the PreRender event looks like this:

```
Dim e As New EventArgs
Me.OnPreRender(e)
```

In C#, the code looks like this:

```
EventArgs e = new EventArgs();
this.OnPreRender(e);
```

Because these events are also visible to code in the host page, calling the OnPreRender method at run time also causes any code on the host page that's tied to your custom control's PreRender event to run twice.

Adding Code to Constituent Controls

If the user changes the text in a text box that you've added to your custom control, you may want to have some code run in your custom control to respond to the text box's TextChanged event. While adding code to the events fired by your custom control or user control is easy (just wire up the event and put the code in the appropriate event routine), how do you add code to the events fired by your constituent controls? For instance, after adding constituent controls to your custom control, you'll probably want to associate some default code with the constituent control's Client-side notification events.

For user controls, adding code to the events for the constituent controls that you've dragged onto the page is easy—it's the same process that you use when creating a Web page. However, if you're creating a custom control or if you've added controls to the Controls collection of a user control, the process isn't as obvious. Those are the scenarios addressed in this section.

Creating the Routine

The first step is to add the routine that you want to have run to your custom control. The following routine is intended to be called when a text box has its TextChanged event fired. The TextChanged event is passed a generic Object (normally called "sender"), and an EventArgs object (normally called "e"). As a result, the routine (here called UpdateTextBox) must be declared with matching parameters:

```
Sub UpdateTextBox(ByVal sender As Object, ByVal e As EventArgs)

End Sub
```

In C#, the routine is defined like this:

```
public void UpdateTextBox(object sender, EventArgs e)
{

}
```

Within the routine, you can use the sender parameter to reference the control that called the routine. Because the sender parameter is declared as type Object, this code needs to convert that reference to a text box:

```
Sub UpdateTextBox(ByVal sender As Object, ByVal e As EventArgs)
Dim txt As WebControls.TextBox

txt = CType(sender, WebControls.TextBox)
   If txt.Text <> "Hello, World" Then
      ...code to validate a changed control...
   End If

End Sub
```

In C#, the routine looks like this:

```
public void UpdateTextBox(object sender, EventArgs e)
{
   WebControls.TextBox txt;

   txt = (WebControls.TextBox) sender;

   if(txt.Text != "Hello, World")
   {
      ...code to validate a changed control...
   }
}
```

Wiring the Routine to the Control

The final step is to attach the UpdateTextBox routine to the text box's TextChanged event. In Visual Basic 2005, the AddHandler associates an event for an object with an EventHandler object. In turn, the EventHandler points to some routine to be run. When you create the EventHandler object, you pass the address of the routine in the custom control to be run when the event is fired.

Because the scenarios that are being covered are the ones where the custom control isn't on a design surface, the text box can't be referred to directly (either with Me.TextBox1 in Visual Basic 2005 or this.TextBox1 in C#). To add an event routine to your constituent controls, you have to get the reference to the constituent yourself.

If you're doing this in the CreateChildControls event, you have a reference to the control available to you. If you're adding event code to a constituent control at some point in the custom control's processing where you don't have a reference to the constituent control, you can retrieve a reference to the control from the WebControl object's Controls collection using the FindControl method (discussed in Chapter 3).

Added to the CreateChildControls routine, the Visual Basic 2005 code to connect the text box's TextChanged event to the UpdateTextBox routine looks like this:

```
Dim txt As New System.Web.UI.WebControls.TextBox
Dim ev As EventHandler

txt.Text = "Hello, World"
```

```
    txt.ID = "txtInput"

    ev = New EventHandler(AddressOf UpdateTextBox)
    AddHandler txt.TextChanged, ev

     Me.Controls.Add(txt)
```

In C#, the equivalent operation is handled by assigning a new EventHandler to the event for the object by using the += operator:

```
    System.Web.UI.WebControls.TextBox txt;
    EventHandler ev;

    txt = new System.Web.UI.WebControls.TextBox;

    txt.Text = "Hello, World";
    txt.ID = "txtInput";

    txt.Click += new System.EventHandler(this.UpdateTextBox);

     this.Controls.Add(txt);
```

Creating Custom Methods, Properties, and Events

As described in Chapter 3, the first step in customizing a control consists of overriding the base methods, properties, and events provided by whatever object that you've inherited from. The second step is to add code to the events that make up the control's life cycle.

However, those are only the first steps in customizing your object. You should override the base methods of the inherited object to provide only the functionality necessary to create a control that can work in the ASP.NET environment. And adding code to the control's events allows you to execute code only at specific moments in the control's life cycle. Further, since this code will run every time that the host page loads the control, it can't be controlled by the host page. As discussed at the start of this chapter, code in the events and base methods often is utility code. For your control to be useful in your application, you need to add some functionality that is required by your application, that goes beyond the utility features of an ASP.NET control, and that is under the control of the host page. This means adding new methods, properties, and events to your control.

Access Levels

When you add a method, property, or event to your control, you need to decide what other components can access your code. You can declare a function, subroutine, property, or event in your custom control with five different types of access. However, for routines that you want to be available from the host page, you really have only one choice: you need to use Public (or omit any access information when declaring a subroutine or function — the default is Public). The following table lists the keywords that control access and what their effect is.

Visual Basic 2005	C#	Can Be Called from the Host Page?	What Routines Can Call the Method?
Public	Public	Yes	Any other routine
Protected	Protected	No	Routines in the Class module or in classes that inherit from this class
Friend	Internal	No	Routines in the same assembly/DLL/Project
Protected Friend	Protected internal	No	Can be called from routines in inherited classes, in the same class, and in the same assembly
Private	Private	No	Accessible only from within its module, class, or structure

Custom Properties

Defining properties is only slightly more complicated than defining methods. A property consists of two parts: code to execute when the property is read (the "get" routine) and code to execute when the property is changed (the "set" routine). In the get portion, the property routine acts like a function that's returning a value; in the set portion, the property routine acts like a subroutine that is being passed a value.

The properties on your control can be read or set in a variety of ways, all of which cause the code in your property routine to execute. Here are some examples:

- At run time, code in the host page for your control can read or change the property's value.
- At design time, a developer can change the value of your property by updating the Property List in Visual Studio 2005.
- At run time, if your control supports personalization, a user may set the property by using one of the custom control editors.

The following code shows a property called Text written in Visual Basic 2005 that accepts or returns a string value. When the property is set to some string, the value is passed into the routine using the value parameter, which the code then moves into a module level variable called strText. When the property is read, the code returns the value in the module level variable:

```
Dim strText As String

Property Text() As String

    Get
```

```
        Return strText
    End Get

    Set(ByVal value As String)
        value = strText
   End Set

End Property
```

In C#, the equivalent code looks like this:

```
private string strText;

 public string Text
 {
  get
  {
   return strText;
  }

  set
  {
   strText = value;
  }
}
```

The code to use this property from the hosting page looks like this in Visual Basic 2005:

```
Me.MyControl.Text = "Hello, World"
Me.TextBox1.Text = Me.MyControl.Text
```

In C#:

```
this.MyControl.Text = "Hello, World";
this.TextBox1.Text = this.MyControl.Text;
```

Just like methods, you must declare property routines as Public in order for them to be available to the host page.

ReadOnly Properties

To create a read-only property, you need to omit only the set portion. However, in Visual Basic 2005 you must also indicate on your property's declaration that your property is read-only by using the ReadOnly keyword. No keyword is required in C# for a property without a set portion.

Should you ever need to create a write-only property, omit the get portion and, in Visual Basic 2005, add the WriteOnly keyword to the property declaration.

Here's a read-only property that returns a control's security key:

```
ReadOnly Property SecurityKey() As Guid

    Get
        Return strText
    End Get

End Property
```

In C#, the equivalent code looks like this:

```
public Guid SecurityKey
{
 get
 {
   return strText;
 }
}
```

Indexed Properties

The typical property definition has no parameters for the get portion and one for the set portion. While it's not a common occurrence, you can add parameters to both the get and set portions of your property. The result is a property that, to the developer, looks like an array or a collection (that is, a property that requires an index to get or set the value).

> **Properties that accept parameters cannot be enabled for customization with the WebBrowsable and Personalizable attributes.**

To define a property that requires an index, just add parameters to the get and set portions of the property as in this Visual Basic 2005 code:

```
Dim strTextStrings(5) As String

Property TextStrings(ByVal Position As Integer) As String

  Get
     Return strTextStrings(Position)
  End Get

  Set(ByVal value As String)
     value = strTextStrings(Position)
  End Set

End Property
```

In C#, the equivalent code looks like this:

```
private string[5] strTextStrings;

 public string[] this[int Position]
 {
  get
  {
   return strTextStrings[Position];
  }

  set
  {
   strTextStrings[Position] = value;
  }
}
```

> **There are several important restrictions on using index properties in C#. In C#, you're restricted to having one indexed property (called an *indexer*) per class. As the example the routine doesn't have a real name (instead, the *this* keyword is used).**

This Visual Basic 2005 code demonstrates how the TextStrings property can be used with an index from code on the host page:

```
Me.MyControl.TextStrings(1) = "Hello, World"
Me.TextBox1.Text = Me.MyControl.TextStrings(1)
```

In C#, because there is only one indexer per object, the index is used with the reference to the object rather than with a property:

```
this.MyControl[1] = "Hello, World";
this.TextBox1.Text = this.MyControl [1];
```

Referencing Other Objects by Id

Some properties on your control may reference other objects by returning the ID of the object. As an example, you might have a custom control that returns the ID property of a Customer object rather than returning the Customer object itself. By using the IdReferenceProperty on your property and specifying the type of the object whose ID you are returning, you can configure the property to allow designers and other components to examine properties of the underlying object at design time or run time.

This Visual Basic 2005 example returns the ID property of a Customer object by using the IdReferenceProperty to tie the property to the Customer object:

```
<IDReferenceProperty(GetType(Customer))> _
Public ReadOnly Property CustomerId() As String
  Get
   Dim cust As New Customer
   Return cust.Id
  End Get
End Property
```

In C#:

```
[IDReferenceProperty(typeof(Customer))]
public string CustomerId
{
 get
 {
  Customer cust = new Customer();
  return cust.Id;
 }
}
```

Flagging a property with the IDReferenceProperty signals to .NET components that this is a property that returns an ID. Editors, for instance, can use this feature to provide lists of IDs.

Passing to the attribute the type of the object whose ID property is being returned provides additional functionality. For instance, it allows you to write general purpose code that can retrieve the type of the object being returned. To do that you must first call the GetAttributes method of the TypeDescriptor object and pass a reference to your control to get a collection of the attributes applied to your control. You can then retrieve the IDReferencePropertyAttribute from the Attributes collection by passing the type of IDReferencePropertyAttribute to the collection. Having retrieved the IDReferencePropertyAttribute, you can retrieve the type of the underlying object (in this case, the Customer object) using the attribute's ReferencedControlType property. This Visual Basic 2005 code demonstrates the technique:

```
Dim atts As System.ComponentModel.AttributeCollection
Dim rf As IDReferencePropertyAttribute
Dim typ As Type

  atts = TypeDescriptor.GetAttributes(Me)
  rf = atts(GetType(IDReferencePropertyAttribute))
  typ = rf.ReferencedControlType
```

In C#

```
System.ComponentModel.AttributeCollection atts;
IDReferencePropertyAttribute rf;
Type typ;

atts = TypeDescriptor.GetAttributes(this);
rf = atts(GetType(IDReferencePropertyAttribute));
typ = rf.ReferencedControlType;
```

Saving Design Time Changes

So what happens when a developer using your control changes the value of your property at design time in the Property List? How do you ensure that changes the developer makes survive until the page is used? The short answer is: Most of the time, you don't have to do anything—ASP.NET takes care of it for you.

The long answer is that this discussion applies only to properties that return simple data types (such as string, integer, and so on). Properties that return more complex datatypes (objects with multiple properties) do require some more work and are discussed in Chapter 9.

If the developer changes the value of one of your properties at design time, the new value of the property is automatically saved to the page as an attribute on your control's design time tag. In other words, if you have a control called BookDetail with a custom property called Title, and the developer using your control changes that value in the Property List to "The Wizard of Oz", then the BookDetail tag is written to the page like this:

```
<cc2:BookDetail ID="BookDetail1" Title="Wizard of Oz" runat="server"/>
```

As you can see, the default mode for saving property values is, in XML terms, "attribute-based." You can change the way that a property is saved to one of two element-based modes by using the PersistenceMode attribute. This Visual Basic 2005 example uses the PersistenceMode attribute, passing the PersistenceMode.InnerDefaultProperty as the parameter:

```
<PersistenceMode(PersistenceMode.InnerDefaultProperty)> _
  Public Property Title() As String
```

In C#:

```
[PersistenceMode(PersistenceMode.InnerDefaultProperty)]
  public string Title()
```

Setting PersistenceMode to PersistenceMode.InnerDefaultProperty causes the value of the property to be saved as the text between the open and close tags for the custom control, like this:

```
<cc2:BookDetail ID="BookDetail1" runat="server">Wizard of Oz</cc2:BookDetail>
```

Using PersistenceMode.InnerDefaultProperty also makes the property the default property. As a result, you can use only PersistenceMode.InnerDefaultProperty with one property because you are allowed only one default property in your control.

Passing PersistenceMode.InnerProperty as the parameter to the PersistenceMode attribute causes the value to be saved as the text inside a child element, like this:

```
<cc2:BookDetail ID="BookDetail1" runat="server">
  <Title>
Wizard of Oz</Title>
</cc2:BookDetail>
```

For most cases, the default mode (saving property values as attributes) will work fine for you (actually, you probably don't care how property values are saved). Changing the PersistenceMode may make sense if your control is being saved on a page that will be processed by something other than a browser (for instance, if the page will be read using an XML processor) or is going to be used as input for some other process. For instance, if users will save your page and then import it into some other tool (such as Microsoft Word or Excel) one of the other PersistenceMode formats may be more compatible than the default attribute-based mechanism.

Configuring Your Property

Several other attributes can be applied to properties to control how your properties behave:

- **DefaultValue:** Allows you to set the value that a property will have before it is altered by the developer or host page code.
- **DesignOnly:** When this attribute is applied and set to True, the property can be set only at design time — the property cannot be altered by code in the host page.
- **Themeable:** You can prevent your property from participating in themeing by applying the Themeable attribute to your property and passing False to the attribute.
- **DisplayName:** Using this attribute changes the name of the property — but only in the Property List (not in the IntelliSense drop-down lists or the host page's code). You may use this attribute if you want to sort the property into a special location in the Property List or provide a more descriptive name.

This Visual Basic 2005 example uses attributes to configure a custom Text property called Text. The property's default value is set to "Hello, World", the property cannot be used in themes, the property form cannot be changed at run time, and the name of the property in the Property List is changed to "Title (Deprecated)":

```
<DefaultValue("Hello, World"), Themeable(False), DesignOnly(True),
  DisplayName("Title (Deprecated)")> _
    Public Property Title() As String
```

In C#:

```
[DefaultValue("Hello, World"), Themeable(False)] _
   public string Text
```

- **URLProperty:** If your property will be used to accept URLs, you can apply the URLProperty attribute to control what text may be accepted by the property. The first parameter to the URLProperty attribute provides a filter that controls what text will be accepted; the second, optional, parameter specifies the kind of URL (absolute, root relative, app relative, or doc relative) that can be accepted. This Visual Basic 2005 code specifies that the URL must have a file extension of .htm and be an absolute or app relative path:

```
<UrlProperty("*.htm", UrlTypes.Absolute Or UrlTypes.DocRelative)>  _
   Public Property Text() As String
```

In C#:

```
[UrlProperty("*.htm", UrlTypes.Absolute | UrlTypes.DocRelative)]
   public string Text
```

- **ValidationProperty:** This property allows you to designate which of your properties is to be checked by validation controls that are assigned to validate the control. Just add the ValidationProperty attribute to the control's Class declaration, passing the name of the property that you want Validator controls to check. This Visual Basic 2005 code makes the Title property the property to be validated by any validation controls:

```
<ValidationProperty("Title")> Class BookDetail ()
```

In C#:

```
[ValidationProperty("Title")] public class BookDetail :
```

Shared/Static Methods and Properties

You can also declare your methods or properties as shared (in Visual Basic 2005) or static (in C#). Shared/static routines have an interesting characteristic: They can be called without having to create the object that they are part of. Here's a method in Visual Basic 2005 that's been declared as Shared:

```
Public Shared Sub ProcessData(ByVal Data As String)

End Sub
```

In C#

```
public static void ProcessData(string Data)
{
}
```

Of course, your control will be sitting on a Web page and will be automatically created when the page is requested — so why would a developer need a shared/static routine on your control?

The primary scenario in which shared/static routines are useful is when the host pages contains code that must execute after the HTML has been sent to the browser and the Page object has been removed from memory. For instance, it's possible for the host page's code to call a Web Service so that, when the Web Service returns, a routine in your host page is called (known as a *callback function*). It's entirely possible that by the time the Web Service returns, all the other code on the page will have executed and the Page object been removed from memory. It would still be possible for a developer to call a method on your control, provided that the method was declared as shared/static.

However, there are several important limitations as to what you can do with a shared/static routine:

- You can't declare routines that override default methods or properties.
- You can't, from within a shared/static routine, access anything in your control unless that item exists without the control having been loaded. This means that you can't call other methods on your control or access module level variables (unless they also have been declared static — in which case the variable is shared among all instances of your control).

Configuring Methods and Properties for Visual Studio 2005

There are several attributes that you can apply to your properties and a few that you can apply to methods to control how they are handled in Visual Studio 2005:

- **ParenthesizedPropertyName:** Adding this attribute to a property causes the property to be displayed in the Visual Studio 2005 Property List with parentheses around the name (as the ID property is displayed, for instance). When the Property List is sorted alphabetically, properties with parentheses around their names will be sorted to the top of the list.
- **PasswordPropertyText:** You can prevent text for your property from being displayed in the Property List by applying the PasswordPropertyText attribute to the property. In the Property List, your text will be displayed in the same way that text is displayed in a password-enabled text box.
- **ReadOnly:** Applying the ReadOnly attribute makes your property read-only at design time — developers won't be able to change the value of your property in the Property List (the property will also appear as disabled — grayed out — in the Visual Studio 2005 Property List).

  Don't confuse this attribute with the ReadOnly keyword used when creating a property without a set portion — that keyword makes your property read-only at run time and design time.

In Visual Basic 2005, because ReadOnly is a keyword, it must be enclosed in brackets.

This Visual Basic 2005 code shows a property set to prevent the property from being changed at design time, causes the text to be displayed using the password characters in the Property List, and have the property name displayed in parentheses in the Property List:

```
<[ReadOnly](True), PasswordPropertyText(True), ParenthesizedPropertyName(True) > _
    Public Property Text() As String
```

In C#:

```
[ReadOnly(True), PasswordPropertyText(True), ParenthesizedPropertyName(True)]
   public string Text
```

- **EditorBrowsable:** You can prevent your property or method from being displayed by the editor (in the IntelliSense drop-down lists, for instance) by applying the EditorBrowsable attribute.

  You might use this attribute for properties or methods whose use you want to deprecate but can't remove because the method or property is still in use in support legacy applications. The EditorBrowsable attribute can be set to Never (to prevent the item from being displayed) or Advanced (where the editor will display the item only if the editor is configured for advanced users). This Visual Basic 2005 code prevents a method called Update from being displayed:

```
<EditorBrowsable(EditorBrowsableState.Never)> Public Sub Update()
```

In C#:

```
[EditorBrowsable(EditorBrowsableState.Never)] public void Update()
```

- **Description:** This attribute can be used with events, methods, classes, and properties. The attribute is passed a single string, which an editor may display. For instance, if you use this attribute with a property, the string will be displayed at the bottom of the Property List in Visual Studio 2005 when the developer selects your property. Use this attribute to provide some additional design-time documentation to the developers using your control.

Adding Custom Events

Your custom control can fire events, in the same way that the ASP.NET controls you are already working with fire events. The host page is able to associate code with the events that your control raises like this in Visual Basic 2005:

```
Private Sub BookDetail1_InvalidValue(ByVal value As String) _
        Handles BookDetail1.InvalidValue

End Sub
```

In C#, the host page associates code with the event like this:

```
this.BookDetail1.InvalidValue += new InvalidValueHandler(this.HandleInvalidValue);

private void HandleInvalidValue(string value)
{

}
```

Defining Events

To implement an event you should:

- Use delegates to implement your event
- Use the delegate in your event declaration
- Create a class to hold event information

There is a short and a long description of using delegates. Here's the short description:

To use a delegate to implement an event, you must declare a public delegate in your control. The host page for your control binds a routine to your delegate. When, inside your control, you call the Invoke method for your delegate, the host page's routine that is bound to the delegate executes. The declaration of your delegate specifies the parameters for the routine in the host page.

For the long description, see the sidebar "Introducing Delegates."

Introducing Delegates

To begin with, think of a delegate as a variable that points to a routine in your control, similar to the way an object variable points to an object. To use a delegate you must first declare the delegate and then associate it with a routine in your control (in the same way that you declare an object variable and then associate it with some object).

When you declare a delegate you must specify the kind of routine that the delegate can be associated with. This means that you must specify the signature of the routine that the delegate will work with:

- Whether the routine returns results
- How many parameters the routine accepts
- The datatypes of the parameters to be passed to the routine
- The datatype of the result returned by the function
- Whether parameters are passed by reference or by value

In other words, you declare a delegate with all of the same information that you would specify when declaring a function or a subroutine. As a result, declaring a delegate looks very much like declaring a function or subroutine. Following are two examples of delegate declarations in Visual Basic 2005. The first declares a delegate that can be associated with a function that accepts two parameters (one string and one integer) and that returns a Boolean value. The second declares a delegate that can be associated with a subroutine that accepts no parameters:

```
Delegate Function Sample1(ByVal FirstParameter As String, _
                ByVal SecondParameter As Integer) As Boolean
Delegate Sub Sample2()
```

The same declarations in C# look like this:

```
delegate Boolean Sample1(string FirstParameter,
                        int SecondParameter);
delegate void Sample2();
```

You can use the same declaration attributes (Public, Protected, and so on) with a delegate that you would use with a variable.

Thinking of a delegate as a variable is a simplification. In fact, a delegate is a class. So, to use your delegate you must create an instance of the class using the New keyword and have a variable reference the delegate. You then work with the function through the variable that references the delegate:

```
Variable → Delegate → Function
```

It's when you create the instance of your delegate that you actually associate the delegate with some existing routine (or "bind a routine to the delegate"). You bind the delegate to a routine by passing the address of a routine to the delegate's constructor (in Visual Basic 2005, using the AddressOf operator).

This Visual Basic 2005 example instantiates two copies of the Sample1 delegate declared previously, each pointing to a different routine:

```
Dim del1 As New Sample1(AddressOf FirstRoutine)
Dim del2 As New Sample1(AddressOf SecondRoutine)
```

In C#:

```
Sample1 del1 = new Sample1(FirstRoutine);
Sample2 del1 = new Sample1(SecondRoutine);
```

The signature of the routines bound to the delegate must match the delegate's declaration. In the preceding sample, it means that the FirstRoutine and SecondRoutine must be functions that accept two parameters (one string and one integer) and return a Boolean.

You can now execute the function bound to the delegate by calling the delegate's Invoke method, as the following Visual Basic 2005 sample does. Because the delegate was declared as requiring two parameters, the Invoke method for the delegate must be passed two parameters. And, because the delegate was declared as returning a Boolean value, the delegate's Invoke method returns a Boolean value:

```
Dim bolResult As Boolean
bolResult = del1.Invoke("Peter", 55)
```

In C#:

```
Boolean bolResult;
bolResult = del1.Invoke("Peter", 55);
```

When the Invoke method on the delegate is called, the function bound to the delegate executes and is passed the values that were passed to the Invoke method. The value returned by the function is passed back through the delegate to the calling code.

Delegates used for events cannot have named arguments, ParamArray arguments, or Optional arguments and cannot return values.

When deciding what parameters your event should pass, you should follow the standard for .NET, which is to have your event pass two objects: a reference to the object that fired the event, and an object with properties that hold information relevant to the event. The delegate should return nothing (that is, in Visual Basic 2005 declare the delegate as a subroutine; in C# declare the delegate as returning void).

When defining your delegate's parameters, the first parameter is of type Object. The easiest way to handle the second is make it of type EventArgs, the default type for the second parameter for an event in .NET (you'll see how to handle a more complicated parameter later in this section). The first parameter, by convention, is called sender, and the second parameter is called e.

For instance, this Visual Basic 2005 delegate declaration follows the .NET conventions:

```
Public Delegate Sub EventDelegate(ByVal sender As Object, _
                                  ByVal e As EventArgs)
```

As does this C# declaration:

```
delegate void EventDelegate(Object sender, EventArgs e);
```

Now, in your event declaration you can use your declaration. In Visual Basic, declaring an event that uses a delegate looks like this:

```
Public Event MyEvent As EventDelegate
```

In C#:

```
public event EventDelegate MyEvent;
```

You can use the same delegate in several different events that share a common signature for the routine in the host page.

Of course, somewhere in your code, you still have to raise the event to signal to the host page that something has occurred. This code doesn't change from the version of the event that didn't use delegates. You must still pass the parameters required by the event. In Visual Basic 2005, raising an event that uses the standard .NET event parameters looks like this:

```
Dim e As New EventArgs
RaiseEvent MyEvent(Me, e)
```

In C#:

```
EventArgs e = new EventArgs;
MyEvent(this, e)
```

However, if you don't have any data to pass in the second parameter to the event, you can use the EventHandler delegate that comes with the .NET Framework. Because the EventHandler delegate is provided by the Framework, you don't have to write the code to declare the delegate, making your life a little easier. This Visual Basic 2005 example declares an event using the EventHandler without having to declare a delegate:

```
Public Event MyEvent As EventHandler
```

In C#

```
public event EventHandler MyEvent;
```

You raise the event as you did before, passing EventArgs.Empty as the second parameter. In Visual Basic 2005:

```
RaiseEvent MyEvent(Me, EventArgs.Empty)
```

In C#:

```
MyEvent(this, EventArgs.Empty)
```

Defining the e Parameter

If you do have data that you want to return as part of raising your event, you must define your own object to pass as the second parameter to the event instead of using the default EventArgs class or EventArgs.Empty. Defining your own class allows you to give the class properties that you can set to any values that you want to pass to the host page. While your event class can have any design that you want, your class must inherit from the .NET Framework's System.EventArgs class.

Going back to the database connection routine from the start of this section, the goal was to fire an event when a connection failed. In that event, the host was to be passed the reason for the connection failure and given the opportunity to pass back a command that indicated how the problem was to be handled. This means that the object needs two properties: ErrorCode and Command. The convention for naming event argument classes is to use the event name followed by EventArgs. So this class would be called ConnectionFailedEventArgs. In Visual Basic 2005, the class looks like this:

```
Public Class ConnectionFailedEventArgs
    Inherits System.EventArgs

    Public Command As String
    Public ErrorCode As Integer

End Class
```

In C#:

```
public class ConnectionFailedEventArgs : System.EventArgs
{
 public string Command;
 public int ErrorCode;
}
```

Now you can define a delegate that uses your event arguments class and an event that uses your delegate (the naming convention for delegates is the name of the event with the suffix EventHandler). Here's the code in Visual Basic 2005:

```
Public Delegate Sub ConnectionFailedEventHandler(ByVal sender As Object, _
                                   ByVal e As ConnectionFailedEventArgs)
Public Event ConnectionFailed As ConnectionFailedEventHandler
```

And in C#:

```
delegate void ConnectionFailedEventHandler(Object sender, ConnectionFailedEventArgs
e);
event ConnectionFailedEventHandler ConnectionFailed;
```

Now it's just a matter of raising the event. Create your event argument object first and set its properties before using it in the event. (In this case, that means setting the ErrorCode property to the ErrorCode returned by the OledbException object.) After the event handling code in the host finishes running, check the Command property to see how to handle the failed connection. Here's the code in Visual Basic 2005:

```
Try
...database connection code...
Catch ex As Oledb.OledbException
    Dim e As ConnectionFailedEventArgs
    e = New ConnectionFailedEventArgs
```

```
        e.ErrorCode = ex.ErrorCode

        RaiseEvent ConnectionFailed(Me, e)

        Select e.Command
             Case "Retry"
             ...code to handle connection failure...
         End Select
    End Try
```

In C#:

```
try
 {
  ...database connection code...
 }
 catch (System.Data.OleDb.OleDbException ex)
 {
  ConnectionFailedEventArgs e = new ConnectionFailedEventArgs();
  e.ErrorCode = ex.ErrorCode;

  ConnectionFailed(this, e);
  switch(e.Command)
  {
    case "Retry" :
    ...code to handle connection failure...
  }
 }
```

Creating an Event Routine

It's also a standard practice to create an On* method for each event. The On* method is a subroutine that accepts the event arguments parameter and actually raises the event. In Visual Basic 2005, the standard is to declare this method as Overrideable. In C# the method is declared as virtual. This allows any control that inherits from your control to override your event processing with its own processing by supplying its own version of the On* method.

For instance, for the ConnectionFailed event, the standard practice is to create an OnConnectionFailed method that holds the code to process the event. In your code, you can just call the OnConnectionFailed method. This is a sample Visual Basic 2005 routine:

```
Protected Overrideable Sub OnConnectionFailed(ByVal e As ConnectionFailedEventArgs)
        RaiseEvent ConnectionFailed(Me, e)
End Sub
```

In C#:

```
protected virtual void OnConnectionFailed(EventArgs e)
{
  ConnectionFailed(this, e);
}
```

Now, in your control, instead of raising the event directly, you create the event arguments object and call your On* method, passing the event argument object. In Visual Basic, your code looks like this:

```
Try
...database connection code...
Catch ex As Oledb.OledbException
    Dim e As ConnectionFailedEventArgs
    e = New ConnectionFailedEventArgs
    e.ErrorCode = ex.ErrorCode

    OnConnectionFailed(e)      'replace RaiseEvent
    Select e.Command
         Case "Retry"
         ...code to handle connection failure...
     End Select
End Try
```

In C#, the new version of the code looks like this:

```
try
 {
  ...database connection code...
 }
 catch (System.Data.OleDb.OleDbException ex)
 {
  ConnectionFailedEventArgs e = new ConnectionFailedEventArgs();
  e.ErrorCode = ex.ErrorCode;

  OnConnectionFailed(e);
  switch(e.Command)
  {
    case "Retry" :
    ...code to handle connection failure...
  }
```

You can determine if any of the events that the underlying WebControl fires (Init, Load, and so on) have routines associated with them in the host page by checking the control's HasEvents property.

Simple Events in Visual Basic 2005

In Visual Basic 2005 you have a simple mechanism for defining and raising properties. First you must define the event, giving it a name and specifying what parameters will be passed when the event is raised. This Visual Basic 2005 code declares an event called InvalidValue that will pass a single string value called "text":

```
Event InvalidValue(ByVal text As String)
```

The next step is to raise the event when appropriate. This Visual Basic 2005 code (attached to the TextChanged event of a constituent text box) converts the sender parameter to a TextBox object and then checks the text box's Text property. If the Text property isn't a valid entry, the RaiseEvent command is used to raise the InvalidValue event, passing the invalid value to the host page:

```
Sub TextChanged(ByVal sender As Object, ByVal e As EventArgs)
Dim btn As WebControls.TextBox

  btn = CType(sender, WebControls.TextBox)
  If btn.Text = "" Then
    RaiseEvent InvalidValue(btn.text)
  End If

End Sub
```

Firing Events During Postback Processing

You may want to raise events during postback processing. This is when, for instance, the Click event of an ASP.NET Button or the TextChanged event of an ASP.NET TextBox are fired. As discussed in Chapter 3, by implementing the IPostBackDataHandler, you can create a LoadPostData method that will be called after the data from the browser is posted back to the server (and before the Page's Load event). In the LoadPostData method you can check the data for your control and, potentially, raise an event based on that data. For instance, you might check the data returned from the browser against the data you stored in the ViewState when the control was added to the page that was sent to the browser. This would allow you to fire a changed event.

To signal in the LoadPostData method that you want an event to fire as part of postback processing, simply return True from the method. This causes the RaisePostDataEventChanged method to run later in the control's life cycle. This Visual Basic 2005 code does that:

```
Public Class MyPostBackClass
    Inherits System.Web.UI.WebControls.WebControl
    Implements IPostBackDataHandler

Public Function LoadPostData(ByVal postDataKey As String, _
 ByVal postCollection As Collections.Specialized.NameValueCollection) As Boolean _
                                        Implements IPostBackDataHandler.LoadPostData
  If postCollection(Me.UniqueID) <> Me.ViewState(Me.UniqueID) Then
     Return True
  Else
     Return False
  End If
End Function

End Class
```

In C#:

```
public class MyClass : System.Web.UI.WebControls.WebControl, IPostBackDataHandler
{
 bool IPostBackDataHandler.LoadPostData (string postDataKey,
              Collections.Specialized.NameValueCollection postCollection)
 {
  if(postCollection[this.UniqueID] != this.ViewState[Me.UniqueID].ToString())
  {
   return true;
  }
```

```
    else
    {
     return false;
    }
  }
}
```

If the LoadPostData method returns True, the RaisePostBack method is run. In this method, you can raise any event that you want to signal the conditions discovered in the LoadPostData method. This Visual Basic 2005 example raises an event called Changed:

Even if you don't intend to use the RaisePostBack method, you must implement the RaisePostBack method as part of implementing the IPostBackDataHandler interface. So if you want to use the LoadPostBack method, you must implement at least a stub for the RaisePostDataChangedEvent method.

```
Public Sub RaisePostDataChangedEvent() _
                    Implements IPostBackDataHandler.RaisePostDataChangedEvent
    RaiseEvent Changed(Me, EventArgs.Empty)
End Sub
```

In C#:

```
void IPostBackDataHandler.RaisePostDataChangedEvent()
{
 Changed(this, EventArgs.Empty);
}
```

The division of labor between LoadPostData and RaisePostDataChangedEvent may seem odd. However, this division supports the ASP.NET standard of having all client-side triggered events fired between the Page's Load and PreRender events while still giving you early access to the data returned from the browser. LoadPostData (where you should handle data processing) runs early in both the page's and the control's life cycle: after the Page's InitComplete event, before the Page's PreLoad event, and after your control's Init event. On the other hand, the RaisePostDataChangedEvent executes later in the life cycle: after both the Page's and the control's Load event but before the Page's PreRender event.

You can also raise an event for controls that have AutoPostBack turned on by implementing the IPostBackEventHandler (adding AutoPostBack to a custom control is discussed in Chapter 3). The single method required by the IPostBackEventHandler is the RaisePostBackEvent method, which accepts a single string parameter. If the argument passed to this routine is not empty then it will be set to a value specified when AutoPostBack code was added to the page (as described in Chapter 3). This allows you to check to see which control triggered the postback and raise the event only if specific controls cause postback, as this Visual Basic 2005 code does:

```
Public Class MyControl
    Inherits System.Web.UI.WebControls.WebControl
    Implements IPostBackEventHandler

Public Sub RaisePostBackEvent(ByVal eventArgument As String) _
```

```
                        Implements IPostBackEventHandler.RaisePostBackEvent

If eventArgument = "MainText" Then
   RaiseEvent MyEvent(Me, EventArgs.Empty)
End If

End Sub
```

In C#:

```
class MyControl: System.Web.UI.WebControls.WebControl, IPostBackEventHander
{
 void IPostBackEventHandler.RaisePostBackEvent (string eventArgument)
 {
  if(eventArgument == "MainText")
  {
   MyEvent(this, EventArgs.Empty);
  }
 }
}
```

If your page is posted back as part of AutoPostBack processing, the LoadPostData method still runs before the RaisePostBackEvent method.

Efficient Events in C#

C# provides some features for handling events that aren't available in the Visual Basic 2005 environment.

For instance, if the host page hasn't written a routine to handle your control's event, you can check for the condition and skip calling the event. If your event is set to Null, it indicates that the event has no associated range. This C# example checks for an associated routine and calls the routine only if necessary:

```
if (ConnectionFailed != null)
{
  ConnectionFailed(this, e);
}
```

If you create the On* routine to raise your event, this code goes in the On* routine:

```
protected virtual void OnConnectionFailed(EventArgs e)
{
 if (ConnectionFailed != null)
 {
   ConnectionFailed(this, e);
 }
}
```

If your control has many events, you should use the EventHandlerList available through the control's Events property to hold all of your events (this reduces the amount of memory required by your control). To use the EventHandlerList, when you declare your event you must provide add and remove methods that add your event to the control's EventHandlerList (these methods will be automatically called when the host page associates a routine with the event). Each event is added to the list with an object that acts as the identifier for the event in the collection (you must also declare the object that is used as the key).

This C# example declares an object to use as the identifier for the ConnectionFailed event (the object has been given the name ConnectionFailedKey), and then declares the event with the add and remove methods that are called automatically by .NET when the host page adds a routine to the event:

```
private static readonly object ConnectionFailedKey = new object();

public event ConnectionFailedEventHandler ConnectionEvent
 {
  add
  {
   this.Events.AddHandler(ConnectionFailedKey, value);
  }
  remove
  {
   this.Events.RemoveHandler(ConnectionFailedKey, value);
  }
 }
```

Now, before raising the event, you have to retrieve it from the Events list, using the key for that event. As part of removing the item from the list, you need to set the type of the item. For the ConnectionFailed event, use the ConnectionFailedKey object to retrieve the event and set the type of the object removed to ConnectionFailedEventHandler:

```
ConnectionFailedEventHandler ConnectionFailed =
            (ConnectionFailedEventHandler) Events[ConnectionFailedKey];
ConnectionFailed(this, e)
```

Initialization Events

You can also specify that one of your events is to be fired automatically when your control is initialized. To do this, add the InitializeEvent attribute to your Class declaration, passing the name of the event to be run. This Visual Basic 2005 code declares a delegate for the StartUp event and an event called StartUp. The StartUp event is specified as the event to be run when the object is initialized.

```
<InitializationEvent("Startup")> Public Class MyControl
        Inherits System.Web.UI.WebControls.WebControl

Delegate Sub StartupEventHandler(ByVal sender As Object, ByVal e As EventArgs)
Public Event Startup As StartupEventHandler
```

In C#:

```
 [InitializationEvent("Startup")] public class MyControl :
System.Web.UI.WebControls.WebControl

delegate void StartupFailedEventHandler(Object sender, EventArgs e);
event StartupEventHandler Startup;
```

Configuring Events for Visual Studio

You can add the DefaultEvent attribute to the Class declaration to specify which event is the default for the editor (that is, which event is added to the page's code automatically when a developer double-clicks a control in Visual Studio .NET). This Visual Basic 2005 example makes the ConnectionFailed event the default event for the class:

```
<DefaultEvent("ConnectionFailed"), _
      ToolboxData("<{0}:MyControl runat=server></{0}:MyControl>")> _
Public Class MyControl
    Inherits System.Web.UI.WebControls.WebControl
```

In C#:

```
[DefaultEvent("ConnectionFailed")]
[ToolboxData("<{0}:MyControl runat=server></{0}:MyControl>")]
public class MyControl : System.Web.UI.WebControls.WebControl
{
```

On the event itself you can provide some descriptive text and specify where it should appear in the categorized version of the Property List. The Description attribute enables you to set the text for the event that is displayed in the editor and the Category attribute enables you to specify the area in the Property List. This Visual Basic 2005 example uses both:

```
<Description("A test event"), Category("Action")> _
 Public Event ConnectionFailed As ConnectionFailedEventHandler
```

In C#:

```
[Description("A test event")] [Category("Action")]
public event ConnectionFailedEventHandler ConnectionFailed;
```

Managing Events from Multiple Controls

A custom control may have multiple constituent controls, and it's not unusual to have code in the customer control that should to execute when any constituent control is used. For instance, you might want to add a property called Dirty to your custom control and set that property to True when any constituent control has one of its properties changed (in other words, the Dirty property for your control would be True whenever anything has been updated in one of your constituent controls). In order to implement this property, you need to know when values in your constituent controls have been changed. The good news is that checking for changed data is already supported by the ASP.NET Framework: Your constituent controls typically fire events that indicate that their data has changed (such as the TextChanged event on a text box). Rather than catch each individual control's event, you can bubble events from the constituent controls up to the custom control and centralize processing in a single event. You also pass that event up to the host page.

The following Visual Basic 2005 code creates a button; sets the button's ID, CommandName, and CommandArgument properties; and attaches an event routine (called PassAnEvent) to the button:

```
Dim btn As New System.Web.UI.WebControls.Button
btn.Text = "Click Me"
btn.ID = "btnSubmit"
btn.CommandName = btn.ID
btn.CommandArgument = "Click"
Dim ev As EventHandler
ev = New EventHandler(AddressOf Me.PassAnEvent)
AddHandler btn.Click, ev
Me.Controls.Add(btn)
```

The same code in C# looks like this:

```
System.Web.UI.WebControls.Button btn = new System.Web.UI.WebControls.Button();
btn.ID = "btnSubmit";
btn.CommandName = btn.ID;
btn.CommandArgument = "Click";
System.EventHandler ev;
ev = new System.EventHandler(this.PassAnEvent);
btn.Click += ev;
this.Controls.Add(btn);
```

The PassAnEvent routine looks like this in Visual Basic 2005:

```
Sub PassAnEvent(ByVal sender As Object, ByVal e As EventArgs)
Me.RaiseBubbleEvent(sender, e)
End Sub
```

And in C#:

```
protected void PassAnEvent(Object sender, EventArgs e)
{
 this.RaiseBubbleEvent(this, e);
}
```

As you can see, the PassAnEvent code is very generic. All the routine does is accept the standard parameters for any event (a generic object that points back to the original control and an EventArgs object) and pass those to the RaiseBubbleEvent method. Because the PassAnEvent routine is so generic, it can be attached to the events for any number of constituent controls. The result is that you have a single routine that can be used with all of your custom control's constituent controls.

Where you do need to have different event code for different constituent controls, it still makes sense to finish those routines by calling the RaiseBubbleEvent method. Calling the RaiseBubbleEvent causes the custom control's OnBubbleEvent to be called. The result is that all events are now passed through the OnBubbleEvent event of the custom control where you can put any code to handle common tasks for all the constituent controls (such as setting a Dirty property).

To process the results of the RaiseBubbleEvent, you must override the default OnBubbleEvent. The OnBubbleEvent is passed the object and EventArgs used with the RaiseBubbleEvent that triggered the OnBubbleEvent.

In the sample code you've seen so far, the initial Click event would pass a CommandEventArgs object with CommandName and CommandArgument properties that are copied from the button's CommandName and CommandArgument to the generic PassAnEvent routine. The PassAnEvent routine then bubbled the event up to the custom control. The following Visual Basic 2005 code checks the name of the original control (accessible through the source parameter), and then checks the CommandArgument property to determine what action to take:

```
Protected Overrides Function OnBubbleEvent(ByVal source As Object, _
          ByVal args As System.EventArgs) As Boolean

Dim cbtn As WebControls.Button
```

```
Dim cent As WebControls.CommandEventArgs

  Select Case (source.GetType.Name)
    Case "WebControl.Button"
      cbtn = CType(source, WebControls.Button)
       Select Case cbtn.CommandName
         Case "btnSubmit"
           cent = CType(args, WebControls.CommandEventArgs)
           If cent.CommandArgument = "Click" Then
             Me.Dirty = True
          Else
              Me.Dirty = False
          End If
           ...code for other buttons
      End Select
    Case "WebControl.TextBox"
       ...etc. ...
  End Select

End Function
```

Here's the C# version:

```
protected override bool OnBubbleEvent(object source, System.EventArgs args)
{
 WebControls.Button cbtn;
 WebControls.CommandEventArgs cent;

 switch(source.GetType().Name)
 {
   case "WebControl.Button":
      cbtn = (WebControls.Button) source;
      switch(cent.CommandName)
       {
          case "WebControl.Button":
             cbtn = (WebControls.Button) source;
             switch (cbtn.CommandName)
             {
              Case "btnSubmit":
                cent = (WebControls.CommandEventArgs) args;
                if(cent.CommandArgument == "Click")
                {
                 this.Dirty = true;
                }
                else
                {
                 this.Dirty = false;
                }
                break;
              ...code for other buttons...
             };
         case "WebControl.TextBox":
           ...etc. ...
       }
```

Managing the Controls Collection

Two methods give you the ability to manage your Controls collection when controls are added to it and removed from it: AddedControl and RemovedControl. These methods are automatically called when controls are added or removed from the custom control's Controls collection.

The AddedControl method is called whenever a control is added to the custom control's Controls collection. The method is passed a reference to the added control and the position of the control in the array where the control was added.

While the AddedControl method is run as you add controls to your custom control in the CreateChildControls method, its real usefulness is when the code in the host page attempts to add controls to your custom control. For instance, if the BookDetail control is on a page, code in the host page might attempt to add another control to the custom control's Controls collection. In that case, the host page might have this Visual Basic 2005 code:

```
Dim tb As WebControls.TextBox = New WebControls.TextBox
Me.BookDetail1.Controls.Add(tb)
```

In C#, the equivalent code is:

```
WebControls.TextBox tb = new WebControls.TextBox();
this.BookDetail1.Controls.Add(tb);
```

When this code executes, the AddedControl method in your custom control fires, allowing you to check the control that's being added. This Visual Basic 2005 code assigns a new ID value to text boxes as they are added:

```
Protected Overrides Sub AddedControl(ByVal control As System.Web.UI.Control, _
                                    ByVal index As Integer)
If control.GetType.Name = "TextBox" Then
    control.ID = "NewText" & index.ToString
End If
End Sub
```

This C# code does the same:

```
protected override void AddedControl(System.Web.UI.Control control, int index)
{
    if(control.GetType().Name == "TextBox")
    {
        control.ID = "NewText" + index.ToString;
    }
}
```

The RemovedControl method fires when a control is removed from the Controls collection. Like the AddedControl method, this method is passed a reference to the removed control but, because the control is no longer part of the collection, the method is not passed the control's position in the collection.

Summary

In this chapter you've gone beyond the basics of creating a custom control or user control—you've seen how to add application-specific functionality to your custom control. Specifically, you learned:

- The primary mechanism for adding application-specific functionality is custom methods and properties. Custom methods and properties allow you to provide routines that developers can call when the functionality is needed. You can even create properties that accept parameters (called *indexers* in C#).
- How to have your control fire events that signal to the host page what happened in the browser and to let developers integrate their processing with your routines. By using the controls' ability to bubble events, you can even build a single processing point for all the events fired by your constituent controls.

Most important, this chapter has provided an understanding of what each type of routine (control events, utility methods, custom methods/properties/events) should be used for, including:

- How the events that make up your custom control integrate with the events and constructors of your constituent controls and the host page (and how validation fits into those events).
- Knowing when those events fire (and what resources are available in each event) is an important part of knowing where to put your application code.

In other words, your custom controls and user controls are now full-fledged objects.

In the next chapter you see how to create some special-purpose objects: Validator controls, design-time editors for supporting working with controls in Visual Studio 2005, and templated controls. You also learn how to give your control some special features: databinding and client-side code.

Adding Advanced Functionality

This chapter covers a variety of topics: all tools and technologies that you may find useful in creating custom controls and Web Parts (some even apply to user controls). On the other hand, you might go through your entire career without using any of these specialized techniques. These tools are not necessarily related to each other, but you can think of this as a toolbox that you can reach into to solve particular problems.

In this chapter you see how to:

- Incorporate client-side code into your controls
- Add support to your control for databinding
- Build Validator and templated controls
- Add design-time editors to support developers working with your Web Part

Integrating Client-Side Code

Great Web applications don't consist of just server-side code. To provide users with a responsive user interface, many developers add client-side code to their applications. Not surprisingly, then, great controls often have client-side code in their page in addition to their HTML. In this section, you don't learn how to write client-side code for your application (that's the topic for another book), but you do see how to add client-side code to your page from your server-side code.

> **Adding client-side code to your control is not a decision to be made lightly. Including client-side code increases the chances that your control won't work with every browser. If your control uses client-side code and you expect the control to be used on an Internet site (or any site where users may be using a variety of browsers) then you should plan for an extended testing phase in order to test your code on multiple versions of multiple browsers on multiple operating systems.**

This section takes a look at:

- The three strategies for using client-side code
- Controlling when client-side code executes
- The tools for dynamically adding client-side code to your page

ASP.NET Client-Side Code

There are three strategies for dealing with client-side code, each with its own merits. Each strategy can be illustrated by the way that existing ASP.NET controls use client-side code:

- **Give your code only to clients that can handle it.** This is the strategy used by the ASP.NET Validator controls. The Validator controls add client-side code to the page only when the browser is a recent version of Internet Explorer. (ASP.NET won't even generate client-side validation code for the most recent versions of Netscape Navigator.)
- **Provide only client-side code that every client can execute.** This "least common denominator" approach provides one set of code for all browsers, but provides code that can be executed by any browser. This strategy is demonstrated by the code added when the AutoPostBack property on the control is set to True. Setting AutoPostBack to True generates some very reliable code—it works in browsers as old as Netscape Navigator 4.5, for instance.
- **Let the client machine deal with it.** This strategy, if you can call it that, provides client-side code that may or may not work in every browser. This strategy is exemplified by the ASP.NET LinkButton, which generates client-side code that works in Internet Explorer and Netscape 6.2, but doesn't work in Netscape 4.5.

Picking your strategy is just the first step in deciding how you want to incorporate client-side code. For any of these strategies, you need to choose between dynamic and static code. Static code is written once at design time and is never altered at run time; dynamic code, on the other hand, is generated (at least in part) at run time from your server-side code. For many situations (especially if you're using the third strategy) your needs will be met with static code. For more sophisticated solutions you need to use dynamic code.

Your final consideration in using client-side code is deciding when, and how, the code is to be invoked. As an example, the client-side code generated by the Validator controls is tied to several events fired from several objects on the page. Validator code is run from the onclick event of any submit button and from the onsubmit event of the form, and is also frequently tied to the onblur event of text boxes, for example.

Static and Dynamic Client-Side Code

You can add static client-side code to your user controls in Visual Studio 2005 by going into the Source View of your ASCX page and typing in your code (see Figure 9-1). Visual Studio 2005's Source view of an ASCX file provides IntelliSense support for client-side programmers, including some syntax checking at design time. This is the ultimate in static code: Every browser that requests a page with your user control gets the same code (effectively implementing the third strategy). However, because Web Parts and custom controls have no Source view, you can't use this strategy with them.

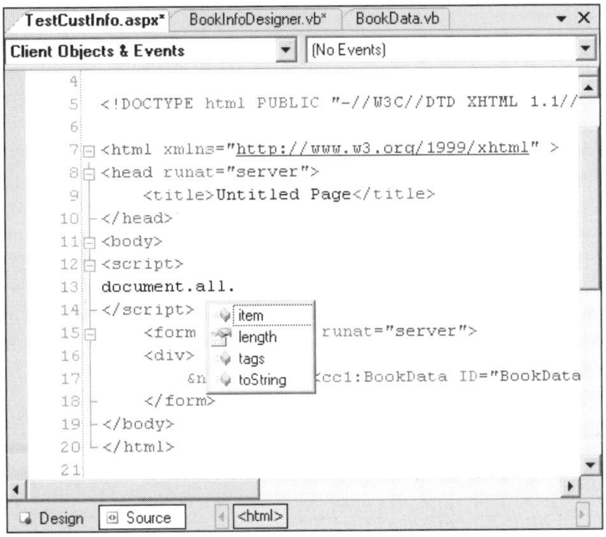

```
4
5  <!DOCTYPE html PUBLIC "-//W3C//DTD XHTML 1.1//
6
7  <html xmlns="http://www.w3.org/1999/xhtml" >
8  <head runat="server">
9      <title>Untitled Page</title>
10 </head>
11 <body>
12 <script>
13 document.all.
14 </script>
15     <form            runat="server">
16     <div>
17         &n           cc1:BookData ID="BookData
18     </form>
19 </body>
20 </html>
21
```

Figure 9-1

A better solution is to move to the lowest level of dynamic code implementation. At this level you check to see what kind of client is requesting your page and provide a standard set of client-side code—but only to those clients that can execute it. If, for instance, your page is being requested by a *crawler* (a program run by a search site to find and index Web pages), you probably want to omit any client-side code that is tied to user activities. This level of dynamic code integration implements the first strategy: "Give your code only to clients that can handle it," and can be used with custom controls, user controls, and Web Parts.

You can check what kind of client you're working with by using the Browser object, which can be retrieved from the ASP.NET Request object. The following Visual Basic 2005 example checks to see if the client is either a crawler or the infamously problematic AOL browser, and omits adding client-side code for either of them (you'll learn about the tools for adding client-side code to your page in the following section):

```
If Me.Page.Request.Browser.Crawler = False Or _
   Me.Page.Request.Browser.AOL = False Then
  ...dynamic client-side code...
End If
```

In C#:

```
if(this.Page.Request.Browser.Crawler == false ||
   this.Page.Request.Browser.AOL == false)
{
  ...dynamic client-side code...;
}
```

This next Visual Basic 2005 example takes an even tougher approach. In this example, code is generated only if the browser is a recent version of Internet Explorer:

```
If Me.Page.Request.Browser.Browser = "IE" And _
   Me.Page.Request.Browser.MajorVersion > 4 Then
  ...dynamic client-side code...
End If
```

In C#:

```
if(this.Page.Request.Browser.Browser == "IE" &&
   this.page.Request.Browser.MajorVersion > 4)
{
  ...dynamic client-side code...
}
```

Triggering Client-Side Code

Assuming that you've added code to your page (either statically in Visual Studio 2005 or dynamically from your server-side code) you need to decide when your code executes. The simplest solution is just to insert a client-side script block into your page, like this:

```
<script language='JavaScript'>
window.alert("Hello, World");
</script>
```

Most browsers will execute this script block as part of loading the page: When the browser reaches this point during the page load process, the browser executes the code and then carries on with loading the page.

For most scenarios in which you want to add client-side code, however, you want to attach the code to some client-side event (for instance, have your code execute in the browser when the user clicks on a button, makes a selection in a list box, or tabs out of a text box). For the following discussion, I assume that the following routine (called SayHello) has been added to the page either statically or dynamically and it's just a matter of calling the function:

```
<script language='JavaScript'>
function SayHello()
  {window.alert("Hello, World");}
</script>
```

Because the code is part of a function, the code won't be executed as part of the page load process. To execute the SayHello routine, it must be associated with ("wired up to") some client-side event. In your server-side code, you can choose which (if any) client-side events will execute this routine.

Most of the events for the HTML controls generated from the server-side WebForm controls aren't exposed directly in the ASP.NET object model. The one exception is the onclick event of a button. To tie a client-side routine to the onclick event of a button, simply set the button's OnClientClick event to the name of the client-side routine, as this Visual Basic 2005 code does in the CreateChildControls method:

```
Protected Overrides Sub CreateChildControls()
Dim btn As New Web.UI.WebControls.Button

  btn.ID = "MyButton"
  btn.Text = "Hello, World"
  btn.OnClientClick = "SayHello();"
  Me.Controls.Add(btn)

End Sub
```

In C#:

```
protected override void CreateChildControls()
{
 Web.UI.WebControls.Button btn = new Web.UI.WebControls.Button();

 btn.ID = "MyButton";
 btn.Text = "Hello, World";
 btn.OnClientClick = "SayHello();";
 this.Controls.Add(btn);
}
```

To use events other than the onclick event of a button, you can add new event attributes to a control's Attributes collection. This Visual Basic 2005 example writes up the SayHello code to the client-side onblur event of a text box by adding the onblur attribute to the control and setting it to the SayHello routine:

```
Dim txt As New TextBox

txt.ID = "TextBox1"
txt.Attributes("onblur") = "SayHello();"

Me.Controls.Add(txt)
```

In C#:

```
TextBox txt = new TextBox();
txt.ID = "TextBox1";
txt.Attributes["onblur"] = "SayHello();";
this.Controls.Add(txt);
```

If your control isn't using constituent controls, you can use the AddAttribute method of the writer object in your control's Render method to add attributes to your control, as this Visual Basic 2005 example does:

```
Protected Overrides Sub Render(ByVal writer As System.Web.UI.HtmlTextWriter)
  writer.AddAttribute("type", "text")
  writer.AddAttribute("id", "txtName;")
  writer.AddAttribute("onblur", "SayHello();")
  writer.RenderBeginTag("input")
  writer.RenderEndTag()
End Sub
```

In C#:

```
protected override void Render(System.Web.UI.HtmlTextWriter writer)
{
  writer.AddAttribute("type", "text");
  writer.AddAttribute("id", "txtName;");
  writer.AddAttribute("onblur", "SayHello();");
  writer.RenderBeginTag("input");
  writer.RenderEndTag();
}
```

With this code, the Web page that the browser gets would include HTML like this:

```
<input type="text" id="txtName" onblur="SayHello();"
```

The events fired in the browser are controlled entirely by the HTML generated by your control. If, for instance, this custom control had written out HTML <span> and <div> tags, the SayHello routine would never run — the browser will never generate an onblur event for <span> and <div> tags.

Rather than wiring up a separate code block to a client-side event, you can insert dynamic client-side code directly into the attribute that you add to the control. The following Visual Basic 2005 code, for instance, adds client-side code directly to the event attribute rather than just adding a call to a function:

```
Me.Attributes("onblur") = _
   "javascript:window.alert('Hello, World');"
```

In C#:

```
this.Attributes["onblur"] =
   "javascript:window.alert('Hello, World');"
```

Adding your code to the events of a control can interfere with ASP.NET's ability to invoke client-side validation code. If a developer uses a Validator control on a page with your control, ASP.NET may concatenate its client-side validation code with your control's client-side code. The semicolon used at the end of the call to SayHello in the previous examples solves this problem by making sure your call is concatenated in a way that allows everyone's code to run. If ASP.NET validation code is added to your client-side code, the result looks like this:

```
<input type="text" id="txtName"
      onblur="return SayHello();if typeof((Page_ClientValidate...
```

Dynamically Generating Code

The next step up the evolutionary ladder of client-side code writing is to dynamically generate your code and insert it into your page. The first step in generating dynamic client-side code is to prepare, in your server-side code, the client-side code to be added to the page and concatenate it into a string variable.

The range of code that you can build is infinite, but I'll stick to the simple SayHello example. This Visual Basic 2005 example puts the SayHello program into a single string:

```
Dim strSayHello As String
strSayHello = "<script>function SayHello(){window.alert(" & _
              "'Hello, World');}</script>"
```

In C#:

```
string strSayHello;
strSayHello = "<script>function SayHello(){window.alert(" +
              "'Hello, World');}</script>";
```

Even if your code is being generated dynamically, it's often a good idea to write an initial, static version of the code in the Source view of your page. This gives you all the IntelliSense support of the Visual Studio 2005 editor plus some syntax checking. It's also a good idea to do some testing with your static code before cutting the code out of your page and incorporating it into your server-side code.

The next step is to add this routine to your page from your server-side code. The simplest way to do this is to use the Response object's Write method, as this Visual Basic 2005 version does:

```
Me.Page.Response.Write(strSayHello)
```

In C#:

```
this.Page.Response.Write(strSayHello);
```

However, there are two problems with this method. The first problem is that you have very little control over where the client-side code is added. Used from the Page_Load event of a WebForm, for instance, the script block is inserted ahead of the HTML and DOCTYPE tags that begin your Web page (the code still executes in Internet Explorer, however).

Typically, there are two places where you want to put your script:

- At the head of the form, so that the code is guaranteed to have been processed by the browser by the time the user works with the control that the code is associated with
- At the end of the form, so that the code can't execute until all of the controls have been successfully loaded

The second problem with using Reponse.Write to add your client-side code to the page is: How do you prevent different copies of your control repeatedly adding the script block to the page? For instance, if you create a control that adds client-side code, there is nothing stopping the developer using your control from putting two or more copies of your control on the page that she is building. If both copies of your control insert client-side code into the page, the results of executing the code are going to be difficult to predict but almost certainly won't be what you want.

The answer to this second problem is to treat the script block in a page as a "library" block: the block contains a variety of useful routines that may be called from all the copies of the control on the page. All you need to do is ensure that, after your library block is added to the page at least once and that no other control adds the library again.

Both the problems of controlling the placement of your code and preventing code from being added several times are handled by the RegisterClientScriptBlock and the RegisterStartUpScript methods of the ClientScriptManager object, which has methods for supporting most client-side scripting activities. You can retrieve the ClientScriptManager for a page from the Page object's ClientScript property.

The difference between the two methods is where the code is placed:

- RegisterClientScriptBlock puts the code immediately after the form open tag that starts the form on your page.
- RegisterStartUpScript puts the code just before the form close tag that ends the form on your page.

RegisterStartUpScript can be used to add script blocks that contain code that isn't in routines—in other words, code that executes as part of the page load process. Because the RegisterStartUpScript code is placed at the end of the form, the controls on the form will have been loaded and be available for processing from your client-side code. This makes RegisterStartUpScript a good choice to add any code that you want to execute before the user has taken any action (such as code to position the cursor in some field when the page is first displayed).

As you'll see in this section, the Page's ClientScriptManager object has a number of methods that are useful when generating client-side code. In ASP.NET 1.*x* some of the methods were available directly from the Page object (RegisterClientScriptBlock and RegisterStartUpScript are two examples). However, those versions of the methods are now marked as obsolete and you should use the versions available from the ClientScriptManager object.

Both of the Register* methods accept four parameters:

- **A system type:** For this parameter you just need to pass the type of your custom control. This parameter allows ASP.NET to keep scripts from different controls separate.
- **The key for the script block:** This key allows ASP.NET to check whether the script block has already been added.
- **The script itself:** This parameter is concatenated into a single string.
- **A Boolean value:** A value that indicates, when True, that this script should be placed inside a <script> element. If you set this parameter to False, you'll need to include the <script> element in your code. This parameter is optional and defaults to False.

If you are generating script blocks for constituent controls, you still want to pass the type of your custom control to the Register event rather than your constituent controls. While your custom control is a unique type, your constituent controls are more likely to be the relatively common TextBoxes, ListBoxes, and other ASP.NET controls.*

This Visual Basic 2005 example places the code for the SayHello routine at the start of the form inside a <script> element:

```
Dim csm As System.Web.UI.ClientScriptManager
csm = Me.Page.ClientScript

csm.RegisterClientScriptBlock(Me.GetType, "PHVBlock", strSayHello, True)
```

In C#:

```
System.Web.UI.ClientScriptManager csm;
csm = this.Page.ClientScript;

csm.RegisterClientScriptBlock(this.GetType(), "PHVBlock", strSayHello, true);
```

The resulting JavaScript code looks like this:

```
<script type="text/javascript">
<!--
function SayHello(){window.alert('Hello, World');}// -->
</script>
```

When adding code to your page, you'll frequently want to incorporate the name of your control into your code. You can retrieve the name of your control at run time from your control's UniqueId property, as discussed in Chapter 3.

If you want your client-side code to manipulate the HTML structure that wraps a Web Part, see Chapter 5 for a description of a Web Part's HTML structure.

In addition to the ClientScript object's RegisterClientScriptBlock and RegisterStartupScriptBlock, you can also use the RegisterOnSubmitStatement to add code to your page. The RegisterOnSubmitStatement adds a script block to your host page that isn't tied to any particular control but executes just before the page is posted back to the server. This Visual Basic 2005 example associates the SayHello routine with the submit event of the page:

```
Dim csm As System.Web.UI.ClientScriptManager
csm = Me.Page.ClientScript

csm.RegisterOnSubmitStatement("PHVSubmitBlock", strSayHello)
```

In C#:

```
System.Web.UI.ClientScriptManager csm;
csm = this.Page.ClientScript;

csm.RegisterOnSubmitStatement("PHVSubmitBlock", strSayHello);
```

The key that you use when adding a script block allows you to check whether the block has already been added by using the Page's IsClientScriptBlockRegistered method (similar Is*Registered methods check for the results of other Register* methods). Passed the key for a script block, the IsClientScriptBlockRegistered method returns True if a client script block with that key has already been added to the page.

This Visual Basic 2005 code takes advantage of the method to avoid adding the SayHello routine if it's already been added:

```
Dim csm As System.Web.UI.ClientScriptManager
csm = Me.Page.ClientScript

If csm.IsClientScriptBlockRegistered("PHVBlock") = False Then
  csm.RegisterClientScriptBlock("PHVBlock", strSayHello)
End If
```

In C#:

```
System.Web.UI.ClientScriptManager csm;
csm = this.Page.ClientScript;

if(csm.IsClientScriptBlockRegistered("PHVBlock") == false)
{
  csm.RegisterClientScriptBlock("PHVBlock", strSayHello);
}
```

Four other notes on using the Register* methods:

- Using the Is*Registered methods is optional. The Register* methods don't add anything if an item with the same key has already been added (and no error will be raised).
- You must call the Register* methods before the Render method (that is, in the PreRender event or earlier).
- All scripts added with any one of the Register methods go into the same <script> element. For instance, all the script code added with the RegisterClientScriptBlock goes into the same <script> element at the start of the form.
- The keys assigned in the RegisterClientScriptBlock, RegisterOnSubmitBlock, and RegisterStartupScript are kept separate from each other. If you add a script block with the key "PHVBlock" with RegisterClientScriptBlock, it won't prevent adding a block with the same key using one of the other Register* methods.

Support for Client-Side Script

ASP.NET provides several other tools to support client-side processing. The following subsections cover these other tools.

Adding Arrays

While your server-side code has access to databases on your server, code executing in the browser does not. The usual solution to this problem is to extract the data from the database in your server-side code and embed that data in a static array in the client-side code. The RegisterArrayDeclaration method not only adds the necessary array to the page, but also flags the array has being added. As a result, controls that share data (for instance, a list of valid customer codes) can avoid adding the data twice.

The RegisterArrayDeclaration accepts two parameters:

- The name of the variable that holds the array in the client-side code
- The string that is used to initialize the array

In this Visual Basic 2005 example, an array called CustStatus is created with four entries ('Rejected', 'Standard', 'Gold', 'Platinum'):

```
Dim csm As System.Web.UI.ClientScriptManager
csm = Me.Page.ClientScript

csm.RegisterArrayDeclaration("CustStatus", _
     "'Rejected', 'Standard', 'Gold', 'Platinum'")
```

In C#:

```
System.Web.UI.ClientScriptManager csm;
csm = this.Page.ClientScript;

csm.RegisterArrayDeclaration("CustStatus",
          "'Rejected', 'Standard', 'Gold', 'Platinum'");
```

The resulting JavaScript code looks like this:

```
<script type="text/javascript">
<!--
   var CustStatus =  new Array("Rejected", "Standard", "Gold", "Platinum");
// -->
</script>
```

Client-Side Includes

Rather than include all the client-side code in the page, a common practice is to place the client-side code in a separate file and reference this file using a <script> tag with an src attribute. The RegisterClientScriptInclude method allows you to add this kind of script tag to reference a script file.

This Visual Basic 2005 example adds a reference to a code file called code.js:

```
csm.RegisterClientScriptInclude("PHVBlock", "code.js")
```

In C#:

```
csm.RegisterClientScriptInclude("PHVBlock", "code.js");
```

The resulting <script> element looks like this:

```
<script src="code.js" type="text/javascript"></script>
```

Using Include files provides a way of implementing the strategy to provide clients with only the client-side code that they can support. It's not unusual to have a set of client-side code that works, for instance, in the latest version of Netscape Navigator but does not work in earlier versions without some modification. To handle these differences, write a version of code for each browser that you intend to support and put each version in a different file. At run time, check the browser type with the BrowserCapabilities object and use RegisterClientScriptInclude to add a reference to the script file that contains code that works on that browser.

The convention for ASP.NET 2.0 is to keep client-side resources (like a script file) in a virtual directory in the root of the Web server called aspnet_client (this virtual directory is created when ASP.NET 2.0 is assigned). You should install your client-side resources:

- In aspnet_client
- In a subfolder named for your application
- In a further subfolder based on the version number of the application

For example, the client-side code file called code.js for version 1.0.0.0 of an application called MyApplication would go in the folder /aspnet_client/MyApplication/1_0_0_0/.

However, rather than keep resources in separate files, you can insert the code file directly into your application's assembly. To embed a file in your application's assembly, just add the file to your project and then (in the file's Properties List) set the file's Build Action to Embedded Resource.

A utility program called WebResource.axd (distributed with the .NET Framework) handles retrieving the embedded resources when requested with a query string that specifies the resource. The RegisterClientScriptResource method generates a script tag with an src attribute that references the WebResource utility and retrieves the resource. This Visual Basic 2005 example retrieves a resource called code.js:

```
csm.RegisterClientScriptResource(Me.GetType, "code.js")
```

In C#:

```
csm.RegisterClientScriptResource(this.GetType(), "code.js");
```

The resulting page would contain this tag:

```
<script src="/WebPartsHostVB/WebResource.axd?d=WylyhFDzry8iRJrQJB9A0hZkD_GD3HHX8pJs
r0kUntA1&amp;t=632482109977226208" type="text/javascript"></script>
```

You can also generate the URL for any resource by using the GetWebResourceURL method, passing the same parameters that you would use to create the resource. This allows you to embed the URL into other attributes than the script tag generated by RegisterClientscriptResource. This Visual Basic 2005 code, for instance, adds the URL to a custom attribute for the control as part of rendering the control's URL:

```
Protected Overrides Sub Render(ByVal writer As System.Web.UI.HtmlTextWriter)
  writer.AddAttribute("type", "text")
  writer.AddAttribute("id", "txtName;")
  writer.AddAttribute("MySrc", Me.Page.ClientScript. _
```

```
                    GetWebResourceURL(Me.GetType,"code.js"))
    writer.RenderBeginTag("input")
    writer.RenderEndTag()
End Sub
```

In C#:

```
protected override void Render(System.Web.UI.HtmlTextWriter writer)
{writer.AddAttribute("type", "text");
  writer.AddAttribute("id", "txtName;");
  writer.AddAttribute("MySrc", this.Page.ClientScript.
                GetWebResourceURL(this.GetType, "code.js"));
  writer.RenderBeginTag("input");
  writer.RenderEndTag();
}
```

Expando Attributes

As the previous example suggested, you can define your own attributes to be added to tags (called *expando* attributes). Expando attributes are implemented as a set of client-side code that is called by the browser when it finds the attribute on a client. The ClientScriptManager's RegisterExpandoAttribute method supports adding the client-side code expando attributes. This Visual Basic 2005 code creates an attribute called EncryptionMethod to be used with <input> tags and sets the attribute's initial value to SHA1:

```
csm.RegisterExpandoAttribute("input", "EncryptionMethod", "SHA1")
```

In C#:

```
csm.RegisterExpandoAttribute("input", "EncryptionMethod", "SHA1");
```

The resulting JavaScript code looks like this:

```
<script type="text/javascript">
<!--
var input = document.all ? document.all["input"] :
                                  document.getElementById("input");
input.EncryptionMethod = "SHA1";
// -->
</script>
```

While this code defines the EncryptionMethod attribute, you still need to add the EncryptionMethod attribute to a tag in your page. You can add attributes to your control (or its constituent controls) using the Attributes collection of a control or one of the methods discussed in Chapter 3 for manipulating attributes on a custom control.

Hidden Fields

Often, client-side code takes advantage of HTML hidden fields (<input> tags with the type attribute set to "hidden"). The RegisterHiddenField adds an HTML hidden field to your page and sets it to some initial value while ensuring that only one copy of the hidden field is inserted. This Visual Basic 2005 code creates a hidden field called BuildQueryString and gives that field an initial value of "?":

```
csm.RegisterHiddenField("BuildQueryString","?")
```

In C#:

```
csm.RegisterHiddenField("BuildQueryString","?");
```

The resulting HTML looks like this:

```
<input type="hidden" name="BuildQueryString" id="BuildQueryString" value="?" />
```

Building CallBack Functions

An important new feature in ASP.NET 2.0 is the capability to create callback functions in client-side code. A callback function is a client-side routine that can call a piece of server-side code and get data back from the server-side code. Client callbacks are supported on most modern browsers (for example, Internet Explorer 6.*x*+, Firefox 1.*x*+, Netscape Navigator 1.*x*+, and Safari 1.*x*+).

Using callback functions to retrieve data from the server eliminates the need to embed arrays of server-side data into your client-side code. Instead, when the client needs the information, code on the client can call a routine on the server that retrieves the data and passes it back to the client.

A typical scenario is to validate a customer number entered in the browser against a database on the server: The user enters some data (including the customer number) into various text boxes in the page and then clicks a button to submit the form. At that point, the processing sequence for a client-side callback is:

1. A function (named RaiseCallbackEvent) in your server-side code is called and passed the value of one variable in the client-side code. You need to add the client-side code to your page to ensure that the customer number is stored in the variable before the server-side code is called.
2. Your RaiseCallbackEvent executes and returns a value. In this example, your RaiseCallBackEvent returns either True or False, depending on whether the customer number is found in the customer table.
3. The value returned by the RaiseCallback event is passed to a client-side routine, which can take whatever action seems appropriate.

I'll now look at implementing this functionality. Before looking at any of the server-side code, I'll show you the client-side code which ensures that the right data is sent to the server and that the results of the server-side processing are handled when the data is returned to the client. Then I'll then look at the server-side code that receives the data from the client and returns a result. Finally, I'll show you how to configure the client so that the server-side code will be called at the right time.

Passing Client-Side Data

Before looking at the code required to implement the callback, let's look at the client-side code needed to ensure the data that your server-side code needs is available. Because only the value of a single client-side variable is passed to your server-side routine, you need to ensure that the variable has been added to your client-side code and set to the correct value.

To support the customer number validation scenario, one solution is to declare a client-side variable that is set to the customer number when the user tabs out of the txtCustomerNumber text box. The page in the browser would look something like this:

```
<script>
var custid;
function CustomerNumber_onBlur() {
custid = document.all.txtCustomerNumber;
}
<script>
<input type="text" id="txtCustomerNumber" onblur="CustomerNumber_onBlur()" ...
```

The code in the CreateChildControl method to insert the client-side script into the page, create the txtCustomerNumber text box, and set the text box's onblur event to call the client-side routine looks like this in Visual Basic 2005:

```
Protected Overrides Sub CreateChildControls()
Dim csm As Web.UI.ClientScriptManager
Dim txt As New Web.UI.WebControls.TextBox

Dim strLoadData As String = "var custid;" & _
                        "function CustomerNumber_onBlur() {" & _
                       "custid = document.all.txtCustomerNumber.value;}"

  csm = Me.Page.ClientScript
  csm.RegisterClientScriptBlock(Me.GetType, "loadCustid", strLoadData, True)

  txt.ID = "txtCustomerNumber"
  txt.Text = ""
  txt.Attributes("onblur") = "CustomerNumber_onBlur();"
  Me.Controls.Add(txt)

End Sub
```

In C#:

```
protected override void CreateChildControls()
{
  Web.UI.ClientScriptManager csm;
  Web.UI.WebControls.TextBox txt = new Web.UI.WebControls.TextBox();

  string strLoadData = "var custid;" + "function CustomerNumber_onBlur() {" +
        "custid = document.all.txtCustomerNumber.value;}";

  csm = this.Page.ClientScript;
  csm.RegisterClientScriptBlock(this.GetType(), "loadCustid", strLoadData, true);

  txt.ID = "txtCustomerNumber";
  txt.Text = "";
  txt.Attributes["onblur"] = "CustomerNumber_onBlur();";
  this.Controls.Add(txt);
}
```

Accepting Server-Side Results

The next step is to create the client-side routine that is called after your server-side code executes. The routine must accept a single parameter that is set to the value returned from your server-side routine.

As an example, this client-side code checks the parameter passed to it and displays a message if the parameter is False:

```
<script>
var custid;
function ReportCustId(IsCustValid) {
  if (isCustValid == false) {
    window.alert("Invalid customer number");}
}
</script>
```

The Visual Basic 2005 code to add this routine to the client looks like this:

```
Dim strCallBack As String = _
        "function ReportCustId(IsCustValid) {" & _
        " if (isCustValid == false) {" & _
        "window.alert('Invalid customer number');}}"

csm.RegisterClientScriptBlock(Me.GetType, "callback", strCallBack, True)
```

In C#:

```
string strCallBack = "function ReportCustId(IsCustValid) {" +
        " if (isCustValid == false) {" +
        "window.alert('Invalid customer number');}}";

csm.RegisterClientScriptBlock(this.GetType(), "callback", strCallBack, true);
```

Implementing Server-Side Processing

With most of the client-side code in place, you can turn your attention to writing the server-side code that accepts the client-side value and returns a value to your client-side routine. In order for your control to take advantage of client callbacks, the control must implement the System.Web.UI.ICallbackEventHandler interface and then implement the RaiseCallbackEvent method and the GetCallBackResult function that are part of the interface. The RaiseCallbackEvent method is called from the client and is passed the data set in the client-side code. Here's a Visual Basic 2005 example of a RaiseCallbackEvent function that tests the CustId passed to the routine and sets the strCustFound string to "true" or "false" depending on the results (the reason for setting a class-level variable in the RaiseCallbackEvent method will be clear shortly):

```
Public Class MyControl _
    Inherits System.Web.UI.WebControls.WebControl
    Implements System.Web.UI.ICallbackEventHandler
Dim strCustFound As String

Public Sub CheckCustId(ByVal CustId As String) _
            Implements System.Web.UI.ICallbackEventHandler.RaiseCallbackEvent
    ...application code to test the CustId parameter...
    If bolCustOK = True Then
```

```
        strCustFound = "true"
    Else
        strCustFound = "false"
    End If

End Sub
```

In C#

```
public class MyControl : Inherits System.Web.UI.WebControls.WebControl,
    System.Web.UI.ICallbackEventHandler
string bolCustFound;

void ICallbackEventHandler.RaiseCallbackEvent(string CustId)
{

   ...application code to test the CustId parameter...
   if (bolCustOK == true)
   {
     strCustFound = "true";
   }
   else
   {
     strCustFound = "false";
   }
}
```

At run time, ASP.NET runs the RaiseCallbackEvent subroutine, passing the client-side variable to it. After your RaiseCallbackEvent finishes executing, the second method in the ICallbackEventHandler interface is called, GetCallbackResult. The GetCallbackResult's job is to return a value to the client-side code (presumably, based on processing in the RaiseCallbackEventHandler). A typical example would look like this, which returns the class-level variable set in RaiseCallbackEvent:

```
Public Function GetCallbackResult() As String _
                        Implements ICallbackEventHandler.GetCallbackResult
    Return strCustFound;
End Function
```

In C#:

```
string ICallbackEventHandler.GetCallbackResult()
 {
  return strCustFound;
 }
```

A bit of history: The original implementation of client-side callbacks used only a single method (the RaiseCallbackEvent function). However, the functionality was broken up into two parts to support controls that implement asynchronous processing.

Wiring up Server and Client Processing

All that you have left to do is tell ASP.NET what client-side variable to pass, what client-side routine to call, and decide what triggers this process.

The connection between your client-side variable, your server-side code, and your client-side routine is handled by some JavaScript client-side code. The good news is that you don't have to write that JavaScript code. Much of the code is general-purpose code that is installed with the .NET Framework and is automatically incorporated into the page with your control. The code that specifically references your client-side routine and variable is generated for you by the ClientScriptManager's GetCallbackEventReference method. This method needs to be passed:

- A reference to the control whose RaiseCallbackEvent method is to be called (normally, you'll pass a reference to your custom control using Me or this).
- The name of the client-side variable to be passed (if there is no client-side variable with this name, then this parameter sets the value to be passed to the client-side routine).
- The name of the client-side routine to be called after the client-side code executes.
- A fourth string parameter set to any value (I'll return to this later).

The code to generate the client-side code that uses the variable and calls the routine inserted with the previous code looks like this in Visual Basic:

```
Dim strCodeString As String

strCodeString = csm.GetCallbackEventReference(Me, "custid", "ReportCustId", "null")
```

In C#:

```
string strCodeString;

strCodeString = csm.GetCallbackEventReference(this, "custid", "ReportCustId",
                                                                      "null");
```

The final step is to add this line of generated script code to your page and associate it with some client-side event. This Visual Basic 2005 code inserts the generated code (after terminating it with a semicolon) and ties it to the onclick event of a button:

```
Dim btn As New Web.UI.WebControls.Button

btn.ID = "clb"
btn.Text = "Check Customer ID"
btn.Attributes.Add("onclick", strCodeString & ";")
Me.Controls.Add(btn)
```

In C#:

```
Web.UI.WebControls.Button btn = new Web.UI.WebControls.Button();

btn.ID = "clb";
btn.Text = "Check Customer ID";
btn.Attributes.Add("onclick", strCodeString + ";");
this.Controls.Add(btn);
```

Reviewing the Process

There were a lot of steps in this process, so a quick review is worthwhile. In order to use client-side callbacks you must:

1. Ensure that the data needed by your server-side routine is loaded into some variable.
2. Add a client-side routine to your page to process the results of your server-side processing. This routine must accept at least one parameter, but other than that single restriction, your client-side routine can do anything that you want.
3. Have your control implement the System.Web.UI.ICallbackEventHandler interface.
4. Write a server-side routine to implement the RaiseCallbackEvent function. This routine is passed the data from the variable you set up in Step 1 and returns the value that is passed to the client-side routine described in Step 2.
5. Generate the code that ties the components together using the ClientScriptManager's GetCallbackEventReference method.
6. Attach the code from the GetCallbackEventReference method to some client-side object's event.

The client callback method gives you tremendous flexibility in what you do both in your client-side code and in your server-side code. For instance,

- While this example used client-side code added to the page dynamically at run time, in a user control you could enter the code directly into the Design view of your ASCX file.
- This example tied the code to a button's onclick event. You could just as easily tie the code to the page's onsubmit event or a list box's SelectedIndexChanged event.
- If the controls that you are loading into the Controls collection implement the ICallback-EventHandler interface, you can pass references to them as the first parameter to the GetCallbackEventReference. This allows your custom control to create client-side routines that interact with your constituent controls.

Things can get more complicated if you want to perform several different actions on the server (for example, validating the data from several different controls). Because only a single variable is passed to the server-side routine, you need to ensure that the necessary data is loaded into the variable at the moment when the server-side code is called. Because only a single server-side routine can be called for your control, you need to ensure that data passed in the parameter to that server-side routine signals what action is to be taken on the server. However, you can pass any data that you can fit into a string (including serialized objects). For a page that is XHTML-compliant, you could pass the whole page back to the server as an XML document, stored in single variable.

Extending Client Callback

A number of options are available to you in doing client callbacks. You can pass two parameters to the client-side routine called after the server-side code: the data from the server-side routine and another parameter whose value is set from the client-side code. Modifying our original client-side code to accept a second parameter gives code like this:

```
function ReportCustId(IsCustValid, ProcessOption) {
```

You specify what is passed as the second parameter to the client-side routine by setting the fourth parameter of the GetCallbackEventReference method (the context parameter). As the name of this parameter suggests, the intent is that you use this parameter to pass control information about the current state of the page to the routine. If the value in the context parameter is the name of a client-side variable, the value of that variable is passed to the client-side routine; if the context parameter's value isn't the name of a client-side value, the value of the context parameter is passed to the client-side code.

In the following Visual Basic 2005 example, the value FailOnError is passed to the second parameter in the client-side code. The client-side code might use this information to decide what is to be done when an invalid customer Id is processed:

```
strCodeString = csm.GetCallbackEventReference(Me, "custid", "ReportCustId", _
                                              "FailOnError")
```

In C#:

```
strCodeString = csm.GetCallbackEventReference(this, "custid", "ReportCustId",
                                              "FailOnError");
```

If you want to have additional code execute along with the code that calls your sever-side routine, you can just append your code to the end of the string returned by the GetCallbackEventReference. This Visual Basic 2005 code calls the InitializeCountries routine after calling the server-side code:

```
btn.Attributes.Add("onclick", strCodeString & "; InitializeCountries();")
```

In C#:

```
btn.Attributes.Add("onclick", strCodeString + "; InitializeCountries();");
```

Because a call to the Web Server can be time-consuming, you may want your client-side processing to continue while the call is being made to the server. You can turn on asynchronous processing by passing True as the fifth parameter to the GetCallbackReference method, as this Visual Basic 2005 code does:

```
strCodeString = csm.GetCallbackEventReference(Me, "custid", "ReportCustId", _
                                              "FailOnError", True)
```

In C#:

```
strCodeString = csm.GetCallbackEventReference(Me, "custid", "ReportCustId", _
                                              "FailOnError", true);
```

As an example, setting the asynchronous processing parameter to True with the version of the code that set the InitializeCountries routine to run after calling the server would cause the InitializeCountries routine to run while waiting for the call to the server-side code to return. Without setting the asynchronous processing option, the browser-side code would pause after calling the server-side code and would continue on to the InitializeCountries routine only after the server-side code has finished processing (and the client-side routine finished running).

If the server-side code fails, you can notify your client-side code of the failure by calling another client-side routine. To implement this client-side error handler, pass the name of the routine to be called on a server-side error as the fifth parameter to the GetCallbackEventReference method (the asynchronous processing parameter becomes the sixth parameter). This Visual Basic 2005 example inserts a client-side routine called ValidationFailed and then, in the GetCallbackEventReference, specifies that the ValidationFailed routine is to be called if server-side processing fails:

```
Dim strErrorCallBack As String = _
              "function ValidationFailed() {" & _
              "window.alert('Unable to Validate Customer Id');}"
csm.RegisterClientScriptBlock(Me.GetType, "callbackerror", strErrorCallBack, True)

strCodeString = csm.GetCallbackEventReference(Me, "custid", "ReportCustId", _
                         "FailonError", "ValidationFailed", True)
```

In C#:

```
string strErrorCallBack = "function ValidationFailed() {" +
              "window.alert('Unable to Validate Customer Id');}";
csm.RegisterClientScriptBlock(this.GetType(), "callbackerror", strErrorCallBack,
                         true);

strCodeString = csm.GetCallbackEventReference(this, "custid", "ReportCustId",
                         "FailonError", "ValidationFailed", true);
```

The error routine is not passed the parameters established in the GetCallbackEventReference method.

The final option with GetCallbackReference is, instead of calling a server-side routine, to have your client call another client-side routine, avoiding the server altogether. To implement this option, pass the name of the client-side routine as the first parameter to GetCallbackReference instead of passing a reference to client-side control. This Visual Basic 2005 example causes a client-side routine called ClientCheck to be run:

```
strCodeString = csm.GetCallbackEventReference("ClientCheck", "custid", _
              "ReportCustId", "FailonError", "ValidationFailed", True)
```

In C#:

```
strCodeString = csm.GetCallbackEventReference("ClientCheck", "custid",
              "ReportCustId", "FailonError", "ValidationFailed", True);
```

The client-side code must accept either one or two parameters (depending on whether the context parameter is set) and return a result that can be used by the client-side routine.

Managing Callbacks

You should be aware that when the server-side code is executed, your control is requested as it would be in other page requests. This means that all of the standard events for your control and for its host page (such as Load, Unload, and PreRender) will execute. There may be code in these events that you don't want to have execute during a callback. You can check to see if your control is being processed because of a callback by checking the Page's IsCallback property, which is set to True during callback processing (the IsPostBack property is also set to True during callback processing).

Your page will not have any of its client-side notification events raised (e.g., the Button's Click event or the TextBox's TextChanged event), nor will the ViewState be updated to reflect the data that the user has entered at the browser.

A control can trigger both postback and a client-side callback (for instance, if the control is a submit button that also has a client-side callback tied to it). In that scenario the page is called twice: first for the callback, and immediately afterward, for the postback. During the first call both IsPostBack and IsCallback are set to True; during the second call, only IsPostBack is set to True.

Because your host page's events also execute during a callback, you should make sure that your documentation makes it clear to developers using your control that you are using callbacks. That way developers using your control can also test for callback processing.

While most browsers support client callback, you should check for that support before inserting your code. You can determine whether a browser supports callbacks by checking the SupportsXmlHttp and SupportsCallback properties of the BrowserCapabilities object. Both properties return True if the browser supports client callbacks. The SupportsCallback property indicates whether the browser supports client callbacks, while the SupportXMLHttp property indicates whether the browser supports sending XML over HTTP (the communication method used by the client callback system).

Currently, both SupportXMLHttp and SupportsCallback return the same value. But, in a later version of ASP.NET, should some other mechanism other than XMLHttp be used to implement client callbacks, the return value from these two properties may differ.

This Visual Basic 2005 code checks to see if the browser supports client callbacks before inserting the client callback code:

```
If Me.Page.Request.Browser.SupportsXmlHttp = True Then
  strCodeString = csm.GetCallbackEventReference(Me, "custid", "ReportCustId", _
                                                                      "null")
  btn.Attributes.Add("onclick", strCodeString & ";")
End If
```

In C#:

```
if(this.Page.Request.Browser.SupportsXmlHttp == true)
{
  strCodeString = csm.GetCallbackEventReference(this, "custid", "ReportCustId",
                                                                      "null");
  btn.Attributes.Add("onclick", strCodeString + ";");
}
```

Interesting fact: Support for client callbacks in Internet Explorer requires loading an ActiveX Control. As a result, Internet Explorer's security settings must allow loading of signed ActiveX Controls from trusted sites (the browser's computer, in this case). Some users may regard this as loosening their security. For other browsers, however, adjustments to the browser's security aren't necessary because callback support is implemented natively.

Using Client-Side Code with WebPart Verbs

Web Parts provide an additional mechanism for calling client-side code. When you create a WebPartVerb in the Verbs property, you can specify the name of the client-side routine to run when the user selects the verb. The client-side routine is specified in either the second or third parameter passed when you create the WebPartVerb (if you want to assign both a server-side routine and a client-side parameter, you pass the address of the server-side code in the second parameter).

This Visual Basic 2005 version of a Web Part's Verb property creates two WebPartVerbs, assigning client-side code as they are created. The vrbEnglish WebPartVerb, for instance, is assigned the id "EnglishChoice" and has the client-side routine "ImplementEnglish" set as the verb's client-side routine:

```
Public Overrides ReadOnly Property Verbs() As _
            System.Web.UI.WebControls.WebParts.WebPartVerbCollection
  Get
   Dim vrbEnglish As New WebControls.WebParts.WebPartVerb( _
                                       "EnglishChoice", "ImplementEnglish")
   Dim vrbFrench As New WebControls.WebParts.WebPartVerb( _
                                       "FrenchChoice", "ImplementFrench")

   vrbEnglish.Text = "English"
   vrbFrench.Text = "French"

   Dim vrbsLanguage(1) As WebControls.WebParts.WebPartVerb
   vrbsLanguage(0) = vrbFrench
   vrbsLanguage(1) = vrbEnglish

   Dim vrbs As WebControls.WebParts.WebPartVerbCollection
   vrbs = New WebControls.WebParts.WebPartVerbCollection(vrbsLanguage)

   Return vrbs

  End Get

End Property
```

In C#:

```
public override System.Web.UI.WebControls.WebParts.WebPartVerbCollection Verbs
{
 get
 {
  WebControls.WebParts.WebPartVerb vrbEnglish = new
       WebControls.WebParts.WebPartVerb("EnglishChoice", "ImplementEnglish");
  WebControls.WebParts.WebPartVerb vrbFrench = new
       WebControls.WebParts.WebPartVerb("FrenchChoice", "ImplementFrench");

  vrbEnglish.Text = "English";
  vrbFrench.Text = "French";
  WebControls.WebParts.WebPartVerb [] vrbsLanguage =
                             new WebControls.WebParts.WebPartVerb[2];
  vrbsLanguage[0] = vrbFrench;
```

```
    vrbsLanguage[1] = vrbEnglish;

    WebControls.WebParts.WebPartVerbCollection vrbs;
    vrbs = new WebControls.WebParts.WebPartVerbCollection(vrbsLanguage);

    return vrbs;
  }
}
```

Of course, it's still necessary to add the client-side routine to the page. This Visual Basic 2005 version of the CreateChildControls routine inserts routines called ImplementEnglish and ImplementFrench:

```
Protected Overrides Sub CreateChildControls()
Dim strImplementFrench As String = _
     "function ImplementFrench(){...clientside code...;}"
Dim strImplementEnglish As String = _
     "function ImplementEnglish(){...clientside code...;}"
Dim csm As ClientScriptManager

  csm = Me.Page.ClientScript

  csm.RegisterClientScriptBlock(Me.GetType, "ImpFrench", strImplementFrench, True)
  csm.RegisterClientScriptBlock(Me.GetType, "ImpEng", strImplementEnglish, True)

End Sub
```

In C#:

```
protected override void CreateChildControls()
{
 string strImplementFrench = "function ImplementFrench(){...clientside code...;}";
 string strImplementEnglish = "function ImplementEnglish(){...clientside
code...;}";
 ClientScriptManager csm;

 csm = this.Page.ClientScript;

 csm.RegisterClientScriptBlock(this.GetType(), "ImpFrench", strImplementFrench,
                                                                          true);
 csm.RegisterClientScriptBlock(this.GetType(), "ImpEng",strImplementEnglish, true);
}
```

Specialized Controls

You can create any custom control that you want. And, as discussed at the start of Chapter 3, you can inherit from any existing control and extend it by adding new methods and properties (or by overriding existing methods and properties). However, the .NET framework comes with several classes that you can use as a base for creating your own controls. In this section, you see how to use two of those classes to create a Validator control. You'll also see how to create a databound and a templated control.

Validator Controls

The .NET Framework provides two classes that you can use to build Validators: BaseValidator and BaseCompareValidator. The general-purpose class is the BaseValidator class; you should use the Base-CompareValidator class as your starting point only when you need to pay attention to the datatypes of the values that you are working with. For instance, the RegularExpressionValidator and Required-FieldValidator both build on the BaseValidator class, while the RangeValidator and CompareValidator build on the BaseCompareValidator class. For the RangeValidator to be able to accurately test if a value is outside of a range, the control must know the datatype of the values—otherwise the control may end up trying to compare the digit 2 to the character "2" and get an incorrect result.

In addition to creating a Validator by building on the BaseValidator or the BaseCompareValidator, you can also start with a WebControl and have it implement the IValidator interface. This strategy requires you to write all the code for all of the methods and properties that define a Validator, rather than just overriding the methods or properties that you want to change or adding any methods or properties that will enhance the control.

Let's start by looking at the methods and properties of the BaseValidator and then look at the single property that the BaseCompareValidator adds.

Writing Validation Code

The key method that you must override in any Validator is the EvaluateIsValid method: This is the method where you put your custom validation code. You flag the results of your custom validation code by returning either True or False from this routine.

To determine what control to test in the EvaluateIsValid method, you can use the BaseValidator's ControlToValidate property, which returns the name of the control that the developer has set your control to validate. To determine what property to test, you can use the GetControlValidationValue method with many controls. Many controls have one of their properties marked as the property to be tested by Validators (for instance, the Text property on a TextBox and the SelectedValue property on a ListBox are marked as the validation property). The BaseValidator's GetControlValidationValue automatically retrieves that value for any control whose name is passed to it. By passing the results of the ControlToValidate property to the GetControlValidationValue method, you can retrieve the value of the validation property. If the GetControlValidationValue doesn't return a value, you could use the name of the Control from the ControlToValidate property to access the control directly as discussed later in this chapter.

A property is marked as the property to be used in validation by using the ValidationProperty attribute on the Class declaration.

Putting this all together, this sample Visual Basic 2005 code tests to make sure that the value in the validation property of the control being validated can be found in a table in the database:

```
Protected Overrides Function EvaluateIsValid() As Boolean
Dim cn As New OleDb.OleDbConnection("strConnection")
Dim cmd As OleDb.OleDbCommand = cn.CreateCommand
Dim strTestValue As String
Dim strTestControl As String
 Try
  strTestControl = Me.ControlToValidate
  strTestValue = Me.GetControlValidationValue(strTestControl)
  cmd.CommandText = "Select count(*) From Table1 Where " & _
```

```
                    "KeyValue = '" & strTestValue & "';"
    If cmd.ExecuteScalar = 0 Then
      Return False
    Else
      Return True
    End If
  Catch
  End Try
End Sub
```

In C#:

```
protected override bool EvaluateIsValid()
{
 OleDb.OleDbConnection cn = new OleDb.OleDbConnection(strConnection);
 OleDb.OleDbCommand cmd = cn.CreateCommand;
 string strTestValue;
 string strTestControl;

 strTestControl = this.ControlToValidate;
 strTestValue = this.GetControlValidationValue(strTestControl);
 cmd.CommandText = "Select count(*) From Table1 Where " + "KeyValue = '"
                                                    + strTestValue + "';";
 cn.Open;
 if(Convert.ToInt32(cmd.ExecuteScalar()) == 0)
 {
  cn.close();
  return false;
 }
 else
 {
  cn.Close();
  return true;
 }
}
```

Ensuring Success

For the previous code to work, three conditions have to be met:

- Your Validator's ControlToValidate property must be set to the name of a control.
- The control named in the ControlToValidate property must exist.
- The control must have a property marked as its validation property.

All of these conditions are beyond your control: The developer using your control is responsible for setting the ControlToValidate property to the name of an existing control, and the developer who built the control being validated must have specified a validation property. However, these conditions are checked for you through the BaseValidator's ControlPropertiesValid method, which is called automatically by ASP.NET. This method returns False and raises an HttpException if any of those three conditions are violated.

In Visual Studio 2005, if the developer sets the ControlToValidate property, Visual Studio 2005 ensures that the property is set to the name of an existing control with a validation property. However, even with Visual Studio 2005, a developer can forget to set the ControlToValidate property, causing the page to fail when ASP.NET calls the ControlPropertiesValid method.

You can check to see if a control has a validation property by calling the BaseValidator's CheckValidation-Property yourself and passing it the name of the control as the first parameter. If the control isn't found or doesn't have a validation property, an HttpException is raised. The second parameter for this method is text that will be incorporated into the message for the HttpException to inform the user which property has a problem. For Validators built on the BaseValidator, you want to pass Control-ToValidate as the second parameter so that the message reads "referenced by the 'ControlToValidate' property."

This Visual Basic 2005 code checks to see if the control referenced in the ControlToValidate property has a validation property:

```
Me.CheckControlValidationProperty(Me.ControlToValidate, "ControlToValidate")
```

In C#:

```
this.CheckControlValidationProperty(this.ControlToValidate, "ControlToValidate");
```

Custom Tests

You can override the ControlPropertiesValid method to create your own test. There are at least three scenarios in which you will want to override the ControlPropertiesValid method and replace it with your own code:

- If you intend to test for a different set of conditions than the default tests provided by the ControlPropertiesValid method.
- If you intend to create a Validator that works with a control that doesn't have a validation property designated, you need to override the ControlPropertiesValid method and provide your own version.
- If you want to add some additional tests beyond the ones performed by the ControlPropertiesValid method.

In the third scenario, you could call the ControlPropertiesValid method to perform the default tests (using either MyBase in Visual Basic 2005 or base in C#) and then execute your additional tests.

If you do override the ControlPropertiesValid method, you should signal that there is a problem by:

- **Throwing an HttpException if your tests fail:** This causes the page with your control to fail (this is what the Validator controls that ship with ASP.NET do).
- **Returning False from the method:** If your version of the ControlPropertiesValid method doesn't return True, your EvaluateIsValid method won't be called.

Returning False and not throwing an HttpException causes your Validator to be omitted from validation processing without causing the page to fail. If you do throw the HttpException, you needn't worry about returning a value from the ControlPropertiesValid method because the page will fail before validation has a chance to execute.

This sample Visual Basic 2005 ControlPropertiesValid routine uses the FindControl method of the Validator to retrieve the control being validated and then checks to see if it is a TextBox. If not, the method throws an HttpException with a message that uses the name of your Validator, as set by the developer. If all the tests are successful, the routine returns True:

```
Protected Overrides Function ControlPropertiesValid() As Boolean
Dim ctr As System.Web.UI.WebControls.WebControl

If Me.ControlToValidate = "" Then
   Throw New System.Web.HttpException( _
        "ControlToValidate property not set for " & Me.UniqueID)
Else
   If Me.Parent.FindControl(Me.ControlToValidate) Is Nothing Then
       Throw New System.Web.HttpException("Control " & Me.ControlToValidate & _
           " found for" & Me.ClientID)
   Else
       ctr = Me.Parent.FindControl(Me.ControlToValidate)
       If ctr.GetType().Name <> "TextBox" Then
          Throw New System.Web.HttpException("Control " & Me.ControlToValidate & _
                " not a textbox for " & Me.ClientID)
       End If
   End If
End If
Return True
End Function
```

In C#:

```
protected override bool ControlPropertiesValid()
{
 System.Web.UI.WebControls.WebControl ctr;

 if(this.ControlToValidate == "")
 {
  throw new System.Web.HttpException("ControlToValidate property not set for " +
                                                          this.UniqueID);
 }
 else
 {
  if(this.Parent.FindControl(this.ControlToValidate) == null)
  {
   throw new System.Web.HttpException("Control " + this.ControlToValidate +
                                              " found for" + this.ClientID);
  }
  else
  {
this.Parent.FindControl(this.ControlToValidate);
   if(ctr.GetType().Name != "TextBox")
   if(ctr.GetType().Name != "TextBox")
   {
    throw new System.Web.HttpException("Control " + this.ControlToValidate +
                                     " not a textbox for " + this.ClientID);
   }
  }
 }
 return true;
}
```

Working with Client-Side Code

You can choose to implement some (or all) of your validation tests in client-side code. To incorporate client-side code into your Validator you need to perform five tasks:

- Check that the browser supports the validation client-side code provided by ASP.NET (and that your control depends on in order to be integrated with client-side validation infrastructure provided by ASP.NET).
- Check that the developer wants to have client-side code added to the host page.
- Wire up your client-side code routine to the ASP.NET client-side Validator code.
- Add the validation-support code that ASP.NET requires.
- Add your client-side code.

The first task in using client-side code is to determine whether the browser calling the page handles client-side validation code by checking the DetermineRenderUplevel property. If the property returns True you can safely add your client-side code.

The DetermineRenderUplevel method doesn't return a valid value at design time so if you put this code in any routine that will be called in Visual Studio 2005, you should check the DesignMode property first and test DetermineRenderUplevel only when DesignMode is False.

If you want to perform your own browser-compatibility tests, you should override the BaseValidator's RenderUplevel method, perform your own tests, and return True if you're willing to add client-side code to the page. The default tests in the BaseValidator check to see if the browser supports Internet Explorer Document Object Model (DOM) version 4 or later and ECMAScript version 1.2 or later. The BaseCompareValidator also returns False if the control uses a non-Gregorian calendar.

The next task is to check if the developer using your control wants to add client-side code. The BaseValidator control supports an EnableClientScript property that allows the developer using your control to suppress client-side code generation. You should check this property also before adding any client-side code so that you won't produce code when the developer wants to suppress it.

After you've determined that you are willing to add client-side code, your next task is to add attributes to your control to wire it up to the validation framework client-side code. The attributes that you need to add to your Validator are:

- **controltovalidate:** The name of the control to be tested
- **evaluationfunction:** The name of your JavaScript function
- **errormessage:** The error message for your Validator
- **display:** The value of the BaseValidator's Display property, which controls how the error message is to display

The final task is to add ASP.NET's validation support code to the page by calling the BaseValidator's RegisterValidatorCommonScript and RegisterValidatorDeclaration methods.

Now you can add your validation routine using the client-side code routines discussed earlier in this chapter. The routine you add must be a function that returns true when the data in the control passes your tests and false when it fails. In order to get the client-side id of the control that you're validating, you can use the BaseValidator's GetControlRenderID method. This method returns the client-side id for the control whose name is passed to the routine. You can use this name in your client-side code to access the control that you're validating.

The following Visual Basic 2005 code puts it all together. Put inside your Validator's Render event, this code checks to see if the browser supports client-side code and that the developer has enabled client-side code. If both of those tests are passed, the code adds the attributes necessary to hook your Validator into the client-side code provided by ASP.NET. The code then adds the necessary validation script blocks. Finally, the code retrieves the client-side name of the control being validated and adds a routine to test the control's value and make sure it's longer than two characters.

```
Protected Overrides Sub Render( _
             ByVal writer As System.Web.UI.HTMLTextWriter)
Dim strName As String
Dim strScript As String
 If Me.DesignMode = False Then
  If Me.DetermineRenderUplevel() And _
     Me.EnableClientScript Then
       writer.AddAttribute("controltovalidate", Me.ControlToValidate)
       writer.AddAttribute("evaluationfunction", "MyControlIsValid")
       writer.AddAttribute("display", Me.Display.ToString())
       writer.AddAttribute("style", "display:none")
       writer.AddAttribute("errormessage", Me.ErrorMessage)

       Me.RegisterValidatorCommonScript()
       Me.RegisterValidatorDeclaration()

       strName = Me.GetControlRenderID(Me.ControlToValidate)

       strScript = "function MyControlIsValid() {if (document.all['" & _
                  strName & "'].length > 2){return true} else {return false};}"
       Me.Page.ClientScript.RegisterClientScriptBlock(Me.GetType, _
                       "val" & Me.ControlToValidate, strScript, True)
  End If
 End If

End Sub
```

In C#:

```
protected override void Render(HTMLTextWriter writer)
{
 string strName;
 string strScript;

if (this.DesignMode == true)
 {
 if(this.DetermineRenderUplevel() && this.EnableClientScript)
 {
  writer.AddAttribute("controltovalidate", this.ControlToValidate);
  writer.AddAttribute("evaluationfunction", "MyControlIsValid");
```

```
    writer.AddAttribute("display", this.Display.ToString());
    writer.AddAttribute("style", "display:none");
    writer.AddAttribute("errormessage", this.ErrorMessage);

    this.RegisterValidatorCommonScript();
    this.RegisterValidatorDeclaration();

    strName = this.GetControlRenderID(this.ControlToValidate);

    strScript = "function MyControlIsValid() {if (document.all['" + strName +
                          "'].length > 2){return true} else {return false};}";

    this.Page.ClientScript.RegisterClientScriptBlock(this.GetType(), "val" +
                          this.ControlToValidate, strScript, true);
   }
  }
}
```

Using the BaseCompareValidator

The second base object that you can build Validator controls on is the BaseCompareValidator object. Fundamentally, the only difference between this class and the BaseValidator class is that the Base-CompareValidator includes the Type property. The developer using your Validator sets the Type property to one of the predefined values in the ValidationDataType enumeration (for example, Currency, String, or Integer). Your code should check the Type property's setting and convert the value of the control that you're validating to a compatible datatype before doing any tests.

The CanConvert method of the BaseCompareValidator can be useful here. If you pass the CanConvert method a string and one of the values from the ValidationType enumerated values, the method will return True if the data can be successfully converted to the specified datatype, False if it cannot. This Visual Basic 2005 code checks to see if the data retrieved through the GetControlValidationValue method can be converted to an Integer value if that was the datatype specified in the control's Type property:

```
Dim strTestControl As String = Me.ControlToValidate
Dim strValue As String = Me.GetControlValidationValue(strTestControl)
Dim intValue As Integer
If Not BaseCompareValidator.CanConvert(strTestValue, _
       ValidationDataType.Integer) = True Then
  BaseCompareValidator.Convert(strTestValue,ValidationType.Integer, intValue)
  If intValue > 0 Then
     Return True
  Else
     Return False
  End If
Else
  Return False
End If
```

In C#:

```
string strTestControl = Me.ControlToValidate;
string strTestValue = Me.GetControlValidationValue(ctrTestControl);
int intValue;
if (this.Type == WebControls.ValidationDataType.Integer)
```

```
{
 if (BaseCompareValidator.CanConvert(strTestValue,
              WebControls.ValidationDataType.Integer) == true)
 {BaseCompareValidator.Convert(strTestValue,
         WebControls.ValidationDataType.Integer, out objValue);
  if (objValue.ToString() == "0")
  {
   return false;
  }
  else
  {
   return true;
  }
 else
 {
  return false;
 }
}
```

If you are doing date comparisons, you should also check the control's CutOffYear property and the GetFullYear method. The CutOffYear returns the last date that can be represented as a two-digit year; the GetFullYear method, when passed a two-digit year, returns the equivalent four-digit year.

It's beyond the scope of this book to discuss all the issues involved in comparing data values in an international environment. However, the BaseCompareValidator does provide a range of methods and properties for dealing with internationalization issues. For instance, depending on how you want to handle tests in international environments, you should consider setting the BaseCompareValidator's CultureInvariantValues property. When set to True, Double, Date, and Currency values are converted to a standard format before they are tested; when set to False, values in those datatypes are left as they were entered in the user interface. The CanConvert method will also accept a third parameter to indicate whether the conversion is to be a culture-neutral format.

Templated Controls

A template control allows the developer to create several different sets of HTML to be used for the control's user interface (UI) in the browser. At run time the control can switch between the different sets of HTML or generate multiple copies of any set of the template. Your control doesn't define the contents of the templates (the developer does that by inserting tags nested inside your control's tags in Source view). Instead, your responsibility is to provide the code that moves the template onto the page to be sent to the browser.

Simple Templates

Templated controls have three parts:

- The control (a user control, a custom control, or a Web Part) that displays the templates
- A class that manages the templates
- A template in HTML

The first step is to create the class to manage your HTML templates. This class inherits from the Control object and must implement the INamingContainer interface, as this Visual Basic 2005 example does:

```
Public Class TemplateManager
    Inherits Control
    Implements INamingContainer

End Class
```

In C#:

```
public class TemplateManager : Control, INamingContainer
{
}
```

Next add a public property to your user control, of type ITemplate, that manages a private module-level variable that represents your template class. This property should have the same name as your template class. This Visual Basic 2005 example shows this property for the TemplateManager class and the module level variable that it manages:

```
Private TemplateHolder As ITemplate = Nothing

Public Property TemplateManager() As ITemplate
    Get
        Return TemplateHolder
    End Get
    Set
        TemplateHolder = value
    End Set
End Property
```

In C#:

```
private ITemplate TemplateHolder = null;

public ITemplate TemplateManager
{
  get
  {
    return TemplateHolder;
  }
  set
  {
    TemplateHolder = value;
  }
}
```

Now tie the template class to the property that manages it by adding the TemplateContainer attribute to the property and passing the type of your template class to the attribute. Revising the property declaration in the earlier Visual Basic 2005 code to tie it to the TemplateManager class would result in code like this:

```
<TemplateContainer(typeof(TemplateManager))> _
   Public Property TemplateManager() As ITemplate
```

In C#:

```
[TemplateContainer(typeof(TemplateManager))]
public ITemplate TemplateManager
{
```

With the infrastructure in place, you can add code in your control to generate as many copies of your template class as required by the host page. Simply generating new copies of the template class won't accomplish much unless the HTML associated with the template is also generated. The HTML for the template is generated and inserted by calling the InstantiateIn method on the module-level variable and passing a reference to the template class.

As you may have noticed, you haven't yet specified what HTML is in the template. The developer using your control will design that HTML when he adds your control to his Web page.

In the same way, generating the HTML isn't much help unless the template class is added to your control's user interface. In a custom control or a Web Part, you add these copies of your Template class to the Controls collection to incorporate the HTML into your user interface. In a user control, you can add your template class to the Controls collection of a PlaceHolder control to put the HTML into your UI.

You can provide any mechanism you want for developers to add new copies of the template to your user control, but the following Visual Basic example arbitrarily creates two copies of the template class, loads them with HTML, and adds the template class to the user interface. In a custom control or Web Part, you would add the templates to the Controls collection of your control. The Visual Basic 2005 code in this example would be the code used in a templated user control and adds the template class to the Controls collection of a PlaceHolder control called DisplayTemplates (this code would be put in the user control's Init or the CreateChildControls event):

```
Dim tm As TemplateManager

  If Not (TemplateHolder Is Nothing) Then
    tm = New TemplateManager
    TemplateHolder.InstantiateIn(tm)
    DisplayTemplates.Controls.Add(tm)

    tm = New TemplateManager
    TemplateHolder.InstantiateIn(tm)
    DisplayTemplates.Controls.Add(tm)
  End If
```

In C#:

```
TemplateManager tm;

  if (TemplateHolder != null)
  {
   tm = new TemplateManager();
   TemplateHolder.InstantiateIn(tm);
   DisplayTemplates.Controls.Add(tm);

   tm = new TemplateManager();
   TemplateHolder.InstantiateIn(tm);
   DisplayTemplates.Controls.Add(tm);
  }
```

A more realistic situation might generate a copy of the template class for every record retrieved from a database.

Using the Templated Control

To use the templated control, a developer drags the control onto the page and then adds a template inside the user control, using tags with the same name as the property in your user control. Assuming that your user control is called TemplateControl, this example shows a TemplateManager template inside of it. In this example, the template just has some constant text ("Hello, World") and a <br> tag:

```
<cc1:TemplateControl runat=server>
   <TemplateManager>
        Hello, World<br/>
    </TemplateManager>
</cc1:TemplateControl>
```

There's one final change you need to make to your control to prevent errors from being generated. As the previous example shows, the user control's tag is going to be broken into two parts and tags that reference the TemplateManager property will be inserted inside of the opened tags. You need to configure the TemplateManager property to support storing the property as a nested tag (by default properties on a control are stored as attributes). Do this by adding the PersistenceMode attribute to the property and passing it the InnerProperty enumerated value. This is the full declaration for the TemplateManager property in Visual Basic 2005 that associates the property with a template class and configures the property to be stored as a nested tag:

```
<TemplateContainer(GetType(TemplateManager)), _
             PersistenceMode(PersistenceMode.InnerProperty)> _
   Public Property TemplateManager() As ITemplate
```

In C#:

```
[TemplateContainer(typeof(TemplateManager))]
[PersistenceMode(PersistenceMode.InnerProperty)]
public ITemplate TemplateManager
{
```

Providing Data to the Template

Frequently, you will want your template class to provide information to the templated HTML. The first step is to add public properties or functions to your template class so that the HTML code can extract information from your template class. This Visual Basic 2005 example has a property (called AProperty) and a function (AFunction) that can be used from the HTML template:

```
Public Class TemplateManager
    Inherits Control
    Implements INamingContainer

    Private APropertyValue As String

    Public Property AProperty() As String
        Get
            Return APropertyValue
        End Get
        Set(ByVal value As String)
```

```
            APropertyValue = value
        End Set
    End Property

    Public Function AFunction() As String
        Return APropertyValue
    End Function

End Class
```

In C#:

```
public class TemplateManager : Control, INamingContainer
{
 private string APropertyValue;

 public string AProperty
 {
  get
  {
   return APropertyValue;
  }
  set
  {
   APropertyValue = value;
  }
 }
 public string AFunction()
 {
  return APropertyValue;
 }
}
```

In the HTML template, the developer using your control can call methods and functions in your template class using the databinding syntax (in the HTML template, the template class is referred to as #Container):

```
<TemplateManager>
  <table>
    <tr>
      <tc>Hello, World</tc>
      <tc><%#Container.AProperty%></tc>
      <tc><%#Container.AFunction%></tc>
    </tr>
  </table>
</TemplateManager>
```

The host page would still need to implement databinding to transfer data from the properties to the page.

This control used only a single template. However, you can add as many template classes (and their associated properties and private module–level variables) to your control as you want.

Databinding to Multiple Records

In this section, you see how to create a control that can consume and display data — a *databinding* control. There are two kinds of databindings:

- **Simple:** The control can be bound to a single field on a single record, and when the DataBind method is called, the control retrieves the data from its field.
- **Complex:** The code can be bound to multiple records, and when the DataBind method is called, the control generates a display that shows all of the records. Controls that support complex databinding expose properties like DataSource, DataKeyField, and DataValueField.

As the previous example showed, a developer can bind to your control just by writing databinding code into his ASPX page. Complex databinding, however, requires that you do some additional work in order to display multiple records.

To create a control that supports complex databinding you must perform four activities:

- Inherit from the System.Web.UI.WebControls.DataBoundControl class.
- Provide a way for developers to set databinding information (the data source to use, the name(s) of the fields to use, and so on).
- Retrieve the data.
- Move the data to the page.

*In .NET 2.0 you don't include the code to retrieve your data in your databound control. Instead, data retrieval is handled by one of the *DataSource objects (e.g., SqlDataSource, ObjectDataSource). Your custom control just has to handle getting the data into the display.*

Much of this work is handled for you when you inherit from the System.Web.UI.WebControls .DataBoundControl class, as in this Visual Basic 2005 example:

```
Public Class MyDataBoundControl
        Inherits System.Web.UI.WebControls.DataBoundControl
```

In C#:

```
class MyDataBoundControl : System.Web.UI.WebControls.DataBoundControl
```

Databinding Properties

Databound controls frequently expose up to seven properties that developers can use to set databinding information. You can decide how many of these you want to implement for your control:

- **DataSourceId:** The value from the Id property of the object that provides the data (frequently a database, but also potentially a list or some other object with an interface that supports databinding). This property is one of the two properties provided by the DataBound class.
- **DataMember:** The name of the data holder within the object providing the data. For instance, if the DataSourceId is the name of a DataSet, then the DataMember is the name of a table within the DataSet. This is the other property provided by the DataBound class.

- **DataTextField:** The name of the field in the data source whose value is to be displayed on the form.
- **DataValueField:** The name of the field in the data source whose value is to be returned when the user selects a displayed item.
- **DataTextFormat:** A format string to be applied to the data retrieved from the field specified in DataTextField.
- **DataValueFormat:** A format string to be applied to the data retrieved from the field specified in DataValueField.
- **DataKeyField:** The name of a field in the data source whose value is associated with the displayed item (usually the primary key field for the data source).

Here's an example of DataTextField property in Visual Basic 2005. In this example, the DataTextField is stored in the ViewState, so the code in the Get and Set portions of the property retrieves and updates the ViewState:

```
Public Property DataTextField() As String
  Get
    Dim strDTF As String
    strDTF = ViewState("DTF").ToString
    If strDTF Is Nothing Then
        Return String.Empty
    Else
        Return strDTF
    End If
  End Get
  Set(ByVal value As String)
     ViewState("DTF") = value
  End Set
End Property
```

In C#:

```
public string DataTextField
{
 get
 {
  string strDTF;
  strDTF = ViewState["DTF"].ToString;
  if(strDTF == null)
  {
   return String.Empty;
  }
  else
  {
   return strDTF;
  }
 }
 set
 {
  ViewState["DTF"] = value;
 }
}
```

It isn't necessary to store the values from the DataTextField and DataValue fields in the ViewState. As described earlier, property values are automatically saved as attributes on the custom control as attributes for the control's take. The ViewState was used in this example to demonstrate how the values might be saved if they were more complex than a simple string. If, for instance, the control supported specifying a series of values for the DataTextField, DataValueField, or DataKeyField, the ViewState would provide better storage for those complex values.

There is a potential problem that can occur when the various databound properties are set. A databound control needs up to seven properties set in order to work effectively and, as a result, changing any one of those properties can change the way that the control should perform databinding. If one of the control's databinding properties is set before data is retrieved, there is no problem: When the control performs databinding the current values of those properties are used to retrieve the data. The problem occurs if the code on the host page changes the values of the databinding properties *after* the data is retrieved. In that situation, you may want to retrieve the data again.

ASP.NET provides two tools to deal with this problem:

- The Initialized property of the Databound class, which is set to true if data has been retrieved (or if the databinding process has been started)
- The OnDataPropertyChanged method, which you can call to signal that a property has changed and cause databinding to be re-executed

You need to signal that the data property has changed only if the control has started retrieving data (that is, when the Initialized property is true. Incorporating this into the DataTextField would mean rewriting the Set portion of the property like this in Visual Basic 2005:

```
Set(ByVal value As String)
  If Me.Initialized = True Then
     Me.OnDataPropertyChanged()
  End If
  ViewState("DTF") = value
End Set
```

In C#:

```
set
{
 if(this.Initialized == true)
 {
  this.OnDataPropertyChanged();
 }
 ViewState("DTF") = value;
}
```

Retrieving Data

You retrieve your data by overriding the PerformSelect method. Before retrieving any data, you should check to see whether the IsBoundUsingDataSourceId property is set to True, indicating that the control has bound to the data specified in the DataSourceId property. If it isn't, you should call the OnDataBinding method, as this Visual Basic 2005 example does (the objects declared at the start of this example will be used later in this section):

```
Protected Overrides Sub PerformSelect()
Dim dsa As System.Web.UI.DataSourceSelectArguments
Dim dsv As System.Web.UI.DataSourceView

  If Me.IsBoundUsingDataSourceID = False Then
     Me.OnDataBinding(EventArgs.Empty)
  End If
```

In C#

```
protected override void PerformSelect()
{
 System.Web.UI.DataSourceSelectArguments dsa;
 System.Web.UI.DataSourceView dsv;

 if(this.IsBoundUsingDataSourceID == false)
 {
  this.OnDataBinding(EventArgs.Empty);
 }
```

The next step is to call the Select method of the DataSourceView (the DataSourceView object can be retrieved through the Databound class's GetData method). The Select method retrieves the data asynchronously, allowing other processing to continue while the data has been retrieved. The select method is passed two parameters:

- A DataSourceSelectArguments object that allows you to tailor the data retrieval settings made in the data source that your argument is bound to. If you don't want to set any special parameters, you can just pass the default object returned by the CreateDataSourceSelectArguments method.
- The routine to call when all the data has been retrieved (the *callback* routine). This routine can perform any processing on the data and will call the routine to move the data to the page.

Two of the DataSourceSelectArguments properties are useful in most scenarios:

- **MaximumRows:** Sets a limit on the maximum number of rows to retrieve.
- **SortExpression:** The string that you set this property to will be passed to the DataSource object that is actually retrieving the data and will be used by the DataSource to sort data. It's your responsibility to make sure that the string is compatible with the DataSource.

Three properties are useful if you want to support paging through the data:

- **RetrieveTotalRowCount:** When set to True, causes the DataSource to return the number of rows that will be retrieved.
- **TotalRowCount:** If RetrieveTotalRow is set to true, this property will, after processing is complete, be set to the total number of rows that the datasource can retrieve. This number is not affected by the MaximumRows setting (for example, if the datasource will return 100 rows and MaximumRows is set to 10, TotalRows is set to 100).
- **StartRowIndex:** The position of the first record to be retrieved.

Not all data sources support all data-related activities. The DataSourceView object has a number of properties that report on what the datasource will (and won't) do for you. For instance, the CanRetrieveTotalRowCount property returns True if the datasource can return the total number of rows to be returned. It's a good practice to check the various Can* properties on the DataSourceView object before setting the properties on the DataSourceSelectArguments.

This Visual Basic 2005 example creates a DataSourceSelectArguments object, sets the maximum rows to be returned to 10, and requests the total rows to be retrieved to be available (if the datasource supports retrieving the total rows). The code then calls the GetData method to retrieve a DataSourceView and calls its Select method. The HandleRetrievedData is specified as the callback routine to be called when the data is retrieved:

```
dsa = New System.Web.UI.DataSourceSelectArguments
dsa.MaximumRows = 10

dsv = Me.GetData
If dsv.CanRetrieveTotalRowCount = True Then
     dsa.RetrieveTotalRowCount = True
End If
dsv.Select(dsa, AddressOf Me.HandleRetrievedData)
```

In C#:

```
dsa = new System.Web.UI.DataSourceSelectArguments();
dsa.MaximumRows = 10;

dsv = this.GetData();
if (dsv.CanRetrieveTotalRowCount == true) {
    dsa.RetrieveTotalRowCount = true;
}
dsv.Select(dsa, this.HandleRetrievedData);
```

When the data has been retrieved, you have three tasks to perform: You should signal to ASP.NET that there is no need to call the PerformSelect method again, ensure that the databinding state is remembered, and provide an opportunity for code to run after the databinding occurs. There are three mechanisms for performing those tasks:

- **RequiresDataBinding:** Setting this property to False prevents ASP.NET from calling the PerformSelect method a second time.
- **MarkAsDataBound:** Updates the ViewState to indicate that the control has been databound.
- **OnDataBound:** Fires the DataBound event so that code in that event can execute. This allows you to associate code with the databinding activity.

This Visual Basic 2005 code carries out all three of those tasks:

```
RequiresDataBinding = False
MarkAsDataBound()
OnDataBound(EventArgs.Empty)
```

In C#:

```
RequiresDataBinding = false;
MarkAsDataBound();
OnDataBound(EventArgs.Empty);
```

It's a good practice to set RequiresDataBinding immediately after calling the Select event to prevent the PerformSelect method from being called again. However, you might want to defer calling MarkAs-DataBound until all of the data has been successfully retrieved and moved to the page. The same is true of calling OnDataBound to fire the DataBound event. In that case, you could perform those tasks in the callback routine.

The callback routine specified in the Select method is passed a single parameter: the data retrieved by the Select method. In the callback routine you can perform any activities that you need before displaying the data (you might want to remove items from the data collection or perform some processing on them).

After you've performed any processing on the data, you are ready to perform the key part of this routine: Call the PerformDataBinding method of the DataBound object. The PerformDataBinding method is where you will move the data onto the page. This Visual Basic 2005 example provides the simplest implementation:

```
Private Sub HandleRetrievedData(ByVal data As IEnumerable)

 PerformDataBinding(data)

End Sub
```

In C#

```
private void HandleRetrievedData(System.Collections.IEnumerable data)
{
 PerformDataBinding(data);
}
```

Displaying Data

To perform the final activity, displaying the data, you must override the PerformDataBinding method called in the callback routine. This method's purpose is very simple: You process all of the retrieved items and do something with the data. In most cases you want to update your user interface with the data that's been retrieved. The sample code that I've presented retrieves only a single value, so my code just moves a single value to the page (other controls might display all the fields or a DataValueField).

The PerformDataBinding method is passed the data extracted from the datasource as a parameter called data. You should begin the routine by calling the underlying PerformDataBinding method to make sure that any utility code in the DataBound class has a chance to execute. You should also make sure that you have actually been passed data before attempting to display it, as this Visual Basic 2005 code does (the variables declared here will be used later in the chapter):

```
Protected Overrides Sub PerformDataBinding( _
                        ByVal data As System.Collections.IEnumerable)
Dim objData As Object
```

```
Dim tb As System.Web.UI.WebControls.TextBox
Dim ctr As Integer
Dim strFieldName as String

   MyBase.PerformDataBinding(data)

   If data IsNot Nothing Then
```

In C#:

```
protected override void PerformDataBinding(System.Collections.IEnumerable data)
{
 System.Web.UI.WebControls.TextBox tb;
 int ctr;
 string strFieldName;

 base.PerformDataBinding(data);

 if(data != null)
  {
```

Now that you know that you have data, you can loop through the data that's been retrieved and process the fields that you want. You can retrieve the data that you want by using the DataBinder object's GetPropertyValue method. The GetPropertyValue must be passed three parameters:

- The data item
- The name of the field to be retrieved
- A format string to control the format of the returned data (developers using your control would expect to set this format using a DataTextFormat property)

In this Visual Basic 2005 example, the field specified in the DataTextField property is retrieved and used to set the value of a TextBox that is added to the Controls collection of the databound control. The parameters passed to the GetPropertyValue method are the data item being processed and the name of the field specified in the DataTextField (no format is provided):

You should check that any properties required to retrieve the data have been set correctly. In the following example, for instance, the DataTextField is checked before it is used to retrieve the data.

```
If DataTextField > "" Then
    strFieldName = DataTextField
    ctr = 0
    For Each objData In data
         tb = New System.Web.UI.WebControls.TextBox
         ctr = ctr + 1
         tb.ID = "tb" & ctr
         tb.Text = System.Web.UI.DataBinder.GetPropertyValue( _
                                   objData, strFieldName, Nothing)
         Me.Controls.Add(tb)
    Next
End If
```

In C#:

```
if(DataTextField.CompareTo("") > 0)
{
 strFieldName = DataTextField;
 ctr = 0;
  foreach (object objData in data)
 {
   tb = new System.Web.UI.WebControls.TextBox();
   ctr = ctr + 1;
   tb.ID = "tb" + ctr;
   tb.Text = System.Web.UI.DataBinder.GetPropertyValue(objData,
                             strFieldName, null);
   this.Controls.Add(tb);
 }
}
```

Performing Updates

Now that you've retrieved your data, you can also provide a way to handle updates. The DataSourceView object provides Update, Delete, and Insert methods that communicate with the datasource to have it carry out any possible updates. As with the Select method, these changes are performed asynchronously.

> **Again, you should check the DataSourceView's CanUpdate, CanDelete, and CanInsert methods before calling the Update, Delete, and Insert methods. Not all DataSources support all activities.**

The three methods accept up to four parameters, the first three of which are lists of name/value pairs:

- The primary keys of the data to be updated (not required for the Insert method)
- The original values for the data (not required for the Insert method)
- The new values (not required for the Delete method)
- A callback function that will be called after the update is complete

The following Visual Basic 2005 code creates a StateBag and then adds name/value pairs consisting of the name of the field and value of the field (retrieved from text boxes on the control). The code then retrieves the DataSourceView object through the GetData method and passes it the array and a function to call after the insert is complete:

```
Public Sub InsertData()
Dim InsertData As New StateBag
Dim dsv As System.Web.UI.DataSourceView

  dsv = Me.GetData
  If dsv.CanInsert = True Then
```

```
        InsertData.Add("CustId", Ctype(Me.FindControl("tb1"), TextBox).Text)
        InsertData.Add("CustName", Ctype(Me.FindControl("tb2"), TextBox).Text)
        dsv.Insert(InsertData, AddressOf Me.HandleInsert)
    End If

End Sub
```

In C#:

```
public void InsertData()
{
 StateBag InsertData = new StateBag;
 System.Web.UI.DataSourceView dsv;

 dsv = this.GetData();
 if(dsv.CanInsert == true)
 {
  InsertData.Add("CustId", ((TextBox) this.FindControl("tb1")).Text);
  InsertData.Add("CustName", ((TextBox) this.FindControl("tb2")).Text);
  dsv.Insert(InsertData, new DataSourceViewOperationCallback(HandleInsert));
 }
}
```

The function used in the last parameter of the Update, Delete, and Insert methods is passed two parameters when it executes after all updates are complete: the number of records affected by the update and an exception object. If there was an error during processing, the exception object is set to the error. This Visual Basic 2005 code checks for an exception object and throws an exception for the application to catch if an error occurred:

```
Function HandleInsert(ByVal affectedRecords As Integer, _
                                        ByVal ex As Exception) As Boolean
    If ex IsNot Nothing Then
        Throw ex
    End If

End Function
```

In C#:

```
public bool HandleInsert(int affectedRecords, Exception ex)
{
 if(ex == null)
 {
  throw ex;
 }
}
```

Design-Time Support

Up until now, you've let ASP.NET generate the tags that define your control at design time and concentrated on how you can manage the HTML generated for the run time display of your control. However, you can take control of the way that property values are stored for your control at design time. This is critical for creating controls whose properties go beyond simple text values.

By default, the property values for your custom control are stored as attributes on your control's tag. This section begins by showing how to implement an alternative way for a custom control to store property settings that supports properties that produce large amounts of text. From there, the section looks at properties that support complex datatypes (for example, properties that return objects) and provides a way for developers to set those properties at design time in source view. This also provides a mechanism for developers to add constituent controls to your control at design time, much like the way you can add new controls to a Panel.

As the design time settings for your control become more complex, both processing those settings at run time and changing those settings at design time become more complex. The next part of this subsection introduces control builders, which support the processing of complex settings for a custom control at run time. Finally, the section finishes by showing how to create designers that make it easier for developers to set the contents of a control at design time.

Handling Complex Properties

By default, the data returned by your control's properties is stored in attributes on your control's tag at design time. For instance, if a control called BookInfo has properties called MainTitle and SubTitle, the design-time tags for that control would look like this:

```
<cc1:BookInfo ID="BookInfo1" runat="server"
                             MainTitle="Custom Controls and Web Parts"
                             SubTitle="ASP.NET 2.0"/>
```

Because the property settings are embedded in the tag for your control, setting the MainTitle and SubTitle properties at design time is easy for developers: they can just rewrite the attribute. Changing the value of a property in Visual Studio 2005's Property List also updates these attributes. However, if a property produces a large amount of text, storing that value in an attribute is awkward. It's more convenient to save large text values as literal text inside an element.

Saving Property Values as Tag Content

For instance, the BookInfo's MainTitle and SubTitle properties could be saved like this:

```
<cc1:BookInfo ID="BookInfo1" runat="server">
  <MainTitle>Custom Controls and Web Parts</MainTitle>
  <SubTitle>ASP.NET 2.0</SubTitle>
</cc1:BookInfo>
```

To implement this design, you need to mark the control as saving its properties as content within the custom control's tag. This is handled by setting four attributes: one on the class declaration and three on the properties themselves. The attributes are:

- **ParseChildren attribute on the class declaration:** This signals to the class that content within the controls tags should be processed and matched to the corresponding properties.

- **PersistenceMode:** This must be set to PersistenceMode.InnerProperty to allow the property to be saved as a nested element.
- **DesignerSerializationVisibility on the property:** This must be set to DesignerSerializationVisibility.Content to cause Visual Studio 2005 to process the contents of the control's tag at design time.
- **NotifyParentProperty on the property:** This causes the property of the custom control to be updated when the nested element is changed.

In Visual Basic 2005, configuring the BookInfo class to save the MainTitle and SubTitle properties as nested tags looks like this:

```
<ParseChildren(True), _
 ToolboxData("<{0}:BookInfo runat=server></{0}:BookInfo>")> _
 Public Class BookInfo
   Inherits System.Web.UI.WebControls.WebControl

Private _MainTitle As String
Private _SubTitle As String

<DesignerSerializationVisibility(DesignerSerializationVisibility.Content), _
 NotifyParentProperty(True), _
 PersistenceMode(PersistenceMode.InnerProperty)> _
 Public Property MainTitle() As String
 ...property code...
 End Property

<DesignerSerializationVisibility(DesignerSerializationVisibility.Content), _
 NotifyParentProperty(True), _
 PersistenceMode(PersistenceMode.InnerProperty)> _
 Public Property SubTitle() As String
 ...property code...
End Property
```

In C#:

```
[ParseChildren(true)]
[ToolboxData("<{0}:BookInfo runat=server></{0}:BookInfo>")]
public class BookInfo : System.Web.UI.WebControls.WebControl
{
 private string _MainTitle;
 private string _SubTitle;

  [DesignerSerializationVisibility(DesignerSerializationVisibility.Content)]
  [NotifyParentProperty(true)]
  [PersistenceMode(PersistenceMode.InnerProperty)]
  public string MainTitle
  {
    ...property code...
  }

  [DesignerSerializationVisibility(DesignerSerializationVisibility.Content)]
  [NotifyParentProperty(true)]
  [PersistenceMode(PersistenceMode.InnerProperty)]
```

```
    public string SubTitle
    {
        ...property code...
    }
  }
```

When you insert the tags to hold property values, you may get spurious errors from Visual Studio .NET saying that the schema doesn't support these nested tags. You can ignore those errors.

Saving Complex Property Values

Saving your property values in attributes or in nested elements works well as long as your property returns simple datatypes that can be easily converted to text. However, for more complex properties (such as objects that have multiple data items associated with a single property) a more sophisticated mechanism is required. You could use a datatype converter to convert the objects to a string (as discussed in Chapter 6). However, by specifying that the data for your property is to be stored in an element, you can enable developers using your control to set those properties at design time in source view.

As an example, the BookInfo custom control needs to be able to handle multiple authors for a single book. To support this, the BookInfo control has an Authors property that accepts an array of Author objects. This Visual Basic 2005 code declares the Author property as an ArrayList:

```
Public Property Authors() As ArrayList
  Get
    Return _Authors
  End Get
  Set(ByVal value As ArrayList)
      _Authors = value
    End Set
End Property
```

In C#:

```
public ArrayList Authors
{
  get
  {
    return _Authors;
  }
  set
  {
    _Authors = value;
}
}
```

A better design would be to use a custom collection instead of an ArrayList to control the type of object passed to the ArrayList. However, that's a topic for a book on best practices in object-oriented design.

Each Author object has multiple properties (for instance, FirstName, LastName). In Visual Basic 2005, the Author class looks like this:

```
Public Class Author
Private _FirstName As String
Private _LastName As String

Public Property FirstName() As String
 Get
   Return _FirstName
 End Get
 Set(ByVal value As String)
    _FirstName = value
 End Set

End Property

Public Property LastName() As String
 Get
   Return _LastName
 End Get
 Set(ByVal value As String)
   _LastName = value
 End Set
End Property

End Class
```

In C#:

```
public class Author
{
 private string _FirstName;
 private string _LastName;

 public string FirstName
 {
  get
  {
   return _FirstName;
  }
  set
  {
    _FirstName = value;
  }
 }
 public string LastName
 {
  get
  {
   return _LastName;
  }
  set
  {
   _LastName = value;
  }
 }
}
```

It would be convenient if Author objects could be added to the Authors property at design time using nested tags within the BookInfo tag, like this:

```
<cc1:BookInfo ID="BookInfo1" runat="server">
  <cc1:Author FirstName="Peter" LastName="Vogel"/>
  <cc1:Author FirstName="Sara" LastName="Shlaer"/>
  <cc1:Author FirstName="Richard" LastName="Purchas"/>
<cc1:BookInfo>
```

To enable this, you must add the ParseChildren attribute to the custom control's class declaration, passing as parameters True and the name of the property to be loaded from the nested elements. By setting the ParseChildren attribute's first parameter to True, you indicate that the values for the property are to be found nested between the open and close tags for the custom control rather than in one of the control's attributes. The second parameter specifies which property is to be set from the nested tags.

The first parameter for the ParseChildren attribute sets the attribute's ChildrenAsControls property. The second parameter sets the attribute's DefaultProperty property.

It is critical that the name of this tag match the name of the object (and *not* the name of the property being loaded). In this example, the class is named Author so the tag used inside the BookInfo element is also named Author. Also, even if your custom control tag contains only a single nested tag, the property that is referenced by the ParseChildren attribute must accept a collection object of some kind (such as an ArrayList).

This Visual Basic 2005 example specifies that the values for the BookInfo object's Authors property are to be found as elements nested within the custom control's open and close tags:

```
<ParseChildren(True, "Authors"), _
ToolboxData("<{0}:BookInfo runat=server></{0}:BookInfo>")> _
Public Class BookInfo
```

In C#:

```
[ParseChildren(true, "Authors")]
[ToolboxData("<{0}:BookInfo runat=server></{0}:BookInfo>")]
public class BookInfo
```

The property specified in the ParseChildren attribute is automatically loaded with the data from between the custom control's open and close tags. In this example, the Authors property is automatically loaded with Author objects with each Author object's properties set from the attributes on the Author tags inside the BookInfo tag.

After the ArrayList is loaded, you can process its contents as you would any other list. For instance, this Visual Basic 2005 code in the Render method iterates through the Authors property using the Author object in order to display author information in an HTML table:

```
Protected Overrides Sub Render(ByVal writer As System.Web.UI.HtmlTextWriter)
  writer.write("<Table>")

  For Each aut As Author In Me.Authors
    writer.Write("<tr>")
    writer.Write("<tc>" & aut.FirstName & "</tc>")
    writer.Write("<tc>" & aut.LastName & "</tc>")
    writer.Write("</tr>")
 Next

 writer.write("</Table>")
End Sub
```

In C#:

```
protected override void Render(System.Web.UI.HtmlTextWriter writer)
{
 writer.Write("<Table>");

 foreach(Author aut in this.Authors)
 {
  writer.Write("<tr>");
  writer.Write("<tc>" + aut.FirstName + "</tc>");
  writer.Write("<tc>" + aut.LastName + "</tc>");
  writer.Write("</tr>");
 }

 writer.Write("</Table>");
}
```

There is one major limitation to this mechanism: Only a single property can be designated as the default property for the ParseChildren attribute. If you have multiple properties with complex datatypes, you need a more sophisticated mechanism. Furthermore, once you designate a default property in the ParseChildren attribute, no other property can store its data in nested tags, as described in the previous section.

One solution is simply to treat the default property as a repository that can hold any kind of object. Provided you specify a default property with the ParseChildren attribute, ASP.NET automatically adds any objects found between your custom control's open and close tags to the collection returned by the default property. It is your responsibility to handle each object type appropriately as you find it in the collection. This approach allows developers to add constituent controls to your custom control by nesting the tags for those controls inside your custom control.

For instance, to add an ASP.NET Label control to the BookInfo control at design time, it would be convenient if a developer could insert a Label tag inside the BookInfo tag:

```
<cc1:BookInfo ID="BookInfo1" runat="server" >
   <asp:Label ID="Label1" runat="server" Text="Your book"></asp:Label>
</cc1:BookInfo>
```

To implement this you need to create a property to hold all the controls that might be added to your custom control. This Visual Basic 2005 property would do the job:

```
Private _ChildControls As ArrayList

 Public Property ChildControls() As ArrayList
   Get
     Return _ChildControls
   End Get
     Set(ByVal value As ArrayList)
       _ChildControls = value
   End Set
End Property
```

In C#:

```
private ArrayList _ChildControls;

public ArrayList ChildControls
{
 get
 {
  return _ChildControls;
 }
 set
 {
  _ChildControls = value;
 }
}
```

On the class declaration, you must specify this "repository" property as the default property for your control, as this Visual Basic 2005 code does:

```
<ParseChildren(True, "ChildControls"), _
 ToolboxData("<{0}:BookInfo runat=server></{0}:BookInfo>")> _
Public Class BookInfo
```

In C#:

```
[ParseChildren(true, "ChildControls")]
[ToolboxData("<{0}:BookInfo runat=server></{0}:BookInfo>")]
public class BookInfo
```

In your Render method, you could iterate through the ChildControls collection, having each control render itself by calling its RenderControl method. In Visual Basic 2005, the code looks like this:

```
Protected Overrides Sub Render(ByVal writer As System.Web.UI.HtmlTextWriter)
  For Each ctl As Control In Me.ChildControls
    ctl.RenderControl(writer)
  Next
End Sub
```

In C#:

```
protected override void Render(System.Web.UI.HtmlTextWriter writer)
{
 foreach(Control ctl in this.ChildControls)
```

```
    {
      ctl.RenderControl(writer);
    }
  }
```

While this provides a simple mechanism for generating constituent controls, it doesn't really address the issue of handling multiple properties with complex datatypes. Instead, it creates a single property to hold all complex objects. It is better to have a dedicated property for each object. It is also better to have some mechanism that allows you to manage the processing of the tags nested in the custom control rather than just blindly rendering them.

Handling Complex Content

The next step is to handle multiple complex properties on a single control and provide a mechanism for managing those elements as they are added. As the example for this section, the BookInfo control is extended to support the following nested tags:

- The Author tag with a first name and a last name
- The Titles tag with the main title and the subtitle
- An ASP.NET Label tag that will be added to the Controls collection of the BookInfo tag and rendered with the control
- A Description tag containing a description of the book

As a result, the BookInfo tag with all of these nested elements looks like this:

```
<cc1:BookInfo ID="BookInfo1" runat="server" >
  <cc1:Author runat="server" FirstName="Peter" LastName="Vogel" />
  <cc1:Titles runat="server" MainTitle="Custom Controls and Web Parts"
                             SubTitle="ASP.NET 2.0" />
  <asp:Label ID="Label1" runat="server" Text="Your book"></asp:Label>
  <cc1:Description runat="server">
  Comprehensive coverage of ASP.NET 2.0 custom controls and web parts.
  </cc1:Description>
</cc1:BookInfo>
```

This design adds a new type of tag to the mix: the Description element, which has no attributes but, instead, has content nested inside the element's open and close tags.

> **To use this mechanism, it's essential that all the controls have prefixes that tie to the Register tag in the page that associates the tag with an assembly and namespace combination that holds the corresponding custom control. The controls must also have the runat attribute.**

To handle multiple nested tags with complex datatypes and nested controls — and do it reliably — you must override your control's AddParsedSubObject method. The AddParsedSubObject method is called each time a new nested tag is processed. The method is passed the object created from the tag being processed. It is your responsibility, as the control developer, both to define the classes to support those tags and to add the code to the AddParsedSubObject method to handle the objects correctly. If, during processing no object is found in the assembly for any tag, the AddParsedSubObject method is passed an ASP.NET LiteralControl containing the text for the tag.

Before looking at the AddParsedSubObject method, then, you need to add the code to define the Author, Titles, Label, and Description objects to the BookInfo control. To simplify the example, I'll just support the Titles and Description tags in the sample code.

To handle the Titles element, you need to define a Titles class so that ASP.NET can create a Titles object from the data in the Titles element. The Titles class has two properties: MainTitle and SubTitle, corresponding to the attributes on the Title element. In Visual Basic 2005, the Title class looks like this:

```
Public Class Titles
Private _MainTitle As String
Private _SubTitle As String

 Public Property Main() As String
  Get
    Return _MainTitle
  End Get
  Set(ByVal value As String)
    _MainTitle = value
  End Set
 End Property

 Public Property SubTitle() As String
  Get
    Return _SubTitle
  End Get
  Set(ByVal value As String)
    _SubTitle = value
  End Set
 End Property

End Class
```

In C#:

```
public class Titles
{
 private string _MainTitle;
 private string _SubTitle;

 public string Main
 {
  get
  {
   return _MainTitle;
  }
  set
  {
   _MainTitle = value;
  }
```

```
    }

    public string SubTitle
    {
     get
     {
      return _SubTitle;
     }
     set
     {
      _SubTitle = value;
     }
    }
   }
```

Because there will be only one Titles element for the BookInfo control, it isn't necessary to create a collection property (as was done for the Authors element). However, you will want to access the values from the Titles tag from within your custom control. A simple solution is to create a MainTitle and SubTitle property and set those properties from the corresponding properties in the Titles object as the Titles objects are processed in the AddParsedSubObject. You can then read those properties from the code in your custom control.

In Visual Basic 2005, the properties to add to the BookInfo custom control look like this:

```
Private _MainTitle As String
Private _SubTitle As String

 Public Property MainTitle() As String
  Get
    Return _MainTitle
  End Get
  Set(ByVal value As String)
    _MainTitle = value
  End Set
 End Property

 Public Property SubTitle() As String
   Get
     Return _SubTitle
   End Get
   Set(ByVal value As String)
      _SubTitle = value
   End Set
 End Property
```

In C#:

```
private string _MainTitle;
private string _SubTitle;

public string MainTitle
{
 get
 {
```

```
      return _MainTitle;
    }
    set
    {
      _MainTitle = value;
    }
  }

  public string SubTitle
  {
    get
    {
      return _SubTitle;
    }
    set
    {
      _SubTitle = value;
    }
  }
```

To handle the Description element with its literal content (an element with text between its open and close tags) all that's necessary is to create a class that inherits from the ASP.NET Literal control. This is the Visual Basic 2005 definition of that object:

```
Public Class Description
  Inherits System.Web.UI.WebControls.Literal

End Class
```

In C#:

```
public class Description : System.Web.UI.WebControls.Literal
{ }
```

You also need to add a Description property to the BookInfo that can be set from the Description tag. In Visual Basic 2005 the property looks like this:

```
Private _Description As String

 Public Property Description() As String
  Get
    Return _Description
  End Get
  Set(ByVal value As String)
    _Description = value
  End Set
 End Property
```

In C#:

```
private string _Description;

public string Description
```

```
{
 get
 {
  return _Description;
 }
 set
 {
  _Description = value;
 }
}
```

With all the groundwork laid, it's time to override the BookInfo's AddParsedSubObject method and add the code to handle these objects. ASP.NET processes each tag, creates the corresponding object, and passes the object to the AddParsedSubObject method. In the AddParsedSubObject, you must determine the kind of object being passed and take the appropriate action. For the BookInfo object those actions are:

- **For an Author element:** An Author object (defined in the previous section) is passed to the AddParsedSubObject method. That object can be added to the Authors property (also defined in the previous section). If the _Authors ArrayList that this method uses hasn't been created, it should be created at this point.
- **For a Titles element:** A Titles object is passed to the method. The values for the Titles object's MainTitle and SubTitle properties can be used to set the corresponding properties on the BookInfo object.
- **For the Label element:** The Label object passed to the method just needs to be added to the BookInfo's Controls collection.
- **For the Description element:** The Text property (inherited from the Literal control) of the Description object can be used to set the BookInfo's Description property.

Any tags that don't have a corresponding object are passed to the AddParsedSubObject method as a LiteralControl object. You can then retrieve the tag's text from the LiteralControl's Text property and parse the tag out.

In Visual Basic 2005, the AddParsedSubObject method looks like this:

```
Protected Overrides Sub AddParsedSubObject(ByVal obj As Object)

 If obj.GetType.Equals(GetType(Description)) Then
   Me.Description = CType(obj, Description).Text
 End If

  If obj.GetType.Equals(GetType(Author)) Then
    If _Authors Is Nothing Then
       _Authors = New ArrayList(2)
    End If
    Me.Authors.Add(obj)
  End If

  If obj.GetType.Equals(GetType(Titles)) Then
     Me.MainTitle = CType(obj, Titles).MainTitle
     Me.SubTitle = CType(obj, Titles).SubTitle
```

```
    End If

    If obj.GetType.Equals(GetType(System.Web.UI.WebControls.Label)) Then
      Me.Controls.Add(obj)
    End If

  End Sub
```

In C#:

```
protected override void AddParsedSubObject(object obj)
{
 if (obj is Author)
 {
  if(_Authors == null)
  {
   _Authors = new ArrayList(2);
  }
  this.Authors.Add(obj);
 }

 if (obj is Titles)
 {
  this.MainTitle = ((Titles) obj).Main;
  this.SubTitle = ((Titles) obj).Subtitle;
 }

 if (obj is Description)
 {
  Description ds;
  ds = (Description) obj;
  this.Description = ds.Text;
 }

 if (obj is Label)
 {
   this.Controls.Add((System.Web.UI.WebControls.WebControl) obj);
 }
}
```

To have the AddParsedSubObject called, the ParseChildren attribute on the BookInfo object must have its first parameter set to False, as in this Visual Basic 2005 code:

```
<ParseChildren(False), _
 ToolboxData("<{0}:BookInfo runat=server></{0}:BookInfo>")> _
 Public Class BookInfo
```

In C#:

```
[ParseChildren(false)]
[ToolboxData("<{0}:BookInfo runat=server></{0}:BookInfo>")]
public class BookInfo
```

While not a good practice, you can include plain text (text outside of any tag) inside your custom control's open and close tags, as in this example:

```
<cc1:BookInfo ID="BookInfo1" runat="server">
  <cc1:Author runat="server" FirstName="Peter" LastName="Vogel"/>
  A comprehensive guide to custom control and web parts.
  <asp:Label ID="Label1" runat="server" Text="Your book"></asp:Label>
</cc1:BookInfo >
```

The text (including all whitespace) from the end of the Author tag to the start of the Label tag is passed to the AddParsedSubObject method as a LiteralControl. The text can be retrieved from the LiteralControl's Text property. However, if all you want is to have the text rendered as a part of the custom control's display, you just need to add the LiteralControl to your custom control's Controls collection, as this Visual Basic 2005 code does:

```
If obj.GetType.Equals(GetType(LiteralControl)) Then
   Me.Controls.Add(obj)
End If
```

In C#:

```
if (obj is LiteralControl)
{
this.Controls.Add((System.Web.UI.WebControls.WebControl) obj)
}
```

Controlling Complex Content

While simply overriding the AddParsedSubObject method will allow you to process complex content, the process, as described so far, has several deficiencies:

- No editing is performed to ensure that only valid tags are present.
- It's not possible to manage the conversion of the nested tags to elements.
- HTML encoding (for example, replacing > with >) is ignored.
- Whitespace between the end of one tag and the start of another is treated as literal text and passed to the AddParsedSubObject method.
- All nested elements must be assigned the appropriate prefix and the runat attribute.

By using a control builder class in conjunction with your custom control, you can take more control over the process of processing tags within your custom control. As ASP.NET processes the tags inside a control, a control builder is called as part of the process before the resulting objects are passed to the AddParsedSubObject method. By tailoring properties on the control builder you can, for instance, eliminate unnecessary whitespace being passed to your AddParsedSubObject method and control the type of object created from the nested tags.

Every ASP.NET control automatically invokes one of the default control builders that comes with ASP.NET or invokes a specialized control builder.

A control builder is a class that inherits from the System.Web.UI.ControlBuilder class, as in this Visual Basic 2005 example:

```
Public Class BookBuilder
  Inherits System.Web.UI.ControlBuilder

End Class
```

In C#:

```
public class BookBuilder : System.Web.UI.ControlBuilder
{
}
```

The control builder is tied to a custom control through the ControlBuilder attribute on the custom control's Class declaration. This attribute must be passed the type of the control builder to be used with the custom control. In Visual Basic 2005, the class declaration to tie the BookBuilder control builder to the BookInfo custom control looks like this:

```
<ControlBuilder(GetType(BookBuilder)), _
ToolboxData("<{0}:BookInfo runat=server></{0}:BookInfo>")> _
Public Class BookInfo
```

In C#:

```
[ControlBuilder(typeof(BookBuilder))]
[ToolboxData("<{0}:BookInfo runat=server></{0}:BookInfo>")]
public class BookInfo
```

You can use the control builder to simplify processing for your AddParsedSubObject method. For instance, by default, the control builder returns all the whitespace from the end of one tag to the start of another as a LiteralControl. In most cases, you won't want to deal with that text in your AddParsedSubObject method. You can suppress whitespace by overriding the control builder's AllowWhitespaceLiteral property and returning False. You can also cause all the HTML literals to be decoded prior to being passed to the AddParsedSubObject method by overriding the HTMLDecodeLiterals method and returning True.

While overriding the AllowWhitespaceLiterals property prevents any blank whitespace from being passed to the AddParsedSubObject method, it doesn't prevent text that's outside of any tag from being passed to the method. Overriding the control builder's AppendLiteralString method prevents literal text from being passed to AddParsedSubObject.

This Visual Basic 2005 example causes HTML to be decoded and prevents both whitespace and literal text from being passed to the custom control's AddParsedSubObject method:

```
Public Class BookBuilder
  Inherits System.Web.UI.ControlBuilder

 Overrides Public Function HtmlDecodeLiterals() As Boolean
   Return True
 End Function

 Public Overrides Function AllowWhitespaceLiterals() As Boolean
```

```
    Return False
  End Function

  Public Overrides Sub AppendLiteralString(ByVal s As String)
  End Sub

End Class
```

In C#:

```
public class BookBuilder : System.Web.UI.ControlBuilder
{
 public override bool HtmlDecodeLiterals()
 {
  return true;
 }

 public override bool AllowWhitespaceLiterals()
 {
  return false;
 }

 public override void AppendLiteralString(string s)
 {
 }
}
```

You can also use the control builder's GetChildControlType method to simplify the tags used inside your custom control or to have different tags processed as the same object. The GetChildControlType method is called once for each tag nested inside your custom control tag and returns the type of object to be used with the tag. The GetChildControlType method is passed the name of the tag and an IDictionary object holding all of the attributes on the tag. This allows you to tailor the objects used with a particular tag, eliminating the need to fully qualify the tag nested inside the custom control. This method also provides a location where you can test for the content found nested in the control and decide what to do with it.

For instance, by using the control builder's GetChildControlType, it is possible to rewrite the nested controls for the BookInfo tag to eliminate the prefixes and runat attributes, as in this example:

```
<cc1:BookInfo ID="BookInfo1" runat="server" >
  <Author FirstName="Peter" LastName="Vogel" />
  <Titles MainTitle="Custom Controls and Web Parts" SubTitle="ASP.NET 2.0" />
  <asp:Label ID="Label1" runat="server" Text="Your book"></asp:Label>
</cc1:BookInfo>
```

As with saving property values as content in the control, you may get spurious errors from Visual Studio .NET saying that the schema doesn't support these nested tags. You can ignore these errors.

In the GetChildControlType method you can examine each tag name and return the object type to be used with the tag (this is the object type that will be passed to the custom control's AddParsedSubObject method). Without this processing, all of the non-ASP.NET tags in the previous example would be treated as literal content because they don't have a prefix or the runat attribute.

This Visual Basic example sets the datatype for each tag and also checks for tags that shouldn't be present:

```
Public Class BookBuilder
  Inherits System.Web.UI.ControlBuilder

 Public Overrides Function GetChildControlType( _
      ByVal tagName As String, ByVal attribs As System.Collections.IDictionary) _
      As System.Type

  Select Case tagName
    Case "Author"
      Return GetType(Author)
    Case "Titles"
      Return GetType(Titles)
    Case "Description"
      Return GetType(Description)
    Case "asp:Label"

    Case Else
       Throw New Exception("Tag " & tagName & " not allowed in this control.")
  End Select
 End Function

End Class
```

In C#:

```
public class BookBuilder : System.Web.UI.ControlBuilder
{
 public override System.Type GetChildControlType(string tagName,
                                           System.Collections.IDictionary attribs)
 {
  switch(tagName)
  {
   case "Author":
     return typeof(Author);
   case "Titles":
     return typeof(Titles);
   case "Description":
     return typeof(Description);
   case "asp:Label":
     return typeof(Label);
     break;
   default:
     throw new Exception("Tag " + tagName + " not allowed in this control.");
  };
 }
}
```

As the sample code shows, the tag name that is passed to the GetChildControlType includes any prefix used with the control.

As part of building a custom control, additional control builders will be called to handle building the custom control's constituent controls. The builders for these constituent controls will either be one of the default builders that come with ASP.NET or a custom builder assigned to the control by the control's developer.

In the AppendSubBuilder method, you can check the control builder being used for each constituent control and throw an exception if the child's control builder doesn't support some functionality that you want. This Visual Basic 2005 example checks whether the control builder being added supports white-space and throws an exception if it does not:

```
Public Overrides Sub AppendSubBuilder( _
 ByVal subBuilder As System.Web.UI.ControlBuilder)

  If subBuilder.AllowWhitespaceLiterals = False Then
    Throw New Exception("Whitespace must be supported.")
  Else
    MyBase.AppendSubBuilder(subBuilder)
  End If

End Sub
```

In C#:

```
public override void AppendSubBuilder(System.Web.UI.ControlBuilder subBuilder)
{
 if(subBuilder.AllowWhitespaceLiterals == false)
 {
  throw new Exception("Whitespace must be supported.");
 }
 else
 {
  base.AppendSubBuilder(subBuilder);
 }
}
```

If you do override the AppendSubBuilder, you should always call the method of the underlying control (unless you are throwing an exception). If you don't, then no builders are added for any child controls.

To support reuse, it makes sense to create your control builders so that each can be used with several types of custom controls. However, there may be specific versions of those controls that a general-purpose control builder may not be able to handle. The ControlBuilder object has a number of properties that allow you to find out information about the control that has called the control builder:

- **HasAspCode:** True if the custom control has ASP code blocks embedded in its source.
- **HasBody:** True if the custom control has both an open tag and a close tag (rather than a single empty tag).
- **ControlType:** The Type object for the custom control the control builder is attached to.

- **ID:** The ID property for the custom control. The control builder can also set this value.
- **TagName:** The tag name for the custom control.
- **FChildrenAsProperties:** This is the property set by the first parameter passed to the ParseChildren attribute and, when true, indicates that automatic parsing of the custom control's content is being performed.
- **InPageTheme:** Returns True if the control is being used to generate a page theme.
- **Localize:** True if the custom control using the builder is localized.

In addition to these properties, you can also retrieve information about the custom control through the control builder's ControlType property, which returns the type of the custom control. A good place to perform checks on the custom control using the control builder is in the control builder's OnAppendToParent method, which is called when the control builder is attached to the custom control.

As an example, this Visual Basic 2005 example checks to see if the control being built is a BookInfo control and, if so, then checks to see if the control has its ChildrenAsProperties property set to True. If the property is set to True the code throws an exception.

```
Public Overrides Sub OnAppendToParentBuilder(ByVal parentBuilder As ControlBuilder)

 If ControlType.Name = "BookInfo" Then
   If Me.FChildrenAsProperties = True Then
       Throw New Exception("This builder should not be used with ParseChildren.")
   End If
 End If

End Sub
```

In C#:

```
public override void OnAppendToParentBuilder(ControlBuilder parentBuilder)
{
 if(ControlType.Name == "BookInfo")
 {
  if(this.FChildrenAsProperties == true)
  {
   throw new Exception(
          "This builder should not be used with ParseChildren enabled.");
  }
 }
}
```

Designers

Given the complexity of the tags that you can put inside a custom control, you're probably thinking that it's unlikely that a typical developer could manage to enter those tags correctly. The solution is to provide the developer with a designer that helps the developer set these properties.

To associate a designer to your custom control, you add the Designer attribute to your class declaration, passing the type of your designer. This Visual Basic.NET example ties the BookInfoDesigner object to the BookInfo Custom Control:

```
<Designer(GetType(BookInfoDesigner)), _
ToolboxData("<{0}:BookData runat=server></{0}:BookData>")> _
 Public Class BookInfo
```

In C#:

```
[Designer(typeof(BookInfoDesigner))]
[ToolboxData("<{0}:BookData runat=server></{0}:BookData>")]
 public class BookInfo
```

You begin building your designer by creating a class that inherits from System.Web.UI.Design. ControlDesigner, and then override the class's GetDesignTimeHTML method. At run time, the GetDesignTimeHTML method for the designer is called instead of the custom control's Render method (within your designer, you can still retrieve the HTML for the custom control by calling the base designer object's GetDesignTimeHTML method).

In order to inherit from the ControlDesigner class, you may need to add a reference to the System.Design library in the .NET tab of the Project | Add Reference dialog box.

Within the GetDesignTimeHTML method, you need to handle three scenarios:

- **The custom control is able to generate its own HTML.** However, you may want to override or modify the HTML generated by the control (for instance, for a databound control, you may not want to access the database at design time and generate a default display instead).
- **The custom control generates an error.** This may occur because some necessary properties haven't been set or the current settings for some properties conflict with each other. You will want to display a message that reflects the error.
- **The custom control does not generate any HTML but no error has occurred.** This can occur when the control is first added to the page and the developer using the control hasn't set any properties yet. A control that generates a table might not display any HTML until the number of rows and columns required are set. You will want to generate some neutral display.

Within the GetDesignTimeHtml method, you can support those scenarios by following this process:

1. Check to see if the control being designed can produce HTML by calling the base object's GetDesignTimeHtml method.
2. If an error is generated, produce the HTML required to display the error. The code to generate the error HTML should be placed in the GetErrorDesignTimeHtml method. This method expects to be passed the exception object for the error.
3. If no error is generated but no HTML is produced, generate the neutral design-time HTML. The code to generate the HTML when the control doesn't generate any HTML should be placed in the GetEmptyDesignTimeHtml method.
4. Generate any custom HTML.
5. Return the HTML.

In Visual Basic 2005, a typical GetDesignTimeHtml routine looks like this:

```
Public Overrides Function GetDesignTimeHtml() As String
Dim strDesignHTML As String

  Try
    ...code to generate custom HTML
    strDesignHTML = MyBase.GetDesignTimeHtml
  Catch ex As Exception
        strDesignHTML = GetErrorDesignTimeHtml(ex)
  End Try

  If strDesignHTML Is Nothing Then
    strDesignHTML = GetEmptyDesignTimeHtml()
  ElseIf strDesignHTML.Length = 0 Then
    strDesignHTML = GetEmptyDesignTimeHtml()
  End If

  Return strDesignHTML

End Function
```

In C#:

```
public override string GetDesignTimeHtml()
{
 string strDesignHTML;
 try
 {
  ...code to generate custom HTML
  strDesignHTML = base.GetDesignTimeHTML()
 }
 catch(Exception ex)
 {
  strDesignHTML = GetErrorDesignTimeHtml(ex);
 }

 if(strDesignHTML == null)
 {
  strDesignHTML = GetEmptyDesignTimeHtml();
 }
 else
 {
  if(strDesignHTML.Length == 0)
  {
   strDesignHTML = GetEmptyDesignTimeHtml();
  }
 }
 return strDesignHTML;
}
```

Under the hood, the base object's GetDesignTimeHTML method calls the custom control's Render method to retrieve the HTML for the control. For some controls, running the Render method may result in some changes being made to the control. Alternatively, you may want to make changes to the control before calling the GetErrorDesignTimeHtml method (for instance, ensuring that all the constituent controls on the form are visible). As a result, you may need to access the custom control and reset some properties on the control after calling the GetDesignTimeHTML method. You can access the custom control through the designer's Component property as discussed later in this section.

For this section's example, you have the BookInfo control generate a custom display at design time that shows the values of the custom control's nested tags. While you'd need to address all of the nested tags in a full implementation, let's concentrate on the Description tag for this section.

To implement the display shown in Figure 9-2, the following Visual Basic 2005 code goes into the GetDesignTimeHTML method (where the comment "code to generate custom HTML" appears in the previous example). This example uses the designer's Component object (which holds a reference to the control that the designer is working with) to retrieve the value of the BookInfo's Description property. The value is then wrapped in an HTML display.

```
Dim bi As BookInfo
  bi = CType(Me.Component, BookInfo)

 If bi.Description > "" Then
   _Description = bi.Description
   strDesignHTML = "<b>Tag Content</b> <br/> " & _
                   "&lt;Description>" & _Description & " &lt;/Description>"
End If
```

In C#:

```
BookInfo bi;
bi =  (BookInfo) this.Component;

if(bi.Description.CompareTo("") > 0)
{
 _Description = bi.Description;
 strDesignHTML = "<b>Tag Content</b> <br/> " + "&lt;Description>" +
                 _Description + " &lt;/Description>";
}
```

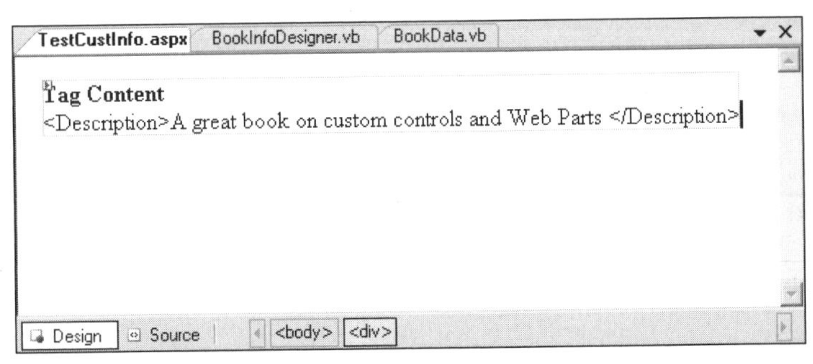

Figure 9-2

A designer should, presumably, allow the developer using the control to make changes to the control. To enable the developer to execute methods in the designer, you must add DesignerVerbs to the control. The text for these verbs will be displayed in the custom control's Common Tasks list and the control's pop-up menu. Figure 9-3 shows a new Verb with the text Set Description in the control's Common Tasks list. Figure 9-4 shows the verb in the custom control's pop-up menu.

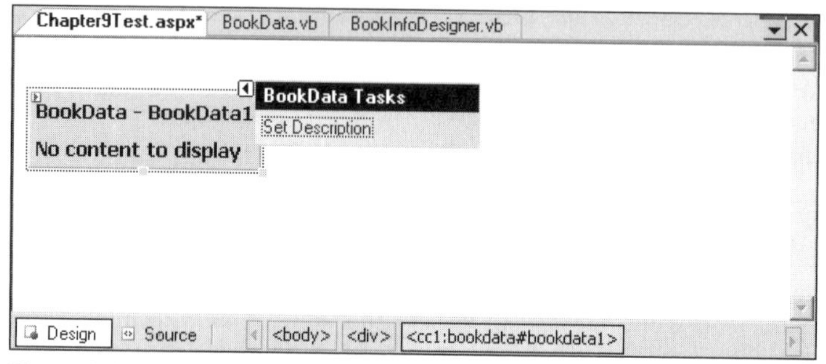

Figure 9-3

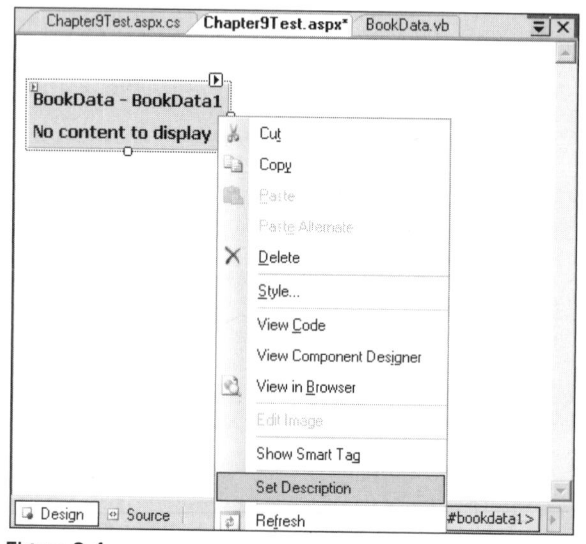

Figure 9-4

Verbs are added to the custom control by overriding the Verbs property of the ControlDesigner object. This property is read-only so you need to provide only a Get portion. The process of adding verbs to a designer is very similar to the process for adding verbs to a Web Part: You must create a DesignerVerb object (passing the text for the verb and the method to be called), add the DesignerVerb to a DesignerVerbCollection object, and then return the DesignerVerbCollection from the property. This Visual Basic 2005 code creates the verb with the Set Description text shown in the previous example:

```
Public Overrides ReadOnly Property Verbs() As _
            System.ComponentModel.Design.DesignerVerbCollection
 Get
   Dim vrbs As New System.ComponentModel.Design.DesignerVerbCollection
   Dim vrb As New System.ComponentModel.Design.DesignerVerb("Set Description", _
                                                        AddressOf GetDescription)

   vrbs.Add(vrb)
   Return vrbs
 End Get

End Property
```

In C#:

```
public override System.ComponentModel.Design.DesignerVerbCollection Verbs
{
 get
 {
  System.ComponentModel.Design.DesignerVerbCollection vrbs = new
     System.ComponentModel.Design.DesignerVerbCollection();
  System.ComponentModel.Design.DesignerVerb vrb = new
     System.ComponentModel.Design.DesignerVerb("Set Description", GetDescription);
  vrbs.Add(vrb);
  return vrbs;
 }
}
```

A routine that is called from a DesignerVerb is declared very much like an event. It is passed two parameters: an object and an EventArgs object. Typically, in one of these routines after retrieving new values from the developer, you should call the control's UpdateDesignTimeHtml method, which will, indirectly, cause the custom control's text to be updated and the GetDesignTimeHtml method to be called to refresh the control's display. This Visual Basic 2005 code uses an InputBox to retrieve a value for the Description property and calls the UpdateDesignTimeHtml method:

```
Sub GetDescription(ByVal sender As Object, ByVal e As System.EventArgs)
   _Description = InputBox("Enter Description", "Description", _Description)
   Me.UpdateDesignTimeHtml()
End Sub
```

In C#:

```
public void GetDescription(object sender, System.EventArgs e)
{
 _Description = Microsoft.VisualBasic.Interaction.InputBox("Enter Description",
                                 "Description", _Description, 0, 0);
 this.UpdateDesignTimeHtml();
}
```

When the UpdateDateDesignTimeHtml method is called, the custom control calls the designer's GetPersistenceContent method to retrieve the tags and text to nest inside the custom controls open and close tags. To implement your changes, you should override the GetPersistenceContent method and return the text that you want inserted into your custom control.

This Visual Basic 2005 example generates the Description tag to go inside the custom control's tags:

```
Public Overrides Function GetPersistenceContent() As String
    Return "<Description>" & _Description & "</Description>"
End Function
```

In C#:

```
public override string GetPersistenceContent()
{
 return "<Description>" + _Description + "</Description>";
}
```

With the code written to handle the process when everything goes right, it's time to write the two methods that are called when the custom control doesn't generate any HTML: the GetEmptyDesignTimeHtml (called when there is no HTML for the custom control and shown in Figure 9-5) and the GetErrorDesignTimeHtml (called when an error is raised and shown in Figure 9-6).

```
Protected Overrides Function GetEmptyDesignTimeHtml() As String
  Return Me.CreatePlaceHolderDesignTimeHtml("<B> No content to display </B>")
End Function

Protected Overrides Function GetErrorDesignTimeHtml(ByVal e As System.Exception) _
                                                                      As String
  Return Me.CreateErrorDesignTimeHtml(e.Message)
End Function
```

In C#:

```
protected override string GetEmptyDesignTimeHtml()
{
 return this.CreatePlaceHolderDesignTimeHtml("<B> No content to display </B>");
}

protected override string GetErrorDesignTimeHtml(System.Exception e)
{
 return this.CreateErrorDesignTimeHtml(e.Message);
}
```

While this example used the base DesignControl, several specialized designers are available in the .NET Framework.

For instance, the ReadWriteControlDesigner allows you to create a designer that a developer can drag controls onto. In the ReadWriteControlDesigner you can determine what controls have been added to the designer and add those controls to your custom control. Earlier in this chapter you saw an example of a control where a ReadWriteControlDesigner would be useful: the version of the BookInfo control that allowed an asp:Label control to be inserted between the BookInfo control's open and close tags. Associating a ReadWriteControlDesigner with the BookInfo control would allow a developer to drag a Label control onto the design surface instead of having to insert tags in Source view.

Similarly, the TemplatedControlDesigner supports creating designers for templated controls so that developers using the control can build the templates in design view instead of in Source view.

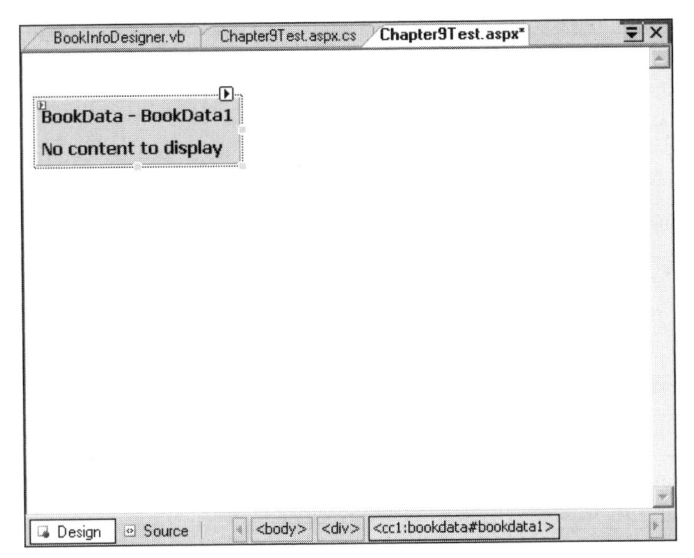

Figure 9-5

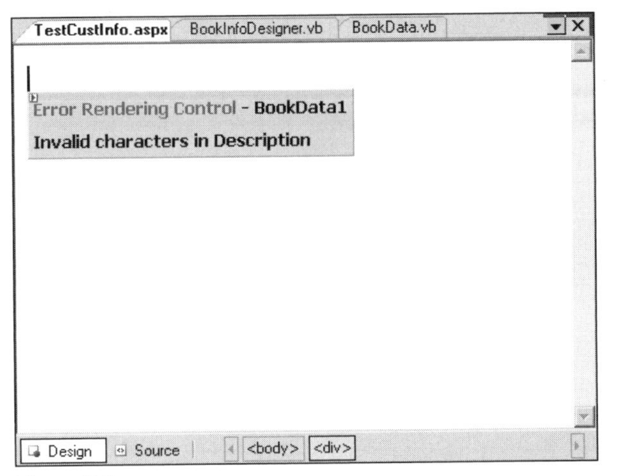

Figure 9-6

Summary

In this chapter you've seen how to:

- Dynamically add client-side code to your custom control and wire it up to the events fired by the HTML generated by your control
- Perform dynamic callbacks from client-side code to access server-side resources
- Create specialized controls: Validators, DataBound, and Templated controls
- Support complex properties at design time by storing settings inside your control's design-time tags
- Process those settings using the AddParsedSubObject method and control builders
- Support developers using your control at design time through designers

As noted at the start of this chapter, you might go your entire career without using all of the technology discussed in this chapter. In the next chapter, you learn about an advanced feature that can be used by Web Parts only: the ability to have two Web Parts communicate with each other to pass data between themselves.

10

Communicating Between Web Parts

One of the most powerful features of Web Parts is their ability to connect to each other both at design time and at run time. This gives you the ability to create a Web Part (a provider) that retrieves data and passes it on to some other Web Part (a consumer) that can be used to create a formatted display for the data. By providing your user with a set of providers and consumers, users are able, at run time, to pick the provider that they want and connect it with the consumer that they want.

As an example, let's return to the book sales site described in Chapter 1; users might pick among Search Providers: One provider might provide many search options while another has only a few and others offer specialized searches aimed at, for instance, the academic market. Having selected a Search Provider, users could connect that part to one of several Search Consumers that provided several different ways of viewing the information: basic information, detailed information, with or without book covers, information for specialized audiences (such as a list of citations for academic audiences).

In this chapter you see how to make all that happen, including how to:

- Create provider Web Parts that can send data to other Web Parts
- Create consumer Web Parts that can request that data
- Create transformers that allow you to connect Web Parts not designed to work together
- Make connections at design time or at run time — or let your users make the connections

Using Connectable Parts

Before I discuss how to create connectable Web Parts, you should first see how to connect Web Parts on a page. Let's assume that two parts already exist:

- A book detail display Web Part (BookDetail)
- A Web Part that lists books (BookList)

A user can select a book from the list and have the detail Web Part display information about the book.

Setting up the Page

To create a page where users can connect Web Parts, you first need to drag the following onto the page:

- A WebPartManager
- At least one WebPartZone
- A ConnectionsZone Web Part

The ConnectionsZone provides the control panel where the user manages connections between Web Parts. Using the ConnectionsZone, the user is able to both make and break connections. The ConnectionsZone won't appear, however, until the WebPartManager is put into the right mode.

To put the page into connections mode, you add a button that the user can click to set the WebPartManager's mode to ConnectDisplayMode. The code in the button's click event looks like this in Visual Basic 2005:

```
Me.WebPartManager1.DisplayMode = WebPartManager.ConnectDisplayMode
```

In C#:

```
this.WebPartManager1.DisplayMode = WebPartManager.ConnectDisplayMode;
```

> **You can't set the WebPartManager's DisplayMode to ConnectDisplayMode unless there is at least one ConnectionsZone on the page.**

Finally, you can drag the provider and consumer Web Parts into the WebPartZone. In the next section, you create a provider part that, when the user provides a book title, retrieves the ISBN for the book (virtually every modern book has a unique ISBN assigned to it). This part is more complex than it seems, as it would have to handle those situations in which the title matches several different books and provide a mechanism in the user interface for the user to select the book that she wants.

You also create a consumer part that retrieves the ISBN from the provider part and uses it to display a book's shipping information.

Making Connections

When the user clicks the button to put the page in connection mode, nothing much changes on the screen. The effect of setting the WebPartManager's DisplayMode property isn't really apparent until the user displays the Verb menu of either the consumer or provider Web Part. As shown in Figure 10-1, when the WebPartManager is in ConnectDisplayMode, a Connect verb is added to the Verb menu of any Web Part that can participate in a connection. When the user selects the Connect verb from one of the Web Parts, the ConnectionsZone on the page is finally displayed, as shown in Figure 10-2.

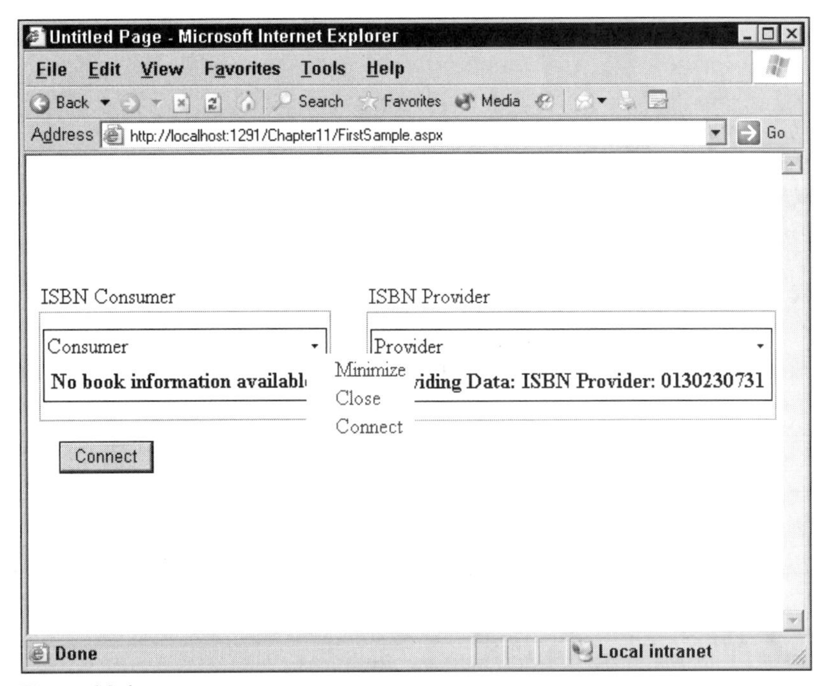

Figure 10-1

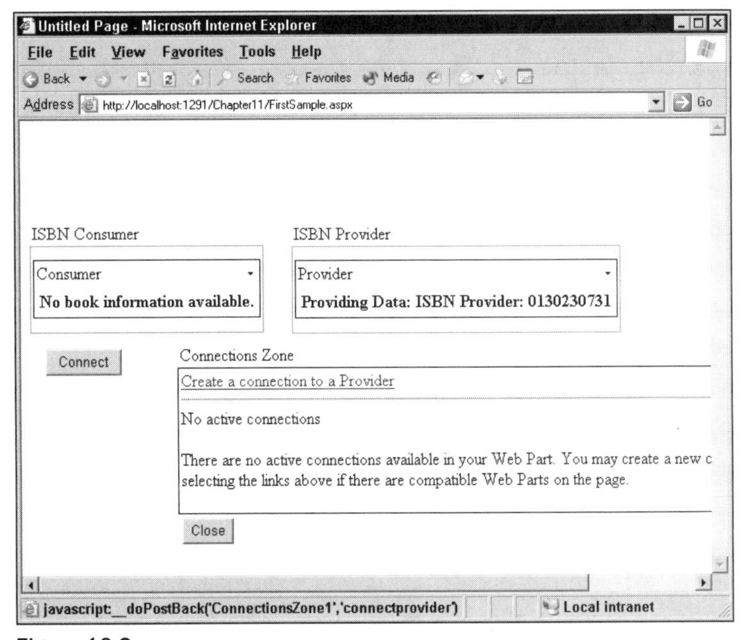

Figure 10-2

Because so little changes on the page when the WebPartManager is put into ConnectDisplayMode, it is a good idea to update the page display yourself to let the user know what to do. After the code that sets the DisplayMode, for instance, you can set the Web Part's Subtitle property to insert some text beside the Verb menu to indicate that new items have been added to the menu (something obvious: "Click the down arrow to make a connection.").

Generally speaking, you don't want to update the Title property. The various Web Part framework controls often use the Title property from Web Parts when displaying lists of Web Parts to the user. As an example, if you start changing the Title property, users won't be able to recognize the part in the list produced by a Catalog Web Part.

The ConnectionsZone displays a hyperlink at the top that allows the user to connect to another Web Part. Under the hyperlink, a list of current connections is displayed. (If there are no connection points, the text "No active connections" is displayed, as shown in Figure 10-2.)

After the user clicks the hyperlink, the ConnectionsZone is redisplayed to allow the user to make a connection to another Web Part. In order for a WebPart to communicate with another WebPart, both WebParts have to implement at least one communication interface. When the ConnectionsZone is displayed, it lists all the communication interfaces for the Web Part.

The ConnectionsZone displays one block for each interface showing the display name for the interface. In Figure 10-3, "Provides ISBN" is the display name for the interface available on the provider whose Connect verb was clicked. (If a consumer Web Part had been selected initially, the word "Get:" would appear instead of "Send:".)

The user can now select from the drop-down list a Web Part to connect to.

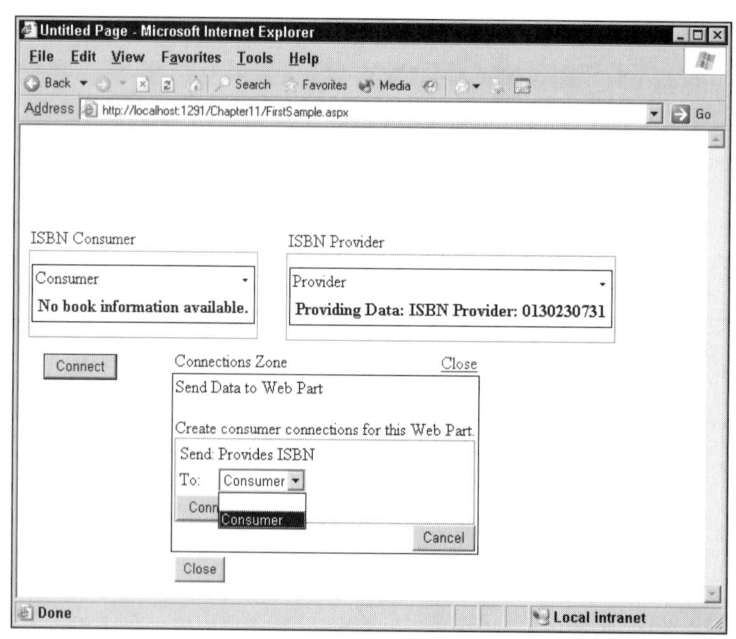

Figure 10-3

The drop-down list of parts to connect to displays the Title property from the available consumer Web Parts — yet another good reason for using titles that are meaningful to your users.

After the user has selected the Web Part to connect to, the user clicks the Connect button to finish making the connection. Once the connection is made, the Web Part consumer automatically pulls the data that it wants from the provider Web Part. At this point, the ConnectionsZone redisplays to show the Web Parts communicating with the current Web Part (see Figure 10-4). With the connection made, the user can then click the Close button at the bottom of the ConnectionsZone or the Close hyperlink at the top of the zone to close the ConnectionsZone.

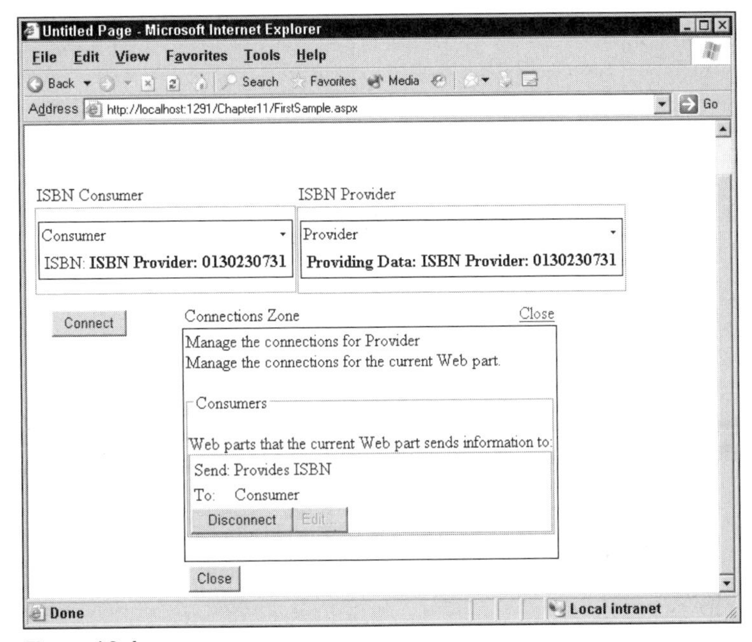

Figure 10-4

Managing Connections

To manage the connection, the user can redisplay the ConnectionsZone at any time by putting the page back in connect display mode. If the user clicks the Connect verb for a Web Part that's involved in a connection, the ConnectionsZone is displayed as it was after the connection was made (as in Figure 10-4).

At its top, the ConnectionsZone displays the name of the Web Part whose Connect verb was clicked (below this is the line, "Manage the connections for the current Web Part."). In the lower part of the display are up to two blocks:

- One block is for Web Parts that the Web Part is providing data to. This block has the title "Providers" and the text "Web Parts that the current Web Part gets information from:".
- One block is for Web Parts that it is consuming data from. The Consumer block has the title "Consumers:" and the text "Web Parts that the current Web Part sends information to:".

Within the blocks is a list of parts for that category. For instance, the Provider block has a block for each Web Part providing data to the current Web Part. In these blocks is the name of the Web Part that data is coming from and the interface being used. Also in the block is a Disconnect button that the user can click to break the connection to the Web Part.

Creating Connectable Web Parts

Now that you've seen how Web Parts can be connected on a page, the next step is to create Web Parts that can be connected. This section walks you through the steps you need to create a provider Web Part and a consumer Web Part.

Creating a Provider Web Part

Let's begin by walking through the process required to create a Web Part that can send data to other Web Parts. There are three steps to creating a Web Part that can provide data to another Web Part:

1. Define an interface that specifies what data is to be passed between the Web Parts.
2. Have the Web Part that will be providing the data implement the interface, including writing the code for the interface's methods and properties.
3. Write the routine that handles the connection in the Provider.

Define an Interface

For a Web Part to communicate with other Web Parts, the Web Parts must implement an interface that data can be passed through. In the interface, you specify the methods and properties that must be supported by any object that implements the interface. Let's start with the simplest possible interface, one that has a single property that returns a single string. In Visual Basic 2005, you define interfaces inside an Interface structure:

```
Public Interface IBookInfo
   Property ISBN() As String
End Interface
```

In C#:

```
public interface IBookInfo:
{
   string ISBN
    {
     get;
     set;
    }
}
```

When declaring a property in an interface, you do not specify an actual body for the property. The interface specifies only what properties and methods must be present but doesn't specify any code—the code is the responsibility of the implementing Web Part. The same is true of any methods that you add to the interface, as described later in this chapter.

You can define your interface in any module outside of a Class. However, the best practice is to define your interface in a separate file with the same name as the interface. This makes your interfaces easily visible in Solution Explorer, allows you to manage your interfaces separately from code in a source management tool, and also gives you the ability to copy interfaces between projects (if necessary) just by copying the interface files. However, if you are going to share an interface between projects, it probably makes more sense to place the interface file in a separate project where it can be compiled into its own DLL. Then, other projects that use the interface can just add a reference to the DLL.

In Visual Studio .NET, you can add a new interface file to your project by selecting Project ➪ Add New Item. In the Add New Item dialog box, select Interface from the list, enter the name of your interface, and click the Add button.

The convention is to give interfaces a name that begins with the letter I (for example, IBookInfo).

Implement the Interface

The next step is to modify a Web Part to provide data through the interface. Begin by having the Web Part implement the interface that you just defined. In Visual Basic 2005, you indicate that you want a class to implement an interface by adding the Implements keyword with the name of the interface after the class definition and the Inherits statement, as this code does:

```
Public Class ProviderPart
    Inherits System.Web.UI.WebControls.WebControl
    Implements IBookInfo
```

In C#, you add the interface name to the end of the class definition preceded by a comma, as this code shows:

```
public class ProviderPart : System.Web.UI.WebControls.WebControl, IBookInfo
```

Now that you've specified what interfaces you're implementing in your Web Part, you have to create all the properties or methods specified in the interface (for the IBookInfo interface, that's only a single property). In Visual Basic 2005, you can give the routines that implement the interface any name that you want, although the convention is to give the routines that you write the same name as in the interface. There are two differences between the routines that implement part of an interface and the routines that you've written before:

- The routine has to use the Implements keyword to tie the routine to a method or property in the interface.
- The routine has to have the same signature as the routine in the interface that it's tied to; for instance, if the routine in the interface is a property that accepts no parameters and returns an integer, then the implementing routine has to be a property that accepts no parameters and returns an integer.

The definition of a method or property (the datatype, the number of properties, whether a property is read-only or write-only) is referred to as the signature of the method or property. An interface consists of a series of method and property signatures without any actual code—without an implementation. The methods or properties in your Web Part have the code that actually implements the interface's signatures. For this to work, the signature of the method or property in the Web Part must match the signature of the item in the interface that the method or property implements. In C#, the name of the method or property is part of the signature. In Visual Basic 2005, on the other hand, the name of the method or property is not part of the signature so you can call your method or property anything that you want.

In this Visual Basic 2005 example, we create a routine called BookIdentifier that is tied to the ISBN property in the IBookInfo property. Like the ISBN property, the BookIdentifier routine is a property that returns a string and accepts no parameters:

```
Property BookIdentifier() As String Implements IBookInfo.ISBN
  Get
    Return myData
  End Get

  Set (Value As String)
    myData = Value
  End Set

End Property
```

In C# you don't assign an alias to an interface routine, but the name of the routine must consist of the interface name and the routine name, separated by a period:

```
public class ProviderPart : WebControl, IBookInfo
  {
   string IBookInfo.ISBN
   {
      get
      {
         return MyData;
      }
      set
      {
         MyData = value;
      }
  }
```

Create a Connection Point

Finally, you need to provide a connection point method for the interface. The connection point method is a function that returns a reference to the provider Web Part. The function's return value is the provider's implementation of the interface.

You can give the method any name that you want but, to indicate that the method is a connection point, you need to add the ConnectionProvider attribute to the routine. The ConnectionProvider must be passed a display name (this is the name that is used in the ConnectionsZone user interface). This Visual Basic 2005 example shows the connection point for the IBookInfo interface:

```
<WebControls.WebParts.WebParts.ConnectionProvider("Provides ISBN", _
 "ISBNProvider")> Public Function IBookInfoProvider() As IBookInfo

    Return Me

End Function
```

In C#, the code looks like this:

```
[WebControls.WebParts.WebParts.ConnectionProvider("Provides ISBN", "ISBNProvider")]
public IBookInfo IBookInfoProvider()
{
  return this;
}
```

One convention for naming the connection routine is to use the name of the interface with the word "Provider" appended to it.

Once you've filled in the routine tied to the ISBN property with some real business logic you have a Web Part that can provide data to another Web Part. Now you need to create a consumer Web Part that is able to pull data from your Web Part provider through the interface.

Creating a Consumer Part

Creating a consumer Web Part is considerably easier than creating a provider: All that you have to do is create a connection point method. The connection point method is a subroutine that accepts a single parameter declared as the interface type (such as IBookInfo). The method must be given the ConnectionConsumer attribute (again, this attribute can be passed the display name to be used in the ConnectionsZone user interface). Using the parameter passed to the method, code in the routine can access a provider through the methods and properties in the interface. This Visual Basic 2005 code accesses the provider through the IBookInfo interface to retrieve the value of the ISBN property:

```
<WebControls.WebParts.WebParts.ConnectionConsumer("IBookInfo Consumer")> _
Public Sub IBookInfoConsumer(ByVal bk As IBookInfo)
Dim strISBN As String

   strISBN = bk.ISBN

End Sub
```

In C#:

```
[WebControls.WebParts.WebParts.ConnectionConsumer("IBookInfo Consumer")]
public void IBookInfoConsumer(IBookInfo bk)
{
  string strISBN;
  strISBN = bk.ISBN;
}
```

To access the provider from routines outside the connection routine, just declare a variable at the class level as the interface type. You can set this variable in the connection routine and use that variable outside the connection routine. However, if the consumer part has not been connected to the provider, then the class variable is set to Nothing in Visual Basic 2005, null in C#. To handle this, you should check that the class variable has been set before using it.

This Visual Basic 2005 code declares a variable called ibk as an IBookInfo, sets ibk in the connection routine, and (in the Render routine) accesses the provider using the ibk variable:

```
Private ibk As IBookInfo

<WebControls.WebParts.WebParts.ConnectionConsumer("IBookInfo Consumer")> _
```

```
Public Sub IBookInfoConsumer(ByVal bk As IBookInfo)
   ibk = bk
End Sub

Protected Overrides Sub Render(ByVal writer As System.Web.UI.HtmlTextWriter)

  If ibk Is Nothing Then
     writer.Write("<b>No book information available.</b>")
  Else
     writer.Write("ISBN: <b>" & ibk.ISBN & "</b>")
  End If

End Sub
```

In C#:

```
private IBookInfo ibk;

[WebControls.WebParts.WebParts.ConnectionConsumer("IBookInfo Consumer")]
public void IBookInfoConsumer(IBookInfo bk)
 {
  ibk = bk;
 }

protected override void Render(System.Web.UI.HtmlTextWriter writer)
 {
  if (ibk == null)
  {
     writer.Write("<b>No book information available.</b>");
   }
   else
   {
     writer.Write("ISBN: <b>" + ibk.ISBN + "</b>");
   }
 }
```

You can't take advantage of the interface to the provider until after the connection point routine has run in the consumer. In the consumer Web Part, both when the connection is first made and on subsequent page requests, the connection point routine runs after the consumer's Load event (and the host page's LoadComplete event), and before the page's PreRender event.

The provider's connection routine runs just before the consumer's connection routine rather than at a specific point in the provider's life cycle.

A Two-Way Street

Classifying Web Parts as consumers and providers suggests a one-way flow of information. In fact, communication between Web Parts is more of a two-way street. After a consumer Web Part retrieves a reference to a provider, the consumer can set properties on the provider through the interface in addition to reading properties from the provider. The consumer can also pass parameters to the methods that the consumer calls, providing another way for the consumer to send information to the provider. While code in the consumer initiates most of the interaction in the connection by calling routines on the provider, that doesn't mean that only the consumer can receive information. As you see later in this chapter in the discussion of the IWebPartField interface, it is possible to create a connection where the provider calls routines in the consumer.

A more complex interface might include both methods and properties, as this Visual Basic 2005 example does:

```
Public Interface IBookInfo
   Property ISBN() As String
   Sub UpdateCache(CacheFlag As Boolean)
   Function SortData(Direction As String) As Boolean
End Interface
```

In C#:

```
interface IBookInfo
{
  string ISBN
  {
   get;
   set;
  }
  void UpdateCache(bool CacheFlag);
  bool SortData(string Direction);
}
```

The provider that implemented this interface includes these routines (in Visual Basic 2005):

```
Property BookIdentifier() As String Implements IBookInfo.ISBN
...business logic
End Property

Sub UpdateCache(CacheFlag As Boolean) Implements IBookInfo.UpdateCache
...business logic
End Sub

Function SortData(Direction As String) As Boolean Implements IBookInfo.SortData
...business logic
End Sub
```

In C#:

```
string IBookInfo.ISBN()
{
  ...business logic
}

void IBookInfo.UpdateCache(bool CacheFlag)
{
  ...business logic
}

bool IBookInfo.SortData(string Direction)
```

```
{
  ...business logic
}
```

The consumer that accesses this provider could include this code to set the property and call the methods as this Visual Basic 2005 code does:

```
<WebControls.WebParts.WebParts.ConnectionConsumer("IBookInfo Consumer")> _
Public Sub IBookInfoConsumer(ByRef bk As IBookInfo)
Dim strProviderValue As String
Dim bolSuccess As Boolean

    strProviderValue = "10345329"
    bk.ISBN = strProviderValue
    bk.UpdateCache(True)
    bolSuccess = bk.SortData("Desc")

End Sub
```

In C#:

```
[WebControls.WebParts.WebParts.ConnectionConsumer("IBookInfo Consumer")]
public void IBookInfoConsumer(IBookInfo bk)
{
   string strProviderValue;
   bool bolSuccess;

   strProvider = "10345329";
   bk.ISBN = strProviderValue;
   bk.UpdateCache(true);
   bolSuccess = bk.SortData("Desc");
}
```

As the consumer calls the methods and sets the properties in the interface, the corresponding routines execute in the provider, allowing the consumer to pass data to the provider by setting properties on the interface or parameters passed to interface methods. The provider can return data through return values from functions or properties that can be read by the consumer.

Predefined Interfaces

You're not obliged to create your own interface — the Web Part framework comes with four predefined interfaces: IWebPartField, IWebPartRow, IWebPartTable, and IWebPartParameters. The interfaces provide mechanisms that allow the consumers and providers to find out information about each other and tailor their activity based on that information. As the names of the interfaces imply, IWebPartField is intended to be used to pass a single value, IWebPartRow to pass a single set of data, IWebPartTable to pass multiple rows of data. The IWebPartParameters interface supports the functionality of the other three interfaces and provides a mechanism for the consumer to indicate to the provider what kind of information the consumer expects.

The IWebPartField, IWebPartRow, and IWebPartTable interfaces are sufficiently similar that seeing how to use one shows you how to use all three of them. I'll use the IWebPartField interface to demonstrate all three.

IWebPartField Overview

The IWebPartField interface includes a single method and a single property:

- The method has a single parameter that allows the provider to call some other routine in the consumer.
- The property is read-only and returns an object that describes a property.

The two members of the interface work together to provide data and a description of that data to the consumer. Describing the process makes it sound very complicated, so let's begin with an overview of the steps involved, beginning at the consumer's side:

1. The connection point method in the consumer is invoked by the Web Part that will provide the data. The consumer is passed a reference to the interface used by the provider.
2. The consumer calls the GetFieldValue method on the interface, passing a reference to some other routine in the consumer (this other routine must be a subroutine that accepts a single parameter of type Object). The provider will use this routine to pass data to the consumer.
3. In the provider, the GetFieldValue method now executes and is passed the reference to the routine that exists back in the consumer.
4. The provider calls the routine in the consumer, passing a single parameter (of type Object). It's at this point that the provider actually provides data to the consumer.
5. The routine in the consumer executes, receiving the data passed by the provider.

There is more flexibility in this process than is suggested in this description. For instance, once the provider has received the reference to the routine in the consumer, the provider can call that routine at any time, not just in the GetFieldValue method.

An IWebPartField Provider

While I'll start by looking at the code for a provider, this code won't make much sense unless you understand the code's purpose — how its routines will be used by a consumer using the IWebPartField interface. Some of this code looks similar to what you've seen before. For instance, the provider must include a routine that returns a reference to the provider's implementation of the interface.

When using the IWebPartField interface the consumer initiates the communication process by calling the GetFieldValue method of the IWebPartField interface (different interfaces will have a different initiating method). The consumer passes to the GetFieldValue method a reference that points to the routine in the consumer that's intended to be called from the provider (references to a routine are called *delegates*). The provider can then call that routine in the consumer, passing data back to the consumer. A good place to start writing the provider's code is by creating the method that will be passed a delegate from the consumer. The provider can then, through the delegate, invoke the consumer's routine, passing information to the consumer.

The following Visual Basic 2005 example demonstrates the code for a provider that implements the IWebPartField interface. The FieldValue method in the sample code implements the GetFieldValue method from the IWebPartField interface. This FieldValue routine is the one that will be called by the consumer to pass a delegate to the provider. The FieldValue method must accept a single parameter, which is the delegate from the consumer. In this example, the parameter is named fld.

After the consumer calls the FieldValue method and passes a delegate, the provider can call the routine in the consumer referenced by the delegate fld. To actually call the routine referred to by the delegate, you use the delegate's Invoke method, passing any parameters that the consumer's routine requires. So, in the FieldValue method in this example, the code calls the Invoke method of the fld parameter. The consumer's routine (which you build in the next section) expects to be passed a single parameter so this code supplies a single parameter to the Invoke method. In this example, a property on the provider is being passed to the consumer's method:

```
Implements WebControls.WebParts.IWebPartField

Sub FieldValue(ByVal fld As WebControls.WebParts.FieldCallback) _
                        Implements WebControls.WebParts.IWebPartField.GetFieldValue

    fld.Invoke(Me.BookData)

End Sub

ReadOnly Property BookData() As String
  Get
      Return strBookTitle
  End Get
End Property
```

In C#:

```
void WebControls.WebParts.IWebPartField.FieldValue(
                                         WebControls.WebParts.FieldCallback fld)

 {
   fld.Invoke(this.BookData);
 }

 string BookData
 {
  get
  {
   return strBookTitle;
  }
 }
```

Of course, the Invoke method could just as easily have been passed a variable or a literal instead of a property on the provider. The reason for passing a property is to support the other part of the IWebPartField interface: the Schema property. The Schema property tells the consumer all about the information being returned by the provider. The Schema property must return a PropertyDescriptor, an object that can hold all the information about a property. If the GetFieldValue method is tied to a property, the Schema property in the provider can be tied to the same property using tools built into the .NET Framework. The consumer can then use the Schema property of the IWebPartField interface to get information about the data the consumer will retrieve.

In the following code, the DataDescription routine implements the Schema property of the IWebPartField interface, creates a PropertyDescriptorCollection that includes all the properties for the provider, and then returns a PropertyDescriptor for the BookData property:

```
ReadOnly Property DataDescription() As ComponentModel.PropertyDescriptor _
                              Implements WebControls.WebParts.IWebPartField.Schema
  Get
    Dim pdc As PropertyDescriptorCollection

    pdc = TypeDescriptor.GetProperties(Me)
    Return pdc("BookData")
  End Get

End Property
```

In C#:

```
ComponentModel.PropertyDescriptor
 WebControls.WebParts.IWebPartField.Schema.DataDescription {
  get
  {
   PropertyDescriptorCollection pdc;

   pdc = TypeDescriptor.GetProperties(this);
   return pdc["BookData"];
  }
}
```

The consumer can now use the Schema property to retrieve a property descriptor that describes the data being passed to the consumer, as you see shortly.

An alternative to passing a PropertyDescriptorCollection based on the properties for the consumer is to create a dedicated object to handle the passed data. You can then create a PropertyDescriptorCollection based on this object and pass that to the provider.

Before moving on to look at the consumer's code, for the sake of completeness (and to give you something familiar to review), here's the provider's connection point routine in Visual Basic 2005:

```
<WebControls.WebParts.WebParts.ConnectionProvider("Provides IWebPartField")> _
Public Function IWebPartFieldProvider() As WebControls.WebParts.IWebPartField

  Return Me

End Function
```

And in C#:

```
[WebControls.WebParts.WebParts.ConnectionProvider("Provides IWebPartField")]
public WebControls.WebParts.IWebPartField IWebPartFieldProvider()
{
  return this;
}
```

An IWebPartField Consumer

Code in the consumer has to accomplish two tasks:

- It must include a routine that will be called by the provider.
- It must pass a reference to that routine to the provider.

In the following Visual Basic 2005 example, the routine to be called by the provider is named ReceiveData. The IWebPartFieldConsumer method passes to the provider a delegate that points to the ReceiveData routine by calling the GetFieldValue method of the interface (the interface is passed to the IWebPartFieldConsumer method). In Visual Basic 2005, a delegate is created whenever you use the AddressOf operator; in C# just passing the routine's name creates a delegate for that routine.

To refresh your memory about what is happening on the provider's side: In the sample Visual Basic 2005 provider code in the previous section, the GetFieldValue method was implemented in a method called FieldValue. That routine received the delegate to the consumer's routine and invoked the routine (in this case, the ReceiveData routine) to pass data back to the consumer.

Following the IWebPartFieldConsumer method in the code is the ReceiveData routine that is to be called by the provider. When the provider in the previous example invoked the delegate passed to the provider, it passed data in a single parameter to the consumer's routine. This example shows that routine with its single parameter: the BookTitle parameter of the ReceiveData subroutine. The ReceiveData code uses the interface's Schema property to retrieve a description of the data to be returned by the consumer by retrieving a PropertyDescriptor object. In this example, the PropertyDescriptor returned by the Schema property is used to check that the data being returned from the provider is a string:

```
Dim ifld As WebControls.WebParts.IWebPartField

<WebControls.WebParts.WebParts.ConnectionConsumer("IWebPartField Consumer")> _
Public Sub IWebPartFieldConsumer(ByVal fld As WebControls.WebParts.IWebPartField)

  ifld = fld
  ifld.GetFieldValue(AddressOf ReceiveData)

End Sub

Sub ReceiveData(BookTitle As Object)
Dim pd As PropertyDescriptor

  pd = ifld.Schema
  If pd.PropertyType.Name = "String" Then
     strTitle = BookTitle.ToString
  End If

End Sub
```

In C#:

```
WebControls.WebParts.IWebPartField ifld;

[WebControls.WebParts.ConnectionConsumer("IWebPartField Consumer")]
public void IWebPartFieldConsumer(UI.WebControls.WebParts.IWebPartField fld)
 {
   ifld = fld;
   fld.GetFieldValue(new WebControls.WebParts.FieldCallback(RecieveData));
```

```
}

public void ReceiveData(object BookTitle)
{
 PropertyDescriptor pd;

 pd = ifld.Schema();
 if(pd.PropertyType.Name == "String")
 {
   strTitle = BookTitle.ToString();
 }

}
```

IWebPartTable and IWebPartRow

The IWebPartTable and IWebPartRow interfaces are similar in structure to the IWebPartField interface and are used in a similar way. The major differences are:

- The IWebPartRow and IWebPartTable's Schema properties return a collection of property descriptors (a PropertyDescriptorCollection). This supports passing a variety of data items to the consumer's routine.
- In the IWebPartRow interface, the equivalent method to the GetFieldValue method is GetRowData.
- In the IWebPartTable interface, the equivalent method to the GetFieldValue method is GetTableData.
- In the IWebPartTable interface, the routine in the consumer that is called from the provider must be passed a collection rather than a single object.

IWebPartParameters

The IWebPartParameters interface uses a similar structure to IWebPartField, IWebPartTable, and IWebPartRow but has four differences that are significant enough that it should be discussed separately:

- The equivalent routine to GetFieldValue is GetParametersData.
- The routine in the consumer called by the provider must be passed a Dictionary instance of name-value pairs.
- The Schema property in the provider must return a collection of PropertyDescriptors instead of a single PropertyDescriptor
- The interface includes a third method, SetConsumerSchema, that the consumer must call first.

It's the SetConsumerSchema method that makes the IWebPartParameters a significantly different interface from the other three predefined interfaces. The SetConsumerSchema method is used to let the consumer pass a PropertyDescriptorCollection to the provider to specify the kind of information that the consumer will accept. As you saw, in the IWebPartField interface the Schema property provided the consumer with a method of finding out information about the data being returned by the provider. The SetConsumerSchema method does the reverse — it lets the consumer tell the provider about the data that the consumer expects to get.

In this section, I refer to the "Dictionary object"—this is shorthand. There is no Dictionary object in the .NET Framework. Instead, there are a number of objects that implement the IDictionary interface (such as SortedList or StateBag). Any of these objects can be used with the consumer's routine in the IWebPartParameters interface. However, "Dictionary object" is considerably shorter than saying "any object that implements the IDictionary interface."

The SetConsumerSchema method must be passed a PropertyDescriptorCollection, listing the items that will be accepted. In the provider, the code in the GetParametersData method should use the information passed in SetConsumerSchema to build the Dictionary object that will be passed back to the consumer. The provider, for instance, could loop through the PropertyDescriptorCollection provided through the SetConsumerMethod to determine the names of the properties to be returned (and their datatypes) in the Dictionary object.

It's almost always a good idea, when writing the code for the consumer object, to call the SetConsumerSchema method before calling the GetParametersData method. To take advantage of the IWebPartParameters interface, the provider needs to have access to the PropertyDescriptorCollection object passed from the consumer before the provider calls the routine back in the consumer. The provider can, for instance, use the information in the PropertyDescriptorCollection to determine if the provider actually has any data that the consumer wants. The provider normally calls the consumer's routine during the provider's GetParametersData method. So, to make it possible for the provider to use the information from the consumer, the consumer should call the provider's SetConsumerSchema method, passing the PropertyDescriptorCollection before calling the provider's GetParametersData. If that order isn't followed, the provider won't have the PropertyDescriptorCollection available to analyze in the GetParametersData when building the Dictionary collection to return to the consumer.

The Schema property still has a role to play. While the SetConsumerParameters method lets the consumer specify what data it wants, the Schema property lets the provider respond with a collection of data that it can provide. Typically, in the Schema property, you will check the collection of PropertyDescriptors sent by the consumer and return a PropertyDescriptorCollection of properties that you can actually provide.

In the following Visual Basic 2005 example of a consumer WebPart, the consumer calls the SetConsumerSchema method, passing a PropertyDescriptorCollection that describes all the properties on the consumer. After passing that information to the provider, the code then does a very simple check through the schema property to see if the count of requested properties matches the count of properties to be returned. If there is a match, the consumer calls the GetParametersData method, passing a reference to the routine to be used by the provider (called ReceiveData in this example). The ReceiveData routine, when it is called by the provider, loops through the Dictionary passed to it, retrieving the data in the Dictionary for BookTitle and AuthorName. This sample code includes definitions for BookTitle and BookAuthor to show what the PropertyDescriptorCollection passed to SetConsumerSchema will include:

```
Public Class SampleConsumer _
   Inherits System.Web.UI.WebControls.WebParts.WebPart

 <WebControls.WebParts.ConnectionConsumer("IWebPartParameters Consumer")>_
 Public Sub IWebPartParametersConsumer( _
                  ByVal prm As WebControls.WebParts.IWebPartParameters)
 Dim pdc As PropertyDescriptorCollection
 Dim iprm As WebControls.WebParts.IWebPartParameters

  iprm = prm

  pdc = TypeDescriptor.GetProperties(Me)
```

```
    iprm.SetConsumerSchema(pdc)

    If iprm.Schema.Count = pdc.Count Then
      iprm.GetParametersData(AddressOf ReceiveData)
    End If
  End Sub

  Sub ReceiveData(ByVal BookInfo As IDictionary)
  Dim entry As DictionaryEntry

    For Each entry In BookInfo.Keys
      Select Case entry.Key.ToString
         Case "BookTitle"
           Me.BookTitle = entry.Value.ToString
         Case "BookAuthor"
           Me.BookAuthor = entry.Value.ToString
      End Select
    Next

  End Sub

  Property BookTitle() As String
    ...application logic
  End Property

  Property BookAuthor() As String
    ...application logic
  End Property
```

In C#:

```
public class SampleConsumer : System.Web.UI.WebControls.WebParts.WebPart
{
[WebControls.WebParts.ConnectionConsumer("IWebPartParameters Consumer")]
 public void IWebPartParametersConsumer(
          WebControls.WebParts.IWebPartParameters prm)
 {
   PropertyDescriptorCollection pdc;
   WebControls.WebParts.IWebPartParameters iprm;

   iprm = prm;

   pdc = TypeDescriptor.GetProperties(this);
   iprm.SetConsumerSchema(pdc);
   if (pdc.Count == iprm.Schema.Count)
    {
     iprm.GetParametersData(ReceiveData);
    }
 }

 public void ReceiveData(IDictionary BookInfo)
 {
  foreach(DictionaryEntry entry in BookInfo.Keys)
  {
   switch(entry.Key.ToString)
   {
```

```
      case "BookTitle":
        this.BookTitle = entry.Value.ToString;
        break;

      case "BookAuthor":
        this.BookAuthor = entry.Value.ToString;
    };
  }
}

public string BookTitle
{
 ...application logic
}

public string BookAuthor
{
 ...application logic
}
```

The following example Visual Basic 2005 code goes in a provider that implements the IWebPartParameters interface. The code saves a reference to the PropertyDescriptorCollection passed to the SetConsumerSchema method in a module level variable called pcSchema (the SetConsumerData is implemented here by a method called sc). The code in the Schema property loops through the PropertyDescriptorCollection passed in the SetConsumerSchema method and checks to see if the provider has a corresponding property. If the provider does, the PropertyDescriptor is added to an array of PropertyDescriptors that is eventually converted into a PropertyDescriptorCollection and returned to the Consumer. In the GetParametersData routine (implemented in this sample by the routine gpd), the property collection is used to determine what data to add to the Dictionary object that will be passed to the consumer's routine through the Invoke method. There are several objects that implement the IDictionary interface — this code uses the StateBag object:

```
Dim pcSchema As PropertyDescriptorCollection

Sub sc(ByVal schema As PropertyDescriptorCollection) _
  Implements WebControls.WebParts.IWebPartParameters.SetConsumerSchema

   pcSchema = schema

End Sub

Public ReadOnly Property IParmsSchema() As _
    System.ComponentModel.PropertyDescriptorCollection _
    Implements WebControls.WebParts.IWebPartParameters.Schema
 Get
   Dim pdcMe As PropertyDescriptorCollection
   Dim pdcReturn(pcSchema.Count) As PropertyDescriptor
   Dim ing As Integer

   pdcMe = TypeDescriptor.GetProperties(Me)
   For Each pd As PropertyDescriptor In pcSchema
      If pdcMe(pd.Name) IsNot Nothing Then
           ing += 1
           pdcReturn(ing) = pd
```

```
            End If
         Next

         Return New PropertyDescriptorCollection(pdcReturn)
       End Get

     End Property

     Sub gpd(ByVal prm As WebControls.WebParts.ParametersCallback) _
         Implements WebControls.WebParts.IWebPartParameters.GetParametersData
     Dim dict As New StateBag
     Dim prop As PropertyDescriptor

       For Each prop In pcSchema
         Select Case prop.Name
           Case "BookTitle"
               dict.Add("BookTitle", Me.BookTitle)
           Case "BookAuthor"
               dict.Add("BookAuthor", Me.BooktAuthor)
         End Select
       Next

       prm.Invoke(dict)

     End Sub
```

In C#:

```
PropertyDescriptorCollection pcSchema;

void WebControls.WebParts.IWebPartParameters.SetConsumerSchema
                                        (PropertyDescriptorCollection schema)
{
 pcSchema = schema;
}

System.ComponentModel.PropertyDescriptorCollection
  WebControls.WebParts.IWebPartParameters.Schema
  {
   get
   {
    int ing = 0;
    PropertyDescriptorCollection pdcMe;
    System.ComponentModel.PropertyDescriptor[] pdcReturn;
    pdcReturn = new System.ComponentModel.PropertyDescriptor[pcSchema.Count];

    pdcMe = TypeDescriptor.GetProperties(this);
    foreach(PropertyDescriptor pd in pcSchema)
    {
     if (pdcMe[pd.Name] != null)
     {
      ing += 1;
      pdcReturn[ing] = pd;
     }
```

```
        }

        return new PropertyDescriptorCollection(pdcReturn);
      }
    }

    void WebControls.WebParts.IWebPartParameters.GetParametersData
                            (WebControls.WebParts.ParametersCallback prm)
    {
     StateBag dict = new StateBag();

     foreach(PropertyDescriptor prop in pcSchema)
     {
        switch(prop.Name)
        {
         case "BookTitle":
           dict.Add("BookTitle", this.BookTitle);
           break;

         case "BookAuthor":
           dict.Add("BookAuthor", this.BooktAuthor);
           break;
        };
     }
     prm.Invoke(dict);
    }
```

Handling Incompatible Interfaces

While the predefined interfaces provide a way for providers and consumers from different developers to communicate, you can also create Transformer objects that handle converting incompatible data. ASP.NET automatically invokes the appropriate transformer when the user attempts to connect incompatible parts.

Assume that there exists a Web Part for displaying Author information using the IAuthorInfo interface. It is convenient for this Web Part to be able to be connected to the FindBook part (this lets users display author information for a book that they have found using the FindBook part). Unfortunately, the IBookInfo interface returns the ISBN as a string while the IAuthorInfo interface treats a book's ISBN as a numeric value. A Transformer can handle this conversion for you.

To start creating a Transformer, you need to add a new class module to your project. Adding a WebCustomControl to your project enables you to create the Transformer with the least amount of typing. The Transformer doesn't have to be in the same project as the Web Parts it handles the conversion between, but needs to have access to the definition of the interfaces. So, if the transformer isn't in the same project as the interface definition, the Transformer's project will need a reference to the interface's DLL or project. In the following sample code, I assume that this Transformer is added to a project called BookSiteWP that holds both the Web Parts that use the Transformer and the interface definitions that must be handled.

A Transformer is a class that inherits from the WebControls.WebParts.WebPartTransformer class. The part must implement the interface for the consumer that receives the data. In addition, the class must have the Transformer attribute applied to it. The Transformer attribute must be passed two parameters: the type of each of the two interfaces that the transformer handles conversions between.

The following Visual Basic 2005 code supports transforming data from the format specified by the IBookInfo interface (the source) to the format required by the IAuthorInfo interface (the target). The Transformer attribute specifies the source and target interfaces, with the source interface being converted from first, and the target interface second. Because this transform converts book information to author information, the IBookInfo type is listed first. The routine also implements the IAuthorInfo interface— the interface that the data is being converted to:

```
<WebControls.WebParts.WebPartTransformer(GetType(IBookInfo), _
  GetType(IAuthorInfo))> Public Class BookToAuthorTransform
    Inherits System.Web.UI.WebControls.WebParts.WebPartTransformer
    Implements IAuthorInfo
```

The equivalent C# code looks like this:

```
[WebControls.WebParts.WebPartTransformer(typeof(IBookInfo), typeof(IAuthorInfo))]
public class BookToAuthorTransform :
        System.Web.UI.WebControls.WebParts.WebPartTransformer, IAuthorInfo
{
```

When it's necessary to convert data between the two interfaces, ASP.NET automatically loads the Transform object and calls the Transform method on the Transformer. The method will be passed a reference to the interface that is providing the data.

For this case, the method is passed the IBookInfo interface. Because the Transform method is written to accept an Object, you need to cast the parameter to the correct type (IBookInfo in this case). The reference to the interface is going to be used in several routines in the Transformer so the variable that holds the reference must be declared at the class level. The function also needs to return a reference to the Transformer. This Visual Basic 2005 code demonstrates the code to handle the conversion from the IBookInfo interface:

```
Dim ibk As IBookInfo

Public Overrides Function Transform(ByVal providerData As Object) As Object
  ibk = CType(providerData, IBookInfo)
  Return Me
End Function
```

The equivalent C# code looks like this:

```
IBookInfo ibk;

public override object Transform(object providerData)
 {
  ibk = (IBookInfo) providerData;
  return this;
 }
```

While a Transform object handles transformations between a single pair of interfaces only, you can create as many Transform classes as you want.

Now you have to implement the methods that provide the data. Because the Transformer is intended to provide data to the IAuthorInfo interface, that's the interface whose methods and properties must be implemented (and, of course, because the IAuthorInfo interface was the interface specified in the

Implements keyword at the top of the class module, all of the IAuthorInfo's members must be implemented in the class). In this case, the Transformer must implement the methods and properties of the IAuthorInfo interface, which is just the ISBN property as an integer value.

The code within the routines that implement the interface must provide the appropriate data to the consumer in the appropriate format. This data can be created by reading data from the interface for the provider (the code can also use whatever other methods the programmer wants). In order to produce the ISBN as an integer value, this example reads the ISBN from the provider interface, converts it to an integer, and returns it. The following Visual Basic 2005 code in the ISBN property reads the ISBN from the IBookInfo interface retrieved in the Transform method. In order to support the IAuthorInfo definition of the ISBN, the routine converts the string retrieved from the IBookInfo to an integer before returning it:

```
Property ISBN() As Integer Implements IAuthorInfo.ISBN
  Get
   If (Not (ibk) Is Nothing) Then
     Return Convert.ToInt32(ibk.ISBN)
   End If
  End Get

  Set(ByVal value As Integer)
    ibk.ISBN = value.ToString
  End Set

End Property
```

The equivalent C# code looks like this:

```
int IAuthorInfo.ISBN
 {
  get
  {
   if (ibk  != null )
   {
    return Convert.ToInt32(ibk.ISBN);
   }
   else
   {
    return 0;
   }
  }

  set
  {
   ibk.ISBN = value.ToString;
  }
 }
```

There is one final step before your Web site can use the Transformer. You must update the web.config file to let the site know about the transformer. This is done by adding a <webParts> element after the <authorization> element in the site's web.config file. Inside the <webParts> element, a <transformers> element includes tags that add new transformers to the site. To add a transformer you use an <add> element. The <add> element's name attribute can be set to any string, but the type attribute must have the name of the Transformer.

This example shows how a Transformer called BookToAuthorTransform in a library (project) called BookSiteWP is added to an ASP.NET 2.0 site:

```
<webParts>
  <transformers>
    <add name="Book To Author Transformer"
                 type="BookSiteWP.BookToAuthorTransform"  />
  </transformers>
</webParts>
```

The ASP.NET Framework provides two predefined Transformers—Row to Table and Row to Parameters—to handle the conversion between IWebPartRow and IWebPartField, and between IWebPartRow and IWebPartParameters, respectively.

Connection Point Parameters

In addition to accepting the display name for the connection point, the ConnectionProvider and ConnectionConsumer attributes can also be passed a unique identifier for the interface as their second parameter. If you have multiple connection points in your Web Part (for instance, if you have a consumer that supports multiple interfaces) you must set this parameter so that the connection points have different identifiers (the default for this parameter is "default"). The following Visual Basic 2005 example shows two connection points in the same consumer supporting the IBookInfo and IWebPartField interfaces. In both connection point routines, a reference to the interfaces is retrieved (presumably so that methods and properties of the interfaces can be used elsewhere in the consumer):

```
Public Class SampleMultipleInterface _
  Inherits System.Web.UI.WebControls.WebParts.WebPart
  Implements IBookInfo
  Implements IWebPartField

Dim ibk As IBookInfo
Dim ifld As IWebPartField

<WebControls.WebParts.WebParts.ConnectionConsumer("IBookInfo Consumer", _
  "BookInfo")> Public Sub SetFieldInfo(ByVal bk As IBookInfo)
   ibk = bk
End Sub

<WebControls.WebParts.WebParts.ConnectionConsumer("IWebPartField Consumer", _
  "Field")> Public Sub SetBookInfo(ByVal ifld As IWebPartField)
    ifld = fld
End Sub
```

In C#:

```
class Connection : System.Web.UI.WebControls.WebParts.WebPart,
                  IBookInfo, IWebPartField
{
IBookInfo ibk;
IWebPartField ifld;

  [WebControls.WebParts.WebParts.ConnectionConsumer("IBookInfo Consumer",
    "BookInfo")] public void SetFieldInfo(IBookInfo bk)
```

```
  {
   ibk = bk;
  }

  [WebControls.WebParts.WebParts.ConnectionConsumer("IWebPartField Consumer",
    "Field")] public void SetBookInfo(IWebPartField ifld)
  {
   ifld = fld;
  }
 }
```

Making Your Own Connections

Up until now, I've been assuming that connections are made at run time by the user. However, you can also create connections at run time through code. Instead of having your user work through the multi-step process required by the ConnectionsZone, you can put all the necessary code to make the connection behind a single button.

You can also set up connections at design time in the tags in your ASPX page. This makes sense when you're using a set of reusable Web Parts to create a page and want to connect the parts permanently.

Types of Connections

You can divide connections into three categories:

- **Transient connections** that last only until the page is requested again. These connections can be made through code in your page. You would use these connections to transfer data between Web Parts during one request-response cycle and to prevent data from being transferred in subsequent cycles.
- **Static connections** that will last through multiple requests of the page because they are maintained as part of the page's personalization. These connections are made in your page's definitions rather than using code in your page. These connections are the ones that you create at design time as part of creating the page.
- **Persistent connections** that, like static connections, are maintained in the page's personalization information and last through multiple requests of the page. However, persistent connections can be made through code or by the user interacting with the page. These are the connections that you use as Web Parts are added to and removed from the page.

The WebPartManager has a Connections collection that allows you to manage static and persistent connections, but not transient connections, on the page. This distinction is important because static and persistent connections are managed from your code through the Connections object on the WebPartManager. Transient connections are created outside of the Connections object.

Making Connections Through Code

You can't make static connections through code (instead, you define static connections in the Source view of the ASPX file). You can, however, make both permanent and transient connections from the code in your page.

Making Persistent Connections

To make a connection that is maintained as part of the page's personalization information you must retrieve references to four objects. First, you need to retrieve the two Web Parts that you want to connect. In the following Visual Basic 2005 example, the code retrieves references to Web Parts in a zone called BookSearch, using the zone's WebParts collection. The two Web Parts that this code works with are a provider called FindBook (which finds a book and provides the book's ISBN) and a consumer called DisplayBook (which displays information about the book whose ISBN is passed to it). These two parts pass information through the IBookInfo interface. As the code shows, because the WebParts collection returns a generic WebPart object, you must cast the returned value into the appropriate type:

```
Dim prov As BookSiteWP.FindBook
Dim cons As BookSiteWP.DisplayBook

prov = CType(Me.WebPartZone2.WebParts("Provider1"), BookSiteWP.FindBook)
cons = CType(Me.WebPartZone2.WebParts("Consumer1"), BookSiteWP.DisplayBook)
```

In C#:

```
BookSiteWP.FindBook prov;
BookSiteWP.DisplayBook cons;

prov =  (BookSiteWP.FindBook) this.WebPartZone2.WebParts["Provider1"];
cons =  (BookSiteWP.DisplayBook) this.WebPartZone2.WebParts["Consumer1"];
```

Next, you need references to the connection points in the Web Parts. You can retrieve a collection of all of the connections points of one type (either provider or consumer) for a Web Part by using the Get*ConnectionPoints methods of the WebPartManager object. For instance, the GetProviderConnectionPoints method returns a collection of all the connection points in the Web Part passed to the method. The following Visual Basic 2005 code retrieves the connection points for the two Web Parts retrieved previously:

```
Dim cncp As ConsumerConnectionPointCollection
Dim prcp As ProviderConnectionPointCollection

prcp = Me.WebPartManager1.GetProviderConnectionPoints(prov)
cncp = Me.WebPartManager1.GetConsumerConnectionPoints(cons)
```

In C#:

```
ConsumerConnectionPointCollection cncp;
ProviderConnectionPointCollection prcp;

prcp = this.WebPartManager1.GetProviderConnectionPoints(prov);
cncp = this.WebPartManager1.GetConsumerConnectionPoints(cons);
```

At this point you're ready to connect your Web Parts. There are two related methods of the WebPartManager that you want to use. The CanConnectWebParts method tests to see if two Web Parts *can* be connected, and returns True if they can. The ConnectWebParts method actually makes the connection between the parts.

Both methods accept the same parameters:

- The provider
- The connection point in the provider
- The consumer
- The connection point in the consumer

For the connection point parameters, you can use the connection point collections retrieved from the Get*ConnectionPoints methods. Because the collections represent all the connection points in the Web Part, you must specify which of the connection points you want to use. If a Web Part has a single connection point you can simply specify the connection point in the first position of the collection. You can also retrieve a connection point by name (assuming that you've assigned a name to the connection point in the ConnectionConsumer or ConnectionProvider attributes).

This Visual Basic 2005 code connects the Web Parts retrieved in the earlier code, using the first connection point in each of their connection point collections — but only after checking to see that the Web Parts can be connected:

```
If Me.WebPartManager1.CanConnectWebParts(prov, prcp(0), cons, cncp(0)) Then
    Me.WebPartManager1.ConnectWebParts(prov, prcp(0), cons, cncp(0))
End If
```

In C#:

```
if(this.WebPartManager1.CanConnectWebParts(prov, prcp[0], cons, cncp[0]))
{
  this.WebPartManager1.ConnectWebParts(prov, prcp[0], cons, cncp[0]);
}
```

If you need to use a Transformer to handle conversions between the Web Parts, both the CanConnectWebParts and the ConnectWebParts methods accept a Transformer object as a fifth parameter.

> *When making connections in code you have to specify the Transform class to use. Transforms are automatically invoked only when connections are made by the user in the ConnectionsZone part.*

This Visual Basic 2005 example connects a FindBook part with a DisplayAuthor part:

```
Dim prov As BookSiteWP.FindBook
Dim prcp As ProviderConnectionPointCollection
Dim cons As BookSiteWP.DisplayAuthor
Dim cncp As ConsumerConnectionPointCollection
Dim trs As New BookSiteWP.BookAuthorTransform

  prov = CType(Me.WebPartZone2.WebParts("FindBook1"), BookSiteWP.FindBook)
  cons = CType(Me.WebPartZone2.WebParts("DisplayAuthor1"), _
                                        BookSiteWP.DisplayAuthor)

  prcp = Me.WebPartManager1.GetProviderConnectionPoints(prov)
  cncp = Me.WebPartManager1.GetConsumerConnectionPoints(cons)
```

```
If Me.WebPartManager1.CanConnectWebParts(prov, prcp(0), cons, cncp(0), _
                                                              trs) Then
        Me.WebPartManager1.ConnectWebParts(prov, prcp(0), cons, cncp(0), trs)
End If
```

In C#:

```
BookSiteWP.FindBook prov;
ProviderConnectionPointCollection prcp;
BookSiteWP.DisplayAuthor cons;
ConsumerConnectionPointCollection cncp;
BookSiteWP.BookAuthorTransform trs = new BookSiteWP.BookAuthorTransform();

prov = (BookSiteWP.FindBook) Me.WebPartZone2.WebParts["FindBook1"];
cons = (BookSiteWP.DisplayAuthor) Me.WebPartZone2.WebParts["DisplayAuthor1"];

prcp = Me.WebPartManager1.GetProviderConnectionPoints(prov);
cncp = Me.WebPartManager1.GetConsumerConnectionPoints(cons);
if (this.WebPartManager1.CanConnectWebParts(prov, prcp[0], cons, cncp[0], trs))
{
  this.WebPartManager1.ConnectWebParts(prov, prcp[0], cons, cncp[0], trs);
}
```

When you are dynamically creating connections between Web Parts, there is a real possibility that you might attach a Web Part to a connection that it is already tied to, directly or indirectly. The WebPartTracker object allows you to check for this condition. To test a potential connection, just create the WebPartTracker, passing the WebPart and the connection point that you intend to use in the connection. After the WebPartTracker is created, you can check the WebPartTracker's IsCircularConnection property to determine if it's safe to create the connection, as this Visual Basic 2005 example does:

```
Dim prov As BookSiteWP.FindBook
Dim prcp As ProviderConnectionPointCollection
Dim wpt As WebParts.WebPartTracker

  prov = CType(Me.WebPartZone2.WebParts("FindBook1"), BookSiteWP.FindBook)
  prcp = Me.WebPartManager1.GetProviderConnectionPoints(prov)

  wpt = New WebParts.WebPartTracker(prov, prcp(0))
  If wpt.IsCircularConnection = False Then
    ...create connections
  End If
```

In C#:

```
BookSiteWP.FindBook prov;
ProviderConnectionPointCollection prcp;
WebParts.WebPartTracker wpt;

prov = (BookSiteWP.FindBook) Me.WebPartZone2.WebParts["FindBook1"];
prcp = this.WebPartManager1.GetProviderConnectionPoints(prov);

 wpt = new WebParts.WebPartTracker(wp, prcp[0]);
 if (wpt.IsCircularConnection == false)
```

```
{
 ...create connections
}
```

Making Transient Connections

Transient connections are easier to make than persistent connections and can be made only in code. These connections are not saved as part of the personalization information for the page and won't survive after the currently requested page has been rendered. In addition, these connections won't appear in the WebPartManager's Connections collection. Transient connections allow you to pass data between two parts and then have the connection automatically dropped once the page is sent to the browser.

As with persistent connections, to make a transient connection in code, you need to retrieve references to the consumer part and the provider part. However, once you have those references all you need to do is call the connection point routine on the provider to retrieve a reference to the interface used for the connection and then pass that reference to the connection point on the consumer — the Web Parts take care of the rest.

For FindBook, if you've used the convention in this book of giving the connection routine a name based on the interface name plus "Provider," the connection routine is called IBookInfoProvider. That routine returns the interface, which must be passed to the connection point routine on the consumer (which, following this book's convention, is called IBookInfoConsumer) as this code does:

```
Dim fbk As BookSiteWP.FindBook
Dim dsk As BookSiteWP.DisplayBook
Dim ibk As IBookInfo

  fbk = CType(Me.WebPartZone2.WebParts("FindBook1"), BookSiteWP.FindBook)
  dsk = CType(Me.WebPartZone2.WebParts("DisplayBook1"), BookSiteWP.DisplayBook)

  ibk = fbk.IBookInfoProvider()
  dsk.IBookInfoConsumer (ibk)
```

In C#:

```
BookSiteWP.FindBook fbk;
BookSiteWP.DisplayBook dsk;
IBookInfo ibk;

fbk = (BookSiteWP.FindBook) this.WebPartZone2.WebParts["FindBook1"];
dsk = (BookSiteWP.DisplayBook) this.WebPartZone2.WebParts["DisplayBook1"];

ibk = fbk.IBookInfoProvider();
dsk.IBookInfoConsumer(ibk);
```

Creating Static Connections

You can also create a connection between two Web Parts using tags in your ASPX file. These connections are maintained for all users and are typically created as part of putting the controls on the page. These connections also appear in the WebPartManager's Connections collection, enabling you to manage those connections from the code in your page.

To create a static connection, you first need to add a StaticConnections element inside of your WebPartManager tag. Inside the StaticConnections element, you place one Connection tag for each connection that you want to make. Each tag must have three attributes:

- **id:** A unique name for the tag
- **ProviderId:** The ID attribute of the provider Web Part in the connection
- **ConsumerId:** The ID attribute of the consumer Web Part in the connection

The tags to create the connection between the provider and consumer in the previous code example look like this:

```
<asp:WebPartManager ID="WebPartManager1" runat="server">
  <StaticConnections>
     <asp:WebPartConnection ID="cn1" ProviderID="FindBook1"
ConsumerID="DisplayBook1" />
  </StaticConnections>
</asp:WebPartManager>
```

This example assumes that you haven't assigned names to your connection points in the ConnectionConsumer or ConnectionProvider attributes. If you have, then you need to specify those names in the Connection tag using the ProviderConnectionPointID or ConsumerConnectionPointID attributes. This example works for a provider with a connection point with the name BookInfo (as in the example in the section on connection point parameters earlier in this chapter):

```
<asp:WebPartManager ID="WebPartManager1" runat="server">
  <StaticConnections>
     <asp:WebPartConnection ID="cn1" ProviderID="FindBook1" ConsumerID="DisplayBook1"
            ProviderConnectionPointID="BookInfo"/>
  </StaticConnections>
</asp:WebPartManager>
```

*If you don't set the *ConnectionPointID attribute, the connection looks for a connection point with the name "default"—which is the default name for a connection point. If no suitable connection point is found, an error will occur when the page is requested.*

For any error that occurs as a result of connecting two Web Parts, you can retrieve the error message from the WebPart object's ConnectErrorMessage (e.g., either through Me.ConnectErrorMessage in Visual Basic 2005 or this.ConnectErrorMessage in C#).

If you have placed your Web Parts on a Master Page but want to create static connections on the Content Pages (presumably because you want to create different connections on different pages), you need to use the ProxyWebPartManager. Just drag the ProxyWebPartManager into the content block on your Content Page, switch to Source view, and insert the tags for your static connections between the ProxyWebPartManager's open and close tags. Here's a typical example:

```
<asp:ProxyWebPartManager ID="ProxyWebPartManager1" runat="server">
  <StaticConnections>
     <asp:WebPartConnection ID="cn1" ProviderID="FindBook1" ConsumerID="DisplayBook1"
```

```
                ProviderConnectionPointID="BookInfo"/>
    </StaticConnections>
</asp:ProxyWebPartManager>
```

Managing Persistent and Static Connections

You can break persistent connections (connections made by the user or in code with the ConnectWebParts method) through the Connections collection on the WebPartManager. This Visual Basic 2005 code, for instance, retrieves the first connection on the page:

```
Dim cn As WebParts.WebPartConnection
cn = Me.WebPartManager1.Connections(0)
```

In C#:

```
WebParts.WebPartConnection cn;
cn = this.WebPartManager1.Connections[0];
```

Once you've retrieved a Connection object, you can use the properties on the object to retrieve the Consumer, the Provider, the ConnectionPoint, and other objects involved in the connection. You can also check these status properties:

- **IsActive:** True if one of the methods in the consumer or provider is executing
- **IsShared:** True if the connection is shared among multiple consumers
- **IsStatic:** True if the connection is created through tags in the ASPX file

Almost all of the properties are read-only except for the Connection's ID property. Setting the ID property on a connection allows you to retrieve the connection later by name instead of by position as in the previous code. The Connections collection itself has the usual properties for a collection. The Connection's Count property, for instance, allows you to determine how many connections exist on the page.

This Visual Basic.NET code creates a connection, and then uses the Connection collection's Count property to retrieve the last Connection in the collection and assign a value to the Connection's ID property:

```
Dim idx As Integer
If Me.WebPartManager1.CanConnectWebParts(prov, prcp(0), cons, cncp(0)) Then
    Me.WebPartManager1.ConnectWebParts(prov, prcp(0), cons, cncp(0))
    idx = Me.WebParManager1.Connections.Count - 1
    Me.WebPartManager1.Connections(idx).ID = "NewConnection"
End If
```

In C#:

```
int idx;
if(this.WebPartManager1.CanConnectWebParts(prov, prcp[0], cons, cncp[0])
  == true)
{
 this.WebPartManager1.ConnectWebParts(prov, prcp[0], cons, cncp[0]);
 idx = this.WebParManager1.Connections.Count - 1;
 this.WebPartManager1.Connections[idx].ID = "NewConnection";
}
```

You can use the Disconnect method of the WebPartManager to break connections on the page. The Disconnect method must be passed a Connection on the page in order to delete the connection.

Retrieving a connection by name (possible only if you've assigned a value to the connection's ID property) results in code that is easier to read and maintain. Static connections always have an ID — it's impossible to add a Connections tag without giving it an ID attribute.

This Visual Basic 2005 code, for instance, retrieves the connection called NewConnection and disconnects it:

```
Dim cn As WebControls.WebParts.WebPartConnection

cn = Me.WebPartManager1.Connections("NewConnection")
Me.WebPartManager1.DisconnectWebParts(cn)
```

This C# code does the same:

```
WebControls.WebParts.WebPartConnection cn;

cn = this.WebPartManager1.Connections["NewConnection"];
this.WebPartManager1.DisconnectWebParts(cn);
```

Disconnecting a persistent connection through your code is maintained as part of the page's personalization.

You can delete static connections using the Connections collection by using the Disconnect method. The parts stay disconnected as the user continues to request the page but are not maintained in the page's personalization information — the next time that the user visits the page, the parts are connected.

Connection Events

The WebPartManager fires several events related to connections. The ConnectionsActivating and ConnectionsActivated events fire every time that the page is requested if there is a ConnectionZone on the page — even if there are no connections present. This includes when the page is first requested and when the user clicks the button that changes the DisplayMode of the WebPartManager to enable customization, and after the user selects the Connect option from the Verb menu. The other events fire only while a connection is being made or broken:

- **ConnectionsActivating:** Fires before any of the connection point routines execute.
- **ConnectionsActivated:** Fires after all of the connection point routines have executed.
- **WebPartsConnecting:** Fires after the user clicks the Connect button in the ConnectionsZone WebPart. At this point, the connection that is being made does not yet exist.
- **WebPartsConnected:** Fires after the connection has been made and is available in the WebPartManager's Connections collection.
- **WebPartsDisconnecting:** Fires after the user clicks the Disconnect button in the ConnectionsZone WebPart. At this point, the connection that is being broken is still available in the WebPartManager's Connections collection.
- **WebPartsDisconnected:** Fires after the connection has been broken.

If a connection is made from the user interface, the ConnectionsActivating and Activated events fire after the Disconnected, Disconnecting, Connecting, and Connected events. These events also fire after any client-side events (for instance, after a Button's click event with code that makes connections between Web Parts).

If the connection is made from code, the Connecting, Connected, Disconnecting, and Disconnected events fire after the code that makes or breaks the connection. The Activating and Activated events still fire after all the client-side triggered events.

If you have StaticConnection tags in your form, the ConnectionsActivating event fires just after the control's Load and before the page's LoadComplete event.

Configuring ConnectionsZone Text

In addition to the typical zone-related properties that can be used to configure a ConfigurationsZone (such as CancelVerb) as discussed in Chapter 2, you can also configure the text displayed by the ConnectionsZone in all its various states. Six of the almost two dozen properties in this area are:

- **ConnectToConsumerText and ConnectToProviderText:** The text for the hyperlink at the top of the ConnectionsZone when the zone is initially displayed.
- **ConnectToConsumerTitle and ConnectToProviderTitle:** The title displayed at the top of the status box after the user clicks the hyperlink at the top of the ConnectionsZone.
- **ConnectToConsumerInstructionText and ConnectToProviderInstructionText:** The text displayed in the status box after the user clicks the hyperlink at the top of the ConnectionsZone.

Summary

In this chapter you've seen how to create Web Parts that can communicate with each other. You've seen how to define your own interfaces and how to use the predefined interfaces:

- IWebPartField for passing a single value
- IWebPartRow for passing multiple values
- IWebPartTable for passing a matrix of values
- IWebPartParameters to allow the consumer and the provider to negotiate what data will be passed

In addition to seeing how users can create connections dynamically, you can create connections using

- Tags in your ASPX page
- The ConnectWebPart method of the WebPartManager
- The connection point routines

Finally, at the end of this chapter you learned how you can extract information about your Web Parts, break connections, and assign IDs to connections from your code.

11

Working with the Web Part Architecture

Because this book is focused on *creating* controls, not a lot of time has been spent on how to *use* controls. As an experienced ASP.NET developer, you are already familiar with how to use the various ASP.NET server controls. However, Web Parts present a different issue. Not only are Web Parts the newest part of the ASP.NET toolkit, the way they work together and their dependence on the ASP.NET personalization sub-system make working with Web Parts a different experience than working with other ASP.NET controls.

Chapter 2 described how to design pages with Web Parts and how users interact with them. This chapter describes how a programmer interacts with Web Parts to:

- Control which personalization provider is to be used
- Set whether changes are applied to the current user or all users
- Set and determine which types of changes are permitted on a page
- Implement authorization strategies for your Web Parts by creating a custom WebPartManager
- Monitor and manage personalization changes made by the user by interacting with WebPartManager events
- Dynamically convert standard ASP.NET controls on the page to Web Parts and add them to WebPartZones
- Make personalization changes to the host page from the host page's code
- Import and export personalization settings and support importing/exporting a WebPart that you create

With one exception, none of the material in this chapter directly discusses how to create a control (the one exception is the section on setting attributes to enable exporting for a Web Part). However, the more you know about how developers will expect to use your Web Part, the better job you will do of designing it. And, of course, it's not unlikely that in addition to building Web Parts, you want to use them yourself.

Setting Personalization Options on the WebPartManager

In this section, you learn how to:

- Control the personalization options in the WebPartManager
- Have changes made by one user shared by many users
- Implement authorization for Web Parts

Controlling WebPartManager Personalization Options

You can control much of how personalization is handled by working with the ASP.NET Personalization object, which can be retrieved from the WebPartManager's Personalization property. The methods and properties on this object let you manage the way that personalization is handled on the page:

- **Switching personalization providers:** You can change the personalization provider that is being used by a page by setting the ProviderName property of the Personalization object (setting up personalization providers was discussed in Chapter 7). This Visual Basic 2005 code sets the WebPartManager to use the Access provider:

```
Me.WebPartManager1.Personalization.ProviderName = _
                                "AspNetAccessPersonalizationProvider"
```

  In C#:

```
this.WebPartManager1.Personalization.ProviderName =
                                "AspNetAccessPersonalizationProvider";.
```

- **Discarding personalization changes:** You can return a page to its original state by calling the ResetPersonalizationState method. Before calling this method, you can determine if there are any changes to be backed out by checking the Personalization object's HasPersonalizationState property, which is True if the page has been personalized.
- **Ensuring that changes are allowed:** The Personalization object's EnsureEnabled will be True when the personalization infrastructure is fully enabled and ready to accept changes for the current user. Setting the Personalization object's Enabled property to False prevents personalization changes from being made by the current user. The IsModifiable property allows you to check whether the current user is allowed to make personalization changes.

You can also disable any personalization changes from being made to a page by setting the WebPartManager's Enable property to False.

Applying Changes to Other Users

Personalization changes are made in one of two scopes: shared or user. When the scope is set to user (the default), the changes made by a user affect that page only when it is requested by that user. To put it another way: in user scope, a user's personalization changes are visible to that user only. When the scope is set to shared, however, changes made to the page are made for all users.

You control the scope of a change by calling the ToggleScope method of the Personalization object. Because the ToggleScope method switches the scope from whatever its current state is to the other state, you will usually want to determine the current scope before calling ToggleScope. The current scope can be determined by testing the Personalization object's Scope property against one of the enumerated PersonalizationScope values. Because not all users are allowed to make changes in shared mode, you should also check the Personalization object's CanEnterSharedScope property before calling the ToggleScope method. CanEnterSharedScope returns True if the user is allowed to make shared changes (or if there is some other reason that shared changes can't be made). This Visual Basic 2005 code puts all of these together:

```
Dim prs As System.Web.UI.WebControls.WebParts.WebPartPersonalization

Dim prs As UI.WebControls.WebParts.WebPartPersonalization;
prs = Me.WebPartManager1.Personalization
If prs.CanEnterSharedScope = True Then
  If prs.Scope = PersonalizationScope.User Then
    prs.ToggleScope()
  End If
End If
```

In C#:

```
UI.WebControls.WebParts.WebPartPersonalization prs;
prs = this.WebPartManager1.Personalization;
if(prs.CanEnterSharedScope == true)
{
 if(prs.Scope == PersonalizationScope.User)
 {
  prs.ToggleScope();
 }
}
```

If you do change the WebPartManager's scope, you can determine the original scope for the WebPartManager by reading the Personalization object's InitialState property.

Implementing Authorization

Every Web Part has an AuthorizationFilter property that can be set to any string value. If you want to take advantage of this property, you must create your own WebPartManager and override either its OnAuthorizeWebPart or IsAuthorized method. In these methods, you can add code to check the AuthorizationFilter property on Web Parts and prevent Web Parts from being displayed. These methods are called automatically, as Web Parts are associated with the WebPartManager on the page.

The following example is a Visual Basic 2005 class that inherits from WebPartManager and overrides the OnAuthorizeWebPart method. The e parameter passed to the OnAuthorizeWebPart method references the Web Part being authorized through the WebPart property. You indicate that the Web Part is not authorized by setting the e parameter's IsAuthorized property to False:

```
Public Class PHVWebPartManager
    Inherits System.Web.UI.WebControls.WebParts.WebPartManager

Protected Overrides Sub OnAuthorizeWebPart( _
   ByVal e As System.Web.UI.WebControls.WebParts.WebPartAuthorizationEventArgs)

  If e.AuthorizationFilter <> "Created by PH&V" Then
    e.IsAuthorized = False
  End If
  MyBase.OnAuthorizeWebPart(e)
End Sub

End Class
```

In C#:

```
public class PHVWebPartManager : System.Web.UI.WebControls.WebParts.WebPartManager
{
 protected override void OnAuthorizeWebPart(
              System.Web.UI.WebControls.WebParts.WebPartAuthorizationEventArgs e)
 {
  if(e.AuthorizationFilter != "Created by PH&V")
   {
    e.IsAuthorized = false;
   }
   base.OnAuthorizeWebPart(e);
 }
}
```

While the OnAuthorizeWebPart currently performs no functions, it's a good practice to continue to call the underlying method in case later versions of ASP.NET do implement some default authorization functionality.

The IsAuthorized method calls the OnAuthorizeWebPart method (unless IsAuthorized has been overridden), so overriding OnAuthorizeWebPart effectively overrides IsAuthorized. However, if you prefer to override IsAuthorized, the method is passed four parameters:

- The type of the Web Part
- The path to the Web Part
- The Web Part's AuthorizationFilter
- A Boolean isShared parameter that is set to True if the Web Part has its personalization changes shared among users

In the IsAuthorized method, if the Web Part fails the test, you must return False from the IsAuthorized method:

```
Public Class PHVWebPartManager
    Inherits System.Web.UI.WebControls.WebParts.WebPartManager
  Public Overrides Function IsAuthorized(ByVal type As System.Type, _
         ByVal path As String, ByVal authorizationFilter As String, _
         ByVal isShared As Boolean) As Boolean
    If authorizationFilter <> "Created by PH&V" Then
      Return False
    End If
  End Function
End Class
```

In C#:

```
public class PHVWebPartManager : System.Web.UI.WebControls.WebParts.WebPartManager
{
 public override bool IsAuthorized(System.Type type, string path,
             string authorizationFilter, bool isShared)
 {
  if(authorizationFilter != "Created by PH&V")
  {
   return false;
}
else
{
 return true;
}
```

In order to prevent the AuthorizationFilter from being reset by code on the host page, you need to override your control's AuthorizationFilter and set it to a constant value.

Some history: The AuthorizationFilter property replaces an earlier Roles property in the first Beta of .NET that allowed developers to set the user roles that a Web Part could be used by (for example, Admin or User). The AuthorizationFilter allows developers a more flexible approach to authorization. To duplicate the functionality of the original Roles property, for instance, the OnAuthorizeWebPart method can check the AuthorizationFilter property of the Web Part for the names of the roles that a Web Part can be used by. The OnAuthorizeWebPart can then compare those roles to the role of the currently logged on user.

Managing Personalization for Web Parts

Just because your users can move any Web Part to any WebPartZone doesn't mean that you should let them — it's your application and you need to maintain control over what customizations you permit. Nor is customization restricted to what the user can do in the browser. While up until now I've concentrated on how the user can customize his page by interacting with the page in the browser, you can also customize Web Parts and their pages from your code.

In this section you see how to:

- ❑ Monitor the changes that a user makes while personalizing your page
- ❑ Control what changes you permit your users to make
- ❑ Customize and personalize your page from your code

Much of the work that you can do with Web Parts in your code is done by calling methods and properties of the WebPartManager and interacting with the WebPartManager's events. You've already seen how the DisplayMode property allows you to put the WebPartManager into a mode that allows the user to make changes. The DisplayMode must be set to some object that inherits from the WebPartDisplayMode object (you've seen these objects already also: WebPartManager.DesignDisplayMode, WebPartManager .CatalogDisplayMode, and so on). These objects have five properties that control what personalization is possible:

- ❑ **AllowPageDesign:** When True, indicates that the user can make changes to the page's layout
- ❑ **AssociatedWithToolZone:** When True, indicates that there is a tool zone that must be present for this mode to be used
- ❑ **Name:** The name of the mode
- ❑ **RequiresPersonalization:** When True, indicates that this mode can be used only if Personalization is enabled for the site
- ❑ **ShowHiddenWebParts:** Causes parts that have their Hidden property set to True to be displayed

For example, for the CatalogDisplayMode object, the properties have these settings:

- ❑ **AllowPageDesign:** True
- ❑ **AssociatedWithToolZone:** True
- ❑ **Name:** Catalog
- ❑ **RequiresPersonalization:** True
- ❑ **ShowHiddenWebParts:** True

As an example of the settings for a display mode, the BrowseDisplayMode (the default mode that allows users to just Close and Minimize Web parts) has both its AllowPageDesign and RequiresPersonalization properties set to False.

All of the properties on the DisplayMode object are read-only.

Checking Whether a DisplayMode Is Supported

In addition to the five properties, the various *DisplayMode objects also have an IsEnabled method that, when passed the WebPartManager for the page, returns True if personalization is supported for that DisplayMode. A user may not be permitted to make personalizations, for instance. Passing the page's

WebPartManager to the ConnectDisplayMode allows you to check to see if personalizing connections are permitted, as this Visual Basic 2005 code does before setting the WebPartManager's DisplayMode:

```
If WebPartManager.ConnectDisplayMode.IsEnabled(Me.WebPartManager1) = True Then
    Me.WebPartManager1.DisplayMode = WebPartManager.ConnectDisplayMode
End If
```

In C#:

```
if(WebPartManager.ConnectDisplayMode.IsEnabled(this.WebPartManager1) == true)
{
   this.WebPartManager1.DisplayMode = WebPartManager.ConnectDisplayMode;
}
```

You still need to check if the necessary controls are present on the page. For instance, while personalizing connections may be permitted, if a ConnectionsZone isn't on the page it's not possible for connections to be created. You can check to see if a DisplayMode is supported by using the WebPartManager's SupportedDisplayModes property. You pass the name of a DisplayMode to the SupportedDisplayModes collection and, if the page supports the mode, the DisplayMode will be returned.

More importantly, if the mode *isn't* supported, the SupportedDisplayModes property returns Nothing in Visual Basic 2005 or null in C#. The following Visual Basic 2005 code tests for the Connect mode being supported before attempting to put the WebPartManager in connect mode by using the SupportedDisplayModes property:

```
If Me.WebPartManager1.SupportedDisplayModes("Connect") IsNot Nothing Then
   Me.WebPartManager1.DisplayMode = WebPartManager.ConnectDisplayMode
End If
```

In C#:

```
if(this.WebPartManager1.SupportedDisplayModes["Connect"] != null)
{
   this.WebPartManager1.DisplayMode = WebPartManager.ConnectDisplayMode;
}
```

Don't confuse the SupportedDisplayModes collection with the WebPartManager's DisplayModes collection. The DisplayModes collection lists all the display modes that the manager supports. This list is *not* limited to the display modes that are possible for the current page. For example, while the WebPartManager supports connect mode (so ConnectDisplayMode is found in the DisplayModes collection), the page does not support connect mode if there are no ConnectionsZones on the page (and, as a result, the ConnectDisplayMode cannot be found in the SupportedDisplayModes). Presumably, the DisplayModes property is designed to support the creation of new WebPartManagers that support a different set of modes from the modes supported by the ASP.NET Framework's WebPartManager.

Managing Personalization Changes

When making personalization changes to a page while it's displayed in a browser, it's easy to think that the Web Part is actually closed or moved to a new zone when the user completes the action in the browser. In reality, of course, all that the user can do in the browser is indicate what change she wants made — the actual change is made back at the server. When the user has finished closing a part, or moving it to a new zone, or whatever change the user makes, the data from the page is sent back to the server and ASP.NET starts making the change to the page.

The sequence of events that ASP.NET follows as the user personalizes a page, beginning when the user clicks the button that enables personalization, is:

1. The user clicks the button that puts the WebPartManager into one of the design modes.
2. The page's data is posted back to the server for processing by ASP.NET.
3. The button's Click event executes and the code in the event puts the WebPartManager into one of the design modes.
4. The page is returned to the user.
5. The user performs some personalization activities (for example, dragging a Web Part to another WebPartZone).
6. The page's data is posted back to the server for processing by ASP.NET.
7. ASP.NET implements the changes made by the user in the browser (such as moving the Web Part to the new zone).

After the user puts a page into one of the design modes, the personalization changes that the user makes don't involve performing any of the traditional actions for interacting with ASP.NET (such as clicking a button or selecting items in a list box). Nor do the various user controls, custom controls, or Web Parts have any events related to personalization changes made by the user. If you want to manage the customizations made by your users, you have to use the events fired by the WebPartManager.

WebPartManager Events

To allow you to manage personalization for the page, the WebPartManager fires events as part of implementing the changes the user made in the browser. You can put code into these events to control the personalization performed by the user. These events are also fired when you manage Web Parts from your code (as discussed later in this chapter), so by putting code into the WebPartManager's events you can ensure that your personalization management code manages both changes made by the user of the page and changes made from your code.

For any change to a Web Part, the WebPartManager fires two events: one event that fires before the change takes place (these events have names ending in "ing") and one that fires after the change has taken place (these events have names ending in "ed"). For instance, when the user closes a Web Part, the WebPartClosing event fires before ASP.NET removes the Web Part from the page and the WebPartClosed event fires after ASP.NET has removed the Web Part from the page.

The exceptions to this two-event rule are the events related to connecting, which include events related to the connections on the page in addition to the events related to the Web Parts being connected. Those events are discussed in Chapter 10.

Managing the DisplayMode

Most Web Part personalizations begin with the user clicking a button to run code that changes the WebPartManager's DisplayMode. Two events fire as the WebPartManager's DisplayMode changes: DisplayModeChanging and DisplayModeChanged. The Click event for the button fires after the Page's Load event and before the Page's LoadComplete event (as usual for client-side triggered events). The DisplayMode-related events fire while the code in the Click event executes.

Setting the value of the DisplayMode to its current value does not cause any events to fire. The DisplayModeChanging and DisplayModeChanged events fire only if the WebPartManager's DisplayMode property is set to a new value.

As the code that changes the DisplayMode executes, the DisplayModeChanging event fires. When the first event (DisplayModeChanging) fires, the DisplayMode in the WebPartManager won't yet have been changed. After that first event completes, the DisplayMode is updated to the new value set in the code. After the first event has fired, the second event (DisplayModeChanged) fires. After both of the DisplayMode* events have fired, ASP.NET executes any code that follows the line that changed the DisplayMode. In other words, the process looks like this:

Visual Basic:

```
Protected Sub btnChangeMode_Click( _
   ByVal sender As Object, ByVal e As System.EventArgs) Handles btnChangeMode.Click

  Me.WebPartManager1.DisplayMode = WebPartManager.DesignDisplayMode
      ' WebPartManager_DisplayModeChanging event fires
      ' DisplayMode set to new value
      ' WebPartManager_DisplayModeChanged event fires
  Me.txtMessage.Text = "You can now modify the page."

End Sub
```

The DisplayModeChanging and DisplayModeChanged events also fire when the user changes the display mode as a side effect of some other action. For instance, when the user finishes working with a CatalogEditor as part of adding new parts to the page, the user closes the CatalogEditor by clicking the editor's Close button. In addition to closing down the Catalog Editor, ASP.NET also puts the page back into BrowseDisplayMode, which causes the DisplayModeChanging and DisplayModeChanged events to fire.

As is the case with other .NET events, the WebPartManager's events are passed two parameters. In the first event, the second parameter (the parameter called e) provides you with an opportunity to interrupt the change being made. In addition, the e parameter normally has other properties customized for the different personalization changes.

For example, the e parameter passed to the DisplayModeChanging event has two properties that are useful for managing personalization:

- **Cancel:** Setting this property to True cancels the change to the DisplayMode.
- **NewDisplayMode:** This property returns the value that the DisplayMode is going to be set to. Because the DisplayMode hasn't been changed at this point you can still retrieve the original value of the DisplayMode from the WebPartManager.

As a result, in the DisplayModeChanging event you can test for combinations of the current and future display modes and suppress changes that you don't want to support. More commonly, in the DisplayModeChanging event, these properties allow you to test for a change to a specific DisplayMode and prevent that change under some conditions (you could, for instance, prevent specific users from making some changes). Because the DisplayMode is actually set to an object you can't use an equals sign to compare the NewDisplayMode to one of the predefined DisplayMode values. Instead you use the Equals method of the NewDisplayMode to see if it's the same object as the DisplayMode that you're testing for.

This Visual Basic 2005 example checks to see if the user is going into catalog display mode (which lets the user add new controls to the page). If the user is making that change, the code sets the e parameter's Cancel property to True to suppress the change:

```
If e.NewDisplayMode.Equals(WebPartManager.CatalogDisplayMode) Then
  e.Cancel = True
End If
```

In C#:

```
if(e.NewDisplayMode.Equals(WebPartManager.CatalogDisplayMode))
{
  e.Cancel = true;
}
```

No error is raised when a change is canceled and the DisplayModeChanged event is not fired. If you are using the DisplayModeChanged event to cancel changes under some circumstances, you need to check after any display mode change to check if the change wasn't canceled. A full version of the code in the button's Click event that includes this test looks like this (remember, the DisplayMode* events fire after the DisplayMode is changed and before the next line of code executes):

Visual Basic:

```
Protected Sub btnChangeMode_Click( _
   ByVal sender As Object, ByVal e As System.EventArgs) Handles btnChangeMode.Click

  Me.WebPartManager1.DisplayMode = WebPartManager.CatalogDisplayMode
  If Me.WebPartManager1.DisplayMode.Equals(WebPartManager.CatalogDisplayMode) Then

    Me.txtMessage.Text = "You can now modify the page."
  End If

End Sub
```

In C#:

```
protected void btnChangeMode_Click(object sender, System.EventArgs e)
{
 this.WebPartManager1.DisplayMode = WebPartManager.CatalogDisplayMode;
 if (this.WebPartManager1.DisplayMode.Equals(WebPartManager.CatalogDisplayMode))
{
  this.txtMessage.Text = "You can now modify the page.";
 }
}
```

The e parameter passed to the DisplayModeChanged after the event has occurred has an OldDisplayMode property that holds the value of the WebPartManager's DisplayMode property before the change was made. While this lets you check for specific combinations of changes in the DisplayModeChanged event, you can no longer suppress the change.

You shouldn't try to set the display mode back to its original setting in the DisplayModeChanged event. Even in the DisplayModeChanged event, setting the DisplayMode to a new value will cause the DisplayModeChanging and the DisplayModeChanged events to fire again, potentially putting your page into an endless loop.

Controlling Personalization Changes

For most changes, the user can't make her change until after the page has been put into one of the personalization modes.

There are exceptions: The user can minimize and close a Web Part while the WebPartManager is in its default setting of BrowseDisplayMode.

Once the user makes her change and the page's data is posted back to the server, ASP.NET makes the requested change. The WebPartManager fires events before and after making the change, using the same pattern as the DisplayMode* events: an event whose name ends in "ing" that fires before the changes are made and an event whose name ends in "ed" that fires after the event is changed. The customizations and the corresponding events are as follows:

- If the user closes a Web Part in the browser, the WebPartClosing and WebPartClosed events fire before and after ASP.NET makes the change back on the server.
- After the user clicks the Add button in the CatalogEditor to add a part to a WebZone, the WebPartAdding and WebPartAdded events fire.
- After the user releases the mouse button when dragging a Web Part to a new location, the WebPartMoving and WebPartMoved events fire on the server.

The e parameter for the events that fire *before* the change (the "ing" events) all have a Cancel property that allows you to cancel the change. The other properties on the e parameter vary from event to event but will let you determine:

- Before the change, what change is about to take place
- After the event, what WebPart was changed

The events share some characteristics, particularly in the properties found on the e parameter. Based on the properties available on the e parameter, you can organize events into two groups:

- **Adding or moving a Web Part:** The e parameter for the events that fire before the change (WebPartAdding, WebPartMoving) has three useful properties:
    - **WebPart:** Points to the Web Part being added.
    - **Zone:** Points to the target Zone that the part is being added to.
    - **ZoneIndex:** An integer that specifies the position of the Web Part in the zone it's being added or moved to (0 means that the part will appear first in the zone's WebParts collection).

  The e parameter for the event that fires after the change has a WebPart property that points to the moved or added part.
- **Closing, deleting, or changing a Web Part:** The e parameter for both the event that fires before the change and after the change has a WebPart property that points to the Web Part being closed, deleted, or changed.

No events fire when a user minimizes a Web Part.

As an example of how these events can be used, consider a situation in which you want to prevent a specific part from being moved to a specific WebPartZone. For instance, in one of the BookSite pages, there might be several WebZones on the page. However, some of these zones are intended to hold book search parts and other zones are to hold book list parts. To be more specific: The search entry parts might be permitted in zones only on the top and either side of the page, while the listing parts are to be used in zones only in the middle of the page. If you give your users the freedom to drag parts at will, then you need to use the WebPartManager events to prevent the user from dragging search parts to listing zones.

In this Visual Basic 2005 example, the code checks to see if the user is moving the SearchPart to the ListingZone. If the user does try to make that change, the code cancels the change:

```
Protected Sub WebPartManager1_WebPartMoving(ByVal sender As Object, _
 ByVal e As System.Web.UI.WebControls.WebParts.WebPartMovingEventArgs) _
                                          Handles WebPartManager1.WebPartMoving

  If e.WebPart.ID = "SearchPart" And _
     e.Zone.ID = "ListingZone" Then
       e.Cancel = True
  End If

End Sub
```

The same code in C# looks like this:

```
protected void WebPartManager1_WebPartMoving(object sender,
              System.Web.UI.WebControls.WebParts.WebPartMovingEventArgs e)
{
```

```
    if(e.WebPart.ID == "SearchPart" &&
       e.Zone.ID == "ListingZone")
    {
      e.Cancel = true;
    }
  }
```

If you don't want a part to be moved to any zone under any circumstances, you should set the Web Part's AllowZoneChange property to False.

With the Adding and Moving events, you can use the additional properties on the e parameter to manage other aspects of the change. You can use the ZoneIndex property on the e parameter to control where in the zone the Web Part appears. As one example, you can make sure that all new Web Parts are added at the top of the zone by setting the e parameter's ZoneIndex property to 0.

If, in the first event, you set the Cancel property to True, then the second event will not fire. As a result, any code that you want to execute on a successful change can be put in the second event. In this sample Visual Basic 2005 code, code in the WebPartMoved event sets the Title property of the moved Web Part to let the user know which part was just moved:

```
Protected Sub WebPartManager1_WebPartMoved(ByVal sender As Object, _
      ByVal e As System.Web.UI.WebControls.WebParts.WebPartEventArgs) _
                                      Handles WebPartManager1.WebPartMoved
        e.WebPart.Title = "Moved Part"
End Sub
```

In C#:

```
protected void WebPartManager1_WebPartMoved(object sender,
System.Web.UI.WebControls.WebParts.WebPartEventArgs e)
{
  e.WebPart.Title = "Moved Part";
}
```

Managing Edits

When a WebPartManager is put into EditDisplayMode, the user has the opportunity to work with the AppearanceEditor, the BehaviorEditor, and the LayoutEditor. A key part of managing customizations during EditDisplayMode is keeping track of which part is being edited. Before I cover how to determine which part is being processed, let's review the series of events that occurs when a user personalizes a page in edit mode.

From the user's point of view, when a page is put into EditDisplayMode, nothing much on the page changes. The only change on the page isn't very visible: the Web Parts on the page will have a new entry, Edit, on their Verb menus — which won't be displayed until the user clicks the Verb menu's down arrow.

When the user selects the Edit verb for a Web Part, the page is posted back to the server for processing. When the page is redisplayed to the user, any of the editors that are on the page are displayed. The editors display information for the control whose Edit command was selected (for instance, the AppearanceEditor displays that control's Title property). The part whose Edit item was selected and is being processed by the editor is the "selected" Web Part.

The selected Web Part is not a constant during the time the user spends editing the Web Parts on the page. Once the page is in EditDisplayMode, the user can switch to working with another Web Part by selecting the Edit item from the other Web Part's Verb Menu. Effectively, the user has made the other Web Part the selected Web Part.

You can access the currently selected part through the WebPartManager's SelectedWebPart property. Using the SelectedWebPart property enables you to manipulate the Part's properties either before or after the change, and check that the user's changes are ones that you want to allow. For instance, you might want to prevent the user from setting his text color to the same color as the background color.

The SelectedWebPart property on the WebPartManager applies only to Web Parts selected by choosing an item from its Verb menu. For instance, Web Parts that are selected and dragged in order to move them from one zone to another zone are not referenced through the SelectedWebPart.

You can't use the SelectedWebPart property in all of the events fired by the WebForm. The SelectedWebPart property is never set prior to the PreLoad event of the page that the Web Part is on. This means that you can't access the SelectedWebPart property in the PreInit, Init, and InitComplete events (where developers seldom put application code, anyway). To put it another way, prior to the Load event, SelectedWebPart always has a value of Nothing.

Even during the page events following the Load event, the SelectedWebPart property is not always set. When a user selects a Web Part for editing, as is usual, two events are fired on the server: SelectedWebPartChanging and SelectedWebPartChanged. The SelectedWebPartChanging event fires after the page's Load event and the SelectedWebPartChanged event fires immediately afterward. When the user first selects a Web Part by picking Edit from the part's Verb menu, the SelectedWebPart isn't set while the SelectedWebPartChanging event executes. It's not until the SelectedWebPartChanged event fires that the SelectedWebPart property is set to the Web Part that the user selected.

A warning: The following discussion is going to get confusing. Don't panic! A table that summarizes the changes and the code to handle all the conditions are coming up.

The processing is more complicated when the user selects another Web Part. When the user selects a new Web Part, the SelectedWebPart is set by the time the page's Load event fires but points to the part that was selected when the page was first displayed — not to the part that the user has just selected.

In addition, when the user selects a new Web Part, the SelectedWebPartChanging event fires twice: once for the original Web Part and once for the new Web Part. When the SelectedWebPartChanging event fires for the first time, SelectedWebPart still points to the original Web Part. When SelectedWebPartChanging fires again, SelectedWebPart's value is Nothing.

After the SelectedWebPartChanging event has fired twice, the SelectedWebPartChanged event also fires twice: once for the original Web Part and once for the new Web Part. When SelectedWebPartChanged fires the first time, SelectedWebPart still has a value of Nothing; when SelectedWebPartChanged fires the second time, SelectedWebPart is pointing to the newly selected Web Part.

This sequence is shown in the following table, which illustrates the changes to SelectedWebPart as each of the events fires. In the scenario this table charts, the user had previously selected a Web Part called OriginalWP. The user has now selected the Edit item from the Verb menu for a Web Part called NewWP and the page's data has been posted back to the server.

Event	SelectedWebPart
PreInit	Nothing
Init	Nothing
InitComplete	Nothing
Load	OriginalWP
SelectedWebPartChanging	OriginalWP
SelectedWebPartChanging	Nothing
SelectedWebPartChanged	Nothing
SelectedWebPartChanged	NewWP
LoadComplete and following events	NewWP

As the table shows, all of the WebPartManager events related to personalization (events triggered by moving, adding, or connecting Web Parts) fire between the Page's Load and LoadComplete events. This means that in the Page's Load event, the SelectedWebPart always points to the last Web Part that the user selected and in the PreRender event, the SelectedWebPart always points to the newly selected Web Part.

How can this confusing set of changes be understood? Fundamentally, if you put code in the SelectedWebPartChanging or SelectedWebPartChanged events to manipulate the SelectedWebPart, you face these questions:

- Is the event firing for the first time that a Web Part is selected or is it firing because the user is changing Web Parts?
- If the user is switching between parts, which occurrence of each event are you in?
- Is the SelectedWebPart pointing to the old Web Part or the new Web Part?

There is a way to answer all of these questions.

The e parameter in the SelectedWebPartChanging and SelectedWebPartChanged events has one useful property for answering these questions: WebPart, which points to the Web Part that the user has just selected. So, for instance, when the user changes the selected Web Part, in the SelectedWebPartChanging event the SelectedWebPart and e.WebPart will be referencing different Web Parts. By using e.WebPart (and a single Boolean variable), it's possible to distinguish between the various scenarios when the SelectedWebPartChanging event is fired.

This Visual Basic 2005 code skeleton distinguishes between all the scenarios when the two events fire and notes what SelectedWebPart and e.WebPart are pointing to at each point:

```
Dim bolChanging As Boolean

Protected Sub WebPartManager1_SelectedWebPartChanging(ByVal sender As Object, _
    ByVal e As System.Web.UI.WebControls.WebParts.WebPartCancelEventArgs) _
                                       Handles WebPartManager1.SelectedWebPartChanging
```

```
    If Me.WebPartManager1.SelectedWebPart Is Nothing Then
       'The first time that a Web Part has been selected
       'SelectedWebPart is Nothing
       'e.WebPart points to the selected Web Part

    Else

       If e.WebPart.Title <> Me.WebPartManager1.SelectedWebPart.Title Then
           'The user is changing Web Parts and this is the first time that the event
           '   has fired
           'SelectedWebPart points to the old Web Part
           'e.WebPart points to the new Web Part

       Else
           'The user is changing Web Parts and this is the second time that the event
           '          has fired
           'SelectedWebPart points to the old part
           'e.WebPart points to the old part
            bolChanging = True
       End If
    End If
 End Sub

 Protected Sub WebPartManager1_SelectedWebPartChanged(ByVal sender As Object, _
        ByVal e As System.Web.UI.WebControls.WebParts.WebPartEventArgs) _
                                    Handles WebPartManager1.SelectedWebPartChanged

    If Me.WebPartManager1.SelectedWebPart Is Nothing Then
       'The user is changing Web Parts and this is the first time that the event
       '          has fired
       'SelectedWebPart is Nothing
       'e.WebPart is Nothing

    Else

       If bolChanging = False Then
          'The first time that a Web Part has been selected
           'SelectedWebPart points to the Web Part
           'e.WebPart points to the Web Part

       Else
          'The user is changing Web Parts and this is the second time that the event
          '            has fired
          'SelectedWebpart points to the new Web Part
          'e.WebPart points to the new Web Part
          bolChanging = False

       End If
    End If
 End Sub
```

In C#:

```
bool bolChanging;

protected void WebPartManager1_SelectedWebPartChanging(object sender,
            System.Web.UI.WebControls.WebParts.WebPartCancelEventArgs e)
{
 if(this.WebPartManager1.SelectedWebPart == null)
 {
        //The first time that a Web Part has been selected
        //SelectedWebPart is Nothing
        //e.WebPart points to the selected Web Part
 }
 else
 {
  if(e.WebPart.Title != this.WebPartManager1.SelectedWebPart.Title)
  {
       //The user is changing Web Parts and this is the first time the event
       //              has fired
       //SelectedWebPart points to the old Web Part
       //e.WebPart points to the new Web Part
  }
  else
  {
       //The user is changing Web Parts and this is the second time the event
       //              has fired
       //SelectedWebPart points to the old part
       //e.WebPart points to the old part
       bolChanging = true;
  }
 }
}

protected void WebPartManager1_SelectedWebPartChanged(object sender,
              System.Web.UI.WebControls.WebParts.WebPartEventArgs e)
{
 if(this.WebPartManager1.SelectedWebPart == null)
 {
      //The user is changing Web Parts and this is the first time that the event
      //              has fired
      //SelectedWebPart is Nothing
      //e.WebPart is Nothing
 }
 else
 {
  if(bolChanging == false)
  {
      //The first time that a Web Part has been selected
      //SelectedWebPart points to the Web Part
      //e.WebPart points to the Web Part
  }
  else
  {
      //The user is changing Web Parts and this is the second time that the event
      //              has fired
```

```
            //SelectedWebpart points to the new Web Part
            //e.WebPart points to the new Web Part
            bolChanging = false;
        }
    }
}
```

As is usual for the first event of the pair, the e parameter on the SelectedWebPartChanged event has a Cancel property that can be set to True to cancel the change.

Manipulating Web Parts from Code

You can take advantage of Web Parts' flexibility by manipulating Web Parts from your code. From your code you can close Web Parts, move Web Parts between zones, connect zones, or add Web Parts to a zone. You can even create new Web Parts from standard ASP.NET controls.

Manipulating Web Parts from code gives you two capabilities:

- **The ability to simplify personalization changes for your users:** If users have to make customizations themselves they must go through a three-step process: Click a button to enter a design mode, make their design changes, and then click another button to put the page back into browse mode. You can wrap the whole process up into a single button click.
- **The ability to limit the changes that can be made by a user to those customizations that you implement in your code:** If you don't provide the user with the capability to put the WebPartManager into one of the design modes, the user is able to make only the changes that you've decided to support.

The ability to perform these activities is handled through methods and properties of the WebPartManager.

When manipulating Web Parts from code it's not necessary to put the page into one of the design display modes.

Closing a Web Part

You close a Web Part from your code by calling the WebPartManager's CloseWebPart method, passing the Web Part to be closed. This Visual Basic 2005 code closes a Web Part called Search in a WebPartZone called SearchZone:

```
Dim wp As WebPart

  wp = Me.SearchZone.WebParts("Search")

  Me.WebPartManager1.CloseWebPart(wp)
```

In C#:

```
WebPart wp;

    wp = this.SearchZone.WebParts["Search"];

    this.WebPartManager1.CloseWebPart(wp);
```

The WebPartClosing and WebPartClosed events fire after the CloseWebPart method is called and before the next line of code executes.

Moving a Web Part

To move a Web Part from one zone to another, you use the WebPartManager's MoveWebPart method. This method requires three parameters:

- The Web Part to be moved
- The WebPartZone that the part is to be moved to
- An index that specifies the position of the Web Part in the new WebPartZone (an index of 0 makes the Web Part the first Web Part in the zone)

If you set the index to a position that doesn't exist in the WebPartZone (say, specifying an index of 5 for a WebPartZone that has only three Web Parts), the Web Part being moved is put after all the other Web Parts already in the WebPartZone. No error is raised.

This Visual Basic 2005 code moves a Web Part called Search from a zone called SearchZone to the second position in a zone called InventoryZone:

```
Dim wp As WebPart
Dim wz As WebPartZone

    wp = Me.SearchZone.WebParts("Search")
    wz = Me.InventoryZone
    Me.WebPartManager1.MoveWebPart(wp, wz, 1)
```

In C#:

```
WebPart wp;
WebPartZone wz;

wp = this.SearchZone.WebParts["Search"];
wz = this.InventoryZone;
this.WebPartManager1.MoveWebPart(wp, wz, 1);
```

Adding a Closed Web Part

You can add closed Web Parts back to a page using the WebPartManager's AddWebPart method. All of the Web Parts on a page can be accessed from the WebPartManager's WebParts collection, including closed Web Parts. However, adding a Web Part that is already on the page but isn't closed raises an error.

So, for any part retrieved from the WebParts collection, you should check the part's IsClosed property to make sure that the part is closed before adding the part to the page.

This Visual Basic 2005 code puts a closed Web Part back on the page after checking that the part is closed:

```
Dim wp As WebPart
Dim wz As WebPartZone

  wp = Me.WebPartManager1.WebParts("Search")
  wz = Me.SearchZone
  If wp.IsClosed = True Then
     Me.WebPartManager1.AddWebPart(wp, wz, 0)
  End If
```

In C#:

```
WebPart wp;
WebPartZone wz;

  wp = this.WebPartManager1.WebParts["Search"];
  wz = this.SearchZone;
  if(wp.IsClosed == true)
  {
   this.WebPartManager1.AddWebPart(wp, wz, 0);
  }
```

Adding a Web Part from a Catalog

You can also use the PageCatalogPart to add closed WebParts to the page. The process that you use with the PageCatalogPart also works for adding parts held in the DeclarativeCatalogPart. With these catalog parts, you retrieve a Web Part by passing the WebPartDescription object for the Web Part that you want to the catalog's GetWebPart method. The WebPartDescription object holds a Web Part's Id, Description, Title, and CatalogIconImageURL properties, allowing you to specify which Web Part you want.

The functionality of the ImportCatalogPart is handled through the WebPartManager's ImportWebPart method.

You can get a Web Part's WebPartDescription object in several ways. By using a catalog's GetAvailableWebPartDescription method you can retrieve a WebPartDescriptionCollection that contains the WebPartDescription objects for all the Web Parts in the catalog.

The GetAvailableWebPartDescription cannot be used to retrieve Web Parts added to the DeclarativeCatalogControl using the WebPartsListUserControlPath, as described in Chapter 9.

The following Visual Basic 2005 example retrieves the WebPartDescriptionCollection from the first catalog part in a catalog zone, and then searches the list for a Web Part with the title "Search." After the code finds a matching WebPartDescription object, the code uses that description to retrieve the matching Web Part from the collection and add it to a WebPartZone called znSearch:

```
Dim wpd As WebPartDescription
Dim wpdc As WebPartDescriptionCollection
Dim wp As WebPart
wpdc = Me.CatalogZone1.CatalogParts(0).GetAvailableWebPartDescriptions()
For Each wpd In wpdc
   If wpd.Title = "Search" Then
      wp = Me.CatalogZone1.CatalogParts(0).GetWebPart(wpd)
      Me.WebPartManager1.AddWebPart(wp, Me.znSearch, 0)
   End If
Next
```

In C#:

```
WebPartDescriptionCollection wpdc;
WebPart wp;
wpdc = this.CatalogZone1.CatalogParts[0].GetAvailableWebPartDescriptions();
foreach(WebPartDescription wpd in wpdc)
{
 if(wpd.Title == "Search")
 {
  wp = this.CatalogZone1.CatalogParts[0].GetWebPart(wpd);
  this.WebPartManager1.AddWebPart(wp, this.znSearch, 0);
 }
}
```

You can also create a WebPartDescription object by passing the WebPartDescription's constructor either a Web Part or the values for the WebPartDescription's Id, Title, Description, and CatalogIconImageURL properties. Regardless of how the WebPartDescription is created, it can be used with the GetWebPart method to retrieve a matching Web Part from a catalog.

If the GetWebPart method doesn't find a matching Web Part among the controls in a catalog, an error is raised.

This Visual Basic 2005 example creates a WebPartDescription from a WebPart and then places it in the Session object to be used later:

```
Dim wp As WebPart
wp = Me.znSearch.WebParts(0)

Dim wpd As New WebPartDescription(wp)
Me.Session("wpDescription") = wpd
```

In C#:

```
WebPart wp;
wp = this.znSearch.WebParts(0);

WebPartDescription wpd = new WebPartDescription(wp);
this.Session["wpDescription"] = wpd;
```

The following Visual Basic 2005 example creates the WebPartDescription object by setting the Id, Title, Description, and CatalogIconImageURL properties when the object is created. When you create a

WebPartDescription you must provide values for the Id and Title (the first two parameters) but you can pass zero length strings for the Description and CatalogIconImageURL parameters, as this example does for the CatalogIconImageURL parameter:

```
Dim wp As WebPart
wp = Me.znSearch.WebParts(0)

Dim wpd As New WebPartDescription("wpSearch","Search", "Search for Books","")
Me.Session("wpDescription") = wpd
```

In C#:

```
WebPart wp;
wp = this.znSearch.WebParts[0];

WebPartDescription wpd = new WebPartDescription(
                         "wpSearch","Search", "Search for Books","");
this.Session["wpDescription"] = wpd;
```

The WebPartDescription properties that identify the Web Part (Title, Id, and so on) cannot be changed after the WebPartDescription object is created.

Creating a Web Part

In addition to adding closed Web Parts to the page, you can also convert standard controls into Web Parts using the CreateWebPart method, and then add them to the page. The CreateWebPart creates a new instance of the control and wraps the control in a GenericWebPart object (much like what happens when you drag a standard control from the Toolbox and into a WebPartZone at design time). After the Web Part is created you can use the AddWebPart method to add the new Web Part to a WebPartZone. This Visual Basic 2005 code demonstrates the technique by creating a new Web Part from a control on the page called btnAdd:

```
Dim wp As GenericWebPart
Dim wz As WebPartZone

  wp = Me.WebPartManager1.CreateWebPart(Me.btnAdd)
  wz = Me.WebPartZone1
  Me.WebPartManager1.AddWebPart(wp, wz, 0)
```

In C#:

```
GenericWebPart wp;
WebPartZone wz;

wp = this.WebPartManager1.CreateWebPart(this.btnAdd);
wz = this.WebPartZone1;
this.WebPartManager1.AddWebPart(wp, wz, 0);
```

The same technique can be used with dynamically created controls; however, you must assign a value to the control's ID property before wrapping it in a Web Part. This Visual Basic 2005 code creates an ASP.NET control, wraps it in a Generic Web Part, and then adds it to a zone after assigning the part an ID:

```
Dim wp As GenericWebPart
Dim wz As WebPartZone
Dim txt As TextBox

  txt = New TextBox
  txt.ID = "AddButton"
  wp = Me.WebPartManager1.CreateWebPart(txt)
  wz = Me.WebPartZone1
  Me.WebPartManager1.AddWebPart(wp, wz, 0)
```

In C#:

```
GenericWebPart wp;
WebPartZone wz;
TextBox txt;

  txt = new TextBox();
  txt.ID = "AddButton";
  wp = this.WebPartManager1.CreateWebPart(txt);
  wz = this.WebPartZone1;
  this.WebPartManager1.AddWebPart(wp, wz, 0);
```

You can retrieve the GenericWebPart that a standard control has been wrapped in by using the WebPartManager's GetGenericWebPart method and passing it the standard ASP.NET control. This Visual Basic 2005 code builds on the previous examples to retrieve the GenericWebPart that the ASP.NET control has been wrapped in:

```
Dim wp2 As GenericWebPart
wp2 = Me.WebPartManager1.GetGenericWebPart(txt)
```

In C#:

```
GenericWebPart wp2;
wp2 = this.WebPartManager1.GetGenericWebPart(txt);
```

Exporting and Importing Web Parts

In addition to creating Web Parts at run time from standard controls, you can also create Web Parts by importing from files of Web Part information. Importing a Web Part creates a new Web Part of the type specified in the file and sets most of the Web Part's properties based on the information in the file (among other properties, the new Web Part's Id property is not set).

The easiest way to create a file of Web Part information is to export from an existing Web Part. Before a Web Part's information can be exported, the Web Part must:

- Be part of a WebPartZone on a page (that is, you can't export a Web Part that you've just created using CreateWebPart).
- Be marked as Personalizable.
- Have its ExportMode set to something other than None (more on this property later in this section).

Also, before you can export Web Parts, you must enable exporting for your site. You enable exporting by inserting a WebParts tag into the site's Web.Config site and setting the tag's enableExport attribute to true, as in this example: <webParts enableExport="true"/>.

Using the ExportWebPart Method

To export a Web Part you use the WebPartManager's ExportWebPart method. This method has to be passed two parameters:

- ❑ The Web Part to be exported.
- ❑ Some object that inherits from XmlWriter. The XmlTextWriter object that is part of the .NET Framework is one example of an XmlWriter object.

The following Visual Basic 2005 code exports a Web Part to a file on the server. The code first creates an XmlWriter that writes to a file called OutputPart.wpc. The code then retrieves a reference to a WebPart called DisplayBookInfo and uses the Web Part and the XmlTextWriter with the ExportWebPart method. The ExportWebPart method opens the writer, but it's the routine's responsibility to close the writer (failing to close the writer results in nothing being written to the file):

In these examples, because the second parameter to the XmlTextWriter's constructor is set to Nothing or null, the encoding for the output file will default to UTF-8.

```
Dim wrt As New System.Xml.XmlTextWriter("c:\OutputPart.wpc", Nothing)

   wp = Me.WebPartManager1.WebParts("DisplayBookInfo")
   Me.WebPartManager1.ExportWebPart(wp, wrt)
   wrt.Close()
```

In C#:

```
System.Xml.XmlTextWriter wrt =
            new System.Xml.XmlTextWriter(@"c:\OutputPart.wpc", null);

  wp = this.WebPartManager1.WebParts["DisplayBookInfo"];
  this.WebPartManager1.ExportWebPart(wp, wrt);
  wrt.Close();
```

When a Web Part is exported, each of its property routines has its Get section executed as the import process reads the data for the property.

Web Part File Format

The contents of an exported Web Part look like this (this example uses a Web Part that can draw information from another Web Part so the type of the WebPart is WPConsumerProvider):

```
<webParts>
  <webPart>
     <metaData>
       <type name="WPConsumerProvider.Consumer, WPConsumerProvider,
```

```
                        Version=1.0.0.0, Culture=neutral, PublicKeyToken=null" />
        <importErrorMessage>Cannot import this Web Part.</importErrorMessage>
      </metaData>
      <data>
        <properties>
          <property name="AllowClose" type="bool">True</property>
          <property name="Width" type="unit">300px</property>
           ...more property tags...
          <property name="ExportMode" type="exportmode">All</property>
        </properties>
      </data>
    </webPart>
  </webParts>
```

The WebPart element begins with a metaData tag that includes the information needed to re-create the Web Part. Following the metadata element, the data element contains all the current property settings for the Web Part inside property elements. Because the property settings are exported with their current values, the Web Part is exported with its current personalizations applied.

Preventing Data from Being Exported

Because data is exported in a plain text format, it's easy for the property values to be read (all you need is Notepad). For privacy and security reasons, it may be important to you to prevent some of your Web Part properties from being exported. The Web Parts framework lets you distinguish between two kinds of properties that you don't want to export: properties not to be exported under any circumstances, and properties to be exported only under specific circumstances.

To prevent a property from being exported, the simplest solution is to not mark the party as personalizable (only personalizable properties can be exported). This Visual Basic 2005 code demonstrates a property with personalization turned off by passing False to the Personalizable attribute:

```
<Web.UI.WebControls.WebParts.Personalizable(False)> _
Public Property Data() As String

   Get
      Return _Data
   End Get
   Set(ByVal value As String)
      _Data = value
   End Set

End Property
```

In C#:

```
[Web.UI.WebControls.WebParts.Personalizable(false)]
public string Data
{
 get
 {
  return _Data;
 }
 set
```

```
    {
      _Data = value;
    }
  }
```

To create a property that is to be exported only under some circumstances, you must set the second parameter of the Personalizable attribute to False. This ensures that a property will be exported only if the WebPart's ExportMode property explicitly specifies that sensitive data are to be written. However, in order to set the second parameter, you must set the first parameter of the Personalizable attribute to indicate whether personalization changes are to be shared among all users or remain private to the user who makes them. This Visual Basic 2005 code creates a property whose personalization is shared among all users, but whose data is exported only when the Web Part's ExportMode is set to export sensitive data:

```
<Web.UI.WebControls.WebParts.Personalizable( _
            WebControls.WebParts.PersonalizationScope.Shared, False)> _
Public Property Data() As String
```

In C#:

```
[Web.UI.WebControls.WebParts.Personalizable(
                 WebControls.WebParts.PersonalizationScope.Shared, false)]
public string Data
```

To export sensitive data, the Web Part's ExportMode must be set to All, as in this Visual Basic 2005 code:

```
wp.ExportMode = WebPartExportMode.All
```

In C#:

```
wp.ExportMode = WebPartExportMode.All;
```

To export only data that isn't sensitive, the ExportMode must be set to NonSensitiveData (the default is None, which prevents the Web Part from being exported at all). You can override the ExportMode property to ensure that the mode is changed only to settings that you approve. This Visual Basic 2005 example, for instance, silently prevents the ExportMode from being set to WebPartExportMode.All:

```
Public Overrides Property ExportMode() As _
                System.Web.UI.WebControls.WebParts.WebPartExportMode
  Get
    Return MyBase.ExportMode
  End Get

  Set(ByVal value As System.Web.UI.WebControls.WebParts.WebPartExportMode)
    If value = WebControls.WebParts.WebPartExportMode.All Then
       MyBase.ExportMode = WebControls.WebParts.WebPartExportMode.None
    Else
       MyBase.ExportMode = value
    End If
  End Set

End Property
```

In C#:

```
public override System.Web.UI.WebControls.WebParts.WebPartExportMode ExportMode
{
 get
 {
  return base.ExportMode;
 }
 set
 {
  if(value == WebControls.WebParts.WebPartExportMode.All)
  {
   base.ExportMode = WebControls.WebParts.WebPartExportMode.None;
  }
  else
  {
   base.ExportMode = value;
  }
 }
}
```

Exporting Remotely

You can also trigger exports on other pages by requesting the page with a URL that includes a querystring that specifies that the Web Part be exported. The querystring must include two parameters:

- **_WEBPARTEXPORT:** Set to "true" to trigger export
- **webPart:** Set to the name of the Web Part to be exported

You can use the querystring with the Response object's Redirect method to trigger a Web Part being exported on a page, as this Visual Basic 2005 code does:

```
Dim strURL As String
strURL = "?_WEBPARTEXPORT=true&webPart=" & strWebPartName
Me.Response.Redirect("AnotherPage.aspx" & strURL)
```

In C#:

```
string strURL;
strURL = "?_WEBPARTEXPORT=true&webPart=" + strWebPartName;
this.Response.Redirect("AnotherPage.aspx" + strURL);
```

Rather than build the URL yourself, you can retrieve the URL to export a Web Part by calling the WebPartManager's GetExportURL method, passing the Web Part that you want to export to the method. This Visual Basic 2005 code retrieves the URL for the first Web Part in the zone znOrders and then stores it in the Session object to be used later:

```
Dim strURL As String
strURL = Me.WebPartManager1.GetExportUrl(Me.znOrders.WebParts(0))
Me.Session("ExportString) = strURL
```

In C#:

```
string strURL;
strURL = this.WebPartManager1.GetExportUrl(this.znOrders.WebParts[0]);
this.Session["ExportString] = strURL;
```

The resulting URL is a relative URL. A typical example looks like this:

```
MySite/MyPage.aspx?__WEBPARTEXPORT=true&webPart=wpOrderList
```

Importing Web Parts

To import a Web Part, you use the ImportWebPart method of the WebPartManager object (normally followed by calling the WebPartManager's AddWebPart method to put the Web Part on the page). This method, like the ExportWebPart method, accepts two parameters:

- An object that inherits from an XMLReader. The XmlTextReader that is part of the .NET Framework is one example.
- A string variable that accepts any error message generated during the import.

An imported Web Part will not have its ID property set.

The following Visual Basic 2005 code creates an XmlTextReader that reads a file called OutputPart.wpc. The routine also declares a string variable to hold any messages returned from the import. After the ImportWebPart method is called, the routine closes the reader and checks the string variable updated by the ImportWebPart method. If the string is Nothing, it indicates that the import was successful (no error is raised if an import fails). In this example, if the string is set to Nothing (null in C#), the code sets the ID property to a value and adds the newly created Web Part to a zone:

To prevent a warning message at compile time, the string variable should be initialized when it is declared.

```
Dim rdr As New System.Xml.XmlTextReader("c:\OutputPart.wpc")
Dim strMessage As String = ""
Dim wp As System.Web.UI.WebControls.WebParts.WebPart

   wp = Me.WebPartManager1.ImportWebPart(rdr, strMessage)
   If strMessage is Nothing Then
       wp.ID = "Search1"
       Me.WebPartManager1.AddWebPart(wp, Me.SearchZone,0)
   End If
```

In C#:

```
System.Xml.XmlTextReader rdr = new System.Xml.XmlTextReader(@"c:\OutputPart.wpc");
string strMessage = "";
System.Web.UI.WebControls.WebParts.WebPart wp;

  wp = this.WebPartManager1.ImportWebPart(rdr, out strMessage);
  rdr.Close;
  if(strMessage == null)
```

```
{
 wp.ID = "Search1";
 this.WebPartManager1.AddWebPart(wp, this.SearchZone, 0);
}
```

When a Web Part is imported, each of its property routines has its Set section executed as the import process sets the data for the property.

A warning: The error messages returned by the ImportWebPart method aren't very helpful in diagnosing what went wrong. Typical examples of messages and the actual problem that triggered the problem include:

- **"The file format is not valid. Try importing a Web Part file (.WebPart)":** The XMLTextReader was closed.
- **"Cannot import this Web Part":** The file did not exist.

Summary

In this chapter you added to your toolkit the tools that you need to manage your user's personalization and customization from your host page's code. You learned how to:

- Use the WebPartManager's events to manage end user personalization
- Implement authorization to control which Web Parts are displayed on the page
- Determine the selected part for Edit activities

You also learned how to implement personalization from your code so that you can:

- Close Web Parts
- Move Web Parts from one zone to another
- Add Web Parts to a page
- Convert ASP.NET controls into Web Parts dynamically at run time
- Import and export Web Parts with their personalization information

The other chapters in this book gave you the capability to create Web Parts. This chapter, on the other hand, has given you the capability to control the Web Parts that you use to create your pages.

Part IV
Controls in Action

12

A Custom Control Case Study

In this chapter you won't learn any new technology. Instead, you see how the tools covered in the previous chapters come together to create a typical custom control. The sample control in this chapter (shown in Figure 12-1) will:

- Accept or display information about a single customer: The customer name, e-mail address, street address, city, province or state, and country. This control can be used any place where customer information should be entered or displayed to provide a standard user interface for customer data.
- Support both a display and an update mode:
  - When in display mode, the control uses labels to display the customer's information.
  - When in update mode, a combination of text boxes and labels allow the user to enter information.
- Raise an event whenever any data in the control is changed to notify the host page of the change, passing the name of the control that was changed and the data from both before and after the change.
- Have properties that allow code in the host page to access the information in the control, including a CustomerId property that allows a developer using the control to specify which customer is to be displayed in the control.

The control also functions as a full-featured Web Part:

- The CustomerId property can be set by the user through a Web Part editor.
- The control has an entry on its Verb menu to support control-specific business functionality.
- The control acts both as a Web Part consumer and provider when communicating with other Web Parts.

When acting as a consumer, the Web Part accepts a CustomerId from other Web Parts and displays the information for that customer; when acting as a provider, the Web Part supplies the CustomerId for the customer currently being displayed.

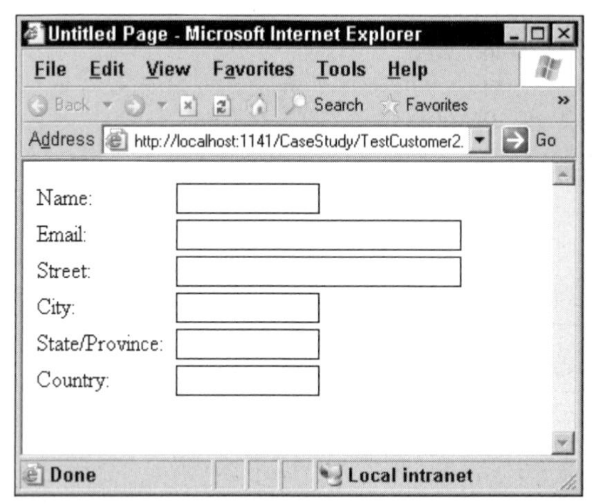

Figure 12-1

Designing the Control

The first decision to make is whether to implement this control as a user control, a custom control, or a Web Part. In this case, deciding not to implement the control as a user control is easy: The custom control is going to be used in several different projects and, because user controls can't be shared among projects, the control can't be implemented as a user control. In addition, because the user interface has to switch between an updateable text box view and a display-only label view at run time, the flexibility of using a custom control is desirable. A custom control builds its user interface at run time while a user control makes life easiest for developers when its user interface is built at design time (although a user control can generate a user interface at run time).

The next decision is whether to implement the control as Web Part or a custom control. Obviously, because the control is to act as a Provider and a Consumer when connected to other Web Parts, the part has to be implemented as a Web Part. However, even if the control wasn't going to use any Web Part–specific features, it would still make sense to implement the control as a Web Part. A Web Part has all the functionality of a custom control plus the Web Part–specific features described in this book. It makes sense, then, to implement all custom controls as Web Parts in case, at some time in the future, you need to add some Web Part–specific feature.

Setting Up the Solution

Because the control is going to be used in multiple projects, it also makes sense to set up a separate project to develop it. That way the control's library can be added to the toolbox for Visual Studio 2005 by the developers who want to use the control. However, you're still going to need a Web site to test your control. That being the case, you should begin creating your solution by creating the site — you can then use this Web site for testing any subsequent controls that you create.

With the Web site created (in the sample code for this book, the site is called CaseStudy), the next step is to add a project for your control. In the Visual Studio Add Project dialog box, select your language, select the Windows subgroup, and select Web Control Library. Give your project a name and add it to your Visual Studio 2005 solution — this is where you create your custom controls (in the sample, the project is called CaseStudyControlsVB or CaseStudyControlsCS).

In the Web site project, you should set up a page for each control that you test. To make it easy to find the right page, it's a good practice to give the page the name of the control that it tests: Delete the Default.aspx page and add a new WebForm with the name of your control (in this sample, that page is CustomerTest). The final configuration change that you have to make to the Web site is to add a reference to your control project on the Projects tab of the Add Reference dialog box, as in Figure 12-2.

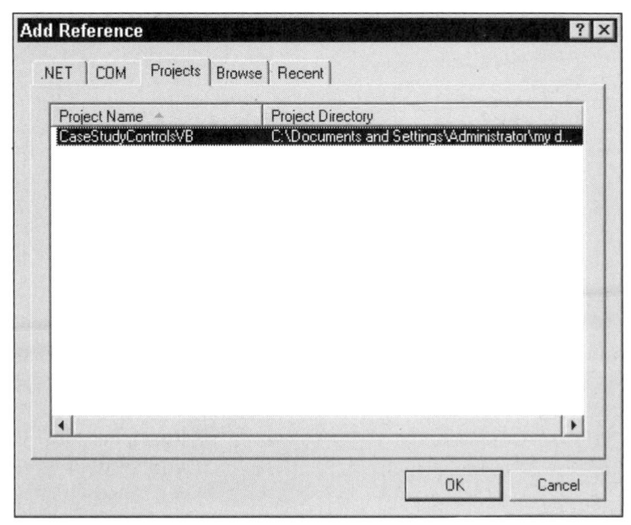

Figure 12-2

In the control project, you should:

1. Delete the default control file and add a new Web Custom Control (called CustomerInformation in this sample).
2. Have the class module inherit from System.Web.UI.WebControls.WebParts.WebPart instead of from System.Web.UI.WebControls.WebControl in the control because you're creating a Web Part.
3. Delete the default code in the class.
4. Delete the DefaultProperty attribute on the Class declaration and (in Visual Basic 2005) delete the square brackets around your class's name in the ToolboxData attribute and in the class name itself.

The result is a solution that looks like the one in Figure 12-3 for Visual Basic 2005 and Figure 12-4 for C#.

If you were creating a templated control, you would implement the INamingContainer interface for the control to ensure that unique names are generated for the controls hosted in the template.

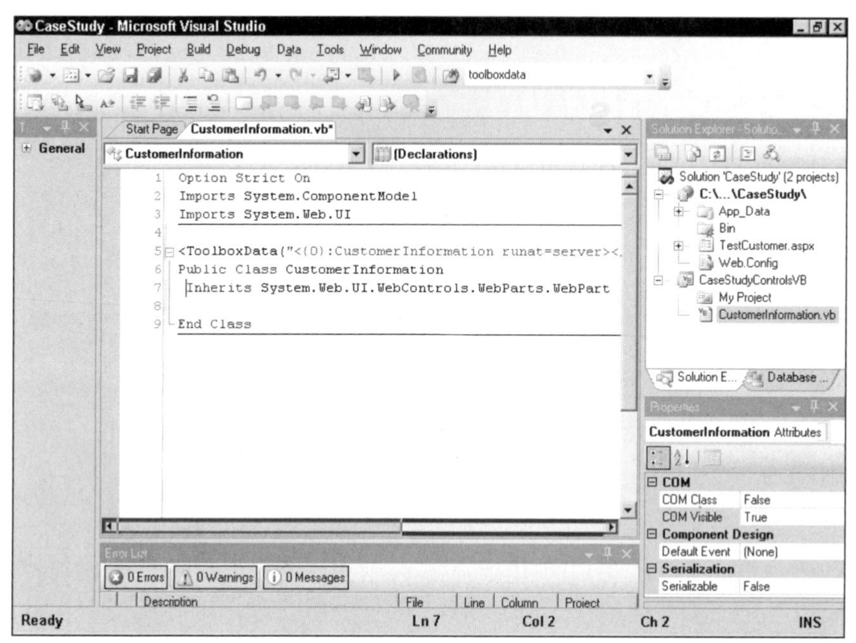

Figure 12-3

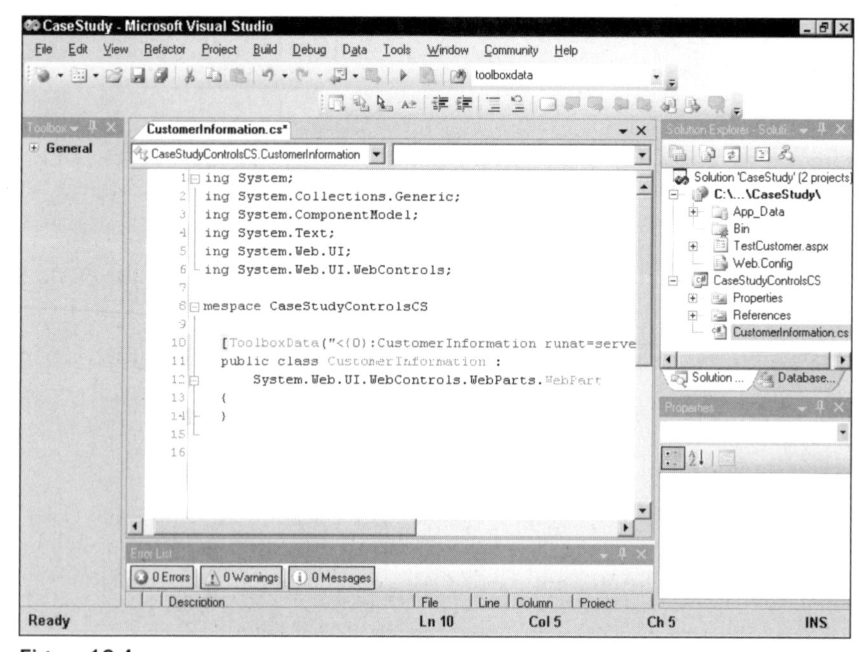

Figure 12-4

If you intend to create multiple projects that you want to have grouped together in the IntelliSense drop-down lists, you should also set your project's Namespace property in the project's Properties dialog box to the name that you want to use for all of your controls.

Adding Controls

The next step in creating your custom control is to override the CreateChildControls method to add the necessary constituent controls to your custom control's user interface. The first version of this code just adds the labels used to display customer data. The control displays the following:

- Customer name
- E-mail address
- Street address
- City
- State/province
- Country

As a result, the control must have twelve labels (six to hold customer information and six to display as labels for the customer information).

In setting properties for the controls, only two properties should be able to be set by the developer:

- The Id property of the text boxes (because they may be accessed in code and should have meaningful names).
- The Text property of the labels (so that they identify the text boxes on the control).

Rather than assign Ids to the Label controls used just as labels, accept the default values generated by ASP.NET. In order to distinguish between the controls that will hold data and the controls that hold labels, the code adds an attribute called DisplayType to the controls; for the labels, that attribute is set to "label" and for the other controls that attribute is set to "data".

Finally, the labels must be added to the custom control's Controls collection, after clearing out any controls that might already be present, as this Visual Basic 2005 code does:

```
<ToolboxData("<{0}:CustomerInformation runat=server></{0}:CustomerInformation>")> _
Public Class CustomerInformation
    Inherits System.Web.UI.WebControls.WebParts.WebPart

Protected Overrides Sub CreateChildControls()
Dim lblName As New System.Web.UI.WebControls.Label
Dim lblEmail As New System.Web.UI.WebControls.Label
Dim lblStreet As New System.Web.UI.WebControls.Label
Dim lblCity As New System.Web.UI.WebControls.Label
Dim lblStateProvince As New System.Web.UI.WebControls.Label
Dim lblCountry As New System.Web.UI.WebControls.Label
Dim lblNameLb As New System.Web.UI.WebControls.Label
Dim lblEmailLb As New System.Web.UI.WebControls.Label
```

```
Dim lblStreetLb As New System.Web.UI.WebControls.Label
Dim lblCityLb As New System.Web.UI.WebControls.Label
Dim lblStateProvinceLb As New System.Web.UI.WebControls.Label
Dim lblCountryLb As New System.Web.UI.WebControls.Label


  lblName.ID = "lblName"
  lblName.Attributes("DisplayType") = "label"
  lblEmail.ID = "lblEmail"
  lblEmail.Attributes("DisplayType") = "label"
  lblStreet.ID = "lblStreet"
  lblStreet.Attributes("DisplayType") = "label"
  lblCity.ID = "lblCity"
  lblCity.Attributes("DisplayType") = "label"
  lblStateProvince.ID = "lblStatProv"
  lblStateProvince.Attributes("DisplayType") = "label"
  lblCountry.ID = "Country"
  lblCountry.Attributes("DisplayType") = "label"

  lblNameLb.Text = "Name:"
  lblNameLb.Attributes("DisplayType") = "data"
  lblEmailLb.Text = "Email:"
  lblEmailLb.Attributes("DisplayType") = "data"
  lblStreetLb.Text = "Street:"
  lblStreetLb.Attributes("DisplayType") = "data"
  lblCityLb.Text = "City:"
  lblCityLb.Attributes("DisplayType") = "data"
  lblStateProvinceLb.Text = "State/Province:"
  lblStateProvinceLb.Attributes("DisplayType") = "data"
  lblCountryLb.Text = "Country:"
  lblCountryLb.Attributes("DisplayType") = "data"

  Me.Controls.Clear
  Me.Controls.Add(lblNameLb)
  Me.Controls.Add(lblName)
  Me.Controls.Add(lblEmailLb)
  Me.Controls.Add(lblEmail)
  Me.Controls.Add(lblStreetLb)
  Me.Controls.Add(lblStreet)
  Me.Controls.Add(lblCityLb)
  Me.Controls.Add(lblCity)
  Me.Controls.Add(lblStateProvinceLb)
  Me.Controls.Add(lblStateProvince)
  Me.Controls.Add(lblCountryLb)
  Me.Controls.Add(lblCountry)

End Sub

End Class
```

In C#:

```
[ToolboxData("<{0}:CustomerInformation runat=server></{0}:CustomerInformation>")]
public class CustomerInformation : System.Web.UI.WebControls.WebParts.WebPart
{
```

```
protected override void CreateChildControls()
{
  System.Web.UI.WebControls.Label lblName = new System.Web.UI.WebControls.Label();
  System.Web.UI.WebControls.Label lblEmail = new
                              System.Web.UI.WebControls.Label();
  System.Web.UI.WebControls.Label lblStreet = new
                              System.Web.UI.WebControls.Label();
  System.Web.UI.WebControls.Label lblCity = new
                              System.Web.UI.WebControls.Label();
  System.Web.UI.WebControls.Label lblStateProvince = new
                              System.Web.UI.WebControls.Label();
  System.Web.UI.WebControls.Label lblCountry = new
                              System.Web.UI.WebControls.Label();
  System.Web.UI.WebControls.Label lblNameLb = new
                              System.Web.UI.WebControls.Label();
  System.Web.UI.WebControls.Label lblEmailLb = new
                              System.Web.UI.WebControls.Label();
  System.Web.UI.WebControls.Label lblStreetLb = new
                              System.Web.UI.WebControls.Label();
  System.Web.UI.WebControls.Label lblCityLb = new
                              System.Web.UI.WebControls.Label();
  System.Web.UI.WebControls.Label lblStateProvinceLb = new
                              System.Web.UI.WebControls.Label();
  System.Web.UI.WebControls.Label lblCountryLb = new
                              System.Web.UI.WebControls.Label();

  lblName.ID = "lblName";
  lblName.Attributes["DisplayType"] = "label";
  lblEmail.ID = "lblEmail";
  lblEmail.Attributes["DisplayType"] = "label";
  lblStreet.ID = "lblStreet";
  lblStreet.Attributes["DisplayType"] = "label";
  lblCity.ID = "lblCity";
  lblCity.Attributes["DisplayType"] = "label";
  lblStateProvince.ID = "lblStatProv";
  lblStateProvince.Attributes["DisplayType"] = "label";
  lblCountry.ID = "lblCountry";
  lblCountry.Attributes["DisplayType"] = "label";

  lblNameLb.Text = "Name:";
  lblNameLb.Attributes["DisplayType"] = "data";
  lblEmailLb.Text = "Email:";
  lblEmailLb.Attributes["DisplayType"] = "data";
  lblStreetLb.Text = "Street:";
  lblStreetLb.Attributes["DisplayType"] = "data";
  lblCityLb.Text = "City:";
  lblCityLb.Attributes["DisplayType"] = "data";
  lblStateProvinceLb.Text = "State/Province:";
  lblStateProvinceLb.Attributes["DisplayType"] = "data";
  lblCountryLb.Text = "Country:";
  lblCountryLb.Attributes["DisplayType"] = "data";

  this.Controls.Clear;
  this.Controls.Add(lblNameLb);
  this.Controls.Add(lblName);
```

```
        this.Controls.Add(lblEmailLb);
        this.Controls.Add(lblEmail);
        this.Controls.Add(lblStreetLb);
        this.Controls.Add(lblStreet);
        this.Controls.Add(lblCityLb);
        this.Controls.Add(lblCity);
        this.Controls.Add(lblStateProvinceLb);
        this.Controls.Add(lblStateProvince);
        this.Controls.Add(lblCountryLb);
        this.Controls.Add(lblCountry);

    }
  }
```

At this point, it's worthwhile to compile your custom control project, and open the test page in your Web site project. You should find your CustomerInformation control waiting for you in your Toolbox, as it is in Figure 12-5.

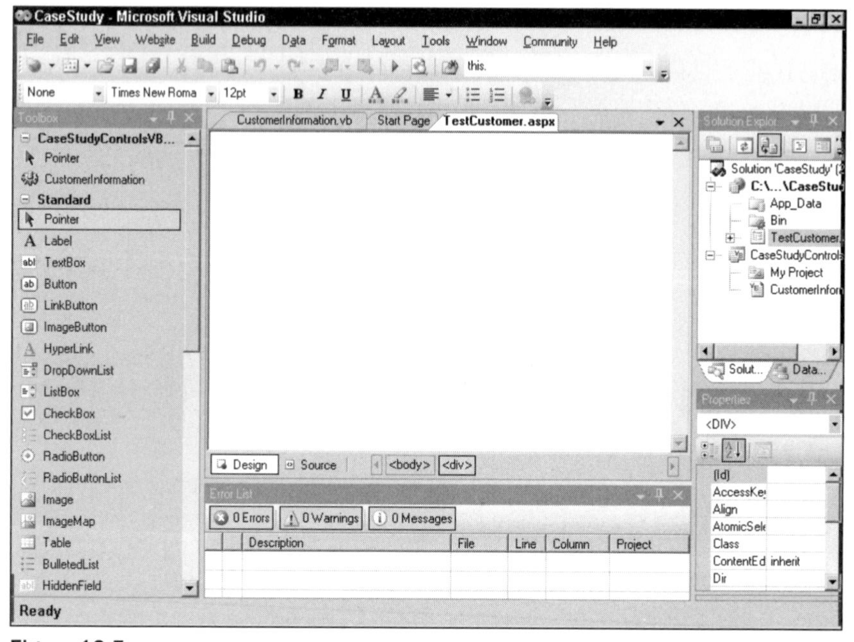

Figure 12-5

However, if you drag your control onto your page at this point, you'll find that it doesn't display your constituent controls. That's because your CreateChildControls method isn't called at design time (if you were to press F5 to test your page, you would find that CreateChildControls is called at run time and your constituent controls are displayed in the browser).

To solve this problem, you can call the CreateChildControls method from your control's OnInit method.

Rather than call the CreateChildControls method directly, the code calls the EnsureChildControls method. The EnsureChildControls method checks to see if the constituent controls have already been created (by testing the ChildControlsCreated property) and skips calling CreateChildControls if the constituent controls have already been added. Also, in the OnInit method, you should call the base control's OnInit method; otherwise the control won't raise its Init event. This is necessary only when the control is being edited, so the code should check the DesignMode property first.

In Visual Basic 2005:

```
Protected Overrides Sub OnInit(ByVal e As System.EventArgs)
  MyBase.OnInit(e)
  If Me.DesignMode = True Then
    Me.EnsureChildControls()
  End If
End Sub
```

In C#:

```
protected override void OnInit(System.EventArgs e)
{
  base.OnInit(e);
  if (this.DesignMode == true)
  {
   this.EnsureChildControls();
  }
}
```

You can also create a routine to handle the control's Init event and call the EnsureChildControls method from that routine (as was done in Chapter 2).

To prevent ASP.NET from calling your CreateChildControls method again, you should set the control's ChildControlsCreated property to True (ASP.NET checks this property before calling the CreateChildControls method and does not call CreateChildControls if the property is set to True). Updating the CreateChildControls method in Visual Basic 2005 gives this code:

```
Protected Overrides Sub CreateChildControls()
    Me.ChildControlsCreated = True
```

In C#:

```
protected override void CreateChildControls()
  {
    this.ChildControlsCreated = true;
```

Now, when you drag the control onto your form you get the display in Figure 12-6.

Obviously, the initial display of the control leaves a great deal to be desired. To begin with, without data, it's difficult to see the labels that will (eventually) display customer information. Also, it's a good idea if each label and text is displayed on a separate line and if there is a gap between the labels and text boxes. The next two sections address those problems.

Figure 12-6

Setting the Default Style

To control the style of the labels that display information to the user, you use a Style object. In dealing with the style of the control, you want to make sure that you don't prevent the developer using your control from being able to set the style of the custom control. So, in the CreateChildControls method, the code begins by checking to see if a style object is available from the control's ControlStyle method (If a Style object has been created for the control, the control's ControlStyleCreated property is set to True.) If the property is set to True, the code extracts the Style object from the ControlStyle property; otherwise the code creates a new Style object.

In Visual Basic 2005:

```
If Me.ControlStyleCreated = True Then
     st = Me.ControlStyle
Else
     st = New System.Web.UI.WebControls.Style
End If
```

In C#:

```
if(this.ControlStyleCreated == true)
{
 st = this.ControlStyle;
}
else
{
 st = new System.Web.UI.WebControls.Style();
}
```

Now that a Style object is available, its properties can be set to create a Style object that can be used with the control as a whole and with its constituent controls. For instance, the labels that display information can be set up to have a thin black border around the control — setting the Style object's BorderStyle, BorderColor, and BorderWidth would meet this goal. If a panel is used to hold all of the constituent controls, as described later in the section "Using Absolute Positioning," the Style object can also be used to set the style of the panel.

While not shown here, the Style object's Font property can also be set to ensure that a standard font is used by all the controls.

To make sure that any settings made by the user aren't overwritten, the code first checks to see if the BorderStyle has been set and sets the other Border-related properties only if the BorderStyle is set to NotSet:

In Visual Basic 2005:

```
If st.BorderStyle = WebControls.BorderStyle.NotSet Then
     st.BorderColor = Drawing.Color.Black
     st.BorderWidth = 1
     st.BorderStyle = WebControls.BorderStyle.Solid
End If
```

In C#:

```
if(st.BorderStyle == WebControls.BorderStyle.NotSet)
{
 st.BorderColor = Drawing.Color.Black;
 st.BorderWidth = 1;
 st.BorderStyle = WebControls.BorderStyle.Solid;
}
```

Positioning the Controls

The initial display of the control, the layout of the constituent controls, leaves a great deal to be desired. There are three ways of managing the layout of the constituent controls:

- Overriding the Render method
- Using a table
- Adding absolute positioning attributes to the constituent control's Style object

Overriding the Render Method

In the Render method, the goal is to place two labels (the label and the customer information) on each line, with a space between the labels. To implement that, the code will:

1. Iterate through each control.
2. Test each control's DisplayType attribute (added to the control when it was created in the CreateChildControls method) to determine if the control is being used as a label or to display information.

3. Call, for each control, the control's RenderControl method to have the control write itself to the page. The RenderControl method must be passed an HtmlTextWriter but, because the Render method you are overriding is passed an HtmlTextWriter, that writer can just be passed to the individual control's RenderControl method.
4. To insert the blank space after a label, the code uses the HtmlTextWriter's Write method to add a blank space to the page.
5. Create a new line after the information control by writing a <br> tag after the information control. To ensure browser compatibility, the code doesn't directly write out the character string "<br>". Instead, the code uses the HtmlTextWriter's WriteBreak method.

If DisplayTypes are added to the control over time, the various DisplayTypes are handled in a Select Case statement that holds all the render activities for each type of control. If a new DisplayType is added in the future, all that's necessary to support the new type is to add a new Case branch to the Select statement.

In Visual Basic 2005:

```
Protected Overrides Sub Render(ByVal writer As System.Web.UI.HtmlTextWriter)

  For Each wc As System.Web.UI.WebControls.WebControl In Me.Controls
    Select Case wc.Attributes("DisplayType")
      Case "data"
         wc.RenderControl(writer)
         writer.WriteBreak
      Case "label"
         wc.RenderControl(writer)
         writer.Write(" ")
    End Select
  Next

End Sub
```

In C#:

```
protected override void Render(System.Web.UI.HtmlTextWriter writer)
{
 foreach(System.Web.UI.WebControls.WebControl wc in this.Controls)
 {
      switch(wc.Attributes["DisplayType"])
      {
       case "data":
          wc.RenderControl(writer);
          writer.WriteBreak;
          break;

       case "label":
          wc.RenderControl(writer);
          writer.Write(" ");
  };
 }
}
```

The result is shown in Figure 12-7. As you can see, the display is ragged. You would want to tweak the Render method code to line up the labels displaying data and to relocate the country data control.

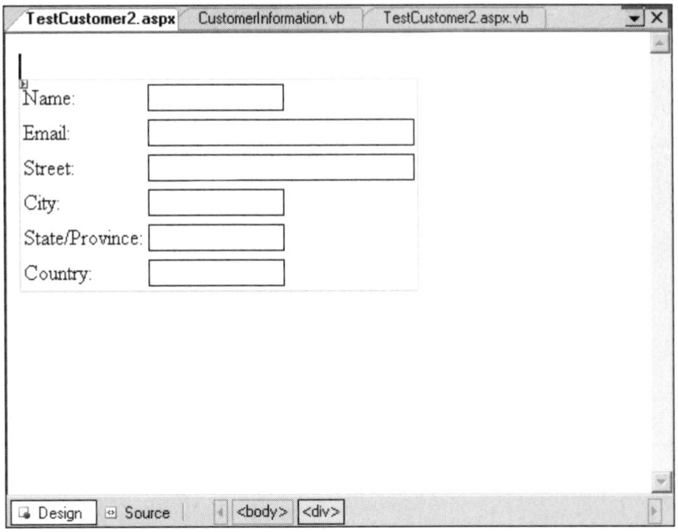

Figure 12-7

Using a Table

Another solution to managing the display of the constituent controls is to use a Table object. In addition to lining up the controls, the HTML that is generated by the Table object is supported in virtually every browser in the same way. To use the Table object, the CreateChildControls method must be updated as follows.

1. Delete the code that added each constituent control to the Controls collection.
2. At the top of the CreateChildControls method, declare a new Table object.
3. Create a TableCell object and place one of the labels in the TableCell by adding it to the cell's Controls collection.
4. Add the cell to a TableRow object.
5. Add the corresponding information label to another TableCell.
6. Add that cell to the TableRow.
7. Add the TableRow to the Table.

In Visual Basic 2005:

```
Dim tbl As New System.Web.UI.WebControls.Table
Dim tc As System.Web.UI.WebControls.TableCell
Dim tr As System.Web.UI.WebControls.TableRow

tr = New System.Web.UI.WebControls.TableRow
```

```
tc = New System.Web.UI.WebControls.TableCell
tc.Controls.Add(lblNameLb)
tr.Cells.Add(tc)

tc = New System.Web.UI.WebControls.TableCell
tc.Controls.Add(lblName)
tr.Cells.Add(tc)

tbl.Rows.Add(tr)
```

In C#:

```
System.Web.UI.WebControls.Table tbl = new System.Web.UI.WebControls.Table();
System.Web.UI.WebControls.TableCell tc;
System.Web.UI.WebControls.TableRow tr;

tr = new System.Web.UI.WebControls.TableRow();
tc = new System.Web.UI.WebControls.TableCell();
tc.Controls.Add(lblNameLb);
tr.Cells.Add(tc);

tc = new System.Web.UI.WebControls.TableCell();
tc.Controls.Add(lblName);
tr.Cells.Add(tc);

tbl.Rows.Add(tr);
```

The final step is to add the Table (rather than the individual controls) to the Control's collection of the custom control as this Visual Basic 2005 code does:

```
Me.Controls.Add(tbl)
```

In C#:

```
this.Controls.Add(tbl)
```

The result is shown in Figure 12-8.

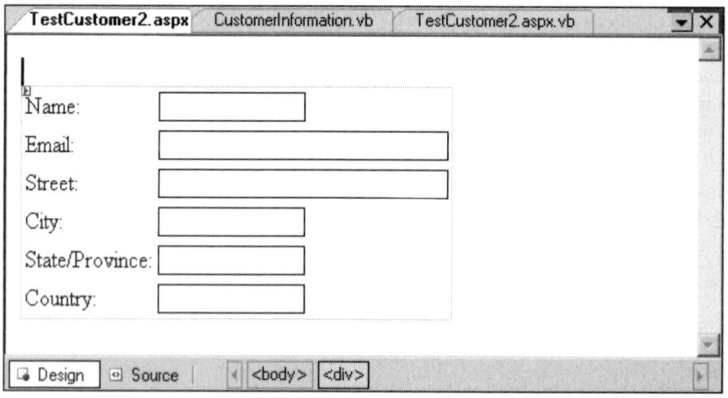

Figure 12-8

Rather than repeat this code over and over, a smarter approach is to write a routine that, when passed two labels and the table, adds the labels to the Table in a new row. The Visual Basic version of that routine looks like this:

```
Private Function AddToTable(ByVal Table As System.Web.UI.WebControls.Table, _
        ByVal Label As System.Web.UI.WebControls.Label, _
        ByVal Data As System.Web.UI.WebControls.Label) As WebControls.Table
Dim tc As System.Web.UI.WebControls.TableCell
Dim tr As System.Web.UI.WebControls.TableRow

  tr = New System.Web.UI.WebControls.TableRow
  tc = New System.Web.UI.WebControls.TableCell
  tc.Controls.Add(Label)
  tr.Cells.Add(tc)

  tc = New System.Web.UI.WebControls.TableCell
  tc.Controls.Add(Data)
  tr.Cells.Add(tc)
  Table.Rows.Add(tr)

Return Table

End Function
```

In C#:

```
private WebControls.Table AddToTable(System.Web.UI.WebControls.Table Table,
          System.Web.UI.WebControls.Label Label,
          System.Web.UI.WebControls.Label Data)
 {
  System.Web.UI.WebControls.TableCell tc;
  System.Web.UI.WebControls.TableRow tr;

  tr = new System.Web.UI.WebControls.TableRow();
  tc = new System.Web.UI.WebControls.TableCell();
  tc.Controls.Add(Label);
  tr.Cells.Add(tc);

  tc = new System.Web.UI.WebControls.TableCell();
  tc.Controls.Add(Data);
  tr.Cells.Add(tc);
  Table.Rows.Add(tr);

  return Table;
 }
```

The routine is called by passing the two labels that go into a row and the table that the row is to be added to. The routine returns the updated Table object so that it can be passed to the routine for the next call (this avoids having to declare the Table object as a module level variable).

In Visual Basic 2005:

```
tbl = AddToTable(tbl, lblNameLb, lblName)
tbl = AddToTable(tbl, lblEmailLb, lblEmail)
...rest of the labels...
```

In C#:

```
tbl = AddToTable(tbl, lblNameLb, lblName);
tbl = AddToTable(tbl, lblEmailLb, lblEmail);
```

Using Absolute Positioning

A third option is to use cascading stylesheet absolute positioning. This option, while providing the finest-grained control, is also the solution most likely to have compatibility problems among browsers (especially, of course, with older browsers that don't support CSS).

In this solution, the code adds three attributes to each constituent control's Style object:

- **absolute:** Set to "position"
- **top:** Set to the distance that the constituent control is to be placed from the top of the custom control
- **left:** Set to the distance that the constituent control is to be placed from the left-hand side of the custom control

This Visual Basic 2005 code positions the data control for the name 5 pixels from the top of the control and 15 pixels from the left-hand edge:

```
lblName.Style.Add("position","absolute")
lblName.Style.Add("top","5px")
lblName.Style.Add("left","15px")
```

In C#:

```
lblName.Style.Add("position", "absolute");
lblName.Style.Add("top", "5px");
lblName.Style.Add("left", "15px");
```

At run time, your custom control is represented by a <span> tag. The positions of your constituent controls will be calculated as offsets from the upper-left corner of your custom control.

Tweaking the various positions of your controls can be time-consuming. A faster method is to open a new form, turn on absolute positioning, and then drag and drop controls onto the user control to match the final layout of your control. You can then, in Source view, read the values generated by Visual Studio 2005 and use those in your code.

While absolute positioning provides a solution for some of the positioning problems in a custom control, there are some problems with using absolute positioning:

- Older browsers may not handle absolute positioning correctly (or at all).
- Controls that use absolute positioning can display oddly in WebPartZones.
- It can be difficult for developers to manipulate controls with absolute positioning in Visual Studio 2005 display controls at design time.

There aren't solutions to the first two problems (other than to use the previous two mechanisms for positioning constituent controls). However, the third problem does have a solution.

At design time, with absolute positioning, your control is represented as a tiny square in the upper-left corner of the control, with the constituent controls spread out below that "anchor" square. Figure 12-9 shows the CustomerInformation control, using absolute positioning. Developers can find it difficult to figure out where to click so that they can drag the control on the page.

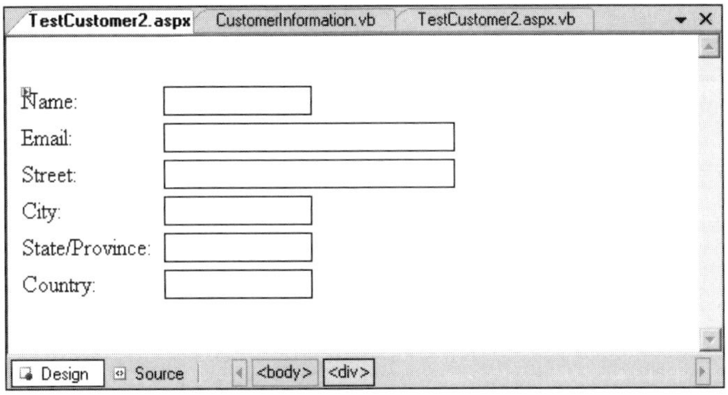

Figure 12-9

If you do decide to use absolute positioning, to make life easier for developers using your control you should consider creating a panel and adding all of your constituent controls to the panel (after setting the constituent control's positioning settings). You need to make sure that you size the panel so that it is large enough to hold all of the controls. After the panel has had the constituent controls added to it, you add the panel to the custom control's Controls collection.

This Visual Basic 2005 code creates a panel, adds the first two labels to it, sets the panel's size, and adds the panel to custom control's Controls collection:

```
Dim pnl As New System.Web.UI.WebControls.Panel

pnl.Controls.Add(lblNameLb)
pnl.Controls.Add(lblName)
...add the rest of the labels to the panel...
pnl.Height = 150
pnl.Width = 320
Me.Controls.Add(pnl)
```

In C#:

```
System.Web.UI.WebControls.Panel pnl = new System.Web.UI.WebControls.Panel();

pnl.Controls.Add(lblNameLb);
pnl.Controls.Add(lblName);
...add the rest of the labels to the panel...
pnl.Height = 150;
pnl.Width = 320;
this.Controls.Add(pnl);
```

The result, at design time, is shown in Figure 12-10. While there is no change to the display in the browser (unless you override the Panel control's default style settings), at design time the control appears with a border around it. Developers can now click the border to drag your control on the page.

Figure 12-10

As with the table-based solution, it makes sense to create a routine that handles positioning the constituent controls. This Visual Basic 2005 routine accepts a number that specifies which line the control appears on and the two labels to be positioned on the line. The code calculates the vertical setting for the control by multiplying the line number by a fixed amount and then sets the positioning properties on the controls passed to the routine:

```
Private Sub AddPositioning(ByVal LineNumber As Integer, _
             ByVal Label As System.Web.UI.WebControls.Label, _
             ByVal Data As System.Web.UI.WebControls.Label)
Dim intVerticalOffset As Integer

   intVerticalOffset = LineNumber * 25
   Label.Style.Add("position", "absolute")
   Label.Style.Add("top", intVerticalOffset.ToString & "px")
   Label.Style.Add("left", "0px")
   Data.Style.Add("position", "absolute")
   Data.Style.Add("top", intVerticalOffset.ToString & "px")
   Data.Style.Add("left", "70px")

End Sub
```

In C#:

```
private void AddPositioning(int LineNumber,
       System.Web.UI.WebControls.Label Label,
       System.Web.UI.WebControls.Label Data)
```

```
{
 int intVerticalOffset;

 intVerticalOffset = LineNumber * 25;
 Label.Style.Add("position", "absolute");
 Label.Style.Add("top", intVerticalOffset.ToString() + "px");
 Label.Style.Add("left", "0px");
 Data.Style.Add("position", "absolute");
 Data.Style.Add("top", intVerticalOffset.ToString() + "px");
 Data.Style.Add("left", "70px");
}
```

The Visual Basic 2005 code to add the name and e-mail text boxes with their labels looks like this:

```
AddPositioning(0, lblNameLb, lblName)
AddPositioning(1, lblEmailLb, lblEmail)
```

In C#:

```
AddPositioning(0, lblNameLb, lblName);
AddPositioning(1, lblEmailLb, lblEmail);
```

Switching Between Display and Update Modes

Because the CustomerInformation control is also intended to allow developers to switch between a display mode and an update mode, the control needs to have a Mode property that allows a developer using the control to change modes. Three design decisions were made when selecting the name for this property:

- Using a generic term such as Mode provides less guidance to developers than using a more specific name (such as DisplayOrUpdate). However, it also makes it possible to add other modes in the future without changing the control's interface to the developer.
- Having a single Mode property ensures that the control can't be given conflicting commands. Conflicting commands would have been possible if, for instance, the control had been given two properties: one to put the control in DisplayMode and one to put the control in UpdateMode.
- Once a noun is chosen to implement mode switching, it makes sense to put the code in a property (most functions have names that begin with verbs). A good case can also be made for creating a method to handle this functionality (for example, ToggleMode or SwitchMode). The code inside the routine would have been very similar in either case.

Because there are only two values (Display and Update), it's a good practice to set up an enumerated value that holds values for those two settings as this Visual Basic 2005 code does:

```
Public Enum ciModeSettings
        ciUpdate
        ciDisplay
End Enum
```

In C#:

```
public enum ciModeSettings
{
 ciUpdate,
 ciDisplay
}
```

In order to store the value of the Mode property, a private variable needs to be declared. In Visual Basic 2005:

```
Private _Mode As ciModeSettings
```

In C#

```
private ciModeSettings _Mode;
```

The Mode property can now be written with Get and Set routines that return the enumerated value, as in this Visual Basic 2005 example:

```
Public Property Mode() As ciModeSettings
    Get
        Return _Mode
     End Get
     Set (value As ciModeSettings)
        _Mode = value
    End Set
End Property
```

In C#:

```
public ciModeSettings Mode
{
 get
 {
  return _Mode;
 }
 set
 {
  _Mode = value;
 }
}
```

Because the Mode property uses this enumerated value, a developer using the control will find the values displayed in the IntelliSense drop-down lists when setting the property (as shown in Figure 12-11) and in the Visual Studio .NET Property List (as shown in Figure 12-12).

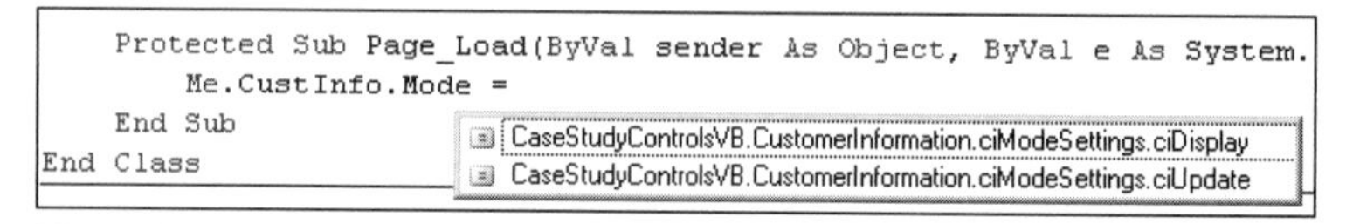

Figure 12-11

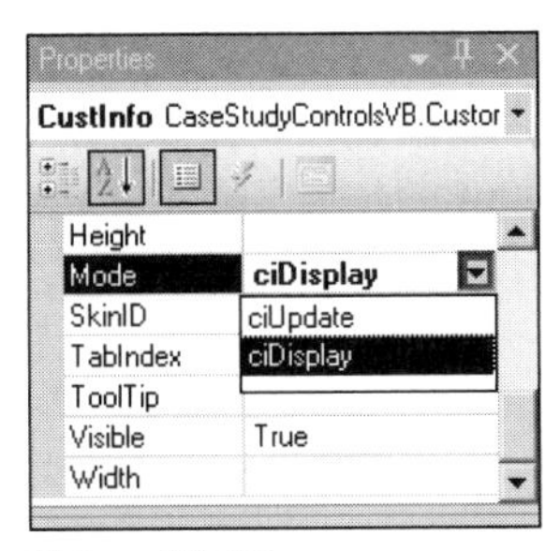

Figure 12-12

In the next section, you see how to add the code to store the control's information. However, for a property like Mode, there's no need to take any action — the property is automatically stored as an attribute on the HTML generated for the control both at design time and at run time. Here's a typical example:

```
<cc1:CustomerInformation ID="CustomerInfo" runat="server" Mode="ciDisplay"
        Style="z-index: 100; left: 38px; position: absolute; top: 15px" />
```

The CreateChildControls routine must include the code to switch between the two modes. The code must check the Mode property and create TextBoxes instead of Labels to hold the customer information. As with the Label controls, the TextBoxes need to have their Id property set and their Style property merged with the ControlStyle object used to format the control.

In Visual Basic 2005:

```
Dim txtName As New System.Web.UI.WebControls.TextBox
Dim txtEmail As New System.Web.UI.WebControls.TextBox
...rest of TextBox declarations...

If Me.Mode = ciModeSettings.ciUpdate Then
   txtName.ID = "txtName"
   txtName.Attributes("DisplayType") = "data"
   txtName.Width = 100
   txtName.MergeStyle(st)

   txtEmail.ID = "txtEmail"
   txtEmail.Attributes("DisplayType") = "data"
   txtEmail.Width = 100
   txtEmail.MergeStyle(st)

   ...rest of textbox controls
Else
   lblName.ID = "txtName"
   lblName.Attributes("DisplayType") = "data"
   lblName.Width = 100
   lblName.MergeStyle(st)

   lblEmail.ID = "txtEmail"
   lblEmail.Attributes("DisplayType") = "data"
   lblEmail.Width = 100
```

```
   lblEmail.MergeStyle(st)

   ...rest of Label controls
End If
```

In C#:

```
System.Web.UI.WebControls.TextBox txtName = new
                         System.Web.UI.WebControls.TextBox();
System.Web.UI.WebControls.TextBox txtEmail = new
                         System.Web.UI.WebControls.TextBox();
...rest of TextBox declarations

if(this.Mode == ciModeSettings.ciUpdate)
{
 txtName.ID = "txtName";
 txtName.Attributes["DisplayType"] = "data";
 txtName.Width = 100;
 txtName.MergeStyle(st);

 txtEmail.ID = "txtEmail";
 txtEmail.Attributes["DisplayType"] = "data";
 txtEmail.Width = 100;
 txtEmail.MergeStyle(st);

  ...rest of TextBox controls
}
else
{
 lblName.ID = "lblName";
 lblName.Attributes["DisplayType"] = "data";
 lblName.Width = 100;
 lblName.MergeStyle(st);

 lblEmail.ID = "lblEmail";
 lblEmail.Attributes["DisplayType"] = "data";
 lblEmail.Width = 100;
 lblEmail.MergeStyle(st);

 ...rest of Label controls
}
```

In the discussion of how to position the controls on the page, I recommended that you set up standard routines to either add controls to a table or to set absolute positioning. Those routines were originally written to accept two Label controls but now need to be extended to handle either a Label or a TextBox control as their second parameter. Because the only properties being manipulated in these routines are the properties common to all WebControls, the simplest solution is just to declare the second parameter of the routines as being of type System.Web.UI.WebControls.WebControl.

Tailoring the Control for the Developer

With much of the control's basic functionality established, now is a good time to set attributes on the control that will make it easier for the developer to use. At the module level, you can insert a TagPrefix attribute to specify the prefix that is to be used when your custom control's tag is generated at run time. The TagPrefix attribute must be passed the Namespace for your control and the prefix to be used. This Visual Basic 2005 example sets the prefix to csc:

```
<Assembly: TagPrefix("CaseStudyControls", "csc")>
<ToolboxData("<{0}:CustomerInformation runat=server></{0}:CustomerInformation>")> _
Public Class CustomerInformation
```

In C#:

```
[assembly: TagPrefix("CaseStudyControls", "csc")]
[ToolboxData("<{0}:CustomerInformation runat=server></{0}:CustomerInformation>")]
public class CustomerInformation
{
```

The HTML for your control at design time now looks like this:

```
<%@ Register Assembly="CaseStudyControlsVB" Namespace="CaseStudyControls"
    TagPrefix="csc" %>

<csc:CustomerInformation ID="CustomerInfo" runat="server"
        Style="z-index: 100;left: 66px; position: absolute; top: 15px" />
```

Without a TagPrefix, the prefix for your control defaults to cc.

When you first create a control, it's hard to predict which properties of the control a developer will use the most. However, for the CustomerInformation control it seems likely that the Mode property will be one that developers will want to set as soon as they add the control to a page. This Visual Basic 2005 code uses the DefaultProperty attribute on the Class declaration to make Mode the default property in the Visual Studio .NET IntelliSense drop-down lists, as shown in Figure 12-13:

```
<DefaultProperty("Mode"), _
 ToolboxData("<{0}:CustomerInformation runat=server></{0}:CustomerInformation>")> _
Public Class CustomerInformation
```

In C#:

```
[DefaultProperty("Mode")]
[ToolboxData("<{0}:CustomerInformation runat=server></{0}:CustomerInformation>")]
public class CustomerInformation
```

On the Mode property itself, the DefaultValue attribute lets you specify an initial value for the Mode property and the Category attribute allows you to specify where the Property appears in the Visual Studio .NET Property List when the list is sorted by category. This Visual Basic 2005 code sets the default value for the control to ciDisplay and puts the property in the Behavior category of the Property List:

```
<DefaultValue(ciModeSettings.ciDisplay), Category("Behavior")> _
    Public Property Mode() As ciModeSettings
```

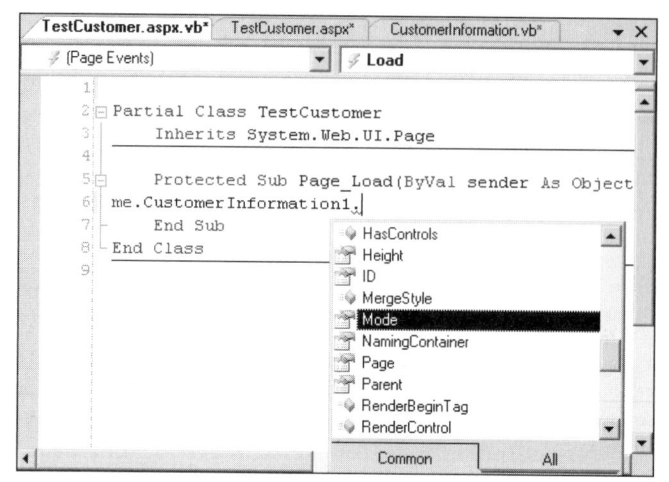

Figure 12-13

In C#:

```
[DefaultValue(ciModeSettings.ciDisplay)]
[Category("Behavior")]
public ciModeSettings Mode
```

Because the Mode property is a critical property for the control, you might want to add the ParenthesizePropertyName attribute, which causes the property name to be enclosed in parentheses (for example, "(Mode)") and, as a result, sort to the top of the Property List when the list is displayed in alphabetical order.

The default toolbox icon for a custom control is a yellow gear-like graphic. If you create a number of custom controls and they all use the default toolbox icon, developers will to find it difficult to locate the control that they want. To solve this problem, use the Project | Add Existing Item menu choice to add a 16 × 16 pixel bitmap to your project. After the bitmap is added, select the bitmap file in Solution Explorer and change its Build Action property to Embedded Resource. This causes your bitmap to be inserted into the assembly for your control when your project is compiled.

With the bitmap now included in your control's assembly you can use the ToolboxBitmap attribute to add the bitmap to the Toolbox by passing two parameters:

- **The type of the assembly to search for the bitmap resource:** Because the bitmap is embedded in your control's assembly, use the GetType function and pass it a reference to your control.
- **The name of the resource to use:** The bitmap's filename.

In Visual Basic 2005, specifying the icon in a file called CustInfoInfo.BMP to be the toolbox icon for the CustomerInformation class looks like this:

```
<System.Drawing.ToolboxBitmap(GetType(CustomerInformation), "CustInfo.BMP"),
 DefaultProperty("Mode"), _
 ToolboxData("<{0}:CustomerInformation runat=server></{0}:CustomerInformation>")> _
Public Class CustomerInformation
```

In C#:

```
[System.Drawing.ToolboxBitmap(GetType(CustomerInformation), "CustInfo.BMP")]
[DefaultProperty("Mode")]
[ToolboxData("<{0}:CustomerInformation runat=server></{0}:CustomerInformation>")]
public class CustomerInformation
```

Saving State

The next piece of the control's basic functionality to add is the code to save the data that is going down to the browser. You can skip this step if, for instance, you're interested only in the data that is sent back up from the browser after the user has entered data. However, you need to override this method if you want to fire events based on the difference between the data sent down to the browser and the data returned from the browser.

Saving the control's state is a four-step process:

1. Define a serializable data structure to hold the data.
2. Declare a variable to use the structure.
3. Store the data for the control in the data structure.
4. Save the data structure to the ControlState.

Defining a Data Structure for Saving State

The first step in saving the data sent to the browser is to create a data structure to hold the customer information. Because the data structure will, eventually be serialized and placed in the ControlState, the structure must be given the <Serializable> attribute, as this Visual Basic 2005 code does:

```
<Serializable> _
Public Structure CustomerInformationData
    Dim Name As String
    Dim Email As String
    Dim Street As String
    Dim City As String
    Dim StateProvince As String
    Dim Country As String
End Structure
```

In C#:

```
[Serializable]
struct CustomerInformationData
 {
  public string Name;
  public string Email;
  public string Street;
  public string City;
```

```
    public string StateProvince;
    public string Country;
  }
```

The second step is to declare a variable that uses the data structure, as this Visual Basic 2005 code does:

```
Private saveData As CustomerInformationData
```

In C#:

```
private CustomerInformationData saveData;
```

Saving to the ControlState

The third step is to notify the host page that the control will be saving data in the ControlState. This notification is handled by calling the Page's RegisterRequiresControlState method and passing a reference to the custom control. Add this to the code already in the OnInit event (Chapter 6 demonstrated how to do this in the Init event):

```
Protected Overrides Sub OnInit(ByVal e As System.EventArgs)
 MyBase.OnInit(e)
 If Me.DesignMode = True Then
    Me.EnsureChildControls()
 End If

 Me.Page.RegisterRequiresControlState(Me)

End Sub
```

In C#:

```
protected override void OnInit(System.EventArgs e)
{
 base.OnInit(e);
 if this.DesignMode == true)
 {
  this.EnsureChildControls()
 }

 this.Page.RegisterRequiresControlState(this);

}
```

The final step is to override the SaveControlState method and save the customer information into the structure defined earlier. After the structure has been loaded with data, that structure must be returned from the function to be stored in the ControlState. In the CustomerInformation control, because the data is being saved in order to support firing the equivalent of the TextBox's TextChanged event, it's necessary to save the data only if the developer has put the control into update mode (the labels used in display mode can't be changed). As a result, the code should check the mode before saving its data. In

Visual Basic 2005, the code to check the mode, retrieve the controls from the custom control's Controls collection, copy the data from the controls into the data structure, and then return the data structure looks like this:

```
Dim cData As New CustomerInformationData

Protected Overrides Function SaveControlState() As Object

 If Me.Mode = ciUpdate Then
   cData.Name = CType(Me.FindControl("txtName"), _
                                  System.Web.UI.WebControls.TextBox).Text
   cData.Email = CType(Me.FindControl("txtEmail"), _
                                  System.Web.UI.WebControls.TextBox).Text
   cData.City = CType(Me.FindControl("txtCity"), _
                                  System.Web.UI.WebControls.TextBox).Text
   cData.Street = CType(Me.FindControl("txtStreet"), _
                                  System.Web.UI.WebControls.TextBox).Text
   cData.StateProvince = CType(Me.FindControl("txtStatProv"), _
                                  System.Web.UI.WebControls.TextBox).Text
   cData.Country = CType(Me.FindControl("txtCountry"), _
                                  System.Web.UI.WebControls.TextBox).Text
   Return cData
 End If
End Function
```

In C#:

```
protected override object SaveControlState()
{
 if (this.Mode == ciUpdate)
  {
   CustomerInformationData cData = new CustomerInformationData();

   cData.Name = ((UI.WebControls.TextBox) this.FindControl("txtName")).Text;
   cData.Email = ((UI.WebControls.TextBox) this.FindControl("txtEmail")).Text;
   cData.City = ((UI.WebControls.TextBox)  this.FindControl("txtCity")).Text;
   cData.Street = ((UI.WebControls.TextBox)
                                        this.FindControl("txtStreet")).Text;
   cData.StateProvince = ((System.Web.UI.WebControls.TextBox)
                                        this.FindControl("txtStatProv")).Text;
   cData.Country = ((System.Web.UI.WebControls.TextBox)
                                        this.FindControl("txtCountry")).Text;
   return cData;
  }
}
```

When the user finishes working with the page and posts back to the server, the control must retrieve the data from the ControlState. This is done in the LoadControlState method and, again, should be done only if the control is in Update mode. This Visual Basic 2005 example retrieves the data from the ControlState and puts the data into the same variable used to hold the data before it was placed in the ControlState:

```
Protected Overrides Sub LoadControlState(ByVal savedState As Object)

  If Me.Mode = ciUpdate Then
    saveData = CType(savedState, CustomerInformationData)
  End If

End Sub
```

In C#:

```
protected override void LoadControlState(object savedState)
{
if (this.Mode == ciUpdate)
 {
 saveData = (CustomerInformationData) savedState;
 }
}
```

Retrieving User Data

With the plumbing for saving the data that is sent down to the browser, it's time to add the code to handle retrieving the user data returned from the browser. In order to retrieve the data that's entered by the user while the control is displayed in the data, your control must implement the IPostBackDataHandler interface. In Visual Basic 2005, this code implements the interface:

```
Public Class CustomerInformation
    Inherits System.Web.UI.WebControls.WebParts.WebPart
    Implements IPostBackDataHandler
```

In C#:

```
public class CustomerInformation : System.Web.UI.WebControls.WebParts.WebPart,
                                   IPostBackDataHandler
```

The user data returned from the browser can be saved in the same data structure as was used to save the data going down to the browser. To keep the user data returned from the browser separate from the control's state data, a new variable needs to be used. This Visual Basic 2005 declares a variable called postData:

```
Private postData As CustomerInformationData
```

In C#:

```
private CustomerInformationData postData;
```

With a variable created to hold the data, the control must implement the LoadPostData method. That method's postCollection parameter is a collection that contains the data entered by the user in the browser. Individual controls can be retrieved from the collection by passing the name of the control to the collection. The name of your control is formed from the name that you assigned it, the unique Id assigned to the custom control by the developer when she dragged your custom control onto the page, and the character being used to separate the two parts of the name. Your custom control's Id can be retrieved through the UniqueId property and the separator from the IdSeparator property.

When a custom control is used inside a WebPartZone, the UniqueId is actually a combination of the custom control's Id and the WebPartManager's Id.

This Visual Basic 2005 code transfers the data from the controls on the form and into the postData structure:

```
Public Function LoadPostData(ByVal postDataKey As String, _
        ByVal postCollection As Collections.Specialized.NameValueCollection) _
        As Boolean Implements IPostBackDataHandler.LoadPostData

  postData.Name = postCollection.Item(Me.UniqueID & Me.IdSeparator & "txtName")
  postData.Email = postCollection.Item(Me.UniqueID & Me.IdSeparator & "txtEmail")
  postData.Street = postCollection.Item(Me.UniqueID & Me.IdSeparator & "txtStreet")
  postData.City = postCollection.Item(Me.UniqueID & Me.IdSeparator & "txtCity")
  postData.StateProvince = postCollection.Item(Me.UniqueID & Me.IdSeparator & _
                                   Me.UniqueID & Me.IdSeparator & "txtStatProv")
  postData.Country = postCollection.Item(Me.UniqueID & Me.IdSeparator & _
                                                               "txtCountry")
```

In C#:

```
public bool IPostBackDataHandler.LoadPostData(string postDataKey, _
                        Collections.Specialized.NameValueCollection postCollection)
{
 postData.Name = postCollection.Item[this.UniqueID & this.IdSeparator & "txtName"];
 postData.Email = postCollection.Item[this.UniqueID & this.IdSeparator &
                                                               "txtEmail"];
 postData.Street = postCollection.Item[this.UniqueID & this.IdSeparator &
                                                               "txtStreet"];
 postData.City = postCollection.Item[this.UniqueID & this.IdSeparator & "txtCity"];
 postData.StateProvince = postCollection.Item[this.UniqueID & this.IdSeparator &
                                                               "txtStatProv"];
 postData.Country = postCollection.Item[this.UniqueID & this.IdSeparator &
                                                               "txtCountry"];
```

The postDataKey parameter holds the name of the custom control. If this were a control that had no constituent controls, you would be able to retrieve the control's data just by passing the postDataKey parameter to the postCollection parameter to retrieve the custom control's data.

The goal is to have the control raise an event, which you define, if there is a difference between the two sets of data. In the next section, the code to raise that event is put in the base object's RaisePostDataChangedEvent method. However, to have the RaisePostDataChangedEvent method invoked, the LoadPostData method must return True. After the user data and the control's state data have been retrieved, it's possible to check the two sets of data and (if there is a difference) return True when they're different.

User data and saved state data must be compared in the LoadPostData method (where the user data is retrieved) because it follows the LoadControlState method (where the control's state data is retrieved).

The data in the two structures can be compared on an item-by-item basis, as this Visual Basic 2005 code does:

```
If saveData.Name <> postData.Name Or _
   saveData.Email <> postData.Email Or _
...
```

This C# does the same:

```
if(saveData.Name != postData.Name ||
   saveData.Email != postData.Email ||
...
```

However, the comparison can be simplified if the CustomerInformationData structure is given a ToString method that returns a unique string for the structure. This Visual Basic 2005 code overrides the structure's default ToString method (which would just return the type name of the structure) to return an XML structure holding the data in the structure:

```
<Serializable> _
Public Structure CustomerInformationData
  Dim Name As String
  Dim Email As String
  Dim Street As String
  Dim City As String
  Dim StateProvince As String
  Dim Country As String

  Overrides Function ToString() As String
   Return "<CustomerInformation>" & _
          "<Name>" & Name & "</Name>" & _
          "<Email>" & Email & "</Email>" & _
          "<Street>" & Street & "</Street>" & _
          "<City>" & City & "</City>" & _
          "<StateProvince>" & StateProvince & "</StateProvince>" & _
          "<Country>" & Country & "</Country>" & _
          "</CustomerInformation>"
  End Function

End Structure
```

In C#:

```
[Serializable]
public struct CustomerInformationData;
  string Name;
  string Email;
  string Street;
  string City;
  string StateProvince;
  string Country;

  override public string ToString()
  {
    return "<CustomerInformation>" +
```

```
            "<Name>" + Name + "</Name>" +
            "<Email>" + Email + "</Email>" +
            "<Street>" + Street + "</Street>" +
            "<City>" + City + "</City>" +
            "<StateProvince>" + StateProvince + "</StateProvince>" +
            "<Country>" + Country + "</Country>" +
            "</CustomerInformation>";
    }
}
```

With this ToString method in place, the two structures can be compared more simply. The end of the LoadPostData routine looks like this in Visual Basic 2005:

```
    If postData.ToString <> saveData.ToString Then
      Return True
    Else
      Return False
    End If

  End Function
```

Raising an Event

In the RaisePostDataChangedEvent, the control should raise an event that can be handled by the host page. For this example, the information that is passed to the host page will be:

- The name of the control whose data was changed
- The saved state data that was sent to the browser
- The user data that was returned from the browser

To put this in focus, let's start with the host page's view. The control fires an event called CustomerInformationChanged when the user changes data while the data is displayed in the browser (the code to check for this condition was described in the previous section). The event handler for the CustomerInformationChanged event is passed a CustomerInformationChangedEventArgs object. The CustomerInformationChangedEventArgs object has three read-only properties that return the name of the data that was changed (e.g., "Name", "Email", "Street"), the data sent to the browser, and the data that the user entered.

The properties are read-only because it wouldn't make sense for the code in the host page to change their values.

The following Visual Basic 2005 code is an example of the code that a host page might put in its CustomerInformationChanged event handler. This code checks to see if the Country text box was changed, and then further checks to see if the country was changed from "United States" to "Canada":

```
Protected Sub CustomerInfo_CustomerInformationChanged( _
  ByVal Sender As Object, _
  ByVal e As CaseStudyControlsVB.CustomerInformationChangedEventArgs) _
                  Handles CustomerInfo.CustomerInformationChanged
```

```
    If e.Id = "Country" Then
     If e.NewText = "Canada" And _
         e.OldText = "United States" Then
           ...special processing for Canada to US change...
      End If
    End If

End Sub
```

The same host page routine in C# looks like this:

```
protected void CustomerInfo_CustomerInformationChanged(
   object Sender, CaseStudyControlsVB.CustomerInformationChangedEventArgs e)
{
 if(e.Id == "Country")
 {
  if(e.NewText == "Canada" && e.OldText == "United States")
  {
     ...special processing for Canada to US change...
  }
}
```

In order to implement this event, the control has to contain code to handle three tasks:

- Define a CustomerInformationChangedEventArgs object to hold the Id, NewText, and OldText properties.
- Define an event that returns the CustomerInformationChangedEventArgs object.
- Add the code to the RaisePostDataChangedEvent method to raise the event.

The convention in .NET is to name the object returned as the second parameter for an event as *nameoftheevent*EventArgs. Because the name of our event is CustomerInformationChanged, the object is named CustomerInformationChangedEventArgs.

Defining a Custom Event Arguments Object

The object used as the event argument must inherit from the System.EventArgs object. To implement the functionality required by the CustomerInformationChanged event, the object needs to implement three read-only properties: Id, NewText, and OldText. Because the properties are read-only, the properties can't have their values set from code. So, the code sets the properties' underlying variables in the object's constructor, which must be passed the three values that the properties return. In the constructor, the code sets three module-level variables that the corresponding properties return from the data passed to it. In Visual Basic 2005 the event arguments object looks like this:

```
Public Class CustomerInformationChangedEventArgs
  Inherits System.EventArgs

Private _Id As String
Private _NewText As String
Private _OldText As String
```

```
    Sub New(ByVal Id As String, ByVal NewText As String, ByVal OldText As String)
      _Id = Id
      _NewText = NewText
      _OldText = OldText
    End Sub

    Public ReadOnly Property Id() As String
      Get
        Return _Id
      End Get
    End Property

    Public ReadOnly Property OldText() As String
      Get
        Return _OldText
      End Get
    End Property

    Public ReadOnly Property NewText() As String
      Get
       Return _NewText
      End Get
    End Property

  End Class
```

In C#:

```
  public class CustomerInformationChangedEventArgs : System.EventArgs
  {
   private string _Id;
   private string _NewText;
   private string _OldText;

   public CustomerInformationChangedEventArgs(string Id, string NewText,
                                              string OldText)
   {
    _Id = Id;
    _NewText = NewText;
    _OldText = OldText;
   }

   public string Id
   {
    get
    {
     return _Id;
    }
   }
   public string OldText
   {
    get
    {
     return _OldText;
```

```
    }
  }

  public string NewText
  {
   get
   {
    return _NewText;
   }
  }
}
```

If this particular event argument is going to be used in the CustomerInformation control only, the code for the CustomerInformationChangedEventArgs object can be placed in the same file as the CustomerInformation control, after the end of the code for the CustomerInformation class.

Defining the Event

The next step is to define the event. This is done by declaring a delegate that returns an Object as the first parameter and the custom event argument as the second parameter. With the delegate declared, the CustomerInformationChanged event can be declared using the delegate. This Visual Basic 2005 code declares both the delegate and the event:

```
Public Delegate Sub CustomerInformationChangedHandler( _
          ByVal Sender As Object, ByVal e As CustomerInformationChangedEventArgs)
Public Event CustomerInformationChanged As CustomerInformationChangedHandler
```

In C#:

```
public delegate void CustomerInformationChangedHandler(object sender,
                                           CustomerInformationChangedEventArgs e);
public event CustomerInformationChangedHandler CustomerInformationChanged;
```

More conventions: The delegate for an event is named nameoftheevent*Handler; the name of the first parameter is Sender; the name of the second parameter is e.*

Raising the Event

With all the preliminary work done, the RaisePostDataChangedEvent method can create the CustomerInformationChangedEventArgs object, pass the necessary data to the object as the object is created, and raise the CustomerInformationChanged event. In this Visual Basic 2005 version of the code, the routine checks to see which data has changed, creates the CustomerInformationChangedEventArgs object, and then raises the event passing a reference to the custom control as the first parameter and the custom event argument as the second parameter:

```
Public Sub RaisePostDataChangedEvent() Implements
        System.Web.UI.IPostBackDataHandler.RaisePostDataChangedEvent
Dim cic As CustomerInformationChangedEventArgs

 If postData.Name <> saveData.Name Then
```

```
    cic = New CustomerInformationChangedEventArgs("Name", postData.Name, _
            saveData.Name)
    RaiseEvent CustomerInformationChanged(Me, cic)
  End If

  ...checking other data items...

End Sub
```

In C#:

```
public void IPostBackDataHandler.RaisePostDataChangedEvent()
{
 CustomerInformationChangedEventArgs cic;

 if(postData.Name != saveData.Name)
 {
  cic = new CustomerInformationChangedEventArgs("Name", postData.Name,
          saveData.Name);
  CustomerInformationChanged(this, cic);
 }

 ...checking other data items...

}
```

Now that the event is defined, it seems likely that when a developer double-clicks your control in design view that he expects Visual Studio .NET to write out the skeleton of the CustomerInformationChanged event (in the same way that double-clicking a button causes Visual Studio .NET to write out the skeleton of the button's Click event). To enable that, you need to add the DefaultEvent attribute to the class definition, specifying the CustomerInformationChanged event. Putting that together with the attributes added earlier gives this in Visual Basic 2005:

```
<DefaultEvent("CustomerInformationChanged"), _

 System.Drawing.ToolboxBitmap(GetType(CustomerInformation), "CustInfo.BMP"), _
 DefaultProperty("Mode"), _
 ToolboxData("<{0}:CustomerInformation runat=server></{0}:CustomerInformation>")> _
Public Class CustomerInformation
```

In C#:

```
[DefaultEvent("CustomerInformationChanged")]
[System.Drawing.ToolboxBitmap(GetType(CustomerInformation), "CustInfo.BMP")]
[DefaultProperty("Mode")]
[ToolboxData("<{0}:CustomerInformation runat=server></{0}:CustomerInformation>")]
public class CustomerInformation
```

Supporting the Next Control Developer

In the same way that you can build a custom control by inheriting from other controls, other developers may want to inherit from your control. If you want to support the "next control developer" (the developer who wants to inherit from your control), there is one more step that you can take when implementing an event.

It is a convention in the .NET Framework to place the code that actually raises an event in a separate routine. This allows developers who inherit from the control to tie code to the event either by overriding the routine that raises the event or by adding an event handler to the event (this convention was discussed in more detail in Chapter 8). The naming convention for this routine containing the code that raises the event is On*nameofevent*. By convention, the On* routine for an event is passed only the event arguments object for the event.

To revise the CustomerInformation object to support this convention, the first step is to remove the RaiseEvent code from the RaisePostDataChangedEvent routine and replace it with a call to a routine called OnCustomerInformationChanged. The OnCustomerInformationChanged event should be passed just the CustomerInformationChangedEventArgs object. This is the revised version of RaisePostDataChangedEvent in Visual Basic 2005:

```
Public Sub RaisePostDataChangedEvent() Implements
        System.Web.UI.IPostBackDataHandler.RaisePostDataChangedEvent
Dim cic As CustomerInformationChangedEventArgs

 If postData.Name <> saveData.Name Then
  cic = New CustomerInformationChangedEventArgs("Name", postData.Name, _
                                              saveData.Name)
  OnCustomerInformationChanged(cic)
 End If

 ...checking other data items...

End Sub
```

In C#:

```
void IPostBackDataHandler.RaisePostDataChangedEvent()
{
 CustomerInformationChangedEventArgs cic;

 if(postData.Name != saveData.Name)
 {
  cic = new CustomerInformationChangedEventArgs("Name", postData.Name,
          saveData.Name);
  OnCustomerInformationChanged(cic);
 }

 ...checking other data items...

}
```

The OnCustomerInformationChanged method must accept the event arguments object and raise the event. In order to allow other developers to override the method, the routine must be marked as Overridable. In Visual Basic 2005, the routine looks like this:

```
Public Overridable Sub OnCustomerInformationChanged( _
    ByVal e As CustomerInformationChangedEventArgs)

  RaiseEvent CustomerInformationChanged(Me, e)

End Sub
```

In C#:

```
public void OnCustomerInformationChanged(CustomerInformationChangedEventArgs e)
{
 CustomerInformationChanged(this, e);
}
```

Displaying User Data on Postback

Having retrieved the user data, it's your code's responsibility to move that data into the constituent controls when the constituent controls are placed back on the page. There are a number of ways to implement this but one way is to attach an event handler to the constituent control's Load event. When the constituent control is added to the Controls collection, the constituent control's Load event fires. In the event handler for the Load event, the control's Text property can be set to the value retrieved in the LoadPostData method. A single routine can be used to handle the Load event for all the controls.

The first step in implementing this functionality is to catch the Load event of the various TextBoxes or Labels and create an event handler for them. In Visual Basic 2005, the code to catch the Load event for each of the TextBoxes and associate an event handler routine called SetData with the events looks like this:

```
If Me.Mode = ciUpdate Then
  AddHandler txtName.Load, AddressOf SetData
  AddHandler txtEmail.Load, AddressOf SetData
  AddHandler txtStreet.Load, AddressOf SetData
  AddHandler txtCity.Load, AddressOf SetData
  AddHandler txtStateProvince.Load, AddressOf SetData
  AddHandler txtCountry.Load, AddressOf SetData
```

In C#

```
if (this.Mode == ciUpdate)
 {
  txtName.Load += new System.EventHandler(this.SetData);
  txtEmail.Load += new System.EventHandler(this.SetData);
  txtStreet.Load += new System.EventHandler(this.SetData);
  txtCity.Load += new System.EventHandler(this.SetData);
  txtStateProvince.Load += new System.EventHandler(this.SetData);
  txtCountry.Load += new System.EventHandler(this.SetData);
```

The SetData routine is passed a reference to the object that fired the Load event. In the SetData routine, the code must check the CustomerInformation's mode (to determine if Labels or TextBoxes are being used). After the type of control has been determined, the Sender object is passed to the SetData routine:

```
Sub SetData(ByVal Sender As Object, ByVal e As System.EventArgs)
Dim txt As System.Web.UI.WebControls.TextBox
Dim lbl As System.Web.UI.WebControls.Label

  If Me.Mode = ciModeSettings.ciUpdate Then
    txt = CType(Sender, System.Web.UI.WebControls.TextBox)

    Select Case txt.ID
        Case "txtName"
           txt.Text = postData.Name

         ...check the remainder of the TextBoxes
    End Select
  Else
    lbl = CType(Sender, System.Web.UI.WebControls.Label)

    Select Case lbl.ID
        Case "lblName"
           lbl.Text = postData.Name

      ...check the remainder of the Labels

    End Select
  End If

End Sub
```

In C#:

```
public void SetData(object Sender, System.EventArgs e)
{
 System.Web.UI.WebControls.TextBox txt;
 System.Web.UI.WebControls.Label lbl;

 if(this.Mode == ciModeSettings.ciUpdate)
 {
  txt = (System.Web.UI.WebControls.TextBox) Sender;

  switch(txt.ID)
  {
   case "txtName":
     txt.Text = postData.Name;
       ...check the remainder of the TextBoxes
  };
 }
 else
 {
  lbl = (System.Web.UI.WebControls.Label) Sender;

  switch(lbl.ID)
  {
   case "lblName":
     lbl.Text = postData.Name;
```

```
    ...check the remainder of the Labels
      break;
    };
  }
}
```

Exposing and Accepting Data

The custom control is going to require some additional properties. Developers using the control will want to be able to extract data from the constituent controls without having to catch the CustomerInformationChanged event. However, because the control provides data for the constituent controls by reading data from the database, most of these properties are read-only. It also seems likely that a developer extracting data from the CustomerInformation control would want the data returned from the user, which is stored in the postData structure.

These are all arbitrary decisions. It's not impossible that in the scenarios where developers are using the CustomerInformation control, the host page needs access to both the original data sent down to the browser and the data the user entered while the control was displayed in the browser. However, for the purposes of this book, these design decisions have the advantage of simplifying the control to let you concentrate on the code required to implement a custom control while ignoring the business-related code that a more full-featured control might require.

The one exception to the properties' being read-only is the CustomerId property. This property allows code in the host page to specify which customer is to be retrieved by the CustomerInformation control. The code to retrieve the customer data is called from the CustomerId property so that, when the CustomerId property is set, the new information is retrieved.

The Visual Basic 2005 version of those properties looks like this:

```
Public Property CustomerId() As String
  Get
    Return _CustomerId
  End Get
  Set(ByVal value As String)
     _CustomerId = value
     GetCustomerInformation(_CustomerId)
  End Set
End Property

Private Sub GetCustomerInformation(_CustomerId As String)
 ...code to retrieve customer information, update postData and constituent controls
End Sub

Public ReadOnly Property Name() As String
  Get
    Return postData.Name
  End Get
End Property

Public ReadOnly Property Email() As String
  Get
```

```
      Return postData.Email
    End Get
  End Property

    ...properties to support the rest of the postData members...
  End Property
```

In C#:

```
  public string CustomerId
  {
   get
   {
    return _CustomerId;
   }
   set
   {
    _CustomerId = value;
     GetCustomerInformation(_CustomerId);
   }
  }

  private void GetCustomerInformation(string _CustomerId)
  {
   ...code to retrieve customer information, update postData and constituent controls
  }

  public string Name
  {
   get
   {
    return postData.Name;
   }
  }

  public string Email
  {
   get
   {
    return postData.Email;
   }
  }

    ...properties to support the rest of the postData members...
    ...properties to support the rest of the postData members...

  }
  }
```

This is only the start of the business-related methods, properties, and events that a complete implementation of the CustomerInformation control might have. For instance, the control should handle a situation in which the customer specified by the CustomerId doesn't exist, perhaps by raising an event. A property that allows a developer using the control to set the connection string for the database server where the customer data is stored would make the control more flexible. It might also be worthwhile to provide a set of properties that return the saved state information in addition to the user-entered data. The control can also be implemented differently. Rather than using the CustomerId property to retrieve customer information, a GetCustomerInformation method can be exposed as part of the control's interface (although this prevents much of the customization options implemented in the next few sections from being implemented). However, all of these decisions depend on the situations where you expect the control to be used and your own development style. More important, implementing these designs doesn't take advantage of the features of a custom control or a Web Part and are outside the scope of this book.

If a developer wants to use a Validator with the CustomerInformation control, the most likely property to be validated is the control's only read-write property: the CustomerId property. It makes sense to flag the CustomerId as the property to be checked by a Validator control (the way that a TextBox's Text property is automatically checked by a Validator control). To flag the CustomerId property as the validation property for the control, you need to add the ValidationProperty to the class declaration and pass the attribute the name of the CustomerId property. Adding this attribute to the attributes already added to the Visual Basic 2005 class declaration gives the following code:

```
<ValidationProperty("CustomerId"), _
 System.Drawing.ToolboxBitmap(GetType(CustomerInformation), "CustInfo.BMP"), _
 DefaultEvent("CustomerInformationChanged"), _
 DefaultProperty("Mode"), _
 ToolboxData("<{0}:CustomerInformation runat=server></{0}:CustomerInformation>")> _
Public Class CustomerInformation
```

In C#:

```
[ValidationProperty("CustomerId")]
[System.Drawing.ToolboxBitmap(GetType(CustomerInformation), "CustInfo.BMP")]
[DefaultEvent("CustomerInformationChanged")]
[DefaultProperty("Mode")]
[ToolboxData("<{0}:CustomerInformation runat=server></{0}:CustomerInformation>")]
public class CustomerInformation
```

Supporting Customization

The CustomerId property is one that a user might want to customize if he wants to view a single customer. If, for instance, the control is used on a page where the customer is to enter information about himself, a user will want to set the CustomerId to their customer id. Alternatively, if the CustomerInformation control is used on a page for sales staff, a sales person who worked with a single large account will want to set the CustomerId to a single customer number.

To make the CustomerId property available to be updated at run time by the user and for those changes to be remembered, both the WebBrowsable and the Personalizable attributes have to be added to the property. This Visual Basic 2005 example shows the CustomerId property with both attributes set:

```
<System.Web.UI.WebControls.WebParts.WebBrowsable(),
 System.Web.UI.WebControls.WebParts.Personalizable()> _
Public Property CustomerId() As String
```

In C#:

```
[System.Web.UI.WebControls.WebParts.WebBrowsable()]
[System.Web.UI.WebControls.WebParts.Personalizable()]
public string CustomerId
```

With these two attributes added to the CustomerId property, the property can now be edited using the PropertyEditor WebPartEditor. Figure 12-14 shows a Web page with the CustomerInformation control in a WebPartZone with the PropertyEditor part displaying the CustomerId property.

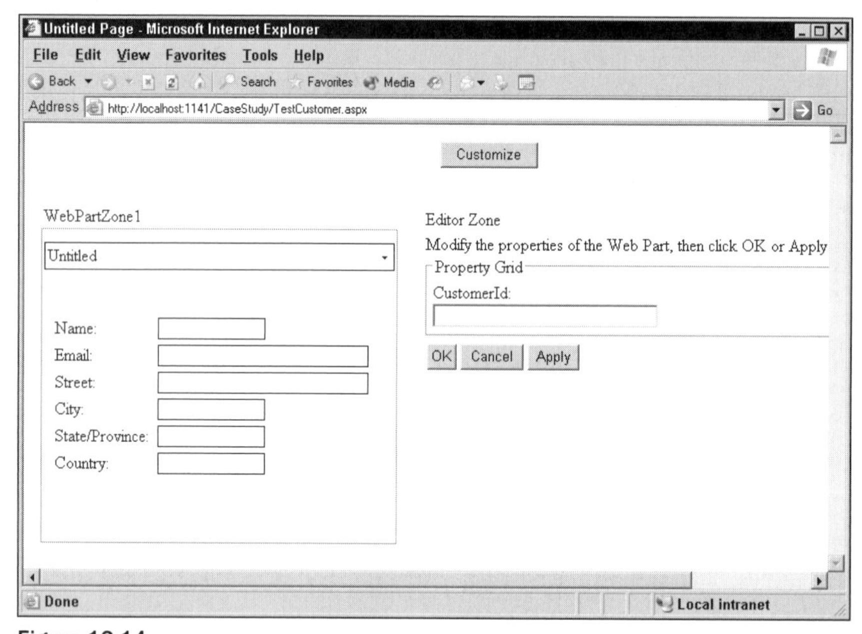

Figure 12-14

Additional Web Part–related properties can make it easier for developers to work with the property. The WebDescription property provides a tooltip when the user hovers his mouse over the data entry area for the property in the PropertyGridEditor. The WebDisplayName value overrides the property name in the PropertyGridEditor, allowing you to provide a user-friendly name. This Visual Basic 2005 example uses both properties (the result can be seen in Figure 12-15):

```
<System.Web.UI.WebControls.WebParts.WebDescription( _
  "Controls the customer displayed."), _
 System.Web.UI.WebControls.WebParts.WebDisplayName("Customer Number"), _
 System.Web.UI.WebControls.WebParts.WebBrowsable(), _
 System.Web.UI.WebControls.WebParts.Personalizable()> _
Public Property CustomerId() As String
```

In C#:

```
[System.Web.UI.WebControls.WebParts.WebDescription(
    "Controls the customer displayed.")]
```

```
[System.Web.UI.WebControls.WebParts.WebDisplayName("Customer Number")]
[System.Web.UI.WebControls.WebParts.WebBrowsable()]
[System.Web.UI.WebControls.WebParts.Personalizable()]
public string CustomerId
```

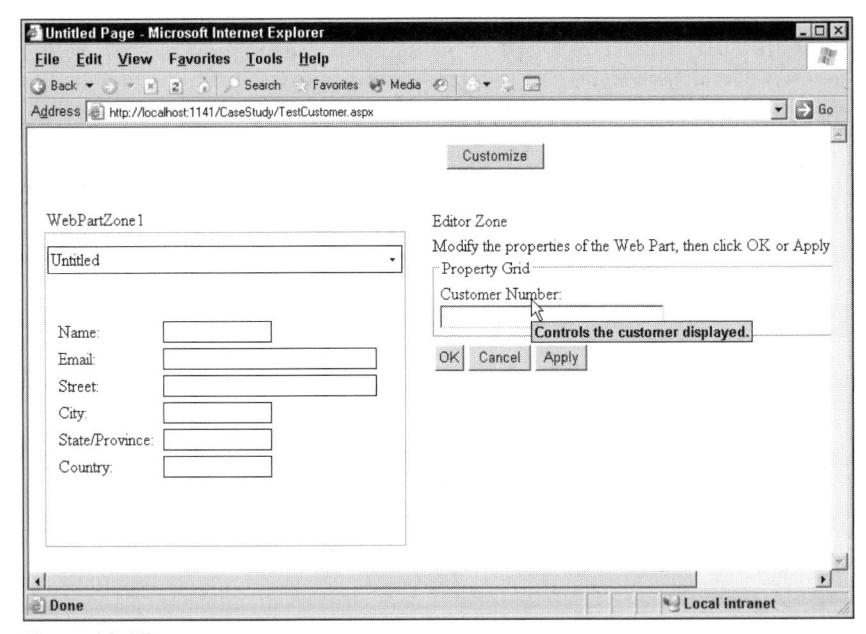

Figure 12-15

Setting the control's Title property allows you to provide a meaningful name for the custom control.

Adding Verbs

In addition to displaying customer information, in update mode the user needs the ability to update customer information. Normally this requires adding various buttons to the control. With a Web Part, however, the ability to update customer information can be provided by adding a verb to the control's Verb menu.

To add a verb to the Verbs menu, the read-only Verbs property must be overridden and code inserted in the Get routine for the property. Within the Verbs menu, a WebPartVerb object has to be created for each verb being created. When a WebPartVerb is created, it must be passed an identifier and a reference to the routine to be run when the user selects the verb. After the verb is created, its Text property can be set to provide a user-friendly name for the menu. Finally, the WebPartVerb must be added to a WebPartVerbs array, the array assigned to a WebPartVerbCollection, and the collection returned from the property. A routine that can be tied to a verb looks very much like a standard .NET event routine: It accepts two parameters with the first parameter (called sender) declared as Object and the second parameter (called e) declared as a System.Web.UI.WebControls.WebParts.WebPartEventArgs object (WebPartVerbs are discussed in detail in Chapter 5).

This Visual Basic 2005 code performs all of those tasks (and also sets the verb's Description property to provide a tooltip for the control):

```
Public Overrides ReadOnly Property Verbs() As _
                WebControls.WebParts.WebPartVerbCollection

  Get
    Dim vrbUpdate As New WebControls.WebParts.WebPartVerb( _
                                    "Update", AddressOf Me.UpdateCustomer)
    Dim vrbsUpdate As WebControls.WebParts.WebPartVerbCollection
    Dim vrbs(0) As WebControls.WebParts.WebPartVerb

    vrbUpdate.Text = "Update Customer"
    vrbUpdate.Description = _
         "Update customer information with data from the control";

    vrbsUpdate(0) = vrbUpdate
    vrbs = New WebControls.WebParts.WebPartVerbCollection(vrbsUpdate)

    Return vrbs

  End Get
End Property

Private Sub UpdateCustomer(ByVal sender As Object, _
        ByVal e As System.Web.UI.WebControls.WebParts.WebPartEventArgs)

   ...code to update the customer information from the postData structure

End Sub
```

In C#:

```
public override System.Web.UI.WebControls.WebParts.WebPartVerbCollection Verbs
{
 get
 {
 System.Web.UI.WebControls.WebParts.WebPartVerb vrbUpdate =
       new System.Web.UI.WebControls.WebParts.WebPartVerb("Update",
                                                     this.UpdateCustomer);
System.Web.UI.WebControls.WebParts.WebPartVerb[] vrbsUpdate =
                new System.Web.UI.WebControls.WebParts.WebPartVerb[0];
 System.Web.UI.WebControls.WebParts.WebPartVerbCollection vrbs;

 vrbUpdate.Text = "Update Customer";
 vrbUpdate.Description = "Update customer information with data from the control";
 vrbsUpdate[0] = vrbUpdate;
 vrbs = new System.Web.UI.WebControls.WebParts.WebPartVerbCollection(vrbsUpdate);

 return vrbs;
 }
}

private void UpdateCustomer(object sender,
```

```
            System.Web.UI.WebControls.WebParts.WebPartEventArgs e)
  {
    ...code to update the customer information from the postData structure
  }
```

Figure 12-16 shows the result.

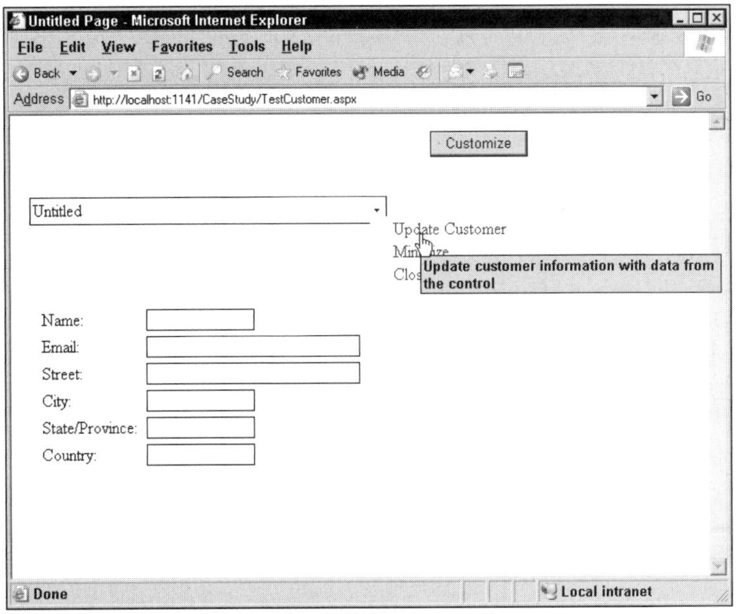

Figure 12-16

Communication

For the last topic in this case study, the control will be extended so that it can act as a provider and a consumer of customer Ids:

- As a provider, when connected to a control that provides a customer Id, the CustomerInformation control displays the customer information.
- As a consumer, when connected to a control that requires a customer id, the control supplies a customer Id.

Defining an Interface

The first step is to create an interface that can be implemented by consumers and providers that will exchange customer information. The interface is simple, consisting of just the customer id. In Visual Basic, the interface (called ICustInfo) looks like this:

```
Public Interface ICustInfo
   Property CustomerId() As String
End Interface
```

In C#:

```
public interface ICustInfo
{
 string CustomerId
 {
        get;
        set;
 }
}
```

Implementing the Provider

To act as a provider of customer Ids, the custom control must implement the interface and a property that the interface defines.

The Visual Basic 2005 code to add the ICustInfo interface to the control (along with the already implemented IPostBackDataHandler interface) looks like this:

```
Public Class CustomerInformation
    Inherits System.Web.UI.WebControls.WebParts.WebPart
    Implements IPostBackDataHandler
    Implements ICustInfo
```

In C#:

```
public class CustomerInformation : System.Web.UI.WebControls.WebParts.WebPart,
                                   IPostBackDataHandler,
                                   ICustInfo
```

Because the CustomerInformation control already has a CustomerId property, all that's necessary is to wire up the existing property to the corresponding member of the interface. To wire up the CustomerId property to the interface in Visual Basic, just add to the property in the custom control the Implements keyword followed by the name of the property in the interface that's being implemented. In this case, the interface is ICustInfo and the property is CustomerId:

```
Public Property CustomerId() As String Implements ICustInfo.CustomerId
```

In C#, even less is required. The property providing the information has to be named to match the interface and the name of the property within the interface that's being implemented:

```
public string ICustInfo.CustomerId
```

The final step is to create a connection point routine. The routine has to be defined as a function (returning the interface) and given the ConnectionProvider attribute. The attribute can be passed a description that will be displayed in the user interface. This Visual Basic 2005 code implements the ICustInfo interface for the CustomerInformation control when the control is acting as a provider:

```
<WebControls.WebParts.ConnectionProvider("Provides Customer Id")> _
Public Function ICustInfoProvider() As ICustInfo

    Return Me

End Function
```

In C#:

```
[WebControls.WebParts.ConnectionProvider("Provides Customer Id")]
public ICustInfo ICustInfoProvider()
{
  return this;
}
```

Implementing the Consumer

After the interface has been defined, to have the custom control act as a consumer all that's necessary is to create a connection point routine. The connection point is a subroutine that accepts a single parameter (of the same type as the interface) and has the ConnectionConsumer attribute applied to it (the ConnectionConsumer attribute can be passed a description). Within the connection routine, the code can access the property defined in the ICustInfo interface. This allows the CustomerInformation control to retrieve a customer id that was being provided by some other control that implemented the ICustInfo interface.

In this Visual Basic 2005 example, the routine accepts the ICustInfo interface and uses it to extract the CustomerId property. After the CustomerId is retrieved, the code passes it to the GetCustomer routine to retrieve the customer information from the ICustInfo interface's CustomerId property:

```
<WebControls.WebParts.ConnectionConsumer("Consumer for CustomerIds")> _
Public Sub ICustInfoConsumer(ByVal cs As ICustInfo)

   _CustomerId = cs.CustomerId
   GetCustomerInformation(_CustomerId)

End Sub
```

In C#:

```
WebControls.WebParts.ConnectionConsumer("Consumer for CustomerIds")]
public void ICustInfoConsumer(ICustInfo cs)
{
 _CustomerId = cs.CustomerId;
 GetCustomerInformation(_CustomerId);
}
```

While this example used an interface with a single property, an interface can include multiple properties and methods. Adding the other properties of the CustomerInformation object (for example, Email, Street) would follow the same pattern as used here: specify the property in the interface and then wire up the already existing property in the CustomerInformation object to the interface. The only difference is that (because the other properties in the CustomerInformation object are marked as read-only) the equivalent entries in the interface must be marked as read-only.

Summary

In this chapter you've seen how to build a custom control that displays multiple pieces of information. In addition, the control acts as a Web Part supporting customization and personalization. At this point, you're ready to start creating your own controls. This case study, in addition to showing how some of the technology in this book can be used, provides you with a framework for creating controls that consist of constituent controls. There are a great many features of custom controls and Web Parts that haven't been discussed in this case study, including creating databound controls and importing/exporting Web Part customizations—but it would be an unusual control that implemented everything in this book.

Index

A

B

C

D

E

N

R

U

V

W

X

Z

GORDON DUTHIE